AN UNHAPPY CIVIL WAR

Other books by John Wroughton:

The Stuart Age, 1603-1714 (1997)

A Community at War: the Civil War in Bath and North Somerset (1992)

King Edward's School at Bath, 1552-1982 (1982)

English Historical Facts, 1603-1688 (with Chris Cook, 1980)

Seventeenth Century Britain (1980)

Documents on World History (2 vols., with Denys Cook, 1976)

Bath in the Age of Reform (1972)

Documents on British Political History (3 vols., 1971)

Smuggling (with John Paxton, 1971)

Plots, Traitors and Spies (1970)

Cromwell and the Roundheads (1969)

AN UNHAPPY CIVIL WAR

The Experiences of Ordinary People in Gloucestershire, Somerset and Wiltshire, 1642-1646

JOHN WROUGHTON

Upon the 30th day of June 1643, there were buried in the churchyard under the west wall three soldiers killed of the Parliament party and one of the Royal party in ***an unhappy civil war****, at the riverside in the Ham meadow in Claverton'.* [Parish registers, Claverton Church, Somerset]

THE LANSDOWN PRESS

First published in 1999 by
The Lansdown Press
41 The Empire Grand Parade
Bath BA2 4DF

ISBN 0 9520249 2 6 (paperback edition)
ISBN 0 9520249 3 4 (cased edition)

Typeset in 10 / 12 New Century.
Tyesetting and origination by
The Lansdown Press.
Printed in Great Britain by
The Cromwell Press, Trowbridge, Wiltshire

Contents

Acknowledgements

The author wishes to thank the following people who have contributed in various ways to the production of this book:

Stephen Beck, a distinguished illustrator of seventeenth-century books, for his imaginative line drawings which accompany the text;
the staff of the British Library and the Public Record Office in London; the Bodleian Library in Oxford; the County Record Offices in Gloucester, Taunton and Trowbridge; the City Record Offices in Bath, Bristol and Wells; the National Portrait Gallery Archive; the Ashmolean Museum; and the Local Studies Libraries in Bath, Bristol, Gloucester, Taunton and Trowbridge - for all their courtesy and helpfulness;
those who have provided valuable references, including Colonel Eric Gruber von Arni, Robert Bell (Bath Archaeological Trust), Ian Chard (Frampton Cotterell Local History Society), Dr Alan Dodge, Marek Lewcun and Richard Salter;
the Bath Archaeological Trust and Dr John Adair for the loan of illustrations; Stuart Crossman for his technical support;
Osprey Publishing Ltd. for permission to reproduce the illustrations by Angus McBride from Elite 25, *Soldiers of the English Civil War 1: Infantry,* © Osprey Publishing Ltd. on the front cover and on pages 43, 59 and 129;
Jane Crompton of Sutton Publishing for her invaluable advice and assistance;
Rodney Morant for his painstaking correction of the typescript; and Professor Ronald Hutton for reading the text and offering helpful and constructive comments - though I would stress that any errors are mine and not theirs.

CHAPTER 1

Forced to Decide: For King or Parliament?

That great God, which is the searcher of my heart, knows with what a sad sense I go upon this service and with what a perfect hatred I detest this war without an enemy...We are both upon the stage and must act those parts that are assigned to us in this tragedy. (Sir William Waller, parliamentarian, to his old friend Sir Ralph Hopton, royalist, 1643)

The Importance of the Three Counties

The level of involvement for ordinary people in the Civil War depended very much on where they lived. For some, living in remote rural villages, the horrors of conflict passed them totally by; whereas for others, based in areas of strategic importance, the war became a day-to-day reality. The hostilities which raged in England between 1642 and 1646 did not involve the civilian population in 'total' war in the modern sense, for it was largely a struggle between two competing armies, which tracked each other around the country, fighting occasional battles and setting up scores of garrisoned bases. Nevertheless, if you lived in these war zones, your life could be made hell by the need of soldiers in search of supplies and the greed of marauders in search of plunder.

Gloucestershire, Somerset and Wiltshire were counties of prime importance to the war effort of both king and parliament. This very fact ensured, from the outset, that ordinary people living in the West would repeatedly experience distress to their livelihood and dislocation to their daily life. Gloucestershire, with a population of around 100,000, possessed an abundant supply of those natural resources which armies coveted - dairy products from the rich pastures of the Vales of Berkeley and Gloucester; fruit and vegetables from the Vale of Evesham, east of Tewkesbury; corn from the Cotswold plateau; timber, iron and coal from the Forest of Dean (with sixteen foundries producing pig iron vital to the manufacture of weapons of war); and cloth from the villages of Stroudwater. Charles I himself noted that 'great quantities of cloth, canvas and lockram are to be had for supplying the great necessities our soldiers have of suits'.

The county was also a centre for trade - and trade produced affluence, which in turn enabled people to pay their taxes! The market towns of Tewkesbury, Chipping Camden, Cirencester, Stroud and Tetbury also gave opportunities for regimental quartermasters to replenish their supplies.

The counties of Gloucestershire, Somerset and Wiltshire in 1642

The river Severn, which ran through Gloucestershire and then linked up with the Avon in Warwickshire, provided a major trade route from Bristol into the Midlands (even though goods needed to be transferred to smaller vessels as they made their way up river). The city of Gloucester guarded that route, as well as the route between the king's headquarters in Oxford and his rich supply and recruiting ground in south Wales. Other major roads, which armies constantly used in the war, passed through the county and were controlled by key towns - Tewkesbury (the road to Worcester); Cheltenham (the road to Coventry); Lechlade (the road to London); and Cirencester (the road to Oxford). The city of Bristol, situated on the southern edge of Gloucestershire with a population of about 15,000, was actually a county in its own right. It contained a wealthy port (with the attraction of lucrative customs duties), a market second only to London, a centre for craftsmen (producing shoes and other valuable items for soldiers) and a base for the manufacture of weapons of war. Both Bristol and Gloucester were therefore regarded by king and parliament alike as prizes of the greatest worth. (1)

Somerset with an estimated population of 196,000 in 1642, was also a county of considerable agricultural wealth. When, in October 1644, Sir William Waller was considering the possibility of attacking the royalist stronghold of Bristol, he looked forward to the prospect with considerable relish because he would have 'as fruitful parts as are in England to quarter in'. Whereas the northern parts of the county specialised in dairy farming and corn, the moors and pasture lands to the south and west gave rise to a lucrative trade in cattle and sheep. Nevertheless, the local economy was not dependent on agriculture alone. Mining, too, was important - lead in the Mendips, alabaster near Minehead, coal around Stratton-on-the-Fosse, Kilmersdon, Ashwick, Timsbury and Paulton, and stone at Doulting and Ham. Traditionally much of the county's wealth had also been drawn from the cloth industry with a large band of broadcloth production in its north-eastern corner around Bath, Frome and Shepton Mallet. Another area in the south and west, which specialised in kersey-broadcloths, was based around the towns of Taunton, Bridgwater, Chard and Wellington. The walled city of Bath, a bustling centre of some 2,000 people, was a place of considerable affluence, thanks partly to the healing qualities of its hot waters, which had brought it national fame as a health resort. The combined riches of the county found outlets at the many markets which thrived in such places as Bath, Wells, Taunton, Yeovil, Somerton, Frome, Warminster and Langport. Cloth and other products could be exported further afield from the larger ports of Minehead and Bridgwater and the smaller ones of Dunster and Watchet. (2)

In Wiltshire, with a population estimated at 113,000 in 1642, the county's agricultural wealth was divided between, on the one hand, the 'chalk country' of the Wiltshire downlands (the Marlborough Downs, Salisbury Plain and the extreme northern tip of the county) - an area of arable farming, based on the old open fields, and sheep grazing; and, on the other, the 'cheese country 'of the north-west, which specialised in cattle-raising and dairy farming. It included a broad band of clothing villages (such as Bradford-on-Avon, Corsham and Broughton Gifford), which spilled over into north-east Somerset, and areas of woodland (such as the forests of Melksham, Braydon and Chippenham). (3)

As the war progressed, Somerset and Wiltshire together became an important thoroughfare for armies on the move - Sir Ralph Hopton's newly-recruited royalist army on its way from Cornwall to Lansdown in 1643, the king's army as it played cat-and-mouse with the parliamentary forces of the Earl of Essex in and out of Cornwall in 1644 and Sir Thomas Fairfax's New Model Army as it chased the remnants of Lord George Goring's royalists in the final mopping-up operations of 1645. Major field armies like these all needed food, clothing, supplies and lodging *en route* as they marched along the roads from Oxford and London to Bristol and the South-West, sweeping through places like Devizes, Chippenham, Bath, Wells, Shepton Mallet, Ilchester, Chard, Taunton and Wellington. The countryside around, therefore, became both a storehouse and a granary. Such valuable lines of communication, of course, needed to be protected by networks of garrisons assembled at strategic points - hence the proliferation of fortified castles, manor houses and towns over both counties. These, too, drew heavily on the villages in their allotted catchment areas to supply their needs throughout the war.

The Sufferings of Ordinary People, 1620-1640

By the 1620s, many ordinary people in the three counties were suffering greatly from a whole variety of economic problems. An explosion in the population had seen an estimated total of 2 million people resident in England in 1500 rise to 5.5 million by 1650. In Wiltshire, for instance, the population increased by 45 per cent in the sixteenth century alone. This trend had created an ever-increasing mass of landless labourers, often living in rough cottages on the edge of forests, who flocked to areas with flourishing labour-intensive industries. The cloth industry around Stroudwater in Gloucestershire and Frome in Somerset, together with the tobacco industry in the Vale of Evesham provided classic examples of this pattern.

However, the precarious existence of these landless labourers was seriously threatened during the first part of the seventeenth century by a general depression, which hit the west country broadcloth industry, thus throwing thousands out of work; and by frequent corn shortages, caused both by low production and repeated harvest failure, which ensured that bread prices remained high. In Somerset, the city of Bath was reported to be 'a very little poor city' in 1622 'and clothing much decayed'. Nearby, the Vicar of Frome and his congregation petitioned the county magistrates about their desperate plight. They explained that the parish had depended almost entirely upon the cloth trade for survival and that many people had 'planted themselves there in the forest attracted in by the prospect of work in weaving, fulling and spinning'. But now, with the decay of that trade, 'the cry of the poor' had grown 'very great and the burden upon the inhabitants unsupportable'. A special survey of the parish had revealed that the 'multitude of the poor' amounted to five hundred men, women and children. It was even worse in Salisbury in Wiltshire, where some 2,300 people were reported as requiring relief in 1626 (or one-third of the population). (4)

The plight of all these people had been further aggravated by schemes for the disafforestation of the royal forests in an attempt by Charles I to raise money. In 1627, for instance, he had given up his right to the Frome Selwood Forest in return for a one-third share of the land, which was subsequently sold off and enclosed. The remainder of the land was allocated to local freeholders in compensation for their loss of grazing rights in the forest, thus enabling further enclosure to take place. The folk who suffered most in this operation were the cottagers living on waste at the edge of the forest - the very same people who were already suffering badly from unemployment in the cloth industry. In hard times they had relied on the forest to provide firewood, timber for building, grazing for a few animals and game for the pot. Enclosure inevitably resulted in the total loss of these unofficial benefits and their own ejection from the huts. Resistance to this policy was inevitable, as fences were increasingly torn down by angry protesters. In 1631, Thomas Carr defied an eviction order and hold out for two weeks until the authorities managed to secure a cannon from the Bristol armoury. This 'miniature civil war' was marked by a noticeable lack of co-operation towards the authorities by influential local people - including Sir Edward Baynton, who refused the sheriff's call for assistance, telling him 'that he did not much fancy that service'. (5)

Exactly the same pattern developed in the Forest of Dean in Gloucestershire where, in 1640, the king accepted a scheme for disafforestation. In exchange for a lump sum of £10,000 and a yearly rent of £16,000, Sir John Winter of Lydney was given the right to extract the mineral and timber resources of the forest for the supply of his iron industry, much to the anger of local cottagers and forest miners. Government policy of a different kind, also in Gloucestershire, contributed to the rise of poverty and unemployment in the Vale of Evesham. Throughout the 1620s, an attempt was made to protect the tobacco crop in the recently-established colony of Virginia by banning its production in England. Local magistrates were therefore expected to supervise the cutting down of tobacco plants - a policy which exacerbated distress in Winchcombe, where 'near four thousand beggars' had already been reported, and upset the officials who had been given this distasteful policy to enforce. (6)

Misery brought about by shortage of work was quickly compounded by shortage of food. The problem became particularly acute in the late 1620s and early 1630s when a series of bad harvests seriously affected the situation. Between 1626 and 1630, for instance, the price of wheat in Wiltshire rose by 40 per cent. In north Somerset, local magistrates sent reports to the Privy Council in London giving an account of the grave crisis facing the community in 1631, when there was very little corn left. The situation was especially severe in the hundred of Frome *[i.e. the area of local administration, containing a group of parishes]*, where it was predicted that the remaining 200 quarters of wheat and rye would feed the 6,500 inhabitants there for less than a fortnight.

The desperate plight of people like this had already provoked food riots in the locality in November 1630. For several years Somerset magistrates had expressed fears that 'the multitudes of poor spinners and weavers in the county, now without work, tend to mutiny'. Their worst fears were realised when three separate incidents involving attacks on licensed corn carriers were reported near Midford in Somerset. In the first of these, William Lansdown of Keynsham was travelling up Midford Hill on his way between Warminster and Bristol with five horseloads of wheat when he was 'set upon by a great number of men and women' who, making threats of violence, pulled down his sacks and made off with them. Food riots in England were not uncommon. The purchase of substantial amounts of grain in the markets by dealers, intent on transporting the stock outside the area (where greater profits could be made), caused local shortages and high prices. Riots therefore ensued as the poor and unemployed attempted to prevent this movement of grain. In Gloucestershire, the river Severn, a route for shipments between the west Midlands and Bristol, was a frequent target for attacks. (7)

In addition to their own problems, the farm labourers, spinners and weavers, who made up much of the village population, heard the constant grumbling of their landlords and employers during the 1630s, when Charles I governed without parliament. These complaints centred inevitably on government policies concerning forced loans, ship money, monopolies and the volume of petty restrictions imposed on the cloth industry. Indeed, the inhabitants of Bradford-on-Avon in Wiltshire witnessed at first hand an angry confrontation between the town's clothiers and Anthony Wither, the government's inspector, who had arrived to enforce the regulations. Men of comparatively few words, they emphasised their argument by simply throwing him into the river. (8)

News and gossip also filtered down into the west country from London, concerning the growing clash between the king and parliament - a clash in which men with strong local connections played a major part (including John Pym, Denzil Holles, Thomas Pury and William Lenthall). Of far greater importance to their own immediate lives, however, than all the debates over the privileges of parliament, were the controversial reforms introduced into church life by William Laud, Archbishop of Canterbury. In many parts of Gloucestershire, Somerset, and Wiltshire, these changes were felt deeply by local people, who bitterly resented what they perceived as a return to catholicism.

The Puritan Revolution and the People, 1600-1640

Even by 1620, large districts within the three western counties area were already under the tight control of the puritans, who had launched a powerful campaign to establish a moral reformation. Evidence for this was particularly apparent in north Somerset and west Wiltshire. Unsatisfactory clergy, for instance, had been removed for lax behaviour, like the Rector of Wootton Rivers in Wiltshire, who was charged with 'behaviour not befitting a minister of the gospel' for condoning the playing of cards in the parsonage, the playing of skittles in the churchyard on Sundays and the selling of 'metheglin' by his wife; or the curate of Stanton Drew in Somerset, who had not only left the parishioners 'without prayer' on several sabbath days, but was also 'very deaf, a user of alehouses and a keeper of drunkards' company'.

Preaching at an open-air conventicle. (Author's collection)

At the same time, a much greater emphasis had been placed on scripture-based preaching at the expense of the communion service. By 1640, puritan ministers had been installed in all the key parishes in north Somerset, including Bath, Frome, Kilmersdon, Mells, Saltford, Stratton and Keynsham. Several towns (including Bath) had established a system of mid-week lectures by visiting puritan divines (who abandoned ceremonial and the wearing of surplices), often attended by the Mayor and Corporation. Where sermons were not available in the parish church, local puritans (often those of more humble birth) had staged a boycott and went, in the words of their opponents, 'gadding to sermons' outside the parish - as happened in Wiltshire at Broughton Gifford and Melksham and at Farrington Gurney in Somerset. By 1604, several of the clothing villages had established non-conformist conventicles, which were separate from the church, including Bradford-on-Avon, Slaughterford, Horningsham and Broughton Gifford.

The sabbath, too, had been given much greater protection. In particular, a determined effort had been made to stamp out the playing of unlawful games on Sunday. Those found guilty were presented to the bishop's visitation for punishment, like those involved in playing skittles at Bradford-on-Avon; those caught breaking church windows during a snowball fight at Bromham; a group of young people charged at Keevil with 'being at a dancing match upon a Sunday after evening prayer'; Eleanor Gibbons of Widcombe for causing her mill to grind on Sunday mornings; and Thomas Clement of Keynsham for bowling in the church yard on the sabbath day. The fact that few such presentments were made is an indication that the puritan grip had already tightened.

Alehouses were regarded with deep suspicion by the puritans, because they were seen to corrupt the young and undermine family discipline. By 1623, therefore, the Mayor of Bath had suppressed all unnecessary and disorderly alehouses. In Bradford-on-Avon complaints had been raised in 1628 denouncing alehouses for 'enticing poor workmen and day labourers' to drown their sorrows while their wives and children starved - one of many petitions to the justices about the disastrous impact of alehouses on the poor. Similarly the ban on Church Ales, with their drunken merry-making round the maypole in annual celebration of the foundation of the parish church, had been rigorously enforced.

Similar concern had been shown for breaches of sexual morality, especially regarding the activities of unruly women who were involved in brawls or were unfaithful in marriage. Bath Corporation, therefore, kept its ducking stool in good repair so that it could shame such transgressors by giving them a good ducking in the river. The same sort of concern also led to the segregation of sexes for the first time in the city's hot water baths. The Privy Council in London had already expressed anxiety about 'the great disorders committed in the common use of the baths by men and women together' - a practice which 'drew together a great concourse of wicked persons' and compelled 'grave and sober people to forbear the place'. The Corporation quickly put an end to all that. (9)

The puritans had also begun the process, wherever possible, of purifying the churches of all popish symbols and idols, such as altars, statues,

A seventeenth-century alehouse. (Author's collection)

stained glass and organs. In Salisbury, the puritan elite, led by Recorder Henry Sherfield and Alderman John Ivie, had taken control of the Corporation by 1620. It was Sherfield who noticed on one occasion some women parishioners making low curtsies in St Edmund's Church. When asked why they did it, they replied 'that they made them to their Lord God, and to God the Father in the glass window'. Sherfield promptly smashed the offending stained glass. (10)

By 1620, therefore, the puritan revolution had succeeded in largely transforming the traditional culture and religion of north Somerset and west Wiltshire. Although largely inspired by the puritan gentry and clothiers who controlled the area, it had widespread support from ordinary local people - weavers, artisans, tradesmen, husbandmen and labourers. The strength of this godly reformation, however, had been sorely tested during the 1630's by a vigorous counter-attack staged by William Laud, Archbishop of Canterbury, who had tried to revive High Church practices

William Piers, Bishop of Bath and Wells (1580-1670). (By courtesy of the Lord Bishop of Bath and Wells from a photograph supplied by the Paul Mellon Centre for Studies in British Art)

within the church. In consequence, he had introduced tight regulations, which sought to stifle the system of lectures by puritan divines; and ordered all clergy to remove communion tables out of the nave (where the puritans had put them) and rail them off instead as altars in the chancel. Rectors were also encouraged to reintroduce ceremonial and to beautify their churches with statues and ornaments. All this was anathema to the puritans, who sensed a return to catholicism.

They were further outraged by the reissue of *The Book of Sports* in 1633, which gave royal approval to the revival of parish festivals and Church Ales, all of which had been virtually eliminated in many areas of Somerset and Wiltshire by the onset of the puritan revolution. In north Somerset, people had also developed a strong dislike of William Piers, Bishop of Bath and Wells, who had introduced Laud's reforms with missionary zeal. So fierce, however, was the opposition to his insistence on railing off of altars that the churchwardens of Beckington, backed by the local gentry and 1000 ordinary local people, defied the Bishop's instruction to remove the communion table and were imprisoned in consequence. This incident vividly illustrates the deep concern that ordinary people felt for their puritan culture and their willingness to defend their faith from outside attack. Exactly similar sentiments were held by many other people living in such places as Gloucester, Tewkesbury, Cirencester, Stroud, Marlborough, Taunton, Bridgwater and Minehead. (11)

The Day of Decision

(a) North Somerset and West Wiltshire: The Mendip Uprising, 1642

In spite of all the suffering and distress, in spite of all the anger over religious policy, civil war was not yet on the agenda in the three western counties by the beginning of 1642. Although the economic situation had been desperate with mass unemployment, grinding poverty and serious shortage of food, English people in the seventeenth century were well accustomed to take natural disasters such as harvest failure in their stride. Even food riots were not necessarily to be regarded the heralds of civil war. Squabbles between king and parliament were also nothing new. Both Elizabeth I and James I, for instance, had had terrible trouble with their parliaments but had survived relatively unscathed. The difference in 1642, however, was that Charles I possessed a stubbornness of character, born of a belief that he had been appointed by God and was therefore only answerable to God for the stewardship of his power - and not to parliament. He consequently lacked the flexibility of mind and will to work out the sort of compromise that could so easily have averted the war. When civil war finally came, it was both unexpected and unwanted.

There was certainly no evidence of war fever spreading through the streets of local towns during the spring of 1642. It is true that the Corporations of Gloucester, Taunton, Devizes, Chippenham, Bath and

Wells, like most corporations throughout the country, were busy restocking their armouries, but this was largely as a precautionary measure for defence against unnamed foes (after all, brief wars had just been fought against the Scots) - or, as was stated in Gloucester, 'by reason [that] the times are dangerous'. Nevertheless, the accumulation of grievances over the previous decade and the acrimonious disputes within the Long Parliament had created an atmosphere of suspicion and anxiety. A nervous edginess prevailed in the West.

Meanwhile, in London, opposition to the king's policies and powers finally reached crisis point in the Commons on 5th January, 1642, when Charles unsuccessfully attempted to arrest five of his most hostile critics (including Wiltshire man Denzil Holles). Shortly afterwards, Charles left his capital for the North, basing himself on York until 22nd August, when the royal standard was finally raised in Nottingham to signal the official start of the Civil War.

During those months, a crucial struggle had developed for control of the militia (or trained bands), as both king and parliament sought to gain the upper hand. Originally formed as county defence forces in 1573 to offset the expected invasion from Spain, the bands had been allowed to lapse in many counties after the defeat of the Armada in 1588. This was not the case in London, however, or in a number of other counties, including Somerset, Wiltshire and parts of Gloucestershire. These ready-made little armies were therefore viewed with covetous eyes. Consequently, in February, parliament had issued an Ordinance placing all the trained bands under its own control. Most counties (including Somerset and Wiltshire) had already accepted this order by the time the king issued a Declaration (11th June), condemning it as illegal. He went on to counter its impact by granting to loyal supporters in each county a 'commission of array' to raise the trained bands for his own use. Under these circumstances, it was inevitable that each county would quickly become a verbal and legal battleground long before the first drop of local blood was shed. In north Somerset and west Wiltshire, these moves were to spark off a major rising in which ordinary local people played a considerable part.

For them the day of decision came at the end of July 1642 - and the initial confrontation took place in Bath. Long before the first shots were fired in the war at large, both king and parliament made a dash to control Somerset, which was valuable for its natural resources (both mineral and agricultural), the port of Bristol (to which it held the key) and its five regiments of trained bands.

On 12th July therefore, the king sent a Wiltshire man, William Seymour, Marquess of Hertford, and various other west country gentlemen (including Sir Ralph Hopton of Witham Friary in Somerset) with a commission of array to raise the trained bands of both those counties for the king. Hertford decided that Somerset would be his first priority. Eight days later, parliament established a committee of its own to raise

William Seymour, 1st Marquess of Hertford (1588-1660). (By courtesy of the Ashmolean Museum, Oxford. Photograph: Photographic Survey, Courtauld Institute of Art)

Somerset's forces on its behalf, a committee containing many influential local people, including Alexander Popham, MP for Bath and commander of the Bath Regiment of trained bands, Sir John Horner of Mells, Sir Edward Hungerford of Farleigh, William Strode of Street and John Ashe of Freshford. (12)

Both groups then converged on Bath, where the scene was set for a noisy confrontation almost a month before the king raised his standard at Nottingham to signify the official start of hostilities. Bath became the centre for this war of words because, by sheer coincidence, the County Assizes happened to be meeting there at the time. In the seventeenth century, the Assizes provided a great social occasion for all those of any status in the county, including the Sheriff, the Lord Lieutenant, the Deputy Lieutenants, the Bishop, the Justices, the Constables, the Mayor and Corporation. What a place in which to recruit! However, the Marquess of Hertford quickly discovered that his welcome was none too friendly on the narrow streets of Bath. He therefore decided to withdraw and set up his headquarters in Wells, being assured that the more southerly residents of the county were likely to be more sympathetic to the king's cause. The trained bands, together with all his allies and potential supporters, were instructed to follow him there.

Meanwhile, parliament's newly-established committee had not been idle. Responding to the threat posed by the marquess, it had sent out letters around the countryside summoning representatives in to a general meeting at Shepton Mallet on 1st August and promising to provide 'several fat bucks thither for their entertainment'. This decision threw the ordinary inhabitants of Shepton into a state of undisguised panic as they visualised the horror of great hordes descending upon their small village. They had indeed been singled out by chance as the first community in Somerset to experience a foretaste of civil war. The community was immediately split. The rector, John Cooth, and a few of the other inhabitants (though by no means the majority) decided to send a petition to Hertford in Wells, earnestly praying for 'protection from the dangerous tumult' in fear that the meeting 'was to fire their houses and make their streets run with blood'. Hertford duly obliged by sending Hopton with a body of cavalry to investigate.

Arriving at Shepton in the early morning and finding about two hundred

Sir Ralph Hopton (1596-1652) of Witham Friary. Portrait by an unknown artist. (By courtesy of the National Portrait Gallery, London)

men in arms, he rode into the market place, 'faced the unruly rabble' and read out the petition. At this point William Strode, a local member of parliament's committee, burst in upon the town and ordered Hopton to leave. For the time being, however, Hopton had superior strength. Strode was roughly pulled from his horse, as Hopton's men drew their swords. He was immediately arrested for treason and placed in the custody of the village constable. Hopton's glory, however, was short-lived. Hearing of the approach of Popham with a crowd of about one thousand countrymen, he withdrew into a field outside the village. Finally, after the two groups had faced up to each other for several hours in an angry confrontation (without a single shot being fired), Hopton returned to Wells. Strode was released from custody - and the village constable speedily enrolled for parliament! Shepton Mallet would never be quite the same again.

The committee now ordered all its followers to a rendezvous at Chewton Mendip. It was there, on 5th August, that a most remarkable gathering took place, as the men of north Somerset, with enthusiastic support from those in west Wiltshire, rose *en masse* to support parliament's cause. Sir John Horner armed his servants, neighbours and tenants from Mells; Alexander Popham brought the Bath Regiment of trained bands; Bath City Council sent weapons, food, wine and tents; 300 cavalry came over from Wiltshire; 300 men of good rank joined from Bristol; and 300 foot volunteers rode across from Gloucestershire. Sadly however, on 4th August, as John Pyne's group of 600 recruits from west Somerset were heading to support them, they were intercepted at Marshall's Elm, near Street, and routed by Henry Lunsford, one of the few professional soldiers in the area at the time. The first blood of the local war was shed, therefore, with seven men killed and still three weeks to go before the official start of hostilities.

Nevertheless, by 5th August, an enthusiastic rabble of no fewer than 12,000 men had assembled to support parliament's committee, even though they were lacking in experienced soldiers and officers. 'Our men', wrote John Ashe to the Speaker of the Commons, 'were raw, untutored and inexperienced both in the use of their arms and horsemanship'. They were, however, swept up in a great wave of emotion, roused by inspired leadership - and they were impatient for battle. 'Although the soldiers', commented Ashe, 'had neither meat nor drink, they could not be stayed, but would march over the hill, which was near 4 miles, until they came in sight of Wells'. There they pitched camp and would not leave 'but lay all that night upon the hill' fasting and in the cold, and spent the time in prayers and singing psalms. Sir John Horner and others, he said, 'lay all that night in their arms upon furzebushes in the open fields, the old knight saying that his furzebed was the best bed he had ever lay on.' Such was the love of the country people for ten miles around that by dawn they had sent in cartloads of provisions, enough for breakfast and dinner.

Down in Wells, the atmosphere was distinctly gloomy. Only nine hundred had responded to Hertford's original summons. To make matters worse, there were mass desertions during the night as many ran up the hill to join friends and neighbours in the other army. Under these circumstances, Hertford wisely decided to withdraw to Sherborne in Dorset without a battle - but not before before Sir Francis Popham had significantly caused cannon shots to be fired from Mendip Hill against the Bishop's Palace in Wells. By the end of September, the royalist forces had disintegrated; Hertford had disappeared into Wales, while Hopton had ridden into Cornwall in the hope of a more successful recruiting campaign. The ordinary people of the area had united under the local gentry and clothiers in spontaneous and decisive action to expel the royalists.

Why did this remarkable series of events take place? Why did local people declare themselves so decisively for parliament and why did war erupt so quickly in these parts? Some historians have argued that the people merely banded together in this way to defend their county community from an outside threat (namely, the marquess) and that their real desire was to remain neutral. It is true that, in other places throughout the land, ordinary people tried to adopt a peace-keeping role and a policy of non-involvement. As Sir Arthur Haselrig commented at the time, they did not care what government they lived under, so long 'as they may plough and go to market'. But although neutralism was a major factor in many parts of the country, it had no place in the thinking of the community of north Somerset (or, indeed, in puritan-dominated places like west Wiltshire, Gloucester, Stroudwater, Taunton, Bridgwater and Minehead). Their commitment to parliament's cause never wavered and was to endure throughout the war.

Their action in 1642 was clearly designed to defend far more than their own county boundary. Indeed, Somerset's boundary with Wiltshire (from where the marquess had originally hailed) was totally irrelevant in the story. Not only did fervent support spill over onto the Mendips from west Wiltshire, but three of the most prominent leaders in this engagement had a foot on each side of the county boundary - Alexander Popham, who was MP for Bath, but also owner of the Littlecote House estates in Wiltshire; Sir Edward Hungerford, MP for Chippenham in Wiltshire, but also owner of Farleigh Castle in Somerset; and John Ashe, clothier from Freshford and treasurer of parliament's Somerset Committee, but also MP for Westbury in Wiltshire and commander of parliament's Wiltshire forces. (13)

It is true that the spirit of localism helped to motivate them into action - the need to keep outsiders at bay, even if it did mean accepting help from their friends over the border in Wiltshire. But it was not just a matter of keeping the marquess out - it was a matter of keeping out what he stood for. Hertford had come directly from the court, where according to common perception, catholicism now dominated the heart of government, with the queen surrounded by catholic priests openly celebrating mass. Set against the background of the church reforms of Archbishop Laud and Bishop Piers locally in the 1630s, the people of north Somerset believed that the arrival of the Marquess of Hertford in July 1642 would herald the suppression of their puritan culture and the revival of catholicism. The scene on the

Mendips was, therefore, far more like a religious convention than the rendezvous of an army. Later, as Popham's troops descended on Wells, they launched a devastating attack on the cathedral and bishop's palace, destroying as many symbols of catholicism as they could find. A newspaper correspondent noted that many villagers had joined the throng, 'bringing pitchforks, dungpicks and suchlike weapons, not knowing who they were to fight, but supposing they were papists'. And so the people in north Somerset and west Wiltshire rose to support parliament. For them, it was a war of religion. (14)

(b) Elsewhere in Somerset and Wiltshire

The day of decision in Salisbury, as in north Somerset, came at the end of July 1642, when its Recorder and Member of Parliament, Robert Hyde, persuaded the mayor to publish the king's commission of array. The election of Hyde, an ardent supporter of the king and the Anglican Church, to the Long Parliament in 1640 had already been bitterly disputed by the town's puritan faction. Although he had survived that challenge, his attempt to raise Salisbury for the royalist cause precipitated his fall. Summoned back to the Commons, Hyde was expelled for his action and sent to the Tower. Control of the city was, therefore, quickly seized by his enemies, who immediately formed a company of volunteers to support the Lord Lieutenant (the Earl of Pembroke) in raising the county for parliament. Further volunteers were quickly recruited at Chippenham, Marlborough and Devizes, where 'Michael and Whitingham' were paid six pence 'for beating a drum for volunteers'.

By the late autumn of 1642, Wiltshire was almost totally under parliament's control. All the potential royalist leaders of quality (the Marquess of Hertford, the Earl of Marlborough, the Earl of Berkshire) had, for various reasons, left the county; several of the more active royalists (like Sir George Vaughan of Falstone and Sir James Long of Draycott Cerne) had departed to join the king's main field army ; while others (like Sir Walter Smyth of Bedwyn and George Lowe of Calne) were on their way to serve the king at Oxford in a political capacity. As the war progressed, the centre of parliamentary support was largely based in the north-western part of the county, an area of dairy farming and woodland, which contained large numbers of clothing villages. Its influence, however, also stretched out in a band as far as Salisbury, taking in Warminster, Bishopstrow and Heytesbury. Royalist support, which at times was no more than lukewarm, was chiefly found in the sheep-corn region of the downs - though, at the start of the war, active leadership was largely noticeable by its absence. Out of the 29 MPs who represented Wiltshire in 1642, no fewer than 21 pledged their loyalty to parliament, when the time for division came, and just eight followed the king. (15)

In Somerset, outside the northern sector, all the clothing towns and ports had declared for parliament, including Taunton, Wellington,

Bridgwater, Chard, Minehead, Watchet and Dunster. In Dunster, the puritan, Thomas Luttrell, had strengthened his castle and increased the size of his garrison once news reached him that the Marquess of Hertford was heading for Minehead (i.e. after his abortive attempt to raise the county for the king). When, shortly afterwards, sixty of Hertford's men appeared at the gates demanding entrance, Mrs Luttrell ordered the garrison to open fire on them to keep them out. Frustrated by this obstruction, the marquess was forced to quarter his men in the area between Taunton and Wellington, but found the villages there violently hostile 'the whole countryside thereabouts being in continual alarm, ringing their bells backward and making fires to draw the people into an

Areas of Allegiance, 1642-1646

uproar'. They therefore marched to Minehead, hoping to find enough boats in the harbour to convey them into south Wales. To their horror, they only found two 'and could procure no more, the malicious activity of the country being far more powerful against them'. (16)

Outside these more committed districts, amid a haze of neutralism, moderate royalism prevailed, inspired by a number of well-established families, including the Pouletts, the Stawells, the Berkeleys, the Wyndhams, the Dodingtons and the Smyths. Although they did their best to raise troops or companies from among their neighbours and tenants, no particular town emerged as a centre of fervent royalist activity. In Wells, one of the most influential figures was Sir Edward Rodney, the city's MP, a keen royalist who also commanded the city's trained bands. However, although the cathedral population was undoubtedly royalist, the citizens themselves were largely uncommitted. The Corporation preferred neutrality and were horrified at the prospect of street fighting when Hertford based himself in their city. Under pressure from Rodney, they provided powder, bullets and match for his trained bands (but, at the same time, demanding payment) and then reluctantly handed over the keys of the magazine. In other words, they did as they were told under duress. (17)

(c) Gloucestershire

In Gloucestershire, support for parliament was centred largely in the Vale of Berkeley and the Vale of Gloucester - a great central band of territory stretching from Tewkesbury, Cheltenham and Gloucester in the north to Stroud, Tetbury and Chipping Sodbury in the south. This area of pasture and dairy farming, with a heavy concentration of clothmaking in Stroudwater and around Cirencester, was also an area noted for the strength of its puritanism and its hostility to the High Church policies of Archbishop Laud. The king, on the other hand, found most of his loyal supporters to the west in the Forest of Dean, which was firmly under the control of a catholic, Sir John Winter of Lydney; and the Cotswold plateau to the east, which was dominated by Lord George Chandos of Sudeley Castle and the Tracey family of Toddington.

Although there was considerable support for parliament in Gloucestershire, the county differed in two significant ways in 1642 from both Somerset and Wiltshire. To begin with, the war first showed itself in the county not in August 1642, but in February 1643 when Prince Rupert took Cirencester by storm. Although this external pressure prompted a response, internally Gloucestershire was noticeably slow in getting off the mark. Parliament's Militia Ordinance, for instance, was not executed there until late August, whereas Sir John Horner, Alexander Popham, William Strode and others had done so in Somerset in early April and Sir Edward Hungerford and Sir John Evelyn had followed suit in Wiltshire in early July.

Secondly, the leadership of the parliamentary party in Gloucestershire was markedly different from that in the other two counties. Whereas the gentry, with strong backing from clothiers, had led the August rising in north Somerset and west Wiltshire, the gentry in Gloucestershire were largely noticeable by their absence. John Corbet, the puritan chaplain to Sir Edward Massey in Gloucester, later commented that, with a few glorious exceptions, 'the yeomen, farmers, clothiers and the whole middle rank of the people...were the only active men. The gentlemen in general denied their concurrence, deserting their country either by open enmity or detestable neutrality'. (18)

Nevertheless, some activity was evident even before the fall of Cirencester. The city of Gloucester itself reacted quickly and decisively to the growing crisis in the summer of 1642. Already under the firm grip of the puritan revolution (there were four city preachers and several parish lecturers there), its actions were largely orchestrated by the powerful influence of its Member of Parliament, Thomas Pury. It was Pury who had already spoken vigorously in the Long Parliament against episcopacy in the church and had, in February 1641, delivered a petition to the Commons from the county with 3,000 signatures, demanding that the bishops should be swept away 'root and branch'. It is therefore not surprising that the city of Gloucester should nail its colours quickly to the parliamentary mast. Corbet recalled that when parties began to appear throughout the country 'the city of Gloucester determined not to stand neutral in action, but to adhere to one party, with which they resolved to stand or fall'. (19)

Elsewhere, too, men of more humble birth were joining the farmers and clothiers in showing local commitment to the cause. Tewkesbury had already emerged as a centre of puritanism and parliamentary support. As early as the spring of 1642, ordinary people had gathered together on a weekly basis to discuss the national crisis. Some four hundred of them later subscribed to the Protestation against the perceived danger of catholicism at court. For those living in Cirencester, the day of decision came on 9th August, when Lord Chandos arrived bearing a commission of array from the king. As news spread of Chandos's intentions, about a thousand people rushed in from the area to barricade the town. Although they later agreed to admit him so that he could confer with local magistrates at the Ram Inn, he was pressurised by some of the unruly members of the trained bands to promise in writing that he would uphold the privileges of parliament and the liberties of the subject. Anger quickly mounted in the town. An ugly situation, however, was partly averted when some of the more moderate townsmen helped him to slip out of the town undetected, leaving his coach behind outside the inn as a decoy. When they discovered his escape, the soldiers vented their rage on his coach, which was torn apart. (20)

Apart from Thomas Pury in Gloucester, two other energetic puritans were working hard to build up a parliamentary following - Sir Robert Cook of Highnam (MP for Tewkesbury) and Nathaniel Stephens of Chavenage (MP for the county). From August 1642, they established a 'Defence Association' for Gloucestershire aimed at countering the activities of the Marquess of Hertford in the western counties. At a large general meeting, it was agreed to accept parliament's Militia Ordinance, to organise a volunteer force for each of the five divisions in the county and to establish a magazine in Cirencester. By September, companies were being formed for training at both Gloucester and Chipping Sodbury. By October, the Association had collected £15,000 in gifts and loans on the basis of parliament's Propositions (see Chapter 3). By the end of the year, garrisons had been established in Gloucester, Cirencester and Tewkesbury.

The Defence Association was eventually to collapse with the fall of Cirencester in February 1643, partly through lack of support from the gentry. It had been kept going through the zealous commitment of just a handful of leaders, the active involvement of captains drawn essentially from business or the professions, and the loyal support of ordinary people in the south-east and centre of the county. On 6th January 1643, for instance, crowds of countryfolk again flocked into Cirencester carrying 'bills and forks' to help in thwarting Prince Rupert's first attempt to seize the town. A high level of popular support continued throughout the war - a fact noted by Clarendon, who confirmed that the enthusiasm of the yeomen was so alarming that none of the gentry (most of whom were loyal to the king) 'durst stay at their own homes'. Colonel Nathaniel Fiennes made a similar observation in September 1642, when he was besieging Worcester. He sent for the trained bands of Gloucestershire to assist him, adding that the county was 'so firm to the parliament, there is no doubt of their compliance'. (21)

It has to be said, however, that the commitment of ordinary people was not always reliable. After Rupert had taken Cirencester by storm on 2nd February, some of the prisoners captured alleged that they had been pressurised into joining the garrison by certain gentlemen and clothiers, who had threatened them with plundering or the loss of jobs if they did not join. Others claimed that they had been 'violently fetched from their homes' by soldiers or 'dragged from their ploughs'. Some apparently, having arrived in Cirencester innocently on business, had been detained there against their will and 'threatened to be shot' if they tried to escape. Although the reporter of these accusations was himself a royalist, the fact that many of the prisoners later defected on arrival in Oxford is perhaps an indication that loyalty for some was only skin deep. (22)

(d) Bristol

Although three hundred or so well-armed citizens had actively supported the rising on the Mendips while others had sent two waggon loads of ammunition and four small field guns, the mayor and sheriffs (according to John Ashe) 'did hinder and oppose it with all their skill'. Indeed, the Corporation tried desperately to remain neutral, drawing up a petition in favour of reconciliation between king and parliament and banning the wearing of colours and badges in the hats of the inhabitants. Bristol, unlike north Somerset had no deep political, religious or economic grievances in 1642. Indeed, there was little trace of puritanism in the city's eighteen churches, which were decorated and beautified according to the preferred taste of Archbishop Laud. The Council was dominated by merchants who were not closely involved with the gentry from neighbouring counties and were therefore isolated from their radical ideas. For instance, 75 per cent of new Council members came from the merchant community between 1620 and 1642, whereas only 3.2 per cent of new recruits were drawn from the ranks of gentry and yeomen between 1605 and 1642. Consequently, in response to the merchants' fear that the coming of war would bring untold disruption to their trade, the Council decided to strengthen the city's defences against *all* unwelcome visitors.

Meanwhile, the House of Commons, disappointed by the city's lack of enthusiasm for the parliamentary cause, sent its commissioners to investigate. On 17th October, they reported back that, in spite of the Council's outward appearances, they were clearly playing for time. 'We find both the mayor and many others very well affected to the parliament, if we

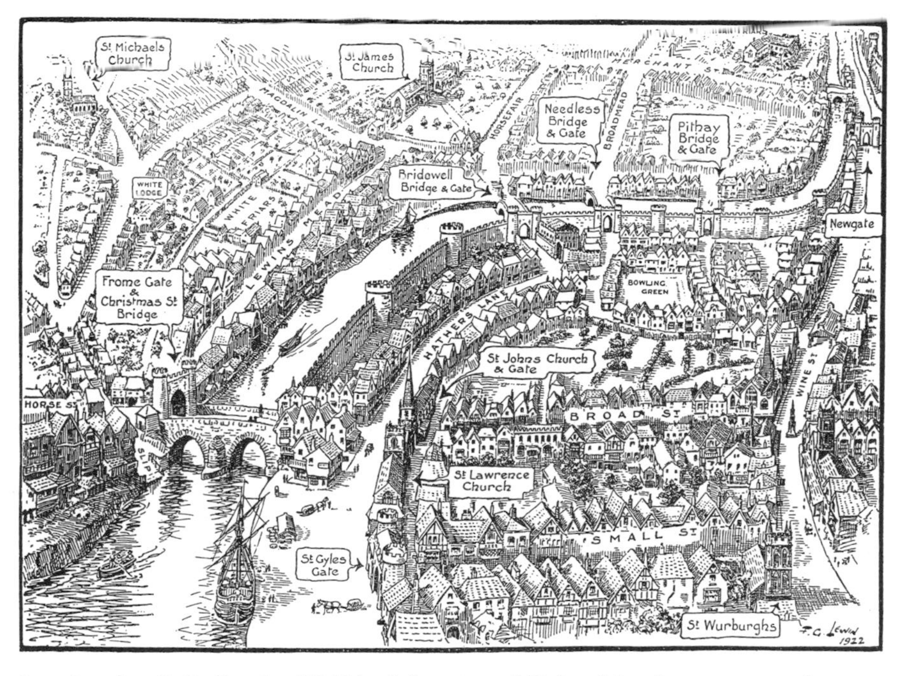

A drawing by F.G. Lewin (1922) of the city of Bristol in the seventeenth century, showing the river Frome which flanked the northern side of the walled area. (By courtesy of the Bristol Central Library)

may judge by verbal expressions - but no horse, plate or money subscribed! ...We assembled the mayor and aldermen today to put them in mind of their duties...After they had heard us with a great deal of regard and attention, they desired time to consider their answer'.

Gradually, however, Bristol was dragged unwillingly into the war, thanks largely to fierce pressure from the puritan gentry of Somerset, Wiltshire and Gloucestershire, who wrote to the Council in October urging them to join their association. The Council again played for time (as councils always do) by setting up a committee, but finally decided to stick to their policy of armed neutrality. The pressure on them, however, became almost irresistible when Popham moved his trained bands to Pensford (just six miles from the city), from where he despatched another strongly-worded request for a meeting, adding somewhat ominously: 'we shall then know who are for us or against us and provide accordingly'. At the same time, the Commons supplied its own weight to the argument by ordering the city to admit forces under the command of Colonel Essex, which were already advancing towards Bristol from Gloucester. The Council, fearful of occupation by these troops from 'foreign' parts, wrote to Popham in a state of panic pleading with him to enter the city before Essex in order to help avert what they termed 'an effusion of blood'. By 8th December, Bristol's armed neutrality was at an end. (23)

The Rise of the Clubmen, 1645

Armed neutrality, however, did have its moment in the three western counties later in the war, when country people again made their views felt and the men and women of north Somerset staged a second great rendezvous on the Mendips. Throughout 1645, in many southern and western counties, ordinary people banded together in a form of self-defence against the atrocities of war. Various 'Clubmen' or 'Peacekeeping' Associations had been formed out of sheer desperation to preserve local communities from 'plunder and all other violence'. In all, Clubmen Associations were formed in Shropshire, Worcestershire and Herefordshire (January to March), Wiltshire, Dorset and Somerset (May to September), Berkshire, Sussex and Hampshire (September to October) and south Wales (August to November). The growth of Clubmen occurred chiefly in those areas which had experienced uncontrolled plunder and attacks on property from large numbers of semi-independent garrisons or from outside armies as they trampled their way in and out of the county. By the spring of 1645, for instance, Goring's unpaid royalist army was running amok in the south-west.

These associations shared a number of characteristics, quite apart from their bitter hostility to soldiers of any kind. First, they were largely neutral, although this principle did not inhibit the formation of tactical alliances (including, for instance, an alliance with Fairfax's New Model Army to eject Goring from Dorset). Secondly, they were drawn essentially from the lower orders of society - the peasantry, the yeomen farmers and the clergy. Thirdly, although the various associations shared some common objectives (especially the need to rid themselves of outside interference and to return 'to known ways'), they differed in their motivation according to the particular nature of local grievances. The Clubmen, therefore, did not represent a unified and organised national movement. (24)

The first of the Clubmen Associations in the western counties, recruited from Dorset and Wiltshire, was established near Wimborne St Giles in late May. By June and July, the movement had spread into Somerset with similar associations formed in the south-east of the county (near Castle Cary), the west (beyond the Quantocks) and the centre (near Bridgwater). Their objectives were much the same - to present peace petitions to both king and parliament, to elect two or three officers from each parish to run the association, to protect themselves from plundering soldiers, to enlist 'uncommitted' men and to raise cash through local rates. The movement, which has been described by one historian as 'the most massive popular movement of the entire Civil War', remained largely neutral throughout both Wiltshire and Somerset, with slight leanings towards the royalists in Wiltshire and in the west and south-west of Somerset and towards parliament in central Somerset.

These local associations were well organised. Each village arranged for a watch to be maintained and for church bells to be rung, whenever groups of marauding soldiers were spotted. The parish officers drew up lists of all able-bodied men, who were expected to rush to the defence of the village when the signal was given, and established a small armoury of weapons and ammunition for use in emergency. Fairfax, in a letter to the Commons, reported that 'they meet with drums and flying colours; and for arms they have muskets, fowling pieces, pikes, halberds, great clubs and such like'. Members often wore white ribbons in their hats, which sometimes carried the motto, 'Peace and Truth'; banners were also spotted, bearing the verse:

> If you offer to plunder or take our cattle
> Be assured we will bid you battle.

The local groups were impressive in both organisation and size. It was estimated that in Wiltshire, for instance, as many as 20,000 people joined the Clubmen. In July 1645, Christopher Dale of Salisbury admitted that, although he had previously been in service with the royalist army, he was now a member of the Clubmen of Salisbury. Their aim, he said, was 'to defend themselves and their goods against all plunderers, but not to oppose either army'. Sixteen men (four per parish) had been chosen in the town to act as leaders of the group, which numbered about 700.

Groups from Wiltshire had joined with similar groups from Dorset to adopt their articles of association at the mass meeting at Gussage Corner, near Wimborne St Giles, on 25th May. Thereafter, they worked hard to present peace petitions to both king and parliament, such as the one organised by Thomas Bennet at a great assembly near Devizes, which called for an end to the 'unnatural wars' and the 'arbitrary power of the sword'. They also strove to act as mediators between the soldiers of both sides. Parliament received a report that 'they take it upon themselves to interpose between the garrisons on either side, and when any of the forces meet in places where they have sufficient power, such as Salisbury and the like, they will not suffer them to fight, but make them drink together'. In June, some of their leaders arranged a meeting between the commanders of two rival garrisons (the royalist one at Longford and the parliamentarian one at Faulston) and persuaded them to declare a temporary cease-fire until an answer had been received to their peace petition. In the meantime, they offered to pay each garrison £50 in maintenance. When necessary, however, the Clubmen were equally prepared to use force themselves to protect their interests. In particular, they had been incensed by the activities of Major Francis Dowett from the royalist garrison at Devizes, who had plundered the countryside around. His movements were, therefore, closely monitored throughout the villages, so that when he was spotted approaching Market Lavington with 40 troopers, the alarm was sounded and he found himself confronted by 1,000 Clubmen in arms. He quickly withdrew.

Nevertheless, in spite of their claims to neutrality, the Wiltshire Clubmen were regarded with deep suspicion by both sides. Fairfax, for instance reported to the Commons that 'they pretended only the defence of themselves from plunder, but not to side either with the king's forces or the parliament's'. He had, however, noticed that the leaders are 'such as have been active in the king's army or those that are known favourers of that party'. His patience with them was therefore quickly exhausted. Although, in July, Fairfax met with their representatives at Broad Chalke (between Salisbury and Shaftesbury), Cromwell eventually arrested their leaders after a dispute. More seriously, in August, when Fairfax was besieging Sherborne Castle, he was threatened by 10,000 Clubmen from Dorset and Wiltshire on Hambledon Hill, near Shaftesbury. Cromwell did his best to pacify them and indeed persuaded some of them to go home. However, when the remainder opened fire and killed several of his soldiers, he had little option but to launch a counter-attack. The Clubmen were no match for the professional soldiers of the New Model Army. Twelve local men were killed in the rout, many more were injured and 400 were taken prisoner. In a letter to Fairfax, Cromwell called them 'poor, silly creatures, whom if you please to let me send home, they promise to be very dutiful'. The Clubmen of Wiltshire crumbled in disarray. (25)

Meanwhile, in Somerset, 5,000 Clubmen had assembled near Castle Cary on 2nd June to draw up a petition denouncing the brutal activities of Goring's soldiers - a petition which was eventually presented to the Prince of Wales in Wells. Others in the area around Langport had banded together to resist similar acts of plunder and violence perpetrated by Mackworth's royalist garrison at Langport. On one occasion they had not only managed to halt the marauding force, but also to capture some prisoners and to advance on Langport itself. They were, however, quickly scattered by cavalry sent out from the town. By the end of June, Humphrey Willis of Woolavington (whose father was a yeoman farmer) had emerged as the leader of the group in mid-Somerset. After his proposals for the association had been accepted at a mass meeting at Pensy-Pound on Sedgmoor, he took 2,000 of his followers to a meeting with Fairfax on Knowle Hill, near Bawdrip. They appeared, much to the general's surprise, carrying white banners made from sheets, just as he was inspecting the New Model Army prior to the siege of Bridgwater. Willis explained that their aim was simply to protect their goods and petition for peace. Although Fairfax did his best to be sympathetic, he was somewhat startled when the Clubmen fired a loud, but chaotic volley of muskets in salute. (26)

There was one other group of Clubmen in Somerset, which turned out to be very different from the rest. The association, which had formed in the north-eastern part of the county by mid-July, was far less neutral in its stance. It very quickly rejected approaches from Prince Rupert, the Governor of Bristol who, in the face of an advance by the New Model Army, was in urgent need of allies. Meeting the Clubmen first at Wraxall, Rupert put on a show of force with one thousand troops and two pieces of ordnance 'partly to flatter and partly to affright'. The local countrymen, however, were made of sturdier stuff and stubbornly refused to acquiesce, either by giving him a volley of shot in submission or by allowing his force to pass through their ranks. This was followed by a further unsuccessful meeting on Lansdown a few days later. Once the New Model Army had arrived in the area, however, the local Clubmen immediately responded to a call from John Ashe and Sir John Horner (two of the leaders who, in 1642, had organised that remarkable rising at Chewton Mendip) to assemble once more on the Mendips - this time to meet with Oliver Cromwell and others sent by Fairfax. It is estimated that between four and five thousand Clubmen arrived for the meeting at the end of August, which was followed by a second gathering a few days later at Dundry. There they readily agreed to lend their support for the recapture of Bristol - a promise which was duly honoured by between two and three thousand of them. By mid-September, Fairfax had appointed Alexander Popham as their commander - the very same man who had led them into action against the Marquis of Hertford at Wells in 1642.

There is clear evidence from the accounts submitted by parishes at the end of the war that support for the Clubmen in north Somerset had been widespread, many villages charging a local rate 'for Clubmen's pay'. Camerton, Dunkerton, Claverton and Thrubwell had all sent contributions to the Clubmen 'then assisting Sir Thomas Fairfax', while Publow had paid four pounds and Chew Stoke five pounds for 'the Clubmen under the command of Colonel Alexander Popham'. Chew Magna, on the other hand, had sent 41 men from the village to assist, whereas Winterstoke had paid 'divers poor men' to go on their behalf, 'when the country was caused to come to Bristol'. Their spontaneous response to Fairfax's invitation represented a reawakening of that allegiance shown at the start of the war - allegiance which had lain dormant during two years of royalist occupation, but which had never been extinguished. As *The King's Weekly Intelligencer* pointed out at the time, these people had been 'active clubbers against Hopton, Stawell and the rest of the incendiaries in the western parts in 1642' and 'active clubbers' they had remained. They had merely awaited the opportunity to serve again (and, in the process, to defend their religion). The thought of neutralism had never entered their minds. (27)

The Tragic Divisions of War

There is no doubt, as we see daily on our television screens, that civil wars tear people asunder. In the summer and autumn of 1642, people living in towns and villages scattered across the three western counties were faced, sooner or later, with the stark choice of supporting either king or parliament. For some living in isolated hamlets, that choice was not presented until much later in the war, if indeed at all. For others, the decision came not as a choice but rather as an imposition by landlords or employers, who merely conscripted them into the ranks of the companies they were raising. There were many, too, who preferred to remain neutral in the conflict (like William Bassett of Claverton or Anthony Stocker of Chilcompton, both of whom tried to act as peace-makers when the war erupted in Somerset), though neutrality seldom remained an option for long. Whether they liked it or not, many ordinary people were quickly swept up into the conflict as armies marched across their fields or raided their barns. For most of those living in Gloucestershire, Somerset and Wiltshire, the day of decision came sooner rather than later. Given the economic and strategic importance of those three counties, there were to be few hiding places to which they could escape.

When the war finally broke out, families were torn apart. In 1644, a royalist musketeer named Hillsdeane was mortally wounded during the storming of Wardour Castle in Wiltshire. As he lay dying, he was suddenly struck by the horrible fact that he had been shot by his own brother, who was a member of the parliamentary garrison. Peter Walkman, Rector of Wootton Rivers in Wiltshire, proudly armed and equipped his two sons (by his second wife) for the king's service. Indeed, when one of them lost his horse and arms in battle, his father 'sent him forth again' with replacements. Much to his dismay, however, a son by his first wife turned out to be sympathetic to parliament's cause. 'I know thou art a roundhead rogue', he thundered at the unfortunate boy, 'and thou wilt go unto the parliament's army; which, if thou dost, thou shalt sink or swim for me; for thou shalt have no maintenance from me'. Some people, of course, found themselves divided from their families through no choice of their own. Edmund White of Broad Chalke in Wiltshire was forcibly conscripted into Hopton's army (much against his will), at a time when his son was fighting for parliament. (28)

The Trevillians, too, found themselves divided by war. Whereas Richard of Mildeney emerged as a keen parliamentarian and a member of its Somerset Committee, the brothers, Thomas of Wick, Robert of Mildeney and John of Kingsbury were arrested at the end of the war as ardent royalists - the latter having stated on one occasion, 'we shall hang the roundheads for twopence a dozen'. Nor is there is any doubt that family divisions caused considerable heartache to those involved. George Trevelyan of Nettlecombe was actively involved in raising men for the king's army, even though his brother, Christopher, was sympathetic to parliament. A keen puritan, Christopher had become a devoted follower of George Newton, the Vicar of St Mary's, Taunton, and had been spotted taking notes in a most meticulous manner as he listened to the thrice-weekly sermons. George Trevelyan's royalist leanings had caused grave concern to his uncle, Thomas Luttrell of Dunster. Writing in May 1643, Luttrell urged his nephew to listen to his advice and pay up the 'voluntary' loan demanded by parliament. He had already used his influence to preserve George's estates from plundering and would willingly put in a word to prevent his imprisonment - but only on condition that he would not persist in his 'former disobedience to parliament'. (29)

Neighbours were also torn apart. The lord of the manor at Claverton in Somerset, Sir William Bassett, eventually - after much wavering - decided to support the king. When, however, he worshipped at the little church next door each Sunday, he went to hear the Rector, Humphrey Chambers, who was a firebrand puritan and a keen supporter of parliament. For some neighbours, the war provided an opportunity to continue traditional feuds and local rivalries, which had built up over the years. In February 1643, a pitched battle took place between 'royalist' supporters from Bruton and their puritan neighbours from Batcombe, who supported parliament. The former triumphantly described their victory in the church registers:

All praise and thanks to God still give
For our deliverance Mathias' Eve.
By his great power we put to flight
Our foes the raging Batcombites,
Who came to plunder burn and slay
And quite consume our town this day.

This episode had far more to do with the tribalism of modern day football violence than with any principles for which the Civil War was fought. (30)

Friends, too, were torn apart. When Sir William Waller (whose first wife had been buried in Bath Abbey) commanded parliament's forces at the Battle of Lansdown in 1643, he came face-to-face with his old friend, Sir Ralph Hopton, who was a royalist. In their youth they had shared many adventures together on the continent, fighting as volunteers in the Thirty Years War. A few days before the battle, Waller wrote a most moving

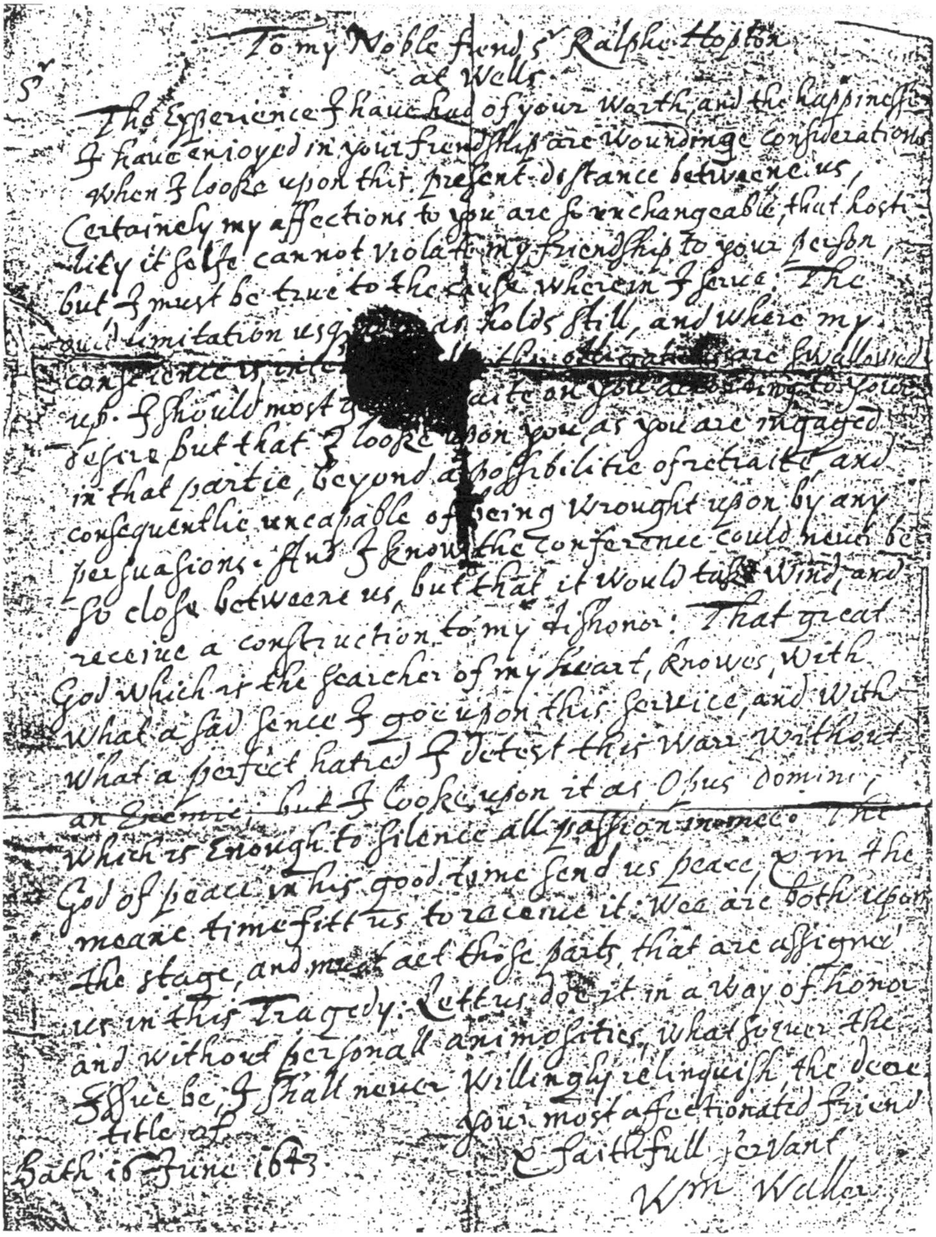
To my Noble frend Sr Ralphe Hopton
at Wells
Sr
The Experience I have had of your Worth and the happinesse
I have enioyed in your friendship are Woundinge considerations
when I looke upon this present distance betweene us,
Certainely my affections to you are so unchangeable, that hostility it selfe cannot violate my friendship to your person,
but I must be true to the cause wherein I serve. The
ould limitation us[illegible] ad aras holds still, and where my
conscience is [illegible] other obligations are swallowed
up. I should most [illegible] waite on you according to your
desire but that I looke upon you as you are ingaged
in that partie, beyond a possibilitie of retraite and
consequentlie uncapable of beinge wrought upon by any
persuasions. And I know the conference could never be
so close betweene us, but that it would take wind and
receive a construction to my dishonor. That great
God which is the searcher of my heart, knowes with
what a sad sence I goe upon this service, and with
what a perfect hatred I detest this Warr without
an Enemie, but I looke upon it as Opus domini,
which is Enough to silence all passion in mee. The
God of peace in his good time send us peace, and in the
meane time fitt us to receive it. Wee are both upon
the stage, and must act those parts that are assigned
us in this Tragedy. Lett us doe it in a way of honor
and without personall animosities, whatsoever the
issue be, I shall never willingly relinquish the deare
title of your most affectionated friend
and faithfull servant
Bath 16 June 1643
Wm Waller

The letter written by Sir William Waller to his old friend, Sir Ralph Hopton, on 15th June 1643, a few days before they met on the battlefield at Lansdown. (By courtesy of Mr P.J.N. Prideaux-Brune of Prideaux Place, near Padstow) letter to Hopton, as the royalist army prepared to advance on Bath - a letter which highlights the human tragedy of war. In it he laments the present distance between them. 'That great God, which is the searcher of my heart, knows with what a sad sense I go upon this service and with what a perfect hatred I detest this war without an enemy, but I look upon it as the work of the Lord...We are both upon the stage and must act those parts that are assigned to us in this tragedy...Whatsoever the issue be, I shall never willingly relinquish the dear title of your affectionate friend...' (31)

Cities were torn apart. When Bath City Council met in the Guildhall, two-thirds of its members supported parliament and one-third supported the king. Furthermore, the Chapman family, which had dominated the Council for years, was split down the middle. Whereas Henry Chapman actively fought for the king, his father (William), brother (Walter) and cousin (Richard) all supported parliament; and, whereas his father-in-law (Robert Fisher) was also a royalist by inclination, his brother-in-law (Matthew Clift) actually led the parliamentarian faction and was heavily involved in county politics. When the Corporation met in Salisbury, the council meetings were dominated by a puritan majority with parliamentarian sympathies, led by Alderman John Ivie. But they were opposed by a formidable coalition of enemies, including the brewers, the cathedral clergy and what Ivie termed 'the great unjust, rude rabble of the town'. More importantly, in 1641, they were opposed by the city's own Recorder and Member of Parliament, Robert Hyde, a keen supporter of the king and cousin to Edward Hyde, future Chancellor to Charles II.

Although the majority of citizens in Gloucester actively supported parliament against the on-going threat of siege, a list was drawn in 1643 up of 104 inhabitants who remained loyal to the king. The people of Cirencester quickly rallied to support parliament in its defence of the town against attacks by Rupert at the start of 1643. Nevertheless, several residents (including Sir William Masters, John James and Robert Keevel) gave valuable information to the royalists about the town's defences, while others acted as guides to lead the attackers in. When Marlborough was taken by storm in December 1642, the success of the royalists was partly attributed to help received from Captain Digges and some members of his trained bands, who had promised that 'they would not shoot' during the attack. According to a contemporary pamphlet, parliamentarian supporters in Bristol were openly abusive to their royalist neighbours, treating them with scorn and spitting at them 'as they passed in the streets'. (32)

***

In September 1644, Colonel Edward Massey (the parliamentarian Governor of Gloucester) led his forces out to attack the village of Beachley, situated at the point where the rivers Severn and Wye merge. Prince

Rupert, who had realised its strategic importance in commanding both the river traffic and the route between Wales and Bristol, had started to fortify it with a royalist garrison of 500 men. John Corbet later described the successful bombardment and assault by Massey's troops, making the point that 'it was performed in the full view of a multitude on the Chepstow side'. The local inhabitants had turned out in force as mere spectators on the river bank to enjoy a grandstand view of the action. Sadly, however, this experience of being passive observers of the conflict was by no means typical. Most ordinary people in the western counties, whatever their own allegiance, soon found themselves personally and inextricably caught up in the horrors of war. (33)

THE HORRORS OF WAR 1

LOYALTY UNREWARDED:

THE CASE OF RICHARD BANASTER

In 1653, seven years after the ending of the Civil War, Major Richard Banaster of Pexton, near Gloucester, was hauled before the Committee for Compounding in London and threatened with sequestration (or confiscation) of his property. Many royalist 'delinquents' had followed the same path for the part they played in the war. This case, however, was somewhat different, because Banaster was a most loyal and active supporter of parliament.

The problem was that he had rented a farm near Gloucester from Lord Craven (an ardent supporter of Charles I) and owed £150 in back rents. Craven himself had been declared a delinquent and his Gloucestershire estates had been duly sequestered in 1652. The state, therefore, now demanded Banaster's unpaid rent, which he was in no position to pay - hence the threat of confiscation hanging over his head. Following his petition against this course of action, commissioners were appointed to hear evidence on his behalf. The witnesses told a remarkable story.

Anne Viner testified that, during the wars, Banaster had been most enthusiatic in stirring up the local people to defend Gloucester against the king's forces and to work on the fortifications there. According to other witnesses, he had personally marched to Worcester with some neighbours at the start of the war to fight royalist troops there and had 'set forth a horse and arms in parliament's service', paying William Roberts out of his own pocket to ride it. Later, he sent Richard Layton, his husbandman, to Colonel Massey in Gloucester with a 'bay gelding' worth £12 14s 0d and '9 loads of hay and 2 fat oxen' worth £16 as contributions to the cause.

This, however, was only the start of his generous support of the war effort. Anne Viner and other neighbours particularly admired his response to a major threat in 1644, when it was widely believed that the royalists, having captured Painswick nearby, would attempt to establish a garrison in Churchdown church. 'At which time', they testified, 'the Major did with 20 foot soldiers secure and defend the said church and preserve it for the parliament against the enemy'.

Shortly afterwards, he raised a foot company of over sixty men to guard the church, keeping them 'at his own charge with meat and drink for nine weeks at least, during which time he killed eight of his own oxen, besides sheep and other provisions'. When the immediate crisis had passed, he decided to mount this troop, if money could be found. His wife then came to his rescue by bringing him £80, which she had hidden in the house - money which the Major immediately 'laid out for the raising of horse and arms for the service of the parliament'. Later, he also sold off some of his own land for £22 to help pay for the cost of maintaining the troop. All this was a huge sacrifice for him and his wife to endure, because they had ten children to support.

Their financial position became more and more acute as they were frequently raided by royalist forces based on Tewkesbury and Sudeley Castle - reprisals, according to Thomas Brosley, for Banaster's 'real affection to the parliament'. As a result, 'he could not keep any considerable stock of cattle about him' (the profit from which would have enabled him to pay his rent), 'but was enforced for a long time to lie out of his house for his own preservation from the late king's soldiers'. During his absence, a troop of cavaliers came from Cheltenham and badly plundered the house, taking away 'five good horses and some muskets, swords and arms, and also 15 pairs of flaxen sheets with a great quantity of other linen, and all the said Major's wearing apparel and all his wines'. During the siege of Gloucester, royalist troops again plundered the house, while they quartered there, seizing 'as much linen clothes as could fill three sacks and 7 fat sheep with great store of pulse and all the provisions he had then in his house'.

Two other vital witnesses spoke in his favour - Thomas Pearce and Nicholas Webb, gentlemen from Gloucester, who had been parliamentary commissioners in 1646-47. They had authorised at that time Banaster's compensation claim for losses sustained in the war, including £628 1s 6d, which he had spent on raising and maintaining his own cavalry troop, and £271 in pay, which was owed to him for his own military service.

In the light of all these testimonies, it was clearly evident that Banaster was broke and unable to pay his back rent - thanks almost entirely to his generosity to parliament's cause and the losses sustained through plunder. When finally he petitioned the Lord Protector, Oliver Cromwell, in January 1655, he asked that the £150 be deducted from the money spent on raising his troop and defending Churchdown church. On 19th January 1656, an Order in Council agreed that the £150 should be remitted, as requested, and that Banaster should be paid the balance due to him of £477 17s 0d. After a ten-year struggle, loyalty had finally been rewarded.

Sources: PRO, SP23.157, Committee for Compounding; *Calandar of the Committee for Compounding*, 1643-1660, pt. 4, pp 3158-9

Soldiers arriving on free quarter.
(Line drawing by Stephen Beck)

CHAPTER 2

Forced to Fight: War-time Conscription

We did lie all night upon the top of this mountain, it being a most terrible tempestuous night of wind and rain, as ever man lay out in, we having neither hedge nor tree to shelter, nor any sustenance of food or fire.
(Sergeant Henry Foster on Prestbury Hill, Gloucestershire, 1643)

The Trained Bands

When the Civil War broke out in England in August 1642, ordinary people in the western counties were quickly caught up in front-line action. There were already some citizens in Gloucestershire, Somerset and Wiltshire country who could be classed as 'trained soldiers'. Although the country did not as yet possess a professional standing army, the City of London and some counties in the provinces still maintained the system of 'trained bands' on which Elizabeth I had based the country's defences from 1573, as she awaited the threatened invasion from Spain. The system was financed by a 'trained-soldiers' rate imposed on each parish (to cover the cost of equipment and routine expenses) and controlled by the Deputy Lieutenants, who were responsible for calling annual musters to ensure that the men were adequately trained. The purpose was to provide an effective home guard, which would defend the county in time of invasion or other danger. As such, the trained bands were not expected to operate beyond their county boundary.

The government, in line with long traditions, expected that all men between the ages of sixteen and sixty should be ready to serve in the defence of the country. In reality, however, Elizabeth's trained band system concentrated its effort on a selected number of men, who had been given a rudimentary knowledge of the use of arms and the tactics of warfare. Although ideally the infantry was to be composed of substantial householders (rather than the dregs of society), this was seldom true in practice. As early as 1590, Lord Burleigh had commented that men of this type were too 'daintily fed and warm lodged' to be of real value in rough conditions. Recruitment was therefore spread more widely among the lower ranks of society. However, with the growth of impressment in the 1620s to enable Charles I to man his foreign expeditions, it was not unknown for more substantial yeomen to volunteer quite suddenly for service in the trained bands - membership of which carried exemption from impressment! Once recruited, the pikemen and musketeers were often equipped with an odd assortment of outdated weapons and armour. They were usually commanded and trained by younger members of the gentry, who were themselves totally inexperienced in warfare (although some of the corporals were old soldiers who had returned from continental campaigns). One of the exceptions in Somerset was Sir Ralph Hopton, who had served as a volunteer in the Thirty Years War.

The trained bands in theory met for one day's training once a month during the summer. According to Colonel Robert Ward, however, these sessions were a waste of time - 'matters of disport and things of no moment'. Writing in 1639, he complained that 'as trainings are now used, we shall, I am sure, never be able to make one good soldier'. The problem was that, by the time that the arms had been issued and inspected, it was almost 'dinner time' - and the officers 'love their bellies so well as they are loath to take much pains about disciplining of their soldiers'. Many of the troops apparently used to slip away to tipple in the local inns instead of training and then 'to fall a drinking after training', so that they were unfit for work next day. Ward strongly advocated the idea of meeting just twice a year for three or four days at a time (preferably in May and September to avoid the harvest) so that the troops could practise with greater intensity.

The highlight of the year for the trained bands was undoubtedly the annual regimental muster in the summer, when more detailed training in tactics could be given. In practice, the musters were often undermined by large-scale absenteeism as a result of their clash with the harvest - even though absentees risked a fine of forty shillings or ten days in gaol. To compensate for the sacrifice of time, members of the Somerset trained bands were paid eight pence per day for the muster weekend - a most generous rate, when compared with labourers' wages at the time (often no more than one-and-a-half pence a day). Prior to the event, warrants were

The trained bands under training. (Line drawing by Stephen Beck)

served by the High Constables of the hundreds on the captains of companies to muster their men and equipment; and on the village constables to produce their weapons from the local armoury and their powder and match from one of perhaps four county magazines.

In July 1632, for instance, the Lord Lieutenant of Wiltshire sent warrants to trained band commanders, instructing them to ensure that their men appeared 'completely furnished' for the muster at Warminster - 'every musketeer bringing with him two pounds of powder and convenient match. And that they do not omit, as most of them have formerly done, to bring with them their [bullet] mould, bullet bag and [musket] rest, that so they may be disciplined and trained'. Those who were absent 'without reasonable cause' would be liable to a forty shillings fine or ten days imprisonment. The muster, which lasted for two days and was held in an open field, was just as unsatisfactory as the monthly training sessions, judging by the experiences of Lord Poulett's regiment at Ilchester in Somerset. The troops always took a long time to dribble onto the site from their various villages; the constables took even longer to arrive with their weapons and powder; then the roll call by the clerks seemed to last an eternity; after which the Deputy Lieutenants insisted in drawing up warrants to be sent to absentees, before they were able to commence the training. It was therefore quite late in the day before Lord Poulett could commence the 'grand review'. (1)

By 1638, the Somerset trained bands (or county militia) numbered 4,000 foot (2,403 musketeers and 1597 pikemen) and 300 horse (82 heavily-armoured cuirassiers and 218 lightly-armoured harquebusiers). The infantry was organised into five regiments, each numbering 800 men, drawn from a particular sector of the county and commanded by a well-known member of the local gentry or nobility. Sir Edward Rodney (the Wells Regiment), Lord John Poulett (the Ilchester Regiment), Sir Ralph Hopton (the Bath Regiment), John Mallet and Sir Thomas Newton were the colonels of infantry. Within a regiment, seven individual companies were each recruited from a group of neighbouring parishes, which helped to produce something of a local spirit. The regiment of cavalry, recruited and equipped largely from the gentry class, was commanded by Sir Charles Berkeley of Bruton.

From a muster roll, dated in Bath on 22nd May, 1639, we know that Sir Ralph Hopton's Bath Regiment was drawn from the north-eastern part of the county. Within that regiment his own double company of two hundred men was given a highly-structured organisation. Hopton was assisted by eleven officers (a lieutenant, a quartermaster, an ensign, four sergeants, a clerk and two drums). Almost half the company's strength was recruited from the Keynsham hundred, the rest coming from places within the hundreds of Bathforum, Frome and Wellow. The infantrymen, divided into 80 pikes and 125 muskets, were drawn from over forty villages each with its own allocation (ranging from eight for the town of Keynsham to just one each for the villages of Widcombe, Nunney and

North Stoke). Although the parish constables were responsible for ensuring that the quotas were maintained, there had clearly been some negligence in the villages of the Bathforum hundred, which had been marked as being '13 men short'. The company met for training in Bath once a month, setting up targets for shooting practice on banks of turf or 'butts' in a close known as 'Butt Haies' and drilling in a meadow outside the West Gate. Their weapons were stored and maintained in the Guildhall, where John Gray, the armourer, was given periodic payments for 'scouring the armour', 'mending the faults in the armoury' or 'a board to set the armour on'. (2)

Once the Civil War had started, both king and parliament made a dash to control the trained bands in those areas which fell under their influence. Inspired by a similar and urgent need to create armies from scratch, both sides turned to groups of influential supporters in each county to raise the militia on their behalf - the king through the issue of commissions of array and parliament through the establishment of County Committees. In Gloucestershire, Somerset and Wiltshire, however, the king's attempts to seize control in 1642 were largely thwarted, thus ensuring that parliament secured initial use of the trained bands in the early months of the war (see Chapter 1).

Their County Committees were also quick to ensure that units were maintained at full strength. In Gloucestershire, for instance, the High Constable of the North Nibley hundred instructed each village constable within his area in August 1642 to recruit between six and eight additional men so that 'defects in the trained bands' could be remedied. The bands were then to muster at The Ridings, near Chipping Sodbury as part of the county's new Defence Association. In Somerset, the Corporation of Wells received a letter from parliament's county commissioners in Somerset in November noting that, whereas the city had previously maintained a force of 44 trained band soldiers, the unit was now 'very defective...by the reason of the death of divers persons that performed those services'. They therefore ordered the Corporation to provide from within the town 'twenty good corslets with swords and pikes and as many muskets with bandoliers, rests, headpieces and swords, assigning and appointing sufficient persons to serve in the said forty arms'. Furthermore, they were to be ready to muster at twenty-four hours notice. The cost of all this equipment, of course, fell heavily on the citizens of Wells - as it did elsewhere in the western counties. The town of Portbury in Somerset, for example, claimed that it had always maintained 'eighteen trained soldiers completely armed' throughout the war, but that their weapons and armour - valued at £30 - had mostly been 'lost in the parliament's service'. (3)

In some cities and counties, the trained band system had fallen into a state of disuse or was not sufficiently strong for the needs of war. A parliamentary Ordinance was therefore quick to plug the gap in Taunton in March 1643, as the city prepared to resist the arrival of Hopton's royalist army from Cornwall, by authorising the establishment of new trained bands. The Mayor and Corporation were granted powers to call, assemble, arm and train 'all persons fit for the war...that shall voluntarily offer themselves to serve in and for the said borough'. They were also ordered to tighten up on the lax attitudes which had previously prevailed, especially with those members of the bands who had 'neglected to make their appearance in arms' when required. The situation was now critical. The officers, therefore, were empowered to draw up a rota of all trained band members so that 'a constant watch or guard both day and night' could be maintained to ensure the safety of Taunton. If any member refused to appear, he was to be fined 2s. 6d. for each offence or face imprisonment. (4)

The city of Bristol, on the other hand, was already much better equipped for war, by the autumn of 1642, with something in the region of 400 troops operating in four companies of trained bands. According to one visitor during the 1630s, the local captains frequently drilled the three foot companies in the Marsh, where the river 'causeth a sweet and pleasant echo of their martial music, drums, fifes and volleys of shot'. There was also apparently a volunteer company 'of gentile, proper, martial and disciplined men, who have their arms lodged in a handsome artillery house, newly built up in the Castle Yard, where once a year, they invite and entertain both earls and lords, and a great many knights and

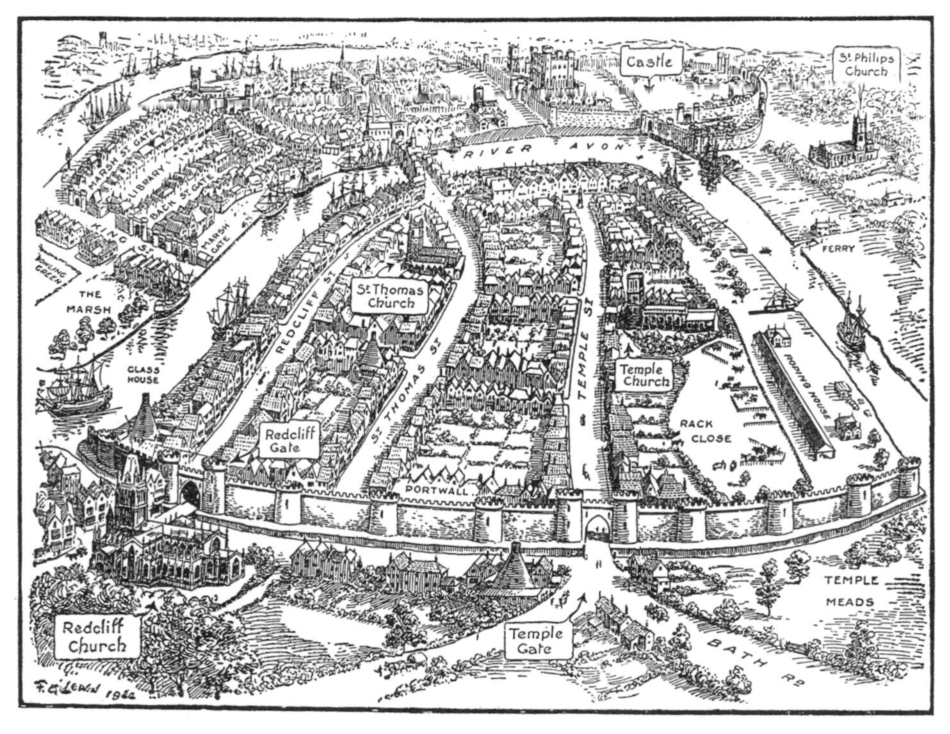

A drawing by F.G. Lewin (1922), showing the walled section of 17th century Bristol to the south of the river Avon with the Marsh on the left. (By courtesy of Bristol Central Library)

gentlemen of rank and quality, at their military feast; and this yard affords them a spacious and a large place to drill and to exercise in'. This was the time of the annual muster, which provided a great social occasion.The Bristol trained bands, however, were also expected to take seriously the task of guarding their city. As hostilities commenced in the country at large, Bristol Corporation stipulated that one hundred musketeers should be on watch duty every night, supervised by five members of the Council; and that every day one company of the bands should be 'in readiness with their arms and be in [the] field'. (5)

The Bath Regiment usually held its muster at Wells, supported heavily by the efforts of the Bath Corporation. In 1642, for instance, they contributed a sum of £4 18s 4d towards the constables' expenses in taking 'the soldiers to Wells and horsehire'. At the same time, they emptied the armoury and paid Thomas Saunders for 'carrying the arms to Wells'. Their metal smith, John Gray, was also sent at their own cost to give what practical help he could in repairing defective arms and armour on site. Furthermore, one of their own members (John Biggs) was despatched with a large supply of wine to entertain 'the colonel and commanders at the General Muster' at a total cost of £6 17s 9d (no mean sum). (6)

During peacetime, membership of the trained bands could often provide an enjoyable pastime - a largely voluntary activity, which brought with it a degree of social recognition. The outbreak of hostilities in 1642, however, quickly brought members of the Somerset militia face-to-face with the stark realities of war. Before August was out, seven of them had been killed (and many more wounded or captured) in a skirmish at Marshall's Elm, near Street. By September, as they helped the Earl of Bedford to lay siege to Sherborne, they had tasted the sheer horror of conflict. According to an eye-witness, they ran 'as if the devil had been in them...when they heard the bullets whistle about their ears'. Over half the 3,000 foot soldiers deserted in terror. In March 1643, those raw and inexperienced members of the bands, who had accompanied Sir William Waller on his mission to capture Malmesbury in Wiltshire, suddenly discovered that they lacked the stomach for bloodshed. In their first attack on the town, 'the falling of some' of his recruits, wounded by musket fire, considerably 'cooled' the enthusiasm of the remainder. Before the summer of 1643 had ended, many of those same trained bands had fought and survived the bloody Battle of Lansdown; but had then gone on to Devizes, where they had been virtually wiped out in the rout of Waller's army. (7)

One interesting and slightly less dangerous task, which was allotted to various companies of the Somerset bands in August 1642, was that of searching for arms. After the local parliamentarians had managed to drive the Marquess of Hertford out of the county and had thereby seized control, the Somerset Committee made out a list of all suspected royalists. Then, backed by detachments of the trained bands, members of the committee made early morning raids on the homes of all suspects in many towns throughout the county, including Taunton, Bridgwater, Wells, Bath,

Glastonbury, Ilchester, Shepton Mallet, Chard, Crewkerne and South Petherton. This mission was highly successful in unearthing weapons, armour and ammunition, which had clearly been stockpiled for future use, including 1,800 sets of armour, 150 saddles, £10,000 in money, 25 light horses and various quantities of muskets, swords, barrels of gunpowder and shot. All this was impounded and sent under escort to the magazine at Taunton Castle. However, although the bands undoubtedly enjoyed this exciting piece of action, some of them were to find that the enemy did not always lie down quite so easily in war. One group, arriving at Lord Poulett's house in Crewkerne, found it barred against them and the servants inside shouting 'be gone' or they would 'let bullets fly amongst them'. Sadly, as the trained bands broke open a door and forced their way in, one of their number was shot dead. (8)

Volunteers

Parliament did its best to ensure that the trained band system continued to operate. A boost was given by the instructions issued to Deputy Lieutenants in both Somerset and Wiltshire, in January 1643, that they were to raise money on the parish rates to ensure that each member of the bands was paid eight pence a day, while on active service. Nevertheless, it quickly became apparent to both sides that the war could never be won on the strength of the trained bands alone. The urgent need for additional forces therefore resulted in a nationwide appeal for more volunteers both to strengthen the county militias and to create large field armies capable of campaigning across the country. On the local level, influential members of the gentry and nobility were quick to offer their services by raising bodies of friends, neighbours and tenants either for king or parliament. In Somerset, for instance, royalist forces were strengthened by Sir John Stawell of Colthelstone, who raised three troops of cavalry and one of infantry in 1643. Similarly, in Gloucestershire, Sir Baynham Throckmorton, the High Sheriff, was given a commission by the king 'to raise and entertain' a regiment of five hundred 'horsemen volunteers' in March of the same year; while, seven months later, Christopher Fawkener received another commission to raise a regiment of 500 'horse volunteers' and a regiment of 1,200 'foot volunteers'.

Earlier still, Lord Chandos had been commissioned to recruit a regiment of horse in the same county. One of the captains he appointed in January 1643 was Richard Atkyns of Tuffley, near Gloucester, who described in his diary the efforts he had made to raise his own troop in support of Chandos. He was so successful in this task that within a month he had mustered '60 men besides officers, and almost all of them well armed'. He scrounged what he could from friends and neighbours, John Dutton giving him 30 steel back-and-breast plates with helmets, plus 'two men and horses completely armed'. There was, nevertheless, an immediate crisis, because no money or quarters had been assigned to support the troop -

with the result that some of the volunteers immediately deserted ('every fourth or fifth man was lost'). Atkyns, like many gentlemen in the war, was therefore forced to dig deep into his own pockets, twice paying his troopers' wages out of his 'own purse'.

Recruiting volunteers, however, could sometimes be a hazardous operation, as Sir Ralph Dutton of Painswick in Gloucestershire found to his cost as hostilities commenced in August 1642. The House of Commons, hearing that Dutton 'beats up a drum in Gloucestershire and Hereford for soldiers', issued an order that he should be apprehended as a delinquent. A few days later, the Gloucestershire Under-Sheriff, accompanied by ten soldiers, made a brave attempt to execute that order. Catching Dutton and a group of his supporters red-handed as they were busy 'raising men against the parliament', they set upon him in earnest. But although two of the cavaliers with him were captured, Dutton narrowly managed to escape by plunging into the river Severn and swimming across to the other bank! Undaunted by his experience, he appeared at the side of the king in Nottingham with his newly- raised regiment, when the royal standard was raised on 22nd August. In order to encourage this tricky process of gaining volunteers, Charles I later promised (in December 1642) that 'whosoever will serve the king as a foot soldier with his own musket' would receive six shillings a week, while a dragoon with a musket would earn twelve shillings and a trooper equipped with horse and pistol would get 17s 6d, plus a joining bonus of £3.00. In March 1643, Sir Samuel Luke noted in his diary that royalist officials did 'beat up drums daily in several towns in Wiltshire' to recruit soldiers, offering them as an inducement eighteen pence per day and two shillings bounty on joining. Sadly, not all promises on pay were honoured. (9)

For parliament, companies of volunteers had been raised in Gloucester, Salisbury and Taunton, even as early as July 1642, while John Pyne had assembled 600 yeomen and cloth workers from west Somerset and Sir John Horner several hundred countrymen from Mells at much the same time. John Ashe, the great clothier from Freshford in Somerset, later claimed that he had 'raised, armed and for many weeks paid a troop of horse, a company of foot and a company of dragoons for ye service of ye west country...and paid for powder, match and bullet expended by them all, which cost him above £3,000'. At the same time, he had raised some dragoons and musketeers for service in Wiltshire at a cost of £200. All this was before the introduction of the weekly assessment in 1643 made possible the official payment of troops. (10)

This spontaneous, but somewhat haphazard response was most commendable, but it hardly solved the overall problem for which more systematic measures were needed. In particular, there was an urgent need for cavalry and dragoons (a specialised form of infantry, who were equipped with horses for speed and manoeuvrability). These were much more expensive to establish and therefore more difficult to assemble on a voluntary basis. Not everyone had either the resources or the generosity of

John Ashe. Parliament therefore issued a series of Ordinances to give a boost to this aspect of recruitment. The 'Propositions' of June, 1642 had encouraged voluntary contributions of money and individual gifts of horses and weapons from all householders. The newly-appointed committee for Somerset therefore set about implementing this order, putting the proceeds towards the raising of a regiment of dragoons under the command of Alexander Popham (who was already commander of the Bath Regiment of trained bands). As the militia increased in size, so the task of training and enlarging it even further was undertaken by four Deputy Lieutenants - Popham and William Strode in the east of the county and John Pyne and Sir John Wroth in the west. In Wiltshire, exactly the same approach was evident when an Ordinance was issued, in January 1643, to raise two regiments of horse and one of dragoons to be financed by voluntary donations, the confiscated estates of royalists and fines imposed on those who had not contributed to the Propositions. By the following month, all these troops In Wiltshire (together with the trained bands) had been placed under the command of Sir Edward Hungerford. Nevertheless, recruitment of county forces at this stage continued to be based on the volunteer. (11)

Local gentry, who had succeeded in raising volunteer troops of horse or companies of foot, usually developed an understandable pride in their new creation. This was, after all, a totally fresh experience in their lives and offered a further dimension to their traditional status in the locality George Trevelyan of Nettlecombe In Somerset, for instance, had raised one such troop for the king in 1643. Anxious to give his men their own identity, he worked out a plan to attach his colours to their coats, so that they would more easily recognise each other on the field of battle. He was, therefore, understandably deflated when a neighbour (John Mallet, a long-standing regimental commander in the trained bands) wrote to him in a condescending manner criticising his scheme. In war, stated Mallet, soldiers were normally identified by attaching their colours to the trim on their weapons or armour. 'The daubing of a coat with lace of sundry colours...I do neither take to be soldier-like, nor profitable for the coat'. Furthermore, when the captaincy of the troop changed, the colours would have to be replaced - 'so he tears off the old colours and often tears coat and all'. Both Trevelyan and Mallet, like most officers at this stage in the conflict, were somewhat inexperienced in the realities of war. Leadership, moreover, was still based on the principle of the glorious amateur. (12)

This was further illustrated in August 1643 by the news that various clergymen in Somerset had 'out of affection to the king 'raised and armed divers men and horses for the royal service'. Many clergymen in the diocese, wary of the puritan drive for reform, pledged themselves to the royalist side - including Christopher Sadbury (Rector of Weston-super-Mare), James Masters (Rector of Bath Abbey) and James Dugdale (Rector of Evercreech). In spite of their commitment to the cause, however, they were the first to admit that they lacked the necessary officer skills. When, therefore, King

Charles discovered that these valuable recruits were still leaderless, he instructed the High Sheriff of Somerset to see that the men were mustered, listed and put under the command of Colonel Horatio Cary, who was himself in the process of raising a regiment. In Wiltshire, too, clergy rallied around the royal standard. Thomas Hickman of Upton Lovell contributed two horses, whereas James Whitney of Donhead St. Mary sent three and Mr Reyley of Newton Tony supplied one. Some were even more generous. Robert Walker of Chilmark despatched one of his servants to undertake duties as the High Sheriff's bodyguard, while Henry Collier of Steeple Langford deserted his church living and, having equipped himself with a horse and armour, rode out to join the king's forces. (13)

The recruitment of field armies (from outside the local county) also relied initially on willing volunteers. The armies tended to recruit as they marched through towns and villages *en route* for their destination. Captain Richard Atkyns, who marched with the Marquess of Hertford's relief force from Oxford to join Sir Ralph Hopton's Cornish army at Chard in the summer of 1643, commented in his diary: 'We did not much in our march, but raise men and arms until we came to Crewkerne'. When the king's own army first took the field, it eventually reached Myddle in Shropshire, where the king's Commissioner of Array had organised a mass meeting of local people. There, according to an eye-witness, the recruiting officer 'with a paper in his hand and three or four soldiers' pikes stuck upright in the ground by him' tempted men to volunteer with the promise of 4s4d a week in wages. Twenty responded to the call. However, as the demands of the military operation grew and the horrors of war were increasingly revealed, this reliance on voluntary effort became more and more unworkable. When Sir William Waller was appointed Major-General of all parliament's western forces in February 1643, he was faced with an order to raise for his field army five new regiments of horse and five new regiments of foot in six western counties (including Gloucestershire, Somerset and Wiltshire) - an extremely difficult assignment, even though parliament normally granted £1,100 'mounting money' to each cavalry captain to help him in equipping a troop and similar 'levy money' to assist colonels in recruiting infantry regiments. (14)

Conscription

It was therefore almost inevitable that, sooner or later, the commanders of both sides would rely increasingly on conscription (or impressment) as the main method of recruitment. Unofficially, royalist commanders had been practising this from the middle of 1643, but the system was not formally ratified by the king until the November of that year, when his council of war recommended the use of conscription on a national basis. This was followed almost immediately in December by the issuing of royal commissions to the High Sheriffs in various counties 'to impress in that county for His Majesty's service so many able men to serve in his army' (the

A recruiting officer at work in 1643. (An original painting by Angus McBride - by courtesy of © Osprey Publishing Ltd.)

actual numbers being specified in a covering letter). In Gloucestershire, for instance, the local commissioners who were charged with the task were instructed to conscript one thousand men from the Berkeley Division of that county for use in the garrisons of Bristol and Thornbury. A month later (January 1644), the king issued specific warrants to Sir William Moreton (High Sheriff of Gloucestershire) and Sir John Penruddock (High Sheriff of Wiltshire) not only authorising impressment, but also severe punishment for those who refused to receive the 'pressed money' or who later deserted from the service. The cost was to be raised from a contribution from parishes and the sale of the property of those who were disaffected. In Wiltshire, this particular commission (renewed in February) concentrated on raising as many men as possible for Hopton's new field army, which was to operate within that county and those immediately adjacent. Hopton pursued his task with vigour, sending out personal instructions and ordering cloth for the uniforms from clothiers in Salisbury and elsewhere. (15)

This policy of conscription was extended by the king's Oxford Parliament in March 1644 to cover the further impressment nationally of 6,000 foot soldiers for the king's own field army. Special committees were established (including one for the western counties) to be responsible for organising the operation and making fair allocations to those counties which were under the king's control. The impact of this decree was immediately felt in Wiltshire, which had been given a quota of 667 men. The commissioners quickly worked out the allocations for the separate hundreds within the county, sending out warrants to the appropriate High Constables who were then responsible for dividing out the total between individual villages, where the detail would be administered by the parish constables. The hundred of Potterne and Cannings, for instance, received a demand for 21 men, which was regarded as 'a proportionable number'. The High Constable was ordered to impress the men immediately and to conduct them to the king's commissioners in Devizes by the following Friday - failure to perform would be at their 'uttermost peril'. They were also given clear guidelines as to the type of soldier they were to recruit. Preference was to be given to single, able-bodied men ('not housekeepers'), who were 'fit to be soldiers and fit for their age'. Ideally, they should be drawn from the ranks of mechanics and tradesmen rather than husbandmen or apprentices - and certainly not seamen. A similar situation prevailed in Gloucestershire, where the Forest of Dean was ordered to provide 600 foot and 180 horse for the king's field army. Other areas suffered too. The High Constable of the Grumbaldash hundred, for instance, received an order in May to make warrants to all the petty officers in the hundred 'for the pressing of 35 men of able and strong body, well clothed, [who] may best be spared and [are] unmarried'. They were to report to The Lamb, outside Lawford's Gate in Bristol, at 9.00 am eleven days later.

The king continued to rely heavily on the goodwill of influential local people in each county to exert pressure on their neighbours for support in the recruiting process. In July, 1644, for example, Sir John Stawell called a meeting at Bridgwater of lukewarm gentry from west Somerset and spent a whole day persuading them to co-operate. Eventually, they agreed to raise through the normal procedure of parish allocations two thousand men 'to be ready within one week of the issuing of warrants'. They apparently then departed 'with a show of much cheerfulness'. Diplomatic methods like these, however, were not always employed to achieve results. There is some evidence that royalist commissioners and their assistants used strong-arm tactics to pressurise and bully local people into service as conscripts.

John Bickham, for instance, employed a good measure of force in 1644, when recruiting for Sir John Stawell's regiment in Somerset. Arriving at Matthew Stile's house in Kingstown with four soldiers, he pulled the man's sick son out of bed to enrol him for the expedition to Lyme. When, however, the son refused to go, Bickham 'plundered his father's house' and seized a horse worth £10 for the use of the regiment. At Broad Chalke in Wiltshire, John Lawes, the royalist tithingman, visited the house of Edmund White, breaking open the door 'with a lever', and impressed him to serve the king in Hopton's army. According to eyewitnesses, Lawes used violence in dragging him out of bed and 'hurt him', even though he was sick and sixty years of age. White was apparently 'in such a fear that he trembled and could neither put off or on his clothing'. He died within six weeks, claiming on his deathbed that Lawes 'had been the death of him'. (16)

Parliament, meanwhile, had reached a similar conclusion about the need to conscript. In August, 1643, they issued an Ordinance which empowered Deputy Lieutenants and committees in each county to raise and impress 'soldiers, gunners and surgeons' with the help of the parish constables. Refusal by individuals to be impressed would result in imprisonment 'until they shall yield obedience or pay the sum of ten pounds to the said committee'. Some people, however, were exempt from impressment - clergy, students at university or the inns of court, members of the trained bands, those with sufficient assets to have been rated for the last subsidy granted by parliament, those with the rank of esquire, those under 18 or over 50, Members of Parliament (and their servants), seamen, fishermen, and the inhabitants of the Isle of Wight, Anglesey or the Cinque Ports.

Later, in August 1644, when parliament established an Association of the Western Counties in an attempt to wrest control of this area from the royalists, the age limits were modified. Parish officers were then instructed to send in lists of all able-bodied people aged 16 to 60 for possible impressment. When a crisis arose, however, parliamentary commanders often ignored official guidelines and attempted a more general recruitment. As early as 12th June 1643, for instance, the Somerset Committee, frightened by the rapid advance of Hopton's army through Somerset, called a rendezvous in Wells 'requiring all from 16 to 60 to come into them with all sorts of arms'. The meeting was, however, frustrated by Hopton's sudden and unexpected arrival in the city. Similarly, in October, 1644, Waller (based in Salisbury) was anxious to strengthen his army as he sought to re-establish control of Wiltshire. According to the Venetian ambassador, 'Every head of a family is commanded either to go himself or to maintain a man at his own cost. They are also pressing in all the streets'. (17)

It is estimated that some 10 per cent of the adult male population found itself under arms at any one time during the years 1643-45 and that 20-25 per cent actually fought for at least a short period during the war. The rapid increase in the size of the armies ensured that a more general cross-section of the lower orders of the village and town population eventually found itself under arms. In order to fill the required numbers quickly, some constables tended to look instinctively towards the prisons, the unemployed or the dregs of society. Barnaby Rich suggested in 1587 that this policy was something of a long-standing tradition: 'In England, when service happens', he wrote, 'we disburden the prisons of thieves, we rob the taverns and alehouse of tosspots and ruffians, we scour both town and country of rogues and vagabonds'. Supply of this kind was soon exhausted, however, and they were quickly forced to look elsewhere. Impressment therefore became a most feared and detested aspect of the war, parishes waiting in dread for the arrival of the next warrant - such as the one received by the constables of Bulkington and Potterne in January 1645. 'I do hereby straightly charge and command you forthwith upon receipt hereof to impress within your precincts two able men for the recruit of his Majesty's army, and to bring them to me to The George in Meere upon Friday next...' (18)

Employers lived in anxiety that their apprentices would be taken, thus draining their businesses of essential labour, just as apprentices feared the loss of their placement when they returned (even though a parliamentary Ordinance had encouraged their recruitment by guaranteeing their immunity from loss of indentures). This was certainly the fate of John Rogers, who had been apprenticed to Thomas Harris, weaver, of Warminster in Wiltshire in 1642. Two years later, according to his petition for relief submitted to the Quarter Sessions at the end of the war, 'he was pressed to be a soldier to serve in the King's army and, having no affection that way, got himself off and went onto ye parliament army and there served till May 1645; after which time your petitioner repaired to his master and tendered his service, who refused the same...for he would make no further use of your petitioner'. (19)

It was of course particularly galling for men like Rogers, who felt a sense of allegiance to one particular side in the conflict, only to be impressed by the other. This was even more the case, if subsequently they were wounded while fighting for the enemy. Richard Ricketts of Rudge, a carpenter by trade, had been impressed by the royalists and by force carried to the Longford garrison in Wiltshire, much against his will. There he had been dangerously wounded, crippled and disabled for all future service or labour, thus driving him to seek the charity of his neighbours in his struggle to support his child. (20)

For the unfortunate wretch who had been singled out for conscription in his village, there were still a number of options open for him to avoid service. Some managed to secure release through their contacts with members of the County Committee or other figures of influence. Others were able to purchase their exemption, as the inhabitants of Publow in Somerset found to their relief in 1643. It cost William Gage and Nathaniel Lott twenty-eight shillings each to be 'freed from the service', plus the donation of either a musket or a pike. The anguish suffered by relatives in war is illustrated by the action of Thomas Elme from the same village, who put up the necessary money together with a musket 'to free his kinsman Wm. Elme from bearing his arms under Col. Popham'. However, these were large sums of money which few could afford. Other options presented themselves elsewhere, because constables had a certain amount

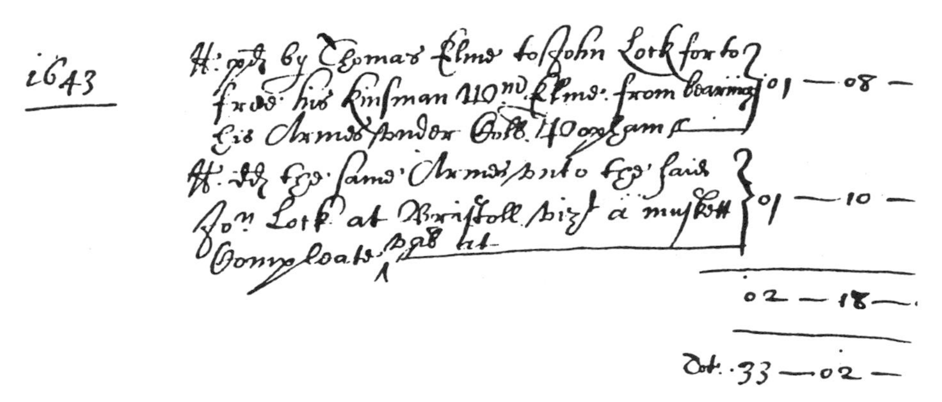
1643 It: paid by Thomas Elmes to John Lock for to free his kinsman Wm Elmes from bearing his Armes under Colo. [illegible] 01 — 08 —
It: for the same Armes unto the said Jon Lock at Bristoll viz a muskett [illegible] 01 — 10 —
02 — 18 —
Tot. 33 — 02 —

Money paid to buy exemption from service for William Elme of Publow. (By courtesy of the Public Record Office - SP28.175)

of freedom in deciding how they would achieve their objective. Sometimes, therefore, it was possible to arrange a substitute (or 'supply') to go in your place. For instance, Thomas King had been conscripted in Brockley, which was in the Chewton hundred in Somerset. After seeing active service for parliament at both Bath and Wells, 'he set forth a supply in his place and the supply was at Sherban [Sherborne] and did continue in the service until after the fight that was at the Vizes [i.e. the Battle of Roundway Down]'. Joseph Durban from the same village had also used this option of providing a replacement after serving part of the commitment himself. (21)

Some people, of course, came up with elaborate excuses which, they hoped would gain them exemption from the service. In January 1644, for instance, Robert Marshman, a tobacco-pipe mender from Bristol, had been visiting friends in the country and was returning home, when he was detained in Bath and forced to accept 'press money' from a royalist recruiting officer. With the Mayor's strong support, he lodged a vigorous appeal against his conscription on the grounds that he was already a petty constable in Bristol, serving the king there by organising the quartering of royalist soldiers. Other people, faced by the threat of impressment, did not wait around to be caught! In June 1644, a scout reported back to Sir Samuel Luke (the parliamentary Governor of Newport Pagnell) that Hopton was busy in Somerset conscripting forces, especially men worth £110 a year in rent. This policy, he said, 'causes many of them to forsake their dwellings'. (22)

Once a man had been conscripted, of course, his only remaining option was to desert at the first opportune moment. Desertion was an enormous problem to the military commanders of both sides. In parliament's army of the Eastern Association, for instance, of 209 conscripted recruits who assembled at the transit camp in Cambridge in July 1644, only 95 actually reached the army itself. So serious did the situation become that stiff punishments were soon ordered for deserters. A parliamentary

Ordinance of March 1645 decreed the death penalty for those found guilty, at the same time threatening fines of £10 on parishes guilty of concealing the runaways and forty shillings per soldier on householders who had offered shelter. Parish officers were instructed to search houses regularly for deserters. (23)

A deserter is arrested.
(Line drawing by Stephen Beck)

The High Constables of the hundred of Potterne and Cannings in Wiltshire were to find, in May 1644, that the royalists could be just as demanding in their concern over deserters. They received an urgent letter from the king's county commissioners alerting them to the fact that four impressed soldiers from their hundred (who were named) had run away. The High Constables were therefore ordered to 'cause all the parishes and tithings to be duly searched' within the hundred and to send them 'with all speed to the Devizes to Captain Robert Skirrowe'. If they could not be found, the constables were to 'impress the same number of men to supply their places'. The letter ended with the sort of threat that was so characteristic of the time - namely, that if they failed in this task, they and the parish constables would be carried off to Oxford to explain themselves to the king's council of war. Later in the year, the policy was further tightened. Faced with an ever-growing number of deserters as the winter closed in, the king issued a proclamation in December ordering their immediate return to duty and warning ordinary residents that they risked £5 fine for providing runaways with shelter (£1 of which would go to the informer!). (24)

The poor parish constable had the most difficult task of all, being subject to all kinds of abuse in the thankless work of organising conscription. Once the recruits had been identified, the constable was responsible for ensuring that they were issued with shoes and other clothing suitable for soldiers on the march (e.g. breeches, shirts, caps and stockings). The warrant issued by royalist commissioners to the High Constables in Wiltshire in April 1644 clearly specified: '...you shall take care that they be conveniently apparelled, either of their own or by the assistance of the parish where they are impressed'. Once they reached their regiment, they were issued only with a coat at the colonel's expense, because the basic costs had already been met by the parish. (25)

By far the worst task for the constable, however, was to ensure that the recruits actually reached the nominated point of rendezvous, where they could be handed over to a captain for escort to their regiment. If any of the conscripts escaped while they were in the custody of the constable, he alone would bear responsibility for finding the same number of replacements. Such was the fear of desertion, that parishes often decided to pay for guards to assist the constable in watching over the recruits in transit. Thus the Marlborough treasurer paid 2s 4d in 1643 'for conducting 6 soldiers to Lavington'; the Guild Steward at Calne in Wiltshire £1 16s 0d in 1644 at 'the press for 10 soldiers for press money, conduct and conductors'; and the parish of Chewton in Somerset £4 0s 0d in May 1646 'for pressing of 4 men, safe keeping and conducting them to Bath'. (26)

Not only was the parish forced to bear the cost of the clothing and the guarding of the recruits, it was also obliged to put up the 'press money' (or small bounty, which the conscripts were given on joining) and to fund any board and lodging required on the journey to the rendezvous. The borough of Calne therefore paid £10 19s 2d 'for 19 soldiers with their press money' and 4s 0d 'for entertaining pressed soldiers'. Sometimes, conscripts who had been handed over by the constables at the rendezvous were forcibly billeted on parishes as they were marched in larger groups under the captain to the army. In May, 1646, for instance, the village of Chewton was called upon to provide one night's lodging for 60 men and 'those that conducted the pressed men to Bath'; while Abraham Hale, keeper of the House of Correction in Devizes, complained that he had been forced to feed and accommodate pressed soldiers at a cost to him of £15 7s 0d. (27)

Increasingly there was an acute shortage of recruits, as armies of both king and parliament competed for the same diminishing supply. This often led to squabbles even between commanders on the same side! For instance, in 1644, Francis Wyndham wrote in a somewhat hurt manner to George Trevelyan complaining that the latter had spoiled his recruitment patch. Trevelyan was new onto the scene, having just been granted a commission by the king to raise a regiment of 1,200 foot in Somerset. Nevertheless, Wyndham, while firmly making his point, did offer a compromise proposal to share out the area. He had, he argued, taken a great deal of trouble to make local people aware of their need to enlist under him for their own security and the protection of the neighbourhood. 'In Watchet and Minehead', he continued, 'I have taken some pains in this business, and shall be unwilling to lose my labour; besides these two places, all I leave to you...' (28)

A similar dilemma faced Colonel Griffin, the royalist Governor of the Longford garrison in Wiltshire, shortly after his appointment in November 1644. The king had clearly tried to map out authorised recruitment areas for each commander to avoid unnecessary competition and had set Griffin the task of increasing his garrison force from 140 men to a full strength of 400. However, although the Governor had been allocated certain hundreds in the county for the purpose of conscription, they were situated some distance from his garrison. In a letter to Lord Digby, Principal Secretary to the king, he therefore complained about their unsuitable location: 'Truly my Lord, they lie so much upon the enemy and so near Hampshire that I am not able to get near the number of the men which is assigned me'. He therefore requested that he should be granted permission 'to press men in these [five] Hundreds which lie far from the enemy and near to the garrison' - plus the city of Salisbury, which was most convenient of all. Such a systematic approach was hardly good news for members of the local community. (29)

The fact that potential recruits were increasingly in short supply created something of a seller's market by encouraging soldiers to desert in search of better terms in other regiments. The problem for ordinary soldiers was that they were often unpaid and seriously lacking in adequate food and clothing. To compound their misery, they were unable to seek their normal entertainment in the inns where, as one of them grumbled, 'nothing will be had without money'. In 1644, Colonel Massey, Governor of Gloucester, complained: 'All my best men run away for lack of clothing and other requisites to protect themselves against the cold, and take service in other parts and associations where they may have a better and surer entertainment'. Newly-raised regiments, anxious to fill their ranks, were apparently quite prepared to take 'all comers' without questions being asked about previous service. This, he said, was extremely bad for morale and was why their armies 'moulder away from great strengths to nothing'. He therefore urged parliament to issue an order to all commanders that no soldier should be accepted into their regiment 'unless furnished with a certificate from their last officer of their leave and dismissal'.

The problem in Gloucester had really rumbled on ever since the conclusion of the siege. Indeed, in December 1643, the signs were already evident in the accounts of Thomas Blayney, treasurer of the garrison, who was clearly making a particular effort to retain the services of their cannoneers - vital specialists, who were often brought into a besieged city from outside and who were usually given favourable treatment in consequence. Against an item in his accounts, regarding 'a week's pay by the Governor's orders' to 16 cannoneers, he had written in the margin: 'Here doth begin their weekly pay, without which they would have been gone'. The problem remained unsolved because recruits, as well as cannoneers, were still at a premium. As late as April 1645, Massey was again complaining about the loss of troops, as they viewed with envious eyes the conditions enjoyed by others. 'Our troops daily leave me - and now they see the Warwick troopers so well clothed and horsed and armed and so well paid'. (30)

Hardships of Service: Exhaustion and Hunger

Once a man had been conscripted for service, he was forced to endure hardships far worse than mere lack of pay, equipment or clothing. Henry Foster, who marched with the London trained bands in the summer of

1643, described some of the rigours encountered when they entered Gloucestershire. As they camped near Stow-on-the-Wold in anticipation of an enemy attack, his regiment was forced to stand in the open field all night, 'having neither bread nor water to refresh ourselves, having also marched the day before without sustenance, neither durst we kindle any fire, though it was a very cold night'. This encounter with the elements was nothing compared with his experience on Prestbury Hill a few days later. Although most of the soldiers had been allocated billets in the local villages, his regiment was responsible for guarding the wagons - and these were stuck in the mud on the top of the hill! They were therefore obliged to 'lie all night upon the top of this mountain, it being a most terrible tempestuous night of wind and rain, as ever men lay out in, we having neither hedge nor tree to shelter, nor any sustenance of food or fire'. When, next day, they finally managed to get down from the hill, they were even more despondent. Though 'wet to the very skin', they could find no shelter or refreshment in the villages, because every house was already packed to the rafters with soldiers.

Cold, drenched and miserable, they were also extremely hungry, having already marched for six days 'with very little provision'. Part of the problem was that the army had deliberately avoided the main roads and

The trained bands exposed to the elements on Prestbury Hill. (Line drawing by Stephen Beck)

chosen a route 'through poor little villages', which were totally incapable ofrelieving a whole army. Some soldiers, in desperation therefore, often ran ahead of the army for half a mile or so in an attempt to beat the others to any small supply of water. By the time that they had drawn up in the field at Prestbury, they were totally exhausted. 'Our soldiers began to complain pitifully, being very worn out and quite spent for want of some refreshing, some complaining that they had not ate or drunk for two days, some [for a] longer time'. (31)

Captain Richard Atkyns had a similar experience of sheer exhaustion in July 1643, when he rode with the royalist horse out of Devizes on a mission to Oxford to gain reinforcements for Sir Ralph Hopton's beleaguered army. He recounts in his diary how he was forced to stop at Lambourne, because his horse had lost two of its shoes. While the blacksmith was replacing them, he leant against a post, but being 'so sleepy, fell down like a log of wood and could not be wakened for half an hour'. He then rode on to Faringdon for the night, but found himself totally exhausted from his exertions in the Battle of Lansdown and the march to Devizes. 'I fell off my horseback twice upon the downs', he wrote, 'before I came to Faringdon, where I reeled upon my horse so extremely that the people of the town took me to be dead drunk'. There he sought out his wife's aunt, who also assumed he was drunk. Nevertheless, she provided him with a bed for the night, where he 'slept for 14 hours together without waking'. Atkyns also experienced serious difficulties over his clothes, which he was unable to change, because his groom had stolen his trunk of personal belongings. Bloodstained and sweaty, he felt thoroughly vile and sickened by the stench. 'For want of a shift [i.e. a change of clothes], my wound having bloodied my linen, I became so lousy in three or four days' he complained, 'that I could not tell what to do with myself'. When eventually he reached Bath, after fighting the Battle of Roundway Down, his shirt was so caked in blood and sweat that, as he pulled it off his back, it completely disintegrated. (32)

Exhaustion of the type described by both Henry Foster and Richard Atkyns was often related to lack of proper sustenance. In the first two years of the war, the armies of both sides seriously lacked a properly-organised commissariat, which ensured that troops were regularly fed. Individual soldiers, therefore, were forced to fend for themselves. Henry Foster described how, on the march to relieve Gloucester, they often had little food 'but what we have brought with us in our snapsacks' (i.e. the backpack in which the soldier carried his food and spare clothing). This flimsy diet could sometimes be supplemented by acts of unauthorised plunder or the official requisitioning of supplies. On the return journey to London, for instance, they had an unexpected windfall near Swindon. 'We drove along with our army about 1,000 sheep and 60 head of cattle, which were taken from malignants and papists in the country for the maintenance of our army'. Foster's own regiment was allocated 87 of the sheep, but sadly lost them all just as the Battle of Newbury was starting.

In theory, royalist commanders were required to issue their men each day with 2lbs of bread, 1lb of meat and two pints of beer, which was reckoned to provide the right amount of energy for a soldier on campaign. In practice, this seldom happened. If lucky, the troops on the march were issued with bread (or biscuit) and cheese, although permanent garrisons could fare considerably better with a more varied diet including peas, beans, oatmeal and fish, as well as cheese, meat and beer (see Chapter 4 - the Chalfield garrison). As a result of all this uncertainty, field armies were increasingly billeted and fed by local householders, in payment for which service the soldier would either settle in cash out of his wages or leave a signed ticket indicating the amount owed (see Chapter 5). With the establishment by parliament of a more professional army (the New Model) in 1645, a real attempt was made to ensure that troops were properly paid so that they could buy food for themselves. Local traders and farmers were therefore encouraged to set up a market to follow the army 'while in march or camp'. The king had already done exactly the same at Matson during the siege of Gloucester in 1643, while in November 1644 he was to show beyond doubt that food supplies were now organised in a much more professional manner. His field army, which was based for several days at Marlborough, greatly benefited from the detailed arrangements made on its behalf by the Chief Commissary (see Chapter 6). (33)

Hardships of Service: Capture and Imprisonment

Another danger facing volunteers and conscripts alike was that of capture, because the fate of prisoners was often uncertain. Within each army, the Provost Marshal (often a civilian) was responsible for the supervision of prisoners. The task was sometimes delegated to assistants or temporary marshals drawn from the locality in which the army was located. Richard Callow of Warminster, for instance, acted in this role for the royalist army in 1643, when he converted the Black Swan in Devizes into a prison for parliamentarians captured in the Battle of Roundway Down. Armies on the march seldom wanted to be burdened by large numbers of prisoners, who needed to be both fed and guarded. They therefore often arranged with the enemy for an exchange of prisoners to take place at some convenient moment. This occurred, in June 1643, when Hopton in Wells and Waller in Bath took advantage of a three-week truce prior to the battle of Lansdown to organise such an exchange. Individual prisoners of military importance or social status were frequently kept for a short period only before being exchanged for a person of similar distinction held by the other side. In 1645, for example, Colonel Nathaniel Stephens, MP for Gloucestershire and parliamentary Governor of Beverstone Castle (who had been captured in February, when royalist forces seized Rowden House in Wiltshire), was exchanged for Sir James Long, the king's High Sheriff in Wiltshire (who had been taken prisoner by Waller at Devizes in March). Similarly, Colonel Edmund Ludlow (who had been captured at the fall of

Wardour Castle in March 1644) was, after a brief imprisonment in Oxford, exchanged for three high-ranking royalist officers. (34)

Sometimes, if an exchange was not appropriate to the circumstances, large numbers of prisoners could be released on a selective basis. In March 1643, for instance, some 1,500 Welsh royalists were captured by Waller at Highnam, near Gloucester. According to one of those who surrendered, so great was the mass of prisoners that, walking in pairs, they stretched in line 'from Highnam almost to Gloucester'. Once they were there, they were dealt with in separate categories. The officers had the choice of either paying ransom money to regain their freedom or submitting to imprisonment in Bristol. The ordinary soldiers could either gain freedom by agreeing to switch sides and fight for parliament or accept imprisonment in the churches of Gloucester. In practice, the latter were only detained for ten days before they were sent back home, after swearing an oath that they would never again 'bear arms against the parliament'.

The fall of a garrison after siege inevitably meant that a large number of soldiers surrendered. The victorious besiegers seldom wanted to imprison the whole garrison force, for the reasons stated above. This usually meant, therefore, that the terms of surrender made specific arrangements for their controlled release. When Bristol was captured by Prince Rupert in 1643, for instance, the common foot soldiers were permitted to march out under escort (without weapons) until they reached Warminster in Wiltshire. There they were released with the promise that they would not be molested in any way by royalist forces over the next three days. Two years later, when the New Model Army captured Bristol, Fairfax agreed to let ordinary soldiers march out under escort (with their swords) to any royalist garrison named by Prince Rupert within a fifty-mile range, with eight days allowed for that march. At the fall of Dunster Castle in 1646, Fairfax gave the captured soldiers the option of either marching in safety to the king in Oxford (with twelve days allowed) or, if they preferred, of receiving individual passes to their homes with full protection against 'the violence of soldiers'. The terms of surrender were even more specific when the garrison of Portishead capitulated in the same campaign. Fairfax on this occasion stipulated, as he released the common soldiers, that 'they should all take oath never to take up arms against the parliament hereafter, but every man go home to his own dwelling and there remain'. (35)

Nevertheless, there are many instances of captured soldiers who lingered in prison, suffering shameful treatment. In May 1644, twenty parliamentarian prisoners, who had been captured at Westbury-on-Severn in Gloucestershire, petitioned Colonel Massey (the Governor of Gloucester) for assistance. They described how they had 'endured a long time of imprisonment' in appalling conditions, first at Bristol and then at Berkeley Castle. Their captors, they complained, had allowed them a diet of bread and cheese, 'but not one drop of drink, unless we pay for it'. This was not easy because they had no money, nor had any been sent to them since their capture. Massey ordered a sum of forty shillings to be sent for their relief. Money of this kind was occasionally sent by families or groups of compassionate neighbours, when they heard of such cases. In August 1644, for instance, the sum of nine pounds was collected around the streets of Bristol and given to Robert Hayes and Edith Jordan to dispense among 'the poor distressed prisoners now in Newgate' (a Bristol prison). Sometimes troop commanders, too, could be compassionate to their men. In April 1643, for instance, Colonel John Fiennes sent five pounds 'to his Cornet Edward Sutton, who lay in prison at Oxford'. (36)

Prison governors were perhaps understandably mean in allocating precious resources to enemy prisoners, especially when many members of their own armies were hungry too. In October 1644, the parliamentary garrison at Gloucester was housing 8 prisoners in the North Gate, 63 in the Castle and 55 in the College. The treasurer allocated to the deputy marshals responsible for these prisons the sum of twelve pence a week for each prisoner - or 1.7 pence per day. Even this was a good deal more generous than the allowance made earlier in March 1643, when some fifteen hundred Welsh prisoners had been held in the churches of St Mary de Lode and Trinity for a period of ten days. According to one of those detained, they were so badly fed that they were 'forced to be glad with turnip tops, cabbage leaves and such things they could get'. Food sent to the prison by friends was immediately confiscated by the guards. The garrison treasurer officially spent the measly sum of £18 19s 0d on distributions of bread to the 1,500 ordinary soldiers - or 0.30 pence per head per day! This was far less than the much-criticised allocation of 1.25 pence per day made to imprisoned parliamentary soldiers by the notorious William Smith, royalist Provost Marshal in Oxford (see The Horrors of War 7). All these pitiful allowances to prisoners must be set for comparison alongside the sum of four pence per day, which was the amount allocated to provide food for each soldier in the Chalfield garrison (see Chapter 4). (37)

St Mary de Lode church, Gloucester, used to house Welsh prisoners taken at Highnam. (Author's collection)

Even this shameful treatment of prisoners pales into insignificance, however, when compared with the fate of the garrison at Woodhouse, near Horningsham in Wiltshire. In June 1644, Major Henry Wansey (a watchmaker from Warminster, who later became a troop commander in Ludlow's cavalry regiment in Wiltshire), had established a parliamentary garrison in the house, which was owned by Thomas Arundel. Hopton, the Governor of Bristol, sent a small force under Sir Francis Dodington (later reinforced by two cannon and troops from the king's own army) to eject Wansey. After driving off Ludlow's relief force, Dodington eventually took Woodhouse by storm, killing twenty of the garrison and capturing a further eighty. Determined to make an example, he gave orders that fourteen of these should be hanged as rebels, later claiming (falsely) that these were renegades who had deserted from the royalist army.

According to Ludlow, one of the selected victims was reported to Dodington by the parson of the parish for threatening 'to stick in his skirts, as he called it' for using the Book of Common Prayer. Hearing this, Dodington 'struck the man so many blows upon the head, and with such force, that he broke his skull'. The poor wretch was then hanged on the same tree as the other thirteen, 'most of them clothiers'. When one of the ropes broke, the man involved pleaded that he might either be spared or be allowed to 'fight against any two for his life'. Dodington refused. Such was his rage that (according to Sir Edward Walker, the king's Secretary) he 'could hardly be induced to spare the rest, who were at length sent prisoners to Bristol'. Dodington's action caused lasting bitterness. Four years later, Agnes Young of Westbury petitioned the Quarter Sessions in great distress, pleading that 'Sir Francis Dodington, (ye bloody tyrant) hanged your petitioner's husband with thirteen more of the garrison', leaving her with five children to support. Nine years later, Alice Gallaway and Alice Moore, whose husbands had also been members of the unlucky fourteen 'murdered at Woodhouse in the service of parliament', were awarded modest maintenance grants to relieve their distress. (38)

In spite of the savagery and brutality, which were sometimes inflicted on prisoners, there was also an underlying code of conduct, based on etiquette, which usually prevailed. Captain Richard Atkyns recalled in his diary the fate of Lieutenant Thomas Sandys (an officer in his cavalry troop), who had been captured during the Battle of Lansdown, only to be shot in cold blood after his surrender by a Scotsman in Sir William Waller's army. Taken down into Bath in a serious condition, he was later interviewed by Waller, who was 'exceeding angry at the inhuman action that befell him and sent for his own surgeon immediately and saw him dressed before he went away; he gave the innkeeper charge that he should have whatever he called for and he would see him paid'. Furthermore, he lent Sandys 'twelve broad pieces for his own private expenses'. When, a few days later, Waller was fleeing for his own life to the safety of the Bristol garrison after defeat at Roundway Down, he nevertheless took time to visit Sandys on his way through Bath. Realising that the man was still too weak to accompany him as his prisoner, Waller accepted his promise that, 'when he was able to ride', he would 'render himself a true prisoner to him at Bristol'. Shortly afterwards, following the arrival of the royalist

Sir William Waller (1579-1668), general of parliament's western forces, 1643. Portrait attributed to E. Bower. (By courtesy of the National Portrait Gallery, London)

army in Bath to claim the city, Sandys insisted that he should be allowed to honour his sworn oath to Waller. Both Atkyns and the Earl of Caernarvon tried their best to persuade him that, as he had now been freed by his own side, the promise had been rendered invalid. When Sandys protested, they even put under arrest to prevent him carrying out his intention. The situation was finally resolved when Bristol fell to the royalists with unexpected speed and Waller fled to London. (39)

One other anxiety facing the conscript was what would happen to his wife and family during his absence at war. Some of the women simply abandoned their homes and joined the ever-growing number of camp followers, who tagged along with baggage train in the wake of the army. These female adherents, who also included a motley collection of vagrants, tinkers, traders, preachers, petty thieves and whores, were forced to fend for themselves. If unattached to a soldier husband, they would try to eke out an existence by selling their wares or services (including cooking, washing, sewing or caring for the wounded) and by clothing themselves in garments stripped from the battlefield dead. They endured all the hazards and discomforts of the conscripts, were prone to starvation and disease and were particularly vulnerable in defeat, when the baggage train was overrun by the enemy. No official provision was made for their accommodation in private houses, as the army passed through the countryside. Indeed, the king's proclamation on arrangements for taking free quarter in Wiltshire, in December 1643, specifically stated that camp followers (including women, boys and children) were not to be granted 'house room', unless the householder agreed. Furthermore, they were often greeted with suspicion and hostility as they entered towns or villages, being viewed as potential paupers, who would become chargeable on the parish. The commanders of both sides frequently expressed embarrassment at the thieving and plundering undertaken by the 'stragglers' who followed the armies - a point emphasised by both Prince Rupert at the siege of Bristol and the king at the siege of Gloucester in 1643. (40)

Women camp followers. (Line drawing by Stephen Beck)

Hardships of Service: Wounded in Action

Another great fear of the conscript was that of being wounded. Quite apart from the horrific nature of wounds inflicted by pike, sword or musket (see Chapter 10), there was an uncertainty and anxiety, as they lay in agony on the battlefield, about what would happen next. Although medicine was still in its early stages, the London Company of Barber-Surgeons was already well established, undertaking considerable research and granting diplomas to those qualified in surgery. By the outbreak of the Civil War, similar companies had been established in provincial centres, including Bristol, where apothecaries, physicians and surgeons enrolled in great numbers for work in the countryside as well as the town. Their headquarters, Barbers' Hall (off Corn Street), contained a fine examination hall as well as a dissecting room. (41)

In the army, each regiment and garrison would include on its strength one surgeon with two assistants, suitably equipped with a 'surgeon's chest' containing medical instruments, ointments, potions and powders. The cost of the latter was often borne by the surgeons, but occasionally covered by the military authorities. In April 1643, for instance, as the Gloucester garrison braced itself for inevitable future attack, the council of war paid Captain Lower the sum of £8 10s 0d 'in lieu of a surgeon's chest'. It was vital that wounded men were treated as quickly as possible to prevent the spread of infection. In consequence, garrison forces often turned to local surgeons to supplement the work of those employed by regiments and thus speed up the process. In October 1644, therefore, the Gloucester

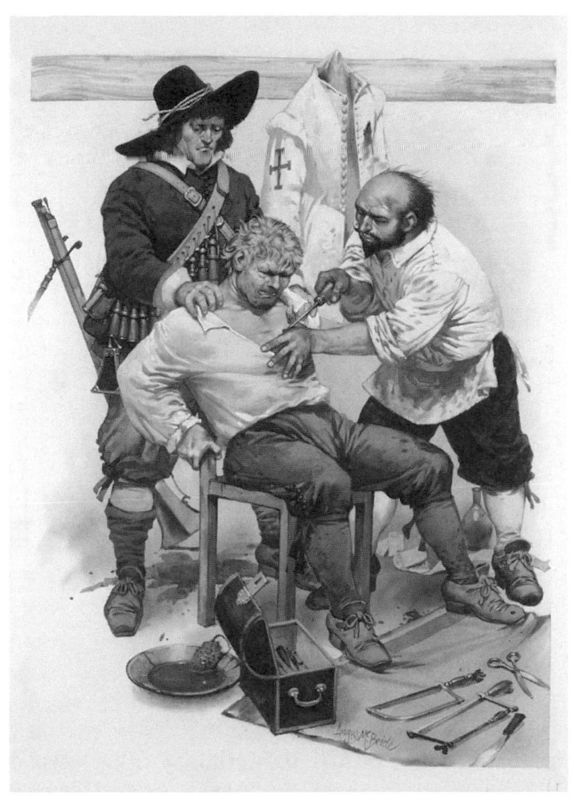

A surgeon removing a musket bullet. (An original painting by Angus McBride - by courtesy of © Osprey Publishing Ltd.)

garrison paid two local surgeons one month's pay for attending and dressing 'the sick and wounded soldiers in the hospital of the militia within this city'. Those soldiers were fortunate not only to be treated quickly, but also to be treated in hospital. (42)

Treatment, whether at the hands of a regimental surgeon or a local one, was always a most unpleasant experience. A soldier, already experiencing intense pain from a musket bullet embedded in his thigh, for instance, was never offered herbs with sedative or pain-killing properties - partly, because surgeons feared accusations of witchcraft and partly, because they believed that pain actually assisted the healing process. The unfortunate patient, therefore, was usually held down by the surgeon's mate, while the surgeon himself applied the relevant range of medical tools from his chest - the probe to locate the bullet; the speculum to open the wound wider; the duck bill to remove debris, which had accompanied the bullet into the flesh (e.g. fragments of clothing) and to take out the bullet itself; the cauterising iron to control the bleeding; the 'tents' of bandage, which were pushed into the wound to prevent premature healing; and the needles and waxed thread to close up the flesh. As he endured his agony, the soldier would doubtless avoid casting his eye at the other tools in the chest, which would be used if amputation was later deemed necessary - the incision knife, the cat lip (or dismembering knife to cut the flesh around the bone), the cerra (or bone saw) and the amputating chisel and mallet (for removing shattered fingers and toes). (43)

Wherever possible at the end of a battle, army commanders would endeavour to transport their wounded soldiers to a hospital in the nearest town under their control. According to two eye-witnesses in March 1643, after a bloody skirmish at Highnam, near Gloucester, 'five wagons full of maimed soldiers were sent to Cirencester for relief' and a further '18 wain loads of maimed men were brought to Oxford'. Five months later, 'thirty cart loads full of maimed soldiers came into Oxford from Prince Maurice out of the west', presumably after their mauling in the Battle of Lansdown. In September of that year, as the king broke up the siege of Gloucester, John Dorney noticed several carts 'laden with sick and maimed soldiers' going down from the royalist army to the river, 'where some boats attended to carry them to Bristol'. Sir Samuel Luke, whose spy also witnessed the scene, put the number of water-borne invalids at four hundred, plus a further three hundred sent 'to Cirencester and thereabouts in forty carts'. The Bristol hospital was also used again in May 1645 following the siege of Taunton, when the royalists despatched 'twelve cartloads of maimed men' for treatment. After Colonel Edmund Ludlow had surrendered Wardour Castle in 1644, his 'sick and wounded men' were initially kept prisoner in the castle. Then, after 'a popish priest had very solemnly, with hands spread over them, cursed them three times', they were 'carried from thence to Bristol'.

Garrison commanders tended to commandeer large buildings to act as temporary hospitals during moments of crisis. This certainly happened in

Bristol in the Autumn of 1645, after its recapture by parliament's New Model Army. Some four hundred men had been wounded as they stormed the outer part of the city and many of these were still receiving treatment two months later. The parliamentary commissioners reported to the Speaker of the Commons on the measures they had taken to help the wounded. 'We appointed an hospital and placed therein so many as the house could contain, with nurses and surgeons fitting for them; and, as our numbers increased, we added house-room and attendants to them'. Nevertheless, the total space available proved to be insufficient, even for the treatment of the infantry. The commissioners had therefore decided to send the wounded cavalry for care and attention into neighbouring villages. Although the army paid householders for the unwelcome task of billeting these troops, the commissioners admitted that the payments made did not cover any element of compensation for the sheer inconvenience, the extra fuel and the soiled bedding - for the men were largely bed-ridden with 'wounds being fractures of bones and dismemberings' caused by musket fire. However, the army's costs in providing all this medical care were heavily subsidised by Bristol City Council which, on 3rd September, had already resolved that it would 'bear the charges of the apothecaries and medicines for any wounded soldiers'. (44)

Wounded soldiers in garrison towns were not always treated in hospitals, but were often billeted out in the homes of ordinary citizens. Lieutenant Joseph Cobbett, who had received 'divers mortal wounds' in the siege of Bristol in 1645, was actually billeted in the house of a surgeon, Lewis Banham. Mostly, however, the physicians would tour around the streets visiting their patients wherever they lodged. One such physician submitted two claims to the garrison treasurer in Gloucester for the 'physic delivered to the sick soldiers and troopers' in May 1644. The first dealt with nine locations (including The Lamb Inn and Goodma Bennett's) and the second covered twenty-three calls. His treatment list for the latter, the cost of which totalled £4 13s 4d, included vomits, purges (i.e. laxatives), cordials, plasters, powders, potions, syrups, juleps (i.e. sweet medicated drinks), electuaries (i.e. powder mixed with honey), decoctions (i.e. extracted essence) and 'a box of pills'. These were all offered in various permutations! (45)

When the system worked at its best, maimed and sick soldiers could find reasonable care and treatment. Not all of them, however, were so fortunate. On many occasions, when armies retreated quickly at the end of a battle, the wounded were simply left in agony on the battlefield to await the mercy of the enemy or local villagers (who were also left to bury the dead). Captain Richard Atkyns, a royalist officer, told in his diary of an accidental explosion of gunpowder after the Battle of Lansdown, which killed or seriously wounded those nearby. The enemy, intent on pursuing the royalist army, appeared before they had time either to bury the dead or to carry away the wounded. Hurriedly, therefore, they packed as many of the maimed soldiers as possible into the Marquess of Hertford's coach and began to carry off the remainder on litters, hastily constructed out of boards. With great reluctance, they decided to leave Major Thomas Sheldon 'to the mercy of the enemy', such were his dreadful injuries. Sheldon, however, had other ideas and made a great 'shift' to join the others, but 'when he found that there was nothing but a cart provided for him', he took one look at it and 'immediately died'.

At Devizes, in 1644, the Corporation paid Mr Jackman five pounds 'for dressing wounded soldiers left by Lord Hopton'. They also paid for the attendance of a surgeon to treat a lame soldier, who had been left at the Bridewell; the costs incurred by Robert Edney for 'physic' and food 'for a soldier that died at his house'; the treatment given to the 'maimed soldiers left in the town, when the first siege was here'; and 'seven shrouds for soldiers' who were beyond medical care. The Corporation at Marlborough, which suffered terribly at times from the war (see The Horrors of War 8), was still not averse to providing 'relief for a sick soldier', 'diet for a sick soldier' or the cost that Widow Phillips incurred 'for keeping a wounded soldier at several times'; but it also did its level best to move these wretches on as quickly as possible. Hence they frequently spent money on such items as 'the carriage of cripples' or 'carrying a sick soldier out of town'. The cost of lengthy treatment could, after all, serve as an endless drain on the town's already limited resources. (46)

Mr Jackman in Devizes could well have been a physician or an apothecary, but much of the treatment offered in local villages was supplied by herbalists or women specialising in traditional remedies! The parliamentary garrison at Chalfield House in Wiltshire clearly enjoyed the services of its own resident surgeon, who had been allocated a room in which he could lock the medicines which regularly arrived from Bath. Nevertheless, the Governor also made frequent use of village women in the area to nurse his sick and wounded soldiers back to health. Some of these provided their services as part of their tax liability - a woman in Holt, for instance, who looked after a soldier for sixteen days; or 'a poor woman' in Broughton Gifford, who tended 'a sick soldier' for three weeks. Others were hired by the garrison to do the same work - 'a woman that tended our sick and wounded men', an entry in the accounts which was frequently repeated. (47)

The soldier, who defied the odds and actually survived both the injury and the treatment, was often left in a disabled condition to fend for himself. Nevertheless, miracles did occasionally occur. The parliamentary commissioners in Bristol claimed in a letter to the Speaker in January 1646 that, out of some four hundred men hospitalised after the siege in the previous September, only four remained - the rest had 'miraculously recovered and returned to their colours'. The majority of those maimed in battle, however, were far less fortunate, finding themselves unable to work and totally dependent on charity for survival. Both sides in the war had offered the promise of support to the wounded and the widowed. As early as October 1642, parliament had instructed parishes to fund pensions of four shillings a week to genuine cases. The king, on the other hand, had initially tried to inspire church collections in aid of the wounded, but by May 1643 had also instructed parishes to pay pensions out of the local rates. In addition, they were to ensure that the maimed were given priority treatment when places were allocated in local almshouses. (48)

In addition to this rather haphazard and unreliable system, army commanders themselves sometimes tried to provide financial assistance to their wounded soldiers. After eight of his men had been wounded in a bloody skirmish on the Mendips in June 1643, royalist cavalry officer Richard Atkyns received 'twenty shillings a man of Sir Robert Long, the Treasurer of the Army'. This beneficence clearly took Atkyns by surprise. It was, he said 'all the money I ever received for myself or my troops during the war!'. Nevertheless, it was not unknown elsewhere. The treasurer of the parliamentary garrison in Gloucester made a number of one-off payments in 1643 and 1644 to soldiers who had been maimed in the fighting - £2 to Cornet Hayes, 'being wounded at Beachley'; £1 to Toby Garbrian, 'who was shot in the time of the siege'; 10s 0d 'to a soldier with one leg' etc. Even civilians qualified, if injured in the call of duty, such as Jane Heards (£1) 'who was wounded in the Friars' Orchard at the time of the siege' (presumably while she was carrying turves for the fortifications).

Sir William Waller also responded to a personal petition from the wife of James Miles, a trooper from the Earl of Stamford's regiment, who had been 'left behind wounded at Hereford'. In spite of Waller's previous help, he was now destitute. She pleaded that the same sort of help should be given to her husband as the general had previously granted 'to others'. His award of five pounds was therefore not entirely without precedent. There is also evidence that officials in the local hundreds were, as instructed, organising a tax from the parish rates. In August 1644, for instance, the Gloucester Committee reminded its treasurer that he had received 26s 6d from the High Constable of the Cirencester hundred, 'which money was due to maimed soldiers'. The treasurer was therefore instructed 'to deliver the said money to Thomas Helmes and Thomas Tymes, being two maimed soldiers and pensioners'. Gloucester Corporation itself had also made a determined effort to organise the collection of a weekly maimed soldiers' rate, in line with parliament's ordinance for the maintenance of orphans and widows 'whose husbands were slain in the parliament's service'. They worked out a rate of between 3d and 5d a week for eleven parishes to produce a total of 3s 3d. However, although the system worked spasmodically, the amounts produced were never sufficient to satisfy demand. The maimed soldiers' rate was just one further burden for parishes to endure - or to avoid! (49)

THE HORRORS OF WAR 2

TAKEN PRISONER

AT CIRENCESTER, 1643

On Thursday 2nd February 1643, royalist forces under Prince Rupert took the town of Cirencester by storm. The 3,500 inhabitants had worked furiously over the previous weeks to strengthen the existing defences, which were somewhat patchy, by blocking streets with metal chains, timber barricades and carts packed with furzebushes. Many of them went on to fight actively in defence of the town as members of the local regiment of trained bands, which formed part of the garrison forces under Lieutenant-Colonel Carr. But although they resisted fiercely, fighting from house to house, they were eventually forced to surrender shortly after the initial breakthrough had taken place. According to eye-witnesses, 'the terror and the fury' of the enemy fire-power greatly contributed to their defeat, with 'grenadoes' launched from mortars setting fire to property and 'bullets', fired at random from cannon into the town, making 'a terrible ruffling among the houses'.

Many of the garrison fled for their lives along the roads to Cricklade and Lechlade, only to be overtaken by Sir John Byron and Prince Maurice. Over a hundred were killed in the chase, but when about three hundred of them fell 'on heaps before the Prince's feet', he was pleased to spare their lives and take them prisoner instead. Altogether some one thousand of the garrison (including 16 wounded) were captured, including the civil governor (John Fettiplace), and about 300 killed. According to John White, a parliamentarian present at the siege, the townsfolk were too terrified to venture out to help the dying. 'There lay some of our men naked four days after they were killed...and none durst bury them'. White also recalled that the prisoners suffered a night of agony crammed into the church. Many of them were stripped 'of their utmost garments'; some were badly wounded; and all were exhausted after the fight. Their friends, however, 'were not suffered to bring them a cup of water into the church that night, but what they thrust in at the backside of the church,

St John the Baptist church, Cirencester, where the prisoners were held overnight.

having broken the windows.

Their ordeal, however, worsened considerably next day, when they set out under escort on a forced march to Oxford. One of the prisoners recalled the horror of their experience: 'Just as they drove us towards Oxford, they gave each of us a small piece of bread and cheese, and then bound us all with match, and so drove us along without stockings on our legs, or shoes on our feet, or hats on our heads, many of us having no doublets, and some gentlemen of good quality without breeches; and so we came to Burford Hill, where the cavaliers gave each of us a little piece of bread, which was all the relief they gave us on our way between Cirencester and Oxford; and for this we waited a long time upon the hill, the wind blowing very cold, and we standing barefoot and bare-legged in the snow. Then we came to Witney, where we lay in the church, and from thence were drove towards Oxford, and about a mile from the city, His Majesty with the Prince and the Duke of York came thither to see us drove along more like dogs and horses than men, up to the knees in mire and dirt, along the horse-way; and abundance of scholars much rejoicing in our misery, calling and abusing us by the names of damned rogues and traitors...'

Once at Oxford, the thousand or so men were imprisoned by the king's Provost Marshal-General (the notorious William Smith) in either the castle or one of the churches. There they were fed on a diet of bread and water 'and almost starved for want of food, clothes and firing' (in spite of the fact that parliament had sent down £100 for their relief). Eventually they were faced with a number of options. Many, to escape the horror of imprisonment, agreed to switch sides and join the king's army. After equipping and training them, Prince Rupert tried the cunning ploy of sending 140 of them to the Reading garrison in exchange for a similar number of their best soldiers. However, the Governor, Sir Arthur Aston, would have none of it and immediately sent them back!

Although the fifty or so prisoners who refused to enlist were generally sentenced to hard labour on the fortifications around Oxford, some were given the option of buying their freedom. Later still, there was another twist to the story. Towards the end of February, forty-seven of the original prisoners submitted a humble petition to the king, craving pardon and asking to be allowed to return home to resume their 'former trades and occupations'. The king granted their petition, promising 'no violency or injury from his soldiers'.

Sources: R.W. Jennings, *The Cotswolds in the Civil War* (Cheltenham, 1976); John Miles Paddock, *The Storing of Cirencester in 1643* (Cirencester, 1993); *Certain Informations*, no.5 (1643) in John Washbourne (ed.), *Bibliotheca Gloucestrensis* (1825), introduction p 32; Falconer Madan, *Oxford Books*, vol.2 (Oxford, 1912), no. 1431; BL, 89 (23), *A Continuation of Certain Special and Remarkable Passages* (1643); BL, E 92 (9), *The Petition of the Inhabitants of Cirencester* (1643); PRO, SP23.114 f 991; BodL, MSS Eng Hist C53 f10, Sir Samuel Luke's Diary, 1643-4; Bulstrode Whitelocke, *Memorials of the English Affairs* (Oxford, 1732 edn.), p 167; SRO, CQ3, 1/94, f 11, Quarter Sessions Petitions

CHAPTER 3

Forced to Pay: War Taxation

I have lent money to both sides
Been plundered by both sides
Been imprisoned by both sides
A mad world!
(William Hill, estate manager at Forthampton, near Gloucester, 1643)

The Tax-Gathering System

Benjamin Franklin once said: 'There are only two certainties in life - death and taxes'. This to many was certainly the fear, if not the personal reality, during the English Civil War. Most ordinary people in the west country, as elsewhere in England, soon discovered that war taxation, in all its various guises, was a many-headed monster - a monster which grew and grew as the war progressed. It mattered little whether they lived in an area controlled by royalist or parliamentarian troops. They nevertheless faced a tax bill and a tax-gathering machine, which seemed very similar to ordinary people at village level.

Both sides worked initially through committees composed of influential local men within each county. Parliament appointed these 'County Committees' on 20th July, 1642 to raise 'horse, horsemen and arms for the defence of the king and both Houses of Parliament' and to receive subscriptions. In Somerset, for instance, twelve local men of standing drawn from the whole length of the county (including Sir John Horner from Mells, John Harington from Kelston, Alexander Popham from Hunstrete and John Ashe from Freshford) were nominated with the power of Deputy-Lieutenants. Although, as hostilities intensified, parliament set up special new committees to collect specific new taxes, they tended to draw the membership of these from exactly the same body of men in each county. Their task, therefore, was to implement a growing number of tax measures authorised by parliamentary Ordinance, reporting back to central committees in London. The system was both arbitrary and efficient. (1)

The king also relied on men of local stature in each county, detailed by name in the 'commissions of array' which he issued from June 1642. (2) From March 1643, these original commissioners were superseded in some counties (including Gloucestershire and Wiltshire) by 'Committees for Guarding the County', although their main work was financial. Their first task was to assess, with the help of local commanders, the amount of cash needed to support the military operation within the county; then, secondly, to agree at meetings with local gentry the actual amount of cash to be raised to cover those needs; and thirdly, to organise the collection of the taxes which had been sanctioned. The system was, therefore, much more localised than the parliamentary equivalent and much more dependent on voluntary agreement.

Nevertheless, there were many similarities and the end result was just the same as far as ordinary farmers, clothworkers, traders and craftsmen were concerned. In each case, committees of local men met to supervise the collection of the tax total which had been allocated to the county, appointing assessors to value property within each hundred. Once a rate had been fixed, which would produce the overall amount of cash required, warrants were issued to the High Constable of each hundred with an allocation for that area; he then worked out the quotas for each parish

John Ashe (1597-1659), clothier of Freshford and treasurer of parliament's Somerset Committee, 1643. (By courtesy of The Methuen Collection, Corsham Court . Photograph: Photographic Survey, Courtauld Institute of Art)

within his hundred, sending them to the village constables (or 'tithingmen'). Before setting about the thankless task of collection, the constable would first liaise with the most prominent members of the parish to work out fair assessments for each individual. A note was made in his returns of any person who had failed to pay his full share.

Although the parliamentary system was probably more ruthlessly efficient, both sides experienced growing difficulty in gathering in the authorised taxes as the war ground on - taxes which were desperately needed to maintain the local county forces on which their defence was dependent. The problem arose partly through the intrusion of main field armies on marches across the county, which tended to take the law into their own hands and undermine official tax policy. Commanders often demanded special levies of cash or supplies of clothing, horse and food; their 'foreign' troops frequently resorted to ruthless plunder of the local population; and, at the same time, the quartermasters demanded 'free quarter' (or forced billeting on householders without immediate payment) because the soldiers had not been paid. Some areas - the 'corridor counties', like Wiltshire - suffered more than others, as armies of both sides crossed and recrossed their territory on their way from London or Oxford to major campaigns and sieges in the West. Another factor, which put further strain on ordinary people, was the demand made by local garrison commanders for extra financial resources to fund the strengthening of fortifications or the purchase of extra munitions - especially if they were based in a 'frontier zone' on the border of enemy territory. People living nearby were therefore subject to additional levies, as the inhabitants of Chippenham in Wiltshire frequently found to their cost.

The consequence of all these extra payments was that the ordinary parishioner was quickly squeezed dry. The instant demand for cash, food, billets and goods, made by soldiers with swords in their hands, often meant that the householder, already drained of what little resources he had, was totally incapable of paying the regular tax, when the village constable called. This seriously undermined the funding of local forces and local garrisons. Then, as the vicious circle continued its course, these local troops (now likewise unpaid) also took the law into their own hands by requisitioning supplies and demanding free quarter from the local community.

By the end of 1643, therefore, both sides tended to modify their system of tax collection in key areas. The royalists, in particular, now employed the garrison governor to take over that task from the County Committee, allocating a specific area in the neighbourhood for his support. Warrants for tax and supplies were henceforth issued by the governor, to whom the village constables made their returns. The governor, as often as not an outsider with no local loyalties to consider, could be much more ruthless in the work of tax collection - supported, if need be, by a troop of soldiers. Main garrisons frequently sprouted smaller satellites in the area around (often in large mansions) to tighten control of available resources and to ensure that these were not snatched by competing forces. The year 1644, therefore, saw a great proliferation in the number of garrisons (both royalist and parliamentarian) in areas of vital importance. Parliament, too, adopted a similar direct system of taxation for certain key garrisons, as we shall discover in the cases of Bristol, Malmesbury and Chalfield, while still retaining a general oversight for the County Committee.

Surviving evidence for the actual implementation of these systems and the collection of war taxes is somewhat patchy for the western counties. Nevertheless, sufficient detail does exist to enable us to estimate something of the financial burden imposed on particular villages with all its attendant human suffering. One main source is provided by the records of the subcommittees of accounts, established in each county by parliament in 1646 to ascertain the wartime losses of each parish community. The Somerset subcommittee, for instance, was composed of local worthies and met regularly in the Guildhall in Bath, during June and July of that year, to receive accounts (or what amounted to compensation claims) from the constables and churchwardens of the area around. These were asked to give details 'of all the arms, horse, plate and monies paid, lent, delivered, taken and received...as also quartering of soldiers to and for the use of parliament since the beginning of this unhappy war'. (3)

These claims for losses sustained by individuals, compiled by 'the churchwardens and two or three of the discreet and honest men of the inhabitants', give a graphic view of the daily misery endured by many during certain phases of the war. They cover only those periods when the West was under parliamentary control, but they extend to free quarter, requisitions and plunder, as well as taxation. The returns for Somerset have survived in fairly substantial detail; those for Gloucestershire are distinctly patchy; while those for Wiltshire have been lost without trace. This source, however, is complemented by a number of corporation account books, warrants, garrison accounts and other miscellaneous documents (some dealing with periods of royalist control), which help to provide a fuller and more balanced picture of wartime experience in the western counties.

Voluntary Payments to the King

From the outset the king, deprived of his traditional method of raising taxes through parliament, relied heavily on voluntary donations. Local commissioners were therefore required at an early stage to assemble groups of wealthy individuals within each county and appeal to them on his behalf. In August 1643, for instance, the king issued a warrant to the High Constable of the Berkeley hundred in Gloucestershire, ordering him to assemble the inhabitants of the 22 villages there and exhort them to pay a contribution of £497 per month towards the £6,000 he needed to support the garrison at Berkeley Castle. Similarly, in September Edward

Wyndham, High Sheriff of Somerset, and other leading gentry were commissioned 'to treat with the inhabitants of that county for a weekly contribution of £2,000 towards the maintaining of His Majesty's army' - a request which was repeated in December of that year. Many responded generously. Money raised was normally despatched to Oxford to support the king's field armies. (4)

Perhaps the most dramatic example of this system at work, however, was given on 6th February 1643 when, after taking Cirencester by storm, Prince Rupert called together leading royalist sympathisers from the Cotswolds gentry. He demanded their help in raising £3,000 immediately from the county of Gloucester, followed by monthly payments of £4,000, for the establishment and maintenance of royalist garrisons at Cirencester, Tewkesbury and Sudeley. Having complied with this request, Lord Chandos, John Tracy, John Dutton, Maurice Berkeley and others were appointed commissioners to put the plan into operation. They immediately set about the task of dispatching a warrant to the High Constable of each hundred within the county, instructing him to 'call and assemble the inhabitants thereof and exhort them for their own good to pay the sums' requested. Their voluntary co-operation would help to avoid 'the calamities of war' and would also ensure that the garrison soldiers would not be forced 'to break out upon the county' and seize whatever they wanted. The initial sum was to be paid directly to the garrisons in two instalments - the first within ten days, followed by the second within ten further days. It was also agreed, however, 'for the ease of the country', that hard-pressed individuals could contribute half their assessment in provisions with an allowance being set against the tax for wheat at 5s 0d per bushel *[i.e. 8 gallons],* beef at 2d per pound, bacon at 5d per pound etc. With a total assessment to find of £159 19s 5d per month, the High Constable of Westminster hundred (having discussed allocations with leading inhabitants) set the monthly rate for each individual parish (e.g. Moreton-in-Marsh £5 18s 11d, Appesley and Wightfield £31 11s 4d etc). (5)

Prince Rupert of the Rhine, commander of the Bristol garrison, 1645. (By courtesy of the National Portrait Gallery, London)

By the beginning of 1644, however, the flow of voluntary cash support had dwindled, causing Charles I's newly-assembled Oxford Parliament to take more positive action. In February, therefore, they agreed to grant the king £100,000, which would be collected by commissioners in each county, who would follow up personal letters from the king to affluent supporters requesting a a specific sum as a loan. These individualised demands were designed to put the optimum pressure on people (many of whom had already contributed) to contribute more. In February of that year, John Grubbe of Potterne in Wiltshire received one such letter. 'Trusty and beloved; we greet you well. Though we are unwilling in the least degree to press upon our good subjects...we must desire you forthwith to lend us the sum of two hundred pounds in money or plate for our necessary support and the maintenance of our army....and we do promise you, in the word of a king, to repay it with interest'. The letter ended on a note of confidence that Grubbe would rally to the call.

However, the fact that these letters were tailored to meet the nature of each individual (probably on the advice of the local commissioners) is well illustrated by a similar letter received in March by one of Grubbe's neighbours, John Harvest. Not only had the amount been reduced to £100 for Harvest, the conclusion to the letter was also much more threatening, presumably because either his loyalty or his generosity was more in doubt. 'If you shall refuse to give us this testimony of your affection, you will give us too great cause to suspect your duty and inclination both to our person and the public cause'.

It was much the same elsewhere in the western counties. In Bristol, merchant William Wyatt received a letter from the king requesting a subscription of £20. The sheriff's endorsement of the document indicates that Wyatt responded by donating eighty ounces of plate, which was valued at £20. In Somerset, George Trevelyan received a letter in March via the High Sheriff, Sir Thomas Bridges, demanding a loan for the king. The threat of further action, if money was not received within seven days, was clearly stated: 'And in case there should be a delay or failing in you, I am required by His Majesty's letters to return your name and to give you notice that you forthwith attend His Majesty at his court in Oxford'. When requesting the loan of £20 from Robert Lucas of Taunton, the king used a totally different argument, basing his case on the monarch's feudal right to demand war service. 'And by law, your personal service attended in a warlike manner for the resistance of this invasion, may be required by us, which we desire to spare, choosing rather to invite your assistance for the maintenance of our army in a free and voluntary expression of your affections to our services'. (6)

Although in theory these requests were for voluntary donations, the Oxford Parliament had already instructed commissioners to cross-examine on the king's behalf any who failed to comply. Indeed, the king had previously decided that contributions would also be required from those who supported parliament. He had therefore issued commissions to Edward Wyndham and other leading allies in Somerset (10th July 1643) and to Sir William Morton and others in Gloucestershire (3rd January 1644) to investigate what persons over the past year or so had 'been in rebellion against His Majesty' or had assisted those who were in rebellion. Having listed all such suspects, they were to make a note of what lands, ready money, cattle and goods they possessed and then await instructions from the king about the seizure of these assets. The commissioners, of course, relied heavily on the front-line help provided by a whole team of assistants, who operated at parish level. These were men of lesser stature drawn from the local community, who knew their neighbours well and were prepared to break ranks by passing on information. It was a highly divisive process and wide open to abuse. Some, like Anthony Cletter of Clyffe Pypard and Henry Ghost of Nene Court in Wiltshire, seized the opportunity to work off old village rivalries by portraying their long-standing opponents as parliamentarian sympathisers, while Francis Baber of Barbadge settled an old score against the village constable by ensuring that royalist troops ransacked his house.

Parish clergy were often used in Wiltshire by commissioners to uncover hidden adversaries. Peter Waterman of Wootton Vizard, actually employed a man on a regular basis to act as a neighbourhood scout 'to enquire out such men as were anyway aiding and abetting the parliament that he might return them to the cavaliers', while Thomas Hickman of Upton Lovell passed on evidence against a number of his parishioners, whose political sympathies 'had thereby corrupted the mind of the people to the prejudice of His Majesty'. They were duly rounded up, plundered and imprisoned. Although many of those who assisted the commissioners in this way were honest and just in their actions, some undoubtedly became obsessed with their newly-discovered power and proceeded to terrorise individuals in a most vindictive manner. Thomas Shoard and John Wansey, constables of Maiden Bradley, persecuted a widow in the village for her parliamentary leanings. Royalist troops were therefore regularly billeted on her without payment (twelve at a time), while the prisoners, the sick and the wounded were routinely dumped at her house for periods of up to ten weeks at a stretch. Her protests were met with scorn and ridicule.(7)

Local officials were expected to co-operate - as John Harvey of Chard found to his cost in June 1643. On refusing to organise a rate for the king, he was threatened by leading royalists that he would be clapped in prison with his head tied to his heels. He quickly gave way in the face of such persuasive arguments. Like Harvey in Somerset, many Wiltshire men also served reluctantly, having been pressurised into acceptance. Some yielded to the threat of reprisals by royalist troops on their property, like Edward Topp of Stockton and Edward Yerbury of Trowbridge. Some, like Richard Goddard of Swindon, only agreed after sustained pressure from neighbours had persuaded them not to risk the severe consequences of refusal. Others accepted in the knowledge that they could use their position as royalist commissioners to work secretly for parliament by protecting parliamentarian sympathisers from heavy assessments, fines or imprisonment and by passing on intelligence of royalist activity. Rowland Plott of Tollard Royal and Charles Seymour of Allington came into this category. (8)

Voluntary Payments to Parliament: the Propositions, 1642

Parliament, meanwhile, had also used the voluntary principle at the beginning of the war, although it was done much more systematically and with the backing of a parliamentary Ordinance. On 9th June, 1642, orders were issued for 'the bringing in of money or plate to maintain horsemen, and arms, for the preservation of the public peace, and for the defence of the king and both Houses of Parliament'. These 'Propositions' encouraged voluntary contributions of money and the gifts of horses and arms by the promise of an eight per cent interest rate (which was never paid).

Once the war had started, the Wiltshire County Committee threw itself wholeheartedly into the task of raising subscriptions. A letter was sent on 3rd October 1642 to all leading gentry, inviting them to a meeting at the Mermaid Inn in Salisbury, when the Propositions would be discussed. The committee then shared out responsibility for the vital task of spearheading the collection, with Sir Edward Hungerford and Sir Edward Baynton leading the effort in the north-west of the county, Sir Neville Poole in the area around Marlborough and Sir John Evelyn in Salisbury. Donations averaged £5 from those able to afford it, with the gentry contributing sums ranging from £15 to £20. In Bristol, the Council responded to an appeal from parliament (24th October) for a house-to-house collection by first raising a subscription amongst themselves (with aldermen giving sums ranging from £5 to £20 and councillors from £4 to £10). Only four members refused to contribute. They then despatched each alderman to visit his own ward in the city, accompanied by the clergy, churchwardens and constables, to collect from those able to contribute. This proved to be greatly successful, a total of almost £2,600 being raised in all. (9)

Meanwhile, the Somerset Committee had got to work under the influential leadership of John Ashe, Alexander Popham and John Horner in the east of the county. Assistant collectors were appointed to visit 'people of ability' and receive their subscriptions. The response was most encouraging. In Keynsham, for instance, forty people lent between them a total of £82 15s 0d 'towards the setting forth of dragoons'. Individual donations varied between five shillings and ten pounds, some of them in the form of plate. A further twenty-eight people combined to provide eighteen horses (most of them fully equipped), twenty-two muskets, eighteen swords, eleven bandoliers, four pistols, five pikes, one halberd, one 'birding piece' and a 'new corslet and head piece' at a total cost of £133 2s 8d. The same pattern was repeated to a greater or lesser extent in many of the Somerset parishes. Widow Elizabeth Jennings of Publow even donated to Nathaniel Fiennes, Governor of Bristol, 'a piece of ordinance'

A Note of the Names of such as sett forth Horses with their furniture, and men with Armes & Monney under the Command of Col: Alexander Popham.

Nathaniell Saunders One Horse & his furniture and 28s to the Rider	5	0	0
and two Musketts and Bandileers	2	0	0
Tho: Pope One Horse with his furniture and a Muskett sworde and Bandileers	4	6	8
Thomas Shephearde One Horse & a Belt	2	0	0
Mr Wm Buckle One Horse with his furniture and 28s to the Rider	5	0	0
Thomas Leman One Horse with his furniture	5	0	0
Mr Flower One horse which cost 6li which with the Armes & other accomodations for the same	8	0	0
and to him that roade the Horse	1	8	0
John Wircombe One horse bridle & Saddle with Pistolls	8	0	0
More a Muskett Bandileers & 3 Swords	2	0	0
More to a man of his owne to ride the Horse	1	8	0
Robert Ford One horse with his furniture	3	10	0
More two Musketts two swordes & Bandileers with 10s in Monney	3	0	0
Mr Bagnall One Horse with his furniture and 28s with Muskett sworde & Bandileers	6	10	0
John Byde One horse with his furniture	8	0	0
Tho: Rawlins One Horse	3	0	0

Contributions made by individuals in Keynsham towards the Propositions, 1642. (By courtesy of the Public Record Office - SP28.175) valued at £20 and belonging to her late husband. The men of Whitchurch provided four horses, seven muskets, two swords and a carbine, as well as sums totalling £23 8s 0d. The village of Paulton claimed later that they had 'lent in money upon the parliament's Propositions and in plate, 5 spoons weighing 6.5 ounces...[total value] £7 10s.' The parish official, desperately fearing that the claim might be questioned through lack of concrete evidence, was quick to add that their donation had been 'paid to Richard Hippesley, which is dead'. Gifts and donations in the north of the county were taken in to the Guildhall in Bath, where John Lock of Pensford received them on behalf of the committee. (10)

A parliamentary Ordinance issued on 27th January, 1643, authorised the County Committee in Somerset to retain any money collected through the Propositions for the support of the local forces which were being raised. This was in the face of 'the ruin and destruction' being threatened by the formation of a new army in Cornwall under Sir Ralph Hopton ('that hellish and accursed crew') and the hostile movement of Welsh forces loyal to the king. Somerset was far too vital to lose - hence this special treatment, which rather established the precedent that local donations and taxes should be used for local defence. The collectors were therefore instructed to pay the money received, not to London as as was the case in the early months of the scheme, but to the County Committee's two treasurers -

The Guildhall in Bath, built in 1625, became a collection point for donations towards the Propositions. Edward Eyre's watercolour, 'High Street Bath, looking towards the Old Guildhall'. (By courtesy of the Victoria Art Gallery, Bath and North-East Somerset Council).

John Ashe of Freshford in the north and Roger Hill of Taunton in the south. The money was used immediately to pay for the setting up and maintenance of a regiment of dragoons under the command of Alexander Popham. (11)

The success of the new arrangements was both impressive and rapid. On the day following the publication of the Ordinance, the accountant of the hundreds of Brent and Brempstone (John Amery of Wrington) handed over the sum of £430, plus 289.5 ounces of plate and two gold rings, to John Ashe, treasurer of the committee. In his detailed accounts, which have survived, Amery gave the overall total raised by the collectors as £463 16s 2d., including a musket valued at 15s 0d. Apart from the lump sum paid to Ashe, he had also made smaller payments for provisions sent directly to the local troops and 2s 0d 'for a money wallet and money bag for Colonel Cole' [probably Richard Cole, merchant, from Nailsea] - a clear sign that colonels were also the paymasters of their regiments. Although John Amery had a balance in hand of £5 1s 9d when he submitted his accounts (towards the latter stages of the war), he begged to be allowed to keep this in payment of his expenses and in compensation for 'having also suffered by fine, plundering and several imprisonments by the king's party for his service and obedience to the parliament'. Such was the fate of tax gatherers, who inevitably attracted growing hostility from the community at large.

This hostility was particularly acute, of course, among those people who tried to avoid payment. Amery listed at the end of his account fourteen people from within the two hundreds who had failed to contribute to the Propositions, including one man for whom he put in a special plea - 'Walter Fayle, a man that was much plundered for his services to the parliament: you shall do well, as I conceive, under favour to spare him'. The implied threat to the other thirteen was no bluff. By the time Amery's accounts were drawn up, the Propositions had lost all sense of voluntary giving. On 27th January, 1643, a parliamentary Ordinance gave the Somerset Committee additional powers to assess and charge those 'malignants' who either had not contributed to the Propositions or had contributed less than their wealth warranted. Offenders were to be fined either a one-twentieth part of their personal estate or a one-fifth part of their yearly revenue. If they refused to co-operate, the committee had authority to raise the appropriate amount by seizing and selling their goods.

This tax, which was known as 'the Fifth and Twentieth Part', had already been applied in London on 26th November 1642 and in Wiltshire on 10th January, 1643 - the latter to provide part of the funding for the raising of two regiments of horse and one of dragoons. Although it is not easy to discover the extent of the success of this tax in Somerset, largely through the destruction of records, some royalists there did suffer in consequence, including Sir Thomas Bridges of Keynsham, who was fined £161. Elsewhere, commissioners sprang into vigorous action to track down defaulters. In Wiltshire, Sir Edward Hungerford visited Salisbury in

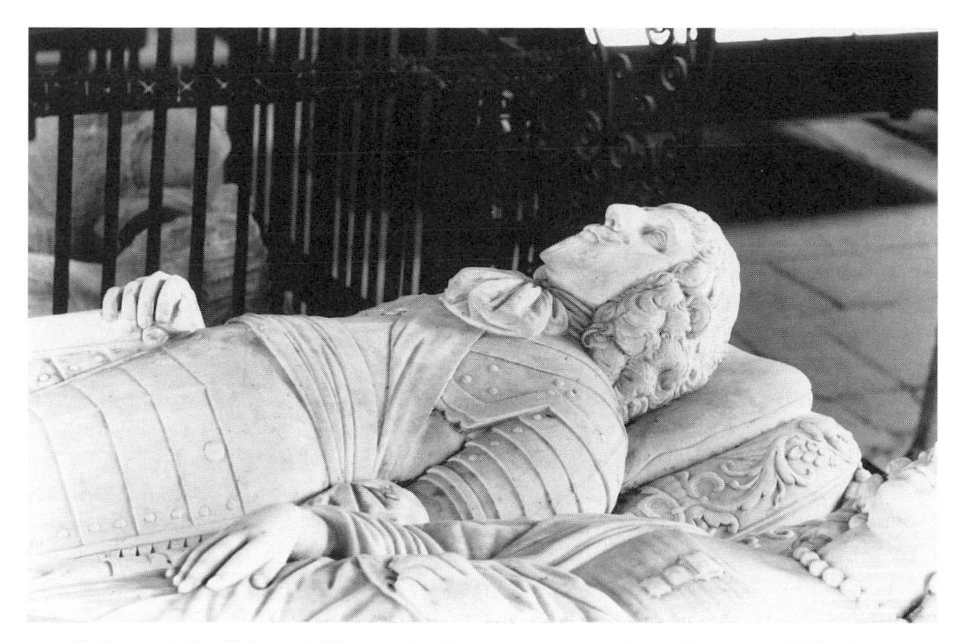

Effigy of Sir Edward Hungerford, commander of parliament's Wiltshire forces in 1643, in the family chapel at Farleigh Castle. (Author's collection)

February 1643 with a body of troops to deal with a number of leading citizens who had failed to contribute to the Propositions. After a series of raids and searches, a total of £500 was collected from individuals, including £20 from Alderman Gauntlett, £8 from Thomas Lawes (the former mayor), £10 from Matthew Bee and £20 each from three members of the Hancock family. (12)

The Propositions and the Fifth and Twentieth Part should not be regarded as a one-off attempt to raise money at the very start of the war, but rather as an on-going campaign to produce a regular income. The collectors never gave up in their attempt to ensure that every householder paid according to his means. Most tax-raising Ordinances of the later war period repeated the call to the County Committees to seek further 'voluntary gifts' at eight per cent interest under the terms of the Propositions; and to seek out those who had not contributed and fine them under the terms of the Fifth and Twentieth Part. This was true in February, 1643, when a new army was to be raised in the West for Sir William Waller; it was true in May, 1644, when parliament sanctioned the raising of extra troops for the Gloucester garrison; and it was true in July, 1644, when further forces were raised for the defence of Wiltshire.

Even as late as 1645 and 1646, the Collector of the garrisons of Chalfield and Malmesbury in Wiltshire was successfully pursuing defaulters at the behest of the County Committee, using troops from the garrisons to assist where necessary. As a result, he managed to raise £56 7s 0d from fifty-eight inhabitants of the area around Chalfield and £53 0s

0d from the Malmesbury district. Indeed, a campaign was conducted throughout Wiltshire from January to June in 1646 to round up non-payers and fine them under the terms of the Fifth and Twentieth Part. Among many individuals to suffer in the process were John Lee of Hamerington (fined £20), John Linch of Downton (a bay gelding worth £7 10s), Thomas Ludlow of Warminster (£5), John Lush of Donhead (2 quarters of oats valued at £2) and Thomas Miles of Wroughton (a black mare valued at £6). Meanwhile, in Gloucestershire, a similar drive had been launched in October 1644 over a wide area around Gloucester, Tewkesbury, Tetbury and Moreton-in-Marsh. In all, some 281 people were fined (mostly sums of £1 in part payment, but ranging upwards to £10 from William Rogers of Dowdesworth). A total of £451 was raised in consequence. (13)

The committee in London, which masterminded these operations and to which the county commissioners reported, was the Committee for the Advance of Money. Established in November 1642, its task was to supervise the receipt of loans under the Propositions and fines under the Fifth and Twentieth Part. From 1645, it was also responsible for unearthing 'concealed delinquencies' (i.e. secret royalists, who had not yet paid their dues). This particular aspect of its work, which dragged on for several years after the ending of the war, relied heavily on local informants to supply vital information. The committee was relentless in pursuit of its victims, helping to ensure a steady flow of revenue throughout the late 1640s.

It was, however, also scrupulously fair in hearing appeals. Some individuals, like John Northover, of Aller in Somerset, had no excuse. He had failed to pay his £100 fine in 1647 and therefore suffered the confiscation of his estates two years later. Some, however, had been wrongly accused through false information, like Robert Hunt of Speckington in Somerset. Originally fined £400 in 1647, he was able to prove that he was not a 'concealed' royalist at all, for he had previously contributed £100 and some horses under the Propositions in Dorset. He was therefore discharged. Others had their fines reduced in view of special circumstances. John Question, a surgeon from Dunster in Somerset, had had his fine originally set at £100 in 1647, but he was able to show that he had 'dressed and cured' many parliamentarian soldiers at the siege of Dunster 'for which he received nothing'. His assessment was reduced to £10. John Carey from Milton in Somerset was in no position at all to pay his fine of £100. Already an old man, he had been held in prison since 1648 with debts of over £1,000 and had a wife and six children to support. He was discharged from the fine in 1651 on payment of £10. Richard Hill of Salisbury in Wiltshire was also discharged from payment. Although his fine had been assessed at £250 in 1644, he was totally devoid of financial means, having been 'driven from his habitation and plundered of his estate'.

Many ordinary local people acted as informants in this process of

Alexander Popham (1605-1669) of Littlecote House, member of parliament for Bath, commander of the Bath Regiment of trained bands and leading member of parliament's county committee in Somerset. (By courtesy of the Royal Armouries - © The Board of Trustees of the Armouries, accession no. I.315)

unearthing 'concealed delinquents'. Their evidence was sometimes malicious, occasionally false and often devastating. Never before had ordinary local people enjoyed so much power in village life. The following are just a few examples taken from hundreds of similar cases dealing with fines under the Fifth and Twentieth Part. John Long of Haw and Monkton in Wiltshire had been reported for two remarks made in casual conversation - 'there were none but rogues and base fellows left in the parliament' and 'hanging was good enough' for all rebels. Sir Edward Fisher of Mickleton in Gloucestershire had been spotted more than once on journeys to Oxford to procure writs with which to sue his neighbours. Village gossip accused Richard Cox of Norton-under-Hampden in Somerset of 'ringing the bells for joy that the cavaliers were coming into these parts', dissuading William Tanner 'from serving parliament' and harbouring 'enemies to parliament' in his house. Local informants in Moreton-in-Marsh in Gloucestershire were scathing in their report on James Beck. He had allegedly persuaded a party of royalist cavalry to take the town constable to Woodstock as their prisoner 'with only his night shirt on, without hose or shoes, on a terribly frosty night, carrying him 14 miles to the king's quarters and using such cruelty that he languished and died in a few days'. John Boxall of Wootton Bassett in Wiltshire had infuriated his neighbours by voluntarily sending 20 cwt of cheese and '30 head of cattle' to Sir Ralph Hopton's forces as they besieged Winchester, some thirty miles away. Without such graphic evidence from people living on the spot, it would have been impossible to proceed against these 'concealed delinquents'. It did little, however, for the future harmony of village life. (14)

Although inevitably the Propositions represented a diminishing asset, as more and more people were eventually ground into submission, it was nevertheless a highly successful tax. It is estimated that over one million pounds was collected from this source alone between 1642 and 1645.

Compulsion: the Weekly Assessment, 1643

By the beginning of 1643, parliament was rapidly coming to the conclusion that voluntary gifts alone would not win the war. Military commanders needed a much more regular and systematic supply of money with which to enlarge and maintain their forces. A compulsory element was therefore added by means of the weekly assessment, imposed by parliamentary Ordinance on 24th February, 1643 and intended to run initially for a period of three months (though in reality it became a permanent tax). It aimed to produce a weekly total figure of £33,518 spread over the country as a whole (at least from those areas under parliament's control), with allocations specified for individual counties and major cities. Gloucestershire was therefore assessed at £750 per week, Somerset £1050, Wiltshire £725, Bristol £55 15s 0d, and Gloucester £62 10s 0d. All persons (and corporations) were to be taxed on the value of their cash, personal property and estates (although the yearly wages of servants were exempt, as were all persons with a yearly income of under £10 or property of less than £100 in value); popish recusants were to pay double and those convicted of evading the tax treble. The Ordinance named committees in each county or city to be responsible for appointing assessors and collectors, who would visit individuals on a weekly basis. In practical terms, the County Committees tended to appoint a subcommittee in each hundred with the High Constable playing a prominent part in working out the assessment for each parish. In the parish itself, groups of prominent and trustworthy members of the community would meet to discuss a fair allocation of the tax for each individual, before handing over the actual collection to the village constable (or 'tithingman'). (15)

The royalists later adopted a similar system of a weekly tax, when they gained control of the western counties from August 1643, usually styling it 'contribution money', although the illusion of the voluntary loan was still maintained and they still sought to gain the agreement of the local people. On 30th November 1643, for instance, it was reported to the king's council of war that the inhabitants of Wiltshire had 'agreed to pay to the king, by way of a loan, for the space of one month, a weekly contribution of £1,200' towards the maintenance of his army there (i.e. compared with the £725 previously charged by parliament). This agreement came as a result of large and passionate meetings in various towns between the king's commissioners and the local gentry, who bitterly complained of the abuses inflicted by soldiers. After further discussion with the king's council of war, the Wiltshire gentry agreed to the new contribution on condition that troops were tightly regulated over requisitions and billeting. Details would be published in all churches and complaints heard in Oxford. (16)

Parliament's system, on the other hand, was far more centralised and less reliant on local agreements. As with the Propositions, it was persistent in ensuring the success of the tax. In an attempt to catch up with tax-dodgers, for instance, an Ordinance was passed on 26th August to deal with those people who had 'covertly conveyed away their goods from their houses and absented their persons to avoid payment of their assessments...and their houses to stand empty'. Local committees were therefore given the power to rent out such houses and apply the money raised to the war effort. In Bristol, the Council had earlier (4th June) issued a warning to those freemen of the city, who had either already left or intended to spend a period out of the city, to ensure that 'the weekly rates laid on them...be paid in and made good from time to time in their absence'. (17)

In the Eastern Division of Somerset, the work of master-minding the operation fell to John Ashe, the treasurer of the committee. Although he applied himself to the task with characteristic energy and persistence, his success was disappointingly uneven, judging by the accounts later submitted by parishes concerned. During the first five months of the operation of the new tax in 1643, for example, the villages of Tickenham, Chelbey and Whitchurch (among others) claimed that they had paid the full amount over all five months; Chew Magna and Foxcote, on the other hand, only claimed payments for four months; Kingston Sutton and Stowey-in-Gentwall for just six weeks; and the parishes of Wellow, Combe Hay and Corston claimed no contributions at all.

Much, of course, depended on the efficiency of the local officials. Some clearly lacked the necessary organisational skills and had lost their original receipts. The constables of Twerton and Newton St. Loe both confessed that 'much more hath been paid before the King's forces took Bristol, but we cannot for the present find out our accounts'. Although some of the villages handed over quite substantial sums during this period (Dunkerton £46 0s 0d, Englishcombe £48 18s 12d, Hinton Charterhouse

£35 9s 2d etc.), the overall success rate was distinctly patchy. Furthermore, even if the parish faithfully made a contribution each week, the total often fell short of the actual assessment because of non-payers within the village. John Amery, the 'accountant' of the hundreds of Brent and Brempstone, recorded in his accounts that he had received £288 14s 0d from the eleven villages in his area, following the Ordinance issued by parliament in May, 1643 to stir collectors into action. However, he then listed the names of eighty-two individuals 'that are behind of their moneys', owing a total of £277 16s 0d (i.e. almost half of the amount which the collectors had targeted). (18)

In Gloucestershire, out of an estimated total of £188,000 levied on the county through the weekly assessment between 1643 and 1647, only £100,000 had been collected by the end of the war in 1646. As elsewhere, the success rate was better in some areas than in others. The parishes of Pebworth and Marston, for instance, raised 80 per cent of their allocation. Similarly, in the twelve months from August 1644, the Gloucestershire hundreds of Tewkesbury, Cleeve, Westminster, Tybaldstone, Cheltenham and Deerhurst paid £4,586 out of their total assessment of £5206 (an 88 per cent collection rate). In the Whitstone hundred, during the six months from February 1644, the High Constable (William Nicolson) managed to collect all but £74 of the assessment total of £1010 (a 93 per cent success

Tax collectors, backed by soldiers, call on villagers for the weekly assessment. (Line drawing by Stephen Beck)

rate). On the other hand, in the Kiftsgate Division *[i.e a group of hundreds in the north of the county]*, the collector (William Neast) only managed to collect 63 per cent of the tax in the eight weeks from August 1644. Variations of this kind were due to a number of factors - the co-operation of local people, the efficiency of the tax collector and the level of enemy operations or military activity in the area.

Tax collection was, of course, a hazardous business and large amounts of cash could be lost in the process. Sir Samuel Luke recalls in his diary how, in April 1643, some of Sir William Waller's troopers, out searching for supplies in the Forest of Dean, intercepted a letter from the royalist leader, Sir John Winter. Addressed to a Mr Moss of Mitchelsdean, it concerned the £910 which Moss was collecting in the area for the maintenance of the king's forces. Whereupon, Waller himself went to Moss's house, pretending to be a royalist officer, and demanded the money in spite of Moss's protests that he had only collected £700 to date. Waller replied that 'it was fit that what he had received should be employed in the king's service and that roundhead Waller was coming that way, who might misemploy it', if he did not not hand it over immediately for safe keeping. Moss meekly complied, only to be arrested when Waller revealed his true identity. (19)

The collectors in fact were finding it more and more difficult to gain the co-operation of local inhabitants who had already been squeezed dry in other ways. A despondent letter written from Bath by John Ashe to Nathaniel Fiennes, Governor of Bristol, on 1st June 1643 illustrates the extent of his problem. It stressed that the continuing demands by local garrison troops for free quarter, cash and supplies clearly made most people feel reluctant to contribute to the weekly assessment in addition. 'The inhabitants and the constables of the hundred of Keynsham', he wrote, 'bring in very little money, alleging that they are eaten up by the Bristol troopers and dragoons'. Such were the complaints about this from the constables in the whole area that Ashe was 'extremely perplexed with them', receiving only ' very small sums'. Surrounded by angry constables as he penned the letter, he was so distraught that he urged Fiennes to 'excuse this scribbling, for it's in the midst of a passionate debate amongst the negligent constables'. (20)

Ashe realised only too well that, if the tax failed to materialise, the soldiers would not be paid, which in turn would result in more plunder and free quarter being taken from the villages by force. The situation was precarious. For instance, the cavalry troop commanded in Bristol by Colonel John Fiennes (brother of the Governor) was based in the city between February and April 1643. Although his 65 men were paid in regular instalments during that period, they were each under-paid by about one-third of the total due. Colonel William Strode was also based in Bristol between March and June 1643 with his cavalry regiment. His carefully-maintained accounts show that, although he paid out on his men's wages and weapons a total of £3,402, he received only £1922 in weekly assessment payments from the local parishes. Nevertheless, he was able to write at the end of the accounts: 'I am in arrears to neither captain nor soldiers...I have charged nothing for my own pay'. Strode, in fact, had made up the considerable shortfall out of his own pocket and the pockets of his local Somerset friends. Other regiments were not so lucky - nor were the ordinary people who were supposed to support them. (21)

Throughout the western counties, the collection of the weekly assessment was being undermined by instant additional demands imposed by both garrison troops and field armies. It was particularly bad in frontier towns like Chippenham in Wiltshire, set in an area which repeatedly changed hands during the war and in a corridor used by armies of both sides as they campaigned westwards. The borough registers tell an amazing story of financial oppression on a huge scale, which was sustained over a period of three years. In 1643, although the Corporation paid a contribution to the weekly assessment on a regular basis throughout the year, the actual size of its payments fell sharply from a total of 16s 0d for the month of February to just 7s 0d for January 1644. There is no doubt that this decline is attributable to the large number of additional demands (23 in all) made by field armies and garrisons of both sides during the same period. These included payments for provisions sent to the garrison at Malmesbury, provisions sent to the king's army at the siege of Gloucester, 'fines' (or lump sums of cash demanded instantly) imposed at different times by Prince Maurice, The Marquess of Hertford and Colonel Massey, 160 dozen loaves of bread despatched to Hertford's army at Devizes prior to the Battle of Roundway Down, 120 dozen loaves sent to Cirencester, the carriage of gunpowder and a large piece of artillery to Devizes and horses for Sir William Waller. Then, on top of all this, additional monthly contributions were sent to maintain the garrison at Malmesbury. (22)

Yelde Hall, a 15th century town hall in Chippenham, contains the original Council Chamber where civil war tax demands were debated. (Author's collection)

These additional demands were usually by special warrant signed by county commissioners or army commanders. Failure to respond would result in a sternly worded reminder, accompanied by undisguised threats of retribution - as the High Constables of the hundred of Potterne and

Cannings in Wiltshire found to their dismay in December 1644. 'Whereas you have received a former warrant for the speedy raising of three-score pounds within your hundred, which you have neglected to do, and given no account thereof, according to your warrant subscribed by Major Nott: These are therefore to require you...without any further delay, to collect the same, and upon pain of plundering to bring it to our quarters at Trowbridge for the use of my Lord Wentworth's brigade, this instant Tuesday...' Parish officials, confronted by a sudden demand like this, would need to impose a village rate quickly. The constable of Stowey-in-Gentwall in Somerset, faced with an instant request for money to assist with the strengthening of the Bristol fortifications in April 1643, simply imposed an additional weekly rate over a seven-week period. (23)

Like Chippenham, the city of Wells had good reason to deplore the draining and exhausting effects of irregular tax demands on the community, especially by armies of both sides passing through the area. Over a period of just two months in the summer of 1644, the Corporation received five major requests of this nature. The king, who was marching into the south-west in pursuit of the army of the Earl of Essex, sent a letter to the mayor, dated 18th July from Mells. Having noted 'the constant readiness and affection of the Corporation of the City of Wells', he asked them to 'speedily furnish' his Treasurer-at-War with the sum of £500 (to be repaid, of course, as soon as possible!). Three days later, he wrote again demanding another favour. Various metal smiths in Wells had apparently responded to the warrant of his General of Artillery and had sent in a supply of horse-shoes for the use of the train. However, in order to avoid inflicting the cost of this on 'these poor men', the king commanded the mayor to make a charge on the city, so that 'satisfaction be given to the said poor smiths for their work'.

Just under a month later, General John Middleton arrived in Somerset with a parliamentarian force, aiming to cut off the supply line to the king's army in Cornwall. He also sent two letters to the Mayor of Wells, the first (on 16th August) demanding sixty horses with saddles and bridles, at a cost of £480, to be supplied within four days; the second, a week later, demanding a levy of £300 to be delivered to Chard within two days. In return, he promised that 'your horses will be protected and your homes kept from plundering'. The councillors were enraged. In a fury, they penned a petition to Middleton, complaining of unfair treatment and urging him 'to consider the poor and desolate estate of the poor borough in these distracted times'. But they had second thoughts. The petition was never sent and the demand was paid. Their suffering, however, was not yet complete. A month later, the king passed through the county again on his return from victory at Lostwithiel. This time, with the need to replenish basic items clothing after a long march, he instructed the city of Wells to supply 500 pairs of shoes and 500 pairs of stockings within six days, storing them in the Town Hall until he sent for them. These were clearly part of an assignment of 6,000 pairs of shoes, 6,000 pairs of stockings,

3,000 suits of clothes and 300 draught horses that the king (in a letter from Chard, dated 29th September) had instructed the High Sheriff of Somerset, Sir John Stawell, to supply from within the county. (24)

Other cities suffered in equal measure. The citizens of Salisbury received a sudden demand from the king on his march through Wiltshire in October 1644 for the sum of £500 - to be paid by the following morning! In Bristol, the Council received a letter from the king on 30th September 1644, requesting 1,500 pairs of shoes and 1,500 pairs of stockings for his army on its return from Cornwall (presumably to supplement those already taken from Wells). The Council decided to pay for these by collecting the money 'out of hand' from the inhabitants through a double payment of the weekly assessment over the next four weeks. They were only just recovering from the shock when, eight days later, they received a further letter demanding £2,000 in ready money for the payment of his troops, plus an additional £1,000 worth of shoes and stockings. After heated debate, the Council resolved to limit their new contribution to £1,000 in total and, not wishing to impose further strain on the inhabitants, to raise it by way of a loan.

Sudden demands like these, however, normally bore most heavily on ordinary individuals. There is no doubt that many people were terrified of the consequences of non-payment with retribution to be expected at the hands of both tax collectors and soldiers. This human anxiety is well illustrated by a letter from William Lawrence to Mr Fletcher (a collector for the Gloucester garrison) in March 1644. Having received a demand for the new weekly assessment, Lawrence wrote in a state of great distress to explain the delay in payment: 'I have sold a mare to the butcher, who promised to fetch it up upon Monday last, but failed. Tomorrow he sendeth me word that he will fetch it without fail. Out of that money, you shall be paid. If any enquiry be made of my payment, I pray you to answer it'. (25)

In spite of the fact that the effectiveness of the weekly assessment was undermined by the sudden imposition of extra demands, the tax nevertheless raised a large amount of money during the war. The inhabitants of the three western counties were perfectly accustomed to the notion of paying taxes both on a regular basis and on extra occasions to cover emergency needs - such as the subsidy of December 1641, granted by parliament for the relief of the army in the North in the war against the Scots. Nevertheless, the weekly assessment was much more persistent and extensive in form than anything they had ever experienced. For instance, the subsidy of 1641 had only cost the village of Englishcombe in Somerset a total of £6 2s 8d, whereas they paid £48 18s 12d in 1643 and £66 8s 0d in 1645-6 towards the weekly assessment. Similarly, the entire hundred of Wellow had paid a combined sum of £83 1s 4d for the 1641 subsidy, compared with a sum of £867 2s 9d for the weekly assessment over two years when parliamentarians were in control. John Morrill has concluded that the weekly assessment 'was the equivalent to a parliamentary subsidy every fortnight', while Alan Everitt has suggested that it represented an income tax of 2s 6d in the pound by 1644-5. (26)

The Introduction of the Excise, 1643

Pressure on the pockets of ordinary people was further intensified by the introduction of the excise by parliament on 22nd July 1643. The tax, which was imposed on the sale of basic commodities (including salt), was organised in London by a group of merchants, who appointed subcommissioners to collect in each of the counties. They were granted powers to search premises and to arrest, fine or imprison defaulters without trial. Local officials were expected to draw up lists of traders and fix rates for commodities on sale. On 8th May 1644, the king copied this method of raising extra revenue by introducing the excise, in areas under his control, on 65 foreign and 21 native goods. An office of excise was established in Oxford with groups of commissioners appointed in major towns (Bristol, Salisbury, Exeter etc) and each English county.

There was widespread opposition to this tax throughout the country and it largely failed to take root. When, for instance, the royalist excise commissioners arrived in Wells in the autumn of 1644, the mayor, Richard Casbeard, could not be persuaded to read the proclamation, while one of his aldermen cried that the commissioners 'came to rob and devour the people'. George Trevelyan and John Bourne, highly respectable members of the local gentry, who had been nominated to serve as commissioners, had already declined to accept the office. Nor was this opposition in Somerset simply limited to the royalist version of the tax. In 1646, there were street demonstrations against parliament's commissioners in Bruton, Somerton and Taunton.

Although the excise was, therefore, generally unsuccessful outside London, there is some evidence that it was made to operate in Bristol. In February 1646, concern was expressed in parliament about the need for greater resources to support the Bristol garrison. The receipts of 'the excise and the new impost within the said city' were therefore to be wholly appropriated for this purpose. On the other hand, there is clear evidence that the tax was efficiently collected over a wide area in Gloucestershire for the maintenance of the Gloucester garrison. The accounts of the Grand Committee there (see below), drawn up by Alderman Pury, show that a total of £282 had been raised by the excise in October 1644 (mainly on the sale of malt, beer, meat and currants) from towns such as Tewkesbury and various places within the Berkeley hundred. Of all districts in the western counties, these had already suffered more than most and were least able therefore to bear this extra burden. (27)

A Change of Tactics: Collection by Garrisons

By 1644, both sides in the war had decided that it would be more efficient to hand over the task of collecting the weekly assessment to the governors of local garrisons. This at least would mean an end to the situation in which two local bodies (the County Committee and the garrison force) were competing for the same limited amount of resources (even if it did not stamp out completely the random demands made by armies from outside the county marching through). The new system did, however, mean that the work of tax collection now fell increasingly into the hands of career soldiers with few local connections, who could therefore view its disagreeable aspects more dispassionately. In practice, important garrisons were allocated a specific area in the vicinity from which to draw their support. These large garrisons often sprouted a number of minor satellite garrisons, quickly established in country mansions throughout the area, to enable the governor to control his resources more tightly in a potentially hostile countryside. The other advantage, which the king in particular appreciated as the war progressed, was that troops could be more easily fed if they were spread around in garrisons, rather than clustered together *en masse* in large field armies. This also enabled them to live off the country at a time when he was almost penniless and therefore unable to pay their wages.

The 15th century North Gate of Sudeley Castle, owned by Lord Chandos, but captured first by Massey and then by Rupert in 1643, before falling to Waller in 1644. (Author's collection)

This new system aimed at not only supporting the garrison forces themselves, but also creating a stockpile for the use of visiting field armies. Winton Castle in Hampshire, for instance, became a depot in 1645 for 15,000 hundredweight of cheese *[with 112 lbs per hundredweight]*, 7,000 hundredweight of biscuits plus large quantities of beef, pork, salt and beer. Even as early as 1643, an interlocking network of thirty-four garrisons had been established in Shropshire, while the parliamentarian garrison at Newport Pagnell had received authority to set up a complicated system stretching over eight counties to support its 1,500 men and visiting troops. Colonel Massey, the Governor of Gloucester, controlled an enormous area around the city through his subsidiary garrisons at such places as Stroud, Dymock, Strensham, Sudeley, Beverstone and Slimbridge. (28)

From 1645, the General Account Book of Marlborough in Wiltshire shows a distinct change in the payment of the weekly contribution. The town had clearly been assigned to support the royalist garrison over the Berkshire border at Faringdon. The entries which refer to '22 weeks contribution to Faringdon', 'Mr Mayor for his expenses to Faringdon', 'Mr Perfitt to carry a letter to Faringdon' etc all suggest that direct payments were now being made to the garrison itself - a garrison which was all too willing to use pressure to secure any initial shortfall in the contribution. On two occasions, therefore, the Mayor was forced 'to make up the rate for Faringdon', costing the borough funds no less than £16 10s 4d in total. (29)

It was a similar story in Chippenham. Whereas, in 1643, the treasurer's accounts tell the story of countless random payments to the armies of both sides in addition to the normal weekly contributions (see above), the accounts for 1644 tell a completely different tale. Gone are virtually all the single payments. Instead, the entries clearly show that the town had taken responsibility for the partial support of three garrisons - Devizes, Lacock and Malmesbury. Although Devizes (a royalist garrison) received comparatively minor help in the form of provisions and supplies, Lacock (another royalist stronghold) was sent 28 weeks of contribution money and substantial assistance towards the strengthening of its fortifications. Malmesbury also received weekly contributions from Chippenham - at first paid to the royalists there and later, when the town fell to Colonel Massey (24th May), to the parliamentarian garrison under Colonel Nicholas Devereux. Indeed, the people around Malmesbury had been among the first to benefit from the new system, following the agreement made between the Wiltshire gentry and the king's commissioners on 30th November 1643 (see above). After furious complaints from local inhabitants, the royalist council of war promised to end all arbitrary demands for cash and supplies (i.e. over and above the weekly tax) and allocate specific areas to each garrison for maintenance. The royalist foot regiment which occupied Malmesbury, therefore, was allocated four hundreds in the immediate vicinity from which to draw its weekly pay of £180 via the regular contribution (with the Calne hundred paying £324 per week, the Chippenham hundred £72, the Damerham North hundred £10 and the Malmesbury hundred £72). (30)

In Gloucestershire, too, similar systems were in operation by royalists and parliamentarians alike by 1644. On 7th April, the king established garrisons at both Sudeley and Tewkesbury, allocating to the former for its support the hundreds of Bradley, Brightwelsbarrow, Cirencester, Crowthorne and Minety, Rapsgate and Slaughter; and to the latter, the hundreds of Cheltenham, Cleeve, Deerhurst, Tewkesbury, Tybaldstone and Westminster. A total of £6,000 a month was calculated for the maintenance of these two garrisons, with half being provided in fresh food supplies. The accounts of Thomas Blayney, treasurer to the parliamentarian garrison of Gloucester, make it abundantly clear that all charges in support of the garrison were applied directly by the Governor. From March 1643 to August 1644, a total of £20,336 was collected in the form of weekly assessments from the parishes in a wide area around the city, voluntary donations, fines of delinquents, rents of royalist lands etc. His regular payments to Robert George for 'carrying warrants to several constables for raising of money' confirm this. Sadly, the new system did not always prevent serious abuse and the infliction of misery on the local population. Some garrisons simply collected the taxes and continued to plunder as before (see below). (31)

Under the new system, demands for taxes or supplies came in the form of warrants, issued either by or on behalf of the garrison governor. The long-suffering High Constable of the hundred of Potterne and Cannings experienced direct pressure of this kind from both sides in the war as Wiltshire increasingly became a battleground in 1644. On 15th July, therefore, he received a warrant from the Governor of Malmesbury, Colonel Devereux, for £240 towards the cost of two months pay for his own regiment of foot and troop of dragoons (who had not been paid for four weeks). The High Constable (John Harvest) was instructed to to bring 'the same pay unto me at my quarters in the said garrison upon Friday next, 19th July'. Nothing could be more direct than that! Earlier, in April, he had received a warrant from the royalist Governor of Devizes, Sir Charles Lloyd - demanding, first, the weekly sum of £20 from the hundred in normal tax; and secondly, the sum of four pounds towards the wages of 'the sentries', to be paid 'weekly and every week' at the house of the governor's collector inside Devizes itself. Shortly afterwards, he received a rather threatening warrant, again from Devizes, demanding an immediate reply to a previous request for help on the fortifications - namely, the use of ploughs and the sum of five pounds 'for the payment of carpenters and sawyers'. Demands for direct payments to the Devizes garrison continued into 1645. In March of that year, the governor's warrant instructed the same hundred to supply a large quantity of butter, cheese, bacon, wheat, malt and peas, to be delivered to the commissary, who would then give them a 'discharge' (i.e. a release from paying their normal assessment). If they were unable to raise the correct amount in provisions, they were 'to gather and receive it in money to the value'. (32)

One of the best examples of the new system of taxation through the garrisons is given by Bristol, a centre vital for the war effort in the West. Under the control of the royalists from July 1643, the Bristol garrison had thrown out a network of satellites with which to control a wide neighbourhood. These included the garrisons at Bath, Farleigh Castle, Nunney Castle and Portishead in Somerset; and Berkeley Castle in Gloucestershire. It was an expensive arrangement. By 1st November 1644, a total establishment of three regiments of foot (with 1,200 men in each regiment) and seven troops of horse (with 60 in each troop) had been assigned to cater for the military requirements of these garrisons, all under the direct control of Bristol. The weekly pay of these combined forces was estimated at a cost of £1,185 19s 0d, with colonels of foot receiving £5, captains £2 10s, corporals 5s 0d, and common soldiers 3s 6d. Nor did that figure include the cost of the garrison officials (treasurer, quartermaster-general, keeper of the stores etc.) or the cost of arms and ammunition. It was estimated, therefore, that the overall sum needed to be raised from the local community for the support of this military operation was no less than £2,000 per week.

Berkeley Castle, owned by Lord Berkeley, was a satellite of the Bristol garrison and changed hands several times during the war. (Author's collection)

Letters patent issued by the king consequently granted full powers to Edmund Turner, treasurer of the garrison network. All sheriffs, mayors and constables were commanded to assist him and his collectors in levying contributions on neigh-bouring districts so that the funding targets, which cut right across county boundaries, could be achieved. Of the £2,000 weekly total, it was stipulated that £150 would be contributed by the City of Bristol, £500 by specified parishes in Wiltshire, £300 by certain parishes in Gloucestershire, £200 by customs duties from the port of Bristol and £850 by listed parishes in the Eastern Division of Somerset (including those in the hundreds of Keynsham, Bathforum, Kilmersdon, Wellow, Chew, Chewton, Bruton, Portbury, Hartcliffe, Winterstoke and Frome, which together bore the brunt of the charge). To help Turner in this challenging assignment, the king instructed local army officers to send out 'such parties of horse or foot as you shall think fit and necessary for the due levying and collecting of the contributions aforesaid'. Two months later, Turner was appointed captain of his own troop of cuirassiers to assist him in this work of tax collection. Strong-arm tactics were not to be discounted as pressure was systematically applied to the local community. The High Constable of the Pucklechurch hundred, for instance, received a warrant on 4th June 1644 for £75 as part of their regular contribution in support of the Bristol garrison. The concluding footnote, however, was ominous. The inhabitants were warned to take this demand for cash seriously so that 'the soldiers, for want thereof, may not be enforced to come and be their own carriers'. Perhaps in the light of this, the news-sheet, *Mercurius Civicus,* was not far off the mark, when it reported that the Governor of Bath (Sir Thomas Bridges) had sent out troops 'who fetched in about 30 of the countrymen thereabouts, and brought them in two by two for not paying the unreasonable taxes assessed upon them'. (33)

By May 1645, however, it was fast becoming clear that they were falling well below their targets for Bristol, in spite of the direct methods being applied. Richard Marsh, Keeper of the King's Stores of Ordnance in Bristol, wrote a pitiful letter to Sir Edward Nicholas, the king's Secretary of State, complaining of the lack of cash. Under the terms of the original establishment, he should have received £350 per week to be spent specifically on ammunition and the making of new weapons for Bristol and its outlying garrisons. But in the first twenty-nine weeks of the scheme, Turner (the Treasurer) had only paid him a total of £2940 instead of the expected sum of £10,150 - i.e. under £90 per week. Apparently the main reason for this was that 'the amounts expected from the customs here and the contribution coming in from Somersetshire are so small.' The inhabitants in the north-east of the county were clearly resisting, partly because they were already impoverished by the war, but partly also because their heart was still with parliament. (34)

After the recapture of Bristol by Sir Thomas Fairfax and the New Model Army on 11th September 1645, parliament soon adopted the royalist scheme for maintaining the garrison. An Ordinance was passed on 3rd December, appointing Major-General Philip Skippon as Governor of Bristol and authorising a total of £3,000 to be raised each month for his support. Of this, £200 a month was to be collected from the City of Bristol, £800 from the parishes in Gloucestershire, £800 from the parishes in Wiltshire and £1,200 from the parishes in Somerset. These amounts were to be taken out of the weekly assessment, which was quickly revived, and paid directly to Bristol. Although there was some variation in collection from village to village, the parish accounts indicate that this time the local officials were much more successful in gathering in payments on a regular basis. The parish constables of the Wellow hundred, with detailed exactions fresh in their memory, are quite specific in the returns for the period August 1645 to September 1646 - Camerton £52 2s 5d (11 months), Dunkerton £45 14s 0d (11 months), Englishcombe £63 8s 0d (9 months), Hinton Charterhouse £52 7s 3d (10 months), and Norton St Philip £43 7s 3d (11 months). Most of these payments were clearly detailed as going to support 'the garrison of Bristol' or 'the Governor of Bath'. (35)

A Change of Attitude: Eliminating Abuse

The new system of centralising the collection of tax through garrison governors undoubtedly made the operation far more effective. It did not, however, automatically eliminate abuse or reduce the suffering of ordinary people in the locality. As late as June 1645, for instance, an inhabitant of the Blackmore Forest, in the parish of Melksham in Wiltshire, wrote to a friend in London that Colonel Lloyd's soldiers from the Devizes garrison 'move about our county, where our misery is such that we are forced to pay them moneys to eat up our provisions of victuals, oats, hay and such like. For we must allow every common soldier six pence by the day, besides diet; twelve pence per sergeant; eighteen pence the lieutenants and captains'.

In October that year, after the siege of Bristol, the parliamentary commissioners wrote to the Speaker of the Commons outlining the terrible hardships inflicted on local people, who were pouring in with their complaints. They had suffered dreadfully during the siege, had had 'their cattle driven, their houses fired, their goods spoiled by the enemy' and what little remained had been ' eaten up' by the large numbers taking part in the siege. Nevertheless, the garrison forces still demanded their weekly contribution and would not make 'any allowance' for their previous losses. To make matters worse, the Gloucester garrison was also making tax demands 'to the very walls of this city', enforcing them by 'imprisoning the persons, beating and wounding such as resist in this violence'. The commissioners urged parliament to ensure in future that each garrison had very firm bounds set for its tax gathering 'that one clash not against the other'. (36)

In the autumn of 1643, a similar story had emerged in the area around Gloucester, where many grievances against the garrison were expressed by local people about the way official overcharged them on their tax assessments and troops continued both to plunder them and to terrorise them with free quarter. Parliament, therefore, set up a committee, under the chairmanship of Alderman Pury, to investigate these complaints (a committee which was later to be re-formed in January 1644 as the Grand Committee). Pury's first decision was to rule that so much had been taken from the populace in free quarter and plunder that most local people were totally incapable of paying their arrears in tax. A new rate was therefore needed, which would be set aside to pay the soldiers' future wages - and not their arrears, which were to be written off. This policy was undoubtedly popular with local people, but it infuriated the Governor, Colonel Massey, who was perpetually confronted by unpaid, semi-mutinous troops. His antagonism towards Pury was later demonstrated in a letter to Sir Samuel Luke (6th November 1644): ' Mr Pury, having for his own pleasure taken a journey some way to London to the old world there; if the parliament desire it, I shall desire that they would be pleased to keep him, for Gloucester finds little need of him'. (37)

The Grand Committee, under Pury's leadership, looked with great compassion on the condition of ordinary people as they investigated abuses and tax arrears, especially in the parishes of the Inshire Division nearest the city, which had been particularly devastated by the war. In March and April 1644, they examined with great care individual petitions received from scores of villagers whose condition was desperate. Thomas Belcher of Tuffley, for instance, was £1 1s 2d in arrears on his tax, but he had billeted soldiers from Colonel Stephens, 'the charge thereof doth amount to more than all his said arrears'. He was therefore totally acquitted. Although Richard Sparke of Great Witcombe had been 'so grievously plundered in his cattle and other goods that thereby he is become exceedingly poor', he had nevertheless shown goodwill by paying his newly-rated tax. The committee therefore decided to cancel his old arrears of £2 15s 0d on condition that he provided the garrison with '4 bushels of beans' at the next harvest. Mrs Lettice Smith of Hempstead was absolved from paying her arrears of £2 8s 1d 'for she hath been plundered of all that she ever had...so that she hath no stock at all upon ye said ground for which she is charged'. Her only duty was to pay the garrison one load of hay at harvest and three bushels of beans at Michaelmas.

Each case was adjudicated, taking individual circumstances into account. Many petitioners had their old arrears cancelled completely, provided that they had a good tax record in the past, had made an attempt to pay the new rate and were considered to be genuine victims of the war. Some were granted partial remission on payment of the remainder; others were simply required to supply hay, beans or oats as a gesture in lieu. The recorded judgments also give vivid glimpses of the misery endured at the hands of soldiers. The following are some of the phrases used to justify a reduction in tax - 'his great losses', 'he hath been deeply plundered', 'his indigent poverty occasioned by plundering', 'we find him to be over-rated', 'the damages and losses he hath sustained by our garrison', 'he hath been plundered of all his goods and cattle, was imprisoned himself and his wife slain by the king's forces and he is utterly undone in respect of a present subsistence'. (38)

There is no doubt that, as a result of the work of the Grand Committee, the lot of ordinary people greatly improved in much of Gloucestershire. Previous demands for supplies and accommodation were in future carefully taken into account when taxes were collected. For instance, the accounts of William Nicholson, High Constable for part of the hundred of Whitstone, for the six months to August 1644, show that £1,010 was due to be collected in weekly tax. However, the parishes concerned were given a credit for almost £750 for costs already expended on quartering troops and horses or providing provisions for Beverstone Castle. The same was increasingly true for the area around Bristol, as the garrison forces gradually took heed of the commissioners' scathing criticism (see above). Thus, in his accounts of January 1645, the constable of Chelbey in the Hartcliffe and Bedminster hundred recorded that, of the five months contribution from August, 'there was none paid', because the cost of accommodation given to troops belonging to Colonels Fleetwood and Cromwell at the siege had now been taken into account. Whereas the tax should have amounted to £20 16s 8d, the cost of quarter had been £23 9s 0d. His calculation had been authorised by Fleetwood's commissioners. For his next accounts of April 1645, the constable had recorded that £8 4s 8d out of the £12 10s 0d due had been 'acquitted by the treasurer, Mr Dennis Hollister, unto the inhabitants' in respect of accommodation given to a troop from Bristol. The remainder of the assessment had been paid, except for £1 10s 0d, which he had been unable to collect. Taxation for local inhabitants, therefore, was slowly becoming much more reasonable. (39)

THE HORRORS OF WAR 3

CRIPPLED BY THE COSTS OF WAR

JOHN CHAMBERLAYNE

John Chamberlayne, farmed his estates at Maugersbury, Stow and Churchdown in Gloucestershire. A royalist by sympathy, he faced charges in 1645 of joining the king's army during the war - an accusation he did not deny. Confronted, therefore, with the certain confiscation (or sequestration) of his property as a delinquent, he ingeniously submitted a carefully-prepared document to the Committee for Sequestrations to illustrate just how much the war effort had already cost him in terms of contributions made to both sides. His *Note of quartering, contribution, and provisions sent to the Armies...since the war begun* provides a revealing insight to the sufferings of major landowners in Gloucestershire as armies marched to and fro.

He had been paid forty visits in all during the war by groups of soldiers in search of free quarter - soldiers who between them stayed a total of 207 nights. By the end of the conflict, he had accommodated and fed no fewer than 63 officers, 742 men and 309 horses at an estimated cost of over £190. Nor did this figure take into account the many occasions when he had 'paid great sums of money to stave off quartering' - presumably by bribing officers to find their billets elsewhere. The longest stay he endured was by 8 men and their horses for 51 consecutive nights. The largest group of soldiers, who stayed at any one time, was a body of 150 officers and men with forty horses from Sir William Waller's army, who were resident for five nights.

Life was certainly not dull with such a rapidly-changing guest list. Chamberlayne must certainly have been kept well informed of the latest military action on the front line, as men arrived from various armies and garrisons of both sides. Groups descended on him from Lord Herbert's Welsh forces (as they attempted to seize Gloucester in February 1643), the king's army (after their withdrawal from the siege of Gloucester), Lord Wilmot's forces (as they endeavoured to block parliament's relief convoy to Gloucester), the king's army (when it was chased by Waller to Worcester), Waller's army (as it played cat-and-mouse with the king), the New Model Army (in its mopping-up operation) and soldiers on the way to the final battle of the war at Stow-on-the-Wold in 1646.

Chamberlayne was also called upon to pay hefty contributions towards the weekly assessment, totalling over £163 in all. In view of the fact that Gloucestershire was heavily disputed territory, he was pressurised by both sides. Some of the money, particularly at the start of the war, was paid directly to regimental commanders - Colonel Gerard, Lord Percy, Sir Thomas Aston and Sir William Vavasour; the remainder, as the war progressed, was collected by local garrisons - Gloucester, Beverstone Castle and Oxford.

Nor did Chamberlayne manage to escape from the demands of quartermasters in search of supplies to requisition or troops in search of goods to plunder. He calculated his losses at over £94. These included, on the one hand, 'bread, beer, cheese, meat and provender' taken by the Earl of Essex's men at the relief of Gloucester; and, on the other, provisions sent on several occasions to the king's forces as they besieged the same city. Then there was the cost of damage twice inflicted on his crops by the careless behaviour of troops. He complained: 'I had corn upon the ground spoiled by the two armies - Prince Rupert facing my Lord the Earl of Essex at Stow - worth £40 at the least' and 'When Sir Wm Waller lay at Stow, the carriage horses were turned in my corn and did me at the least £30 worth of hurt'. Nor did these estimates take into account the theft he sustained of '17 plough horses' taken out of the teams which worked on his fields; and over 100 sheep seized by soldiers.

Although his bill for war costs, therefore, amounted to not much less than £500, he failed to convince the Committee for Compounding that he should be let off lightly. In order to recover his confiscated estates, he was fined a total of £1246 for his delinquency.

Sources: H.P.R. Finberg (ed.), *Gloucestershire Studies* (Leicester, 1957), pp 184-9; GRO, D 621.E2, John Chamberlayne's Accounts; *Calendar for the Committee for Compounding* , vol. 3, pp 279, 1981-4

Line drawing by Stephen Beck

CHAPTER 4

Forced to Support:
A Case Study in Tax Collection

And if a speedy end to these sad times happen not, it will be worse undoubtedly. (Richard Dowdeswell, the Earl of Middlesex's agent at Forthampton, Gloucestershire, July 1644)

The Wiltshire Garrisons of Chalfied and Malmesbury

Although entries in compensation claims and corporation accounts can provide information on how much villages and towns claimed to have paid in weekly assessments, they do not tell us how much they *ought* to have paid - or how much the collectors failed to collect. Fortunately, the accounts of the garrisons of Malmesbury and Chalfield in north-west Wiltshire, which have survived for sixth-month periods during the war, do just that by setting out details of the assessments and payments of each community within their catchment areas. (1)

Malmesbury (see page 148) had been recaptured from the royalists on 24th May 1644 by Colonel Edward Massey, Governor of Gloucester (the sixth and final occasion on which the town changed hands). He immediately established a garrison under Colonel Nicholas Devereux with an estimated 1000 men (including 600 foot, plus horse, dragoons and artillery). Shortly afterwards, on 15th July 1644, parliament passed an Ordinance authorising the Wiltshire County Committee to revive the weekly assessment for the defence and preservation of the county and the garrison of Malmesbury. This was renewed by another Ordinance on 26th August 1645, which authorised the resumption of the weekly assessment for a further six months. The garrison accounts, which concern the period from October 1645 to March 1646, focus on the area assigned to support the garrison by the County Committee. This consisted of 99 towns, villages and hamlets within the hundreds of Chippenham, Malmesbury, Calne, Damerham North and - for the final two months only - Kingsbridge.

Chalfield, a moated manor house owned by Lady Anne Eyre, was an outpost of Malmesbury. Commanded for the period of the accounts (i.e. either October 1644 to March 1645 or January to June 1645) (2) by Lieutenant-Colonel Pudsey, it had an estimated strength of 200 men and 100 horses. It was financed by weekly assessment payments based on the Ordinance of 15th July 1644 and drawn from its allotted area - namely, the 31 towns, villages and hamlets in the hundreds of Bradford and Melksham. The accounts for each of these two garrisons were maintained by William Tarrant, the 'Receiver' or 'Collector', with meticulous detail (but suspect arithmetic!). Together they provide a fascinating insight into the workings of the assessment system and its impact on the local community. Tarrant, who was allowed to keep 3d in the pound of the money he collected to cover his expenses and remuneration, was appointed by the County Committee and (technically) reported back to them. There was no doubt, however, that he was based at each garrison in turn and collected the money directly on their behalf.

The Hall at Chalfield House from a watercolour by J.C. Buckler (1823). By courtesy of Mr Robert Floyd of Great Chalfield Manor

His overall success rate in gathering in the tax is particularly revealing. In the support area for the Malmesbury garrison, he collected £2,076 out of the £2,629 assessed (i.e. 79%), whereas the Chalfield catchment only yielded £868 out of £1,570 demanded (i.e. 55%). One of the major reasons for this sizeable discrepancy is that Tarrant employed a highly successful follow-up procedure for Malmesbury, which he did not apparently operate at Chalfield. This produced an extra £306, without which the Malmesbury total would have fallen to 67%. It is true that troops were used occasionally in tax collection work for the Chalfield garrison, judging by two entries in the accounts for special payments: '2 corporals that went forth and assisted in gathering moneys by the committee's direction...2s 6d': 'for the soldiers...for beer for them, at several times riding abroad with them to collect moneys...10s 0d'. At Malmesbury, however, Tarrant went further and sent out two men quite specifically to chase up defaulters on a regular basis in the hundreds of Chippenham, Malmesbury and Damerham North - an army officer, Cornet John Matravers, who produced an amazing £275, and a civilian, Philip Jenkins, who returned with £31. What methods of persuasion were used is not revealed!

There was a wide variation in payment rates from village to village. In the Chalfield support area, the most reliable contributors were South Wraxall (with 94% of the assessment paid), Atworth (83%), Broughton (81%), Bradford-on-Avon (79%) and Holt (75%). At the other end of the scale were Winckfield and Trowle (40%), Blackmore and Canhold (36%), Melksham (31%) and Woolmer (24%). Tarrant apparently applied constant

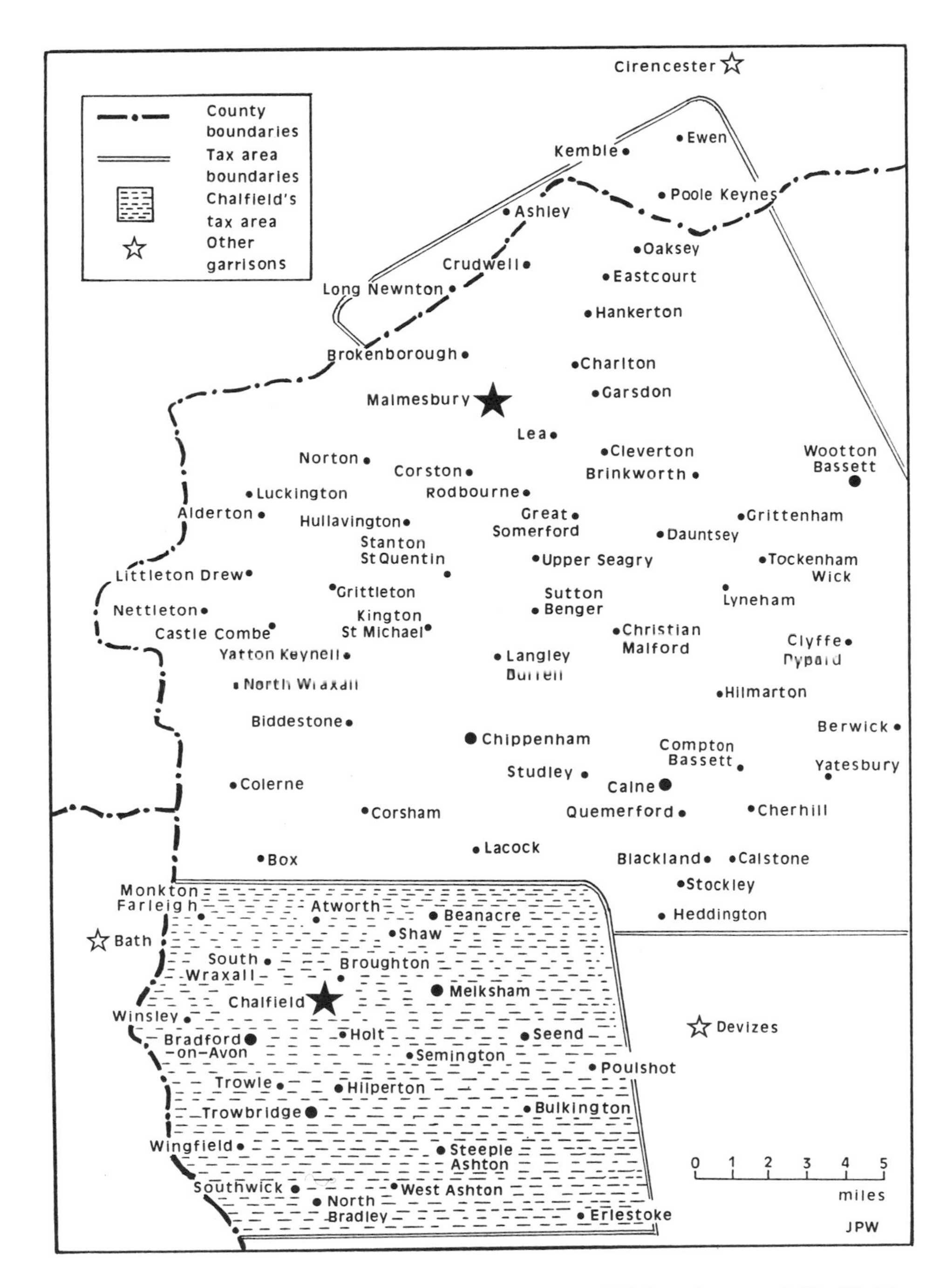

Tax districts allocated to support the garrisons of Malmesbury and Chalfield, 1645-46

pressure to the parish officials in Melksham, sending 'a messenger 3 times to Melksham' in March, ' a soldier that carried a warrant to the Constable of the hundred of Melksham' in April and '2 soldiers for fetching in the tithingman of Melksham' in June. Threats, warnings and reprimands, alas, were apparently to no avail!

In the Malmesbury catchment area, the variation was even more marked. Foxley and Bremnan, Stanton St Quintin, Norton, East Percy and Wetham all recorded 100% payments over the six-month period, whereas Malmesbury, Cole and West Parkes, Langley and Kingswood made no payments at all. It is also noticeable that, from January to March 1646, the Chippenham hundred as a whole produced little money. Out of twenty-nine individual parishes listed, thirteen supplied no tax in January, eighteen none in February and twenty none in March. Indeed in the March of that year, the hundred only managed to pay in total 16% of the assessment.

There were several possible reasons for non-payment of taxes by a town or village in the Civil War. The first was a reluctance to support the side which was regarded as 'the enemy'. But although many communities throughout the country were largely neutral by instinct, the area of north-west Wiltshire (strongly puritan in religion) had keenly supported the cause of parliament throughout the hostilities. The second was genuine impoverishment as a result of wartime hostilities. Indeed, William Tarrant acknowledged in his notes that the inhabitants living around Chalfield were surrounded by five of the king's garrisons within a six-mile radius, all demanding money. This had resulted in local people paying 'some double, some treble contributions' to a mixture of soldiers from both sides.

Great Chalfield Manor with part of the moat and the remains of the front wall. (Author's collection)

Thirdly, there was the inability of the collector to collect because of long-term enemy domination of the locality. The hamlets of Bulkington, Poulshot and Erlestoke, for instance, had been assessed for £197 during the period in question. Their total lack of payments of any kind was explained by Tarrant in a marginal note: 'These 3 tithings, lying remote from the garrison and lying under the enemy's principal garrison of the Devizes, nothing was received from them'. Similarly, the hundred of Wholesdowne had initially been assigned to Chalfield by the County Committee, but only yielded the small pittance of £91 13s 6d. Tarrant wrote against this entry the stark comment: 'This hundred is in the enemy's quarter'.

Fourthly, there was the sudden shift in local control, which caused towns and villages to be temporarily occupied by enemy soldiers. This was a frequent occurrence in Wiltshire in general (a 'corridor' county for marching armies); but it was particularly so in the north-west sector of the county, which was a border zone. Although by October 1644, parliament had established two garrisons (Malmesbury and Chalfield) as forward bases for their Gloucester stronghold, the royalists still dominated the West with garrisons at Bristol, Bath, Farleigh, Highworth, Faringdon, Devizes and Lacock. Apart from Malmesbury, most towns in north-west Wiltshire were open, unwalled sites without formal defences, which could easily be seized by the next cavalry troop passing through. Chippenham was particularly vulnerable in this way and had been suddenly recaptured as late as August 1645 by royalist troops under Colonel James Long.

Fifthly, the garrison towns themselves were often excused tax payments, because of the pressure they faced in many other ways in supporting a garrison. Thus the town of Malmesbury, assessed at £37 7s 0d for the sixth months, paid no weekly assessment at all. The Chalfield hamlet, which had been rated at £48 7s 6d, only contributed a total of £10 14s 0d. It was nevertheless exempted from further payments, because various pasture lands near the garrison, belonging to Lady Eyre, were used as grazing for the garrison's cattle and sheep. This, according to Tarrant, was worth 'the value of all the contribution and more'.

Although soldiers could often be brutal and unsympathetic towards the local population, compassion and understanding could also be shown at times. Tarrant realised that the inhabitants of the area around Chalfield had already been oppressed by royalist garrisons in the neighbourhood and, thus, that his exactions over a sixth-month period, on behalf of his own garrison, would hardly be affordable. With the sanction of the County Committee, therefore, he permitted individual communities either to pay their weekly assessment in cash or 'to pay their contribution in victual, hay and oats' or 'to work it out at the fortifications'. Having part of the allocation paid for in foodstuffs suited the garrison well, because Tarrant's arrangement with the soldiers was that they would receive half their normal pay, plus their meals. [Soldiers normally paid for their own food out of their wages.] In the introduction to his accounts, he therefore recorded with some delight that, because of this arrangement, 'the far greater part was brought in such provisions as they could spare and delivered to Ensign Moyle, who was the Steward of the garrison and who delivered it forth every meal to the soldiers'. Thus many villages paid at least part of their taxes in the produce of their land ('such as they could spare'); an enormous sacrifice, when many families were already on the bread-line. Those who could not spare any food at all, let alone cash, were permitted to offer their labour or their technical skills to assist in strengthening the garrison's fortifications - or, in Tarrant's words, '...and the poorer sort wrought forth theirs'. Whatever was offered was carefully calculated in terms of value to be offset against the village's tax bill.

The garrison could therefore call on teams of labourers, carpenters, 'sawyers' and masons to build a line of earthworks and barricades as a complement to the moat which already existed at Chalfield. At harvest time, they could also draw on the services of 'threshers', together with teams of farmworkers with carts and ploughs, or men to repair the barn. In one case, a metal smith from South Wraxall was tempted to provide his vice 'for the service of the garrison' at a value set against tax of 16s 0d. Village women sometimes secured tax rebates by feeding and nursing sick or wounded soldiers. Most communities (i.e. 65%) in the two hundreds, which were assigned to support the garrison, paid at least part of their assessment in services of this kind with South Wraxall actually contributing over a third of their tax in this way. On the other hand, all the villages and towns combined were only able to find just over 9% of their total assessment in hard cash.

By far the largest part of the contribution came, therefore, in the form of a wide variety of local farm produce - beef, mutton, bacon, beans, beer, malt, fish, spices, wheat (over 230 bushels), bread, butter, eggs and cheese (over 5,370 lbs); together with livestock - turkeys, hens, sheep, cattle, rabbits and ducks; and provender for the horses - hay and oats (over 420 bushels). Some villages seemed to specialise in providing certain items. Bradford-on-Avon, for instance, was the garrison's sole supplier of hops (60lbs), cinnamon, nutmegs, soap and sugar; Trowbridge of paper (95 quires), radishes, carrots, turnips and horses' bridles; and Melksham of fish. In addition, Cheverell could claim to have been the main supplier of cattle (28 in all), Marshfield of salt (18.5 bushels), Holt of cheese (1094 lbs); Broughton Gifford of wheat (79 bushels); and South Wraxall of oats (92 bushels) and malt (37 bushels). (3)

Three villages contributed no cash at all, but rather gained substantial allowances from food supplies and labour (although, in each case, their assessment was not fully paid). These were Whitley and Shaw (which emerged as the sole supplier of candles); Broughton Gifford (which provided substantial work at the fortifications, not to mention its supplies of ducks, rabbits, turkeys and veal); and Holt which, in addition to its cheese, contributed more bacon than most and a great deal of wheat, malt and oats. Furthermore, the village not only placed its tithing ploughs at the disposal of the garrison for five days, but also sent squads of labourers (four, five, six or seven at a time) to work on the defences. This happened on a total of 185 days (in other words, each and every day during the sixth-month period), which resulted in something over 1,000 man-days being worked by the village in all at an enormous cost to their own farming operation. It earned them a total tax remission of just £6 12s 4d from their bill of £72 12s 0d. The pay of a farm worker (as indicated by these accounts) averaged out at no more than 1.5d per day.

In theory at least, local inhabitants would have enjoyed a much more comfortable lifestyle if they had been members of the Chalfield garrison. The pay of a foot soldier at the time was 8d per day, although the troops at Chalfield were, as we have seen, on a 'half pay plus food' arrangement. Even so, 4d a day compares most favourably with the wages received by an agricultural labourer. Furthermore, life in the garrison was really quite comfortable during the period in question - little military activity (apart from one very short siege in April 1645), pleasant surroundings and a good supply of fresh food. It is in fact believed that some of the garrison were local Wiltshire men, who had been added to the original force which Massey had supplied from Gloucester. Sadly for the foot soldiers at Chalfield, however, their wages were not paid on a regular basis and, when they were, they were not always paid in full. Indeed, the accounts reveal that in only eleven weeks of this six-month period were payments made to the infantry, payments ranging in total from £24 to just £10. Worse still, only five weekly payments were made to the dragoons and just two to the cavalry. This enabled Tarrant to balance his books most impressively at the end of the period. Cash receipts of £547 8s 11d and disbursements of £540 13s 0d left a small balance, which Tarrant claimed for himself in fees and expenses. (4)

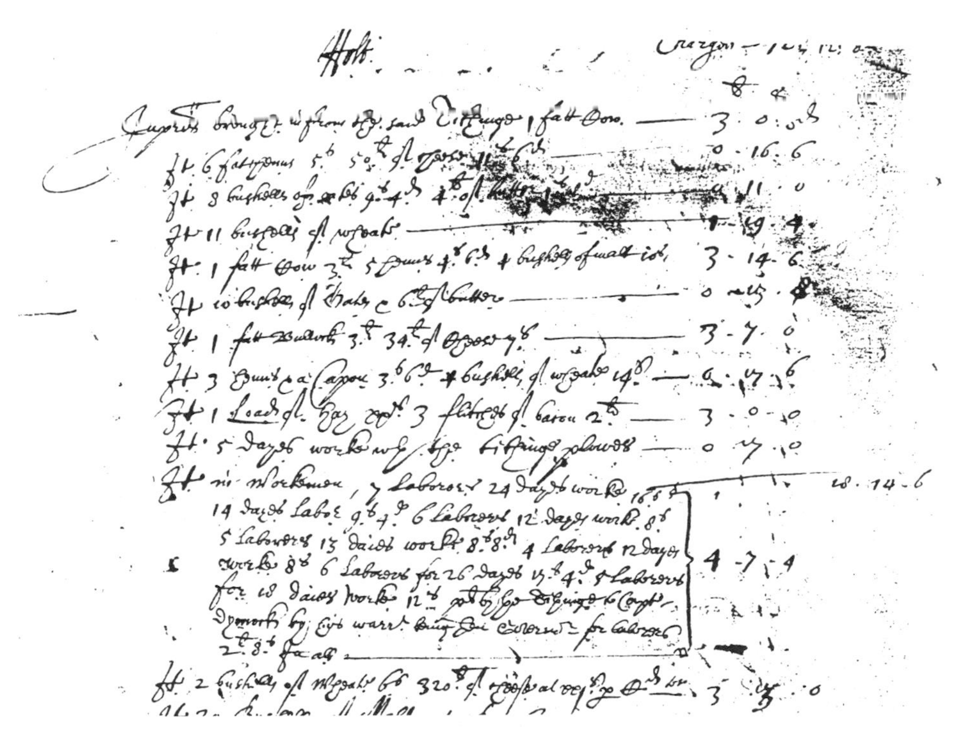

An extract from the accounts of William Tarrant, the Collector, for the garrison of Chalfield, showing payments made in kind or service in lieu of cash by the parish of Holt. (By courtesy of the Public Record Office - SP28.138)

CHAPTER 5

Forced to Provide:
Free Quarter or Billeting

My house is, and hath been, full of soldiers for a fortnight; and such uncivil drinkers and thirsty souls, that a barrel of good beer trembles at the sight of them, and the whole house nothing but a rendezvous of tobacco and spitting. (John Turberville of Somerset to a relative)

The System of Free Quarter

For the ordinary individual living in the western counties, there was nothing more terrifying than the sudden knock on the door, which heralded the arrival of soldiers in search of billets. Although in theory the men were expected to pay for their accommodation out of their wages, in practice this seldom happened. As the war progressed, the military commanders of both sides found themselves so desperately short of money that armies on the march (as well as local garrison forces) were usually weeks behind in their pay. This led to the widespread use of the detested practice of 'free quarter'.

By the spring of 1643, the king had already sanctioned the use of this system by the local county troops, if cash was not available for their wages. He quickly extended the right to colonels of newly-recruited regiments in an attempt to speed up their readiness for action in the field. By the summer, virtually all his forces had adopted the practice. Exactly the same situation had emerged on parliament's side by July 1643, causing the villages of north Somerset to endure a foretaste of greater horrors to come in the weeks prior to the Battle of Lansdown. The inhabitants of Keynsham, for instance, were forced to support 'Captain Rawlins and his troop, being about the number of 50 men and horse for 4 weeks' at an estimated expense of £70. Similarly, the seventy-one householders in Norton St Philip (thirty of them living in impoverished conditions) were faced with the prospect of quartering the whole of Alexander Popham's Bath Regiment, 'being 700 of them'. Although they only stayed for two nights, it cost the village something like £53 in provisions. But this was only the beginning. The next three years were to see a rapid increase in the demands like these made on local people, as the western counties became alive with armies on the march and garrisons sprouting up across the area.

The system of free quarter worked like this. The army's Quarter-Master-General would pinpoint a network of villages and towns which could be used as the army progressed on its march, allocating these to individual regiments. The regimental quartermaster would then go ahead of his troops to select billets in his nominated villages with the help of the local constables. As the regiment marched through, so each soldier was placed with a householder, who had no option but to provide him with board and lodging. At the end of the stay, the householder would be given a ticket, signed by an officer, which detailed the number of men who had been accommodated and the number of nights involved. In theory, these tickets were later redeemed by payments made to the village constables. Although this was sometimes carried out (as in parliament's Eastern Association army, where local people were normally paid well within the year), in practice this seldom happened. The substantial compensation claims for unpaid free quarter bills, made at the end of the war by parishes throughout the region, are testimony enough that the system did not work in the manner intended. There were occasional exceptions in 1643. For instance, Elias Davis was paid 4s 0d and John Fudgell 9s 0d by troops from Colonel Butler's regiment, quartered in the village of Charlcombe, in part payment for their accommodation. This action was sufficiently rare to warrant a special mention in the compensation claim. (1)

Nevertheless, there is evidence that some of the outstanding debts to householders in Somerset were eventually settled. In September 1645, parliament had given authority to Colonel Jepson to quarter his regiment of horse inside the county as he waited embarkation for Munster in Ireland. He was ordered to ensure that his men stayed for no more than two days and nights in any particular house and that they either paid for their accommodation on the spot (at the rate of twelve pence per day for a man and his horse) or left a ticket giving details. In the event, Jepson's regiment hung around in Somerset for four months from December 1645 to March 1646, moving about from hundred to hundred in search of accommodation. They invariably exceeded the specified maximum of two days in each place, normally stretching this to a week. Numbers of men and horses billeted on individual parishes varied from 140 in Shepton Mallet to 40 in Pilton, while the 38 inhabitants of Evercreech were expected to put up a total of 86 soldiers. Although some troops left tickets with their hosts as requested and others departed without leaving any evidence of their stay, no one offered to settle their bill in ready cash. As a result, the inhabitants of Whitstone hundred were £170 19s 2d out of pocket in all by the end of this episode; those in Brent hundred £89 10s 4d; those in Chewton hundred £118 15s 0d; those in Glastonbury hundred £142 16s 0d; and those in Winterstoke hundred £144 11s 0d. Three years later, however, parliament's local committee began investigating their claims and eventually ruled that the debts were to be paid in full out of money set aside for the support of the British army in Ireland. The original tickets (which still survive in the Public Record Office) were carefully examined, as were the cases made by parishes where soldiers had failed to supply such proof. All had received satisfaction by the spring of 1650. (2)

Feb ye 26th 1645

These are to certifie ye committee or collectors whom this shall or may concerne, that the parish of Chewton hath quartered seven score men and horses belonginge to collonell Jephson, for ye space of three nights. which charge I desire may be allowed ye parish out of ye parish assessments –

Tho [illegible] capt
in collonell Jephsons regiment

A billeting note of February 1645 certifying that 'the parish of Chewton hath quartered seven score men and horses belonging to Colonel Jephson, for the space of three nights'. (By courtesy of the Public Record Office - SP28.242, pt. 1)

Attempts to set Free Quarter against Taxation

In order to alleviate the distress caused to householders (who were, of course, also being hit in other ways by taxation, requisitions and plunder), some generals tried hard to ensure that the cost of free quarter was set against the regular bill for taxes. This was certainly the intention of the royalist commander (Sir Ralph Hopton) in October 1643, when he wrote to the Mayor of Wells, warning him of the approach of a regiment in search of free quarter. His letter also sets out a tariff, showing the different rates to be allowed for soldiers and officers: 'I have directed Prince Maurice his Regiment of Foot to quarter in your town till further order. Wherefore pray cause the officers and soldiers thereof to be settled in convenient houses there, according to their qualities and billeted under their rates hereunder mentioned, for which I will cause due allowance to be made out of the weekly contribution of your hundred. The common soldiers at 2s 6d a piece per week. Ensigns and other inferior officers at 3s 6d a piece per week. Superior officers at 6s 0d a piece per week'.

This rate is roughly the same as that listed in a compensation claim, submitted in 1645 by the village of Stanton Prior in Somerset, for unpaid free quarter bills left by parliamentary soldiers - namely 4d per day for each soldier billeted (i.e. 2s 4d per week) and 10d per day for each trooper and horse. By 1645, the allowance for accommodating men in the New Model Army had been increased to 6d a day for ordinary foot soldiers and 8d a day for a trooper plus 4d a night for his horse on hay (or 3d a night on grass). (3)

In December 1643, the king also acknowledged the fact that contributions already made by inhabitants in cash were to be taken into account when considering free quarter. The royalist commissioners, on behalf of the people of Wiltshire, had agreed to contribute £1,200 per week for the period of one month on condition that the king's forces treated householders more fairly. In response to this, a royal proclamation was issued (to be read in all churches) stating that 'no manner of free quarter or billeting' was to be taken by any soldier without immediate payment being made. If a soldier failed to conform, the appropriate sum would instantly be deducted from his wages. Furthermore, the number of soldiers billeted in any one house was to be limited to the number that the house could 'conveniently receive'; no troops were to be forced onto a resident without the involvement of a local parish officer; camp followers (including women, boys and children) were not to be granted 'house-room', unless the owner agreed; and soldiers were to be content with the amount of candles and coal used by the family. (4)

Later in the war, parliament, aware of the growing volume of complaints against this detested practice of free quarter, tried to ban it completely in those areas which were already paying their normal contributions. For instance, the Ordinance which established the Association of Western Counties in August 1644 stipulated quite clearly that 'no free quarter shall be taken in any of the said associated counties'. Quickly retreating from that position, however, it went on to state that if free quarter was taken, then the officers concerned would only be paid one-third of their wages and ordinary soldiers one-half, with the remainder going towards the payment of their free quarter bill. Although parliament itself was becoming more sensitive to the feelings of ordinary people in the counties, front-line field commanders (endlessly strapped for cash) still tended to take the law into their own hands whenever necessity demanded. However, the spirit of reasonableness could prevail at officer level in the villages, when arrangements were being made with local constables. In December 1645, for instance, the village of Blagdon in Somerset received a visitation from a cavalry troop under the command of Captain Bragg (part of the Bristol garrison). He produced a warrant requiring the inhabitants to quarter thirty of his men with their horses for seven days and nights. However, when the constable realised that they were being allocated twelve more than was fair in relation to those being allocated to neighbouring villages, he 'put them away by consent of the captain'. The village accommodated the remaining eighteen with good grace, even though their stay was eventually extended to four weeks! (5)

The idea of setting the cost of free quarter against the weekly assessment was also adopted by officers of parliament's New Model Army when they quartered troops in north Somerset villages prior to the siege of Bristol in 1645. The village of Chelbey in the Portishead hundred, for instance, stated in its compensation claim that it had not paid any of its five months contribution due in August 1645 'because of the free quarter which was given to Major Huntingdon's troop and part of Captain Blissett's troop'. They estimated that, whereas the contribution demand amounted to £20 16s 8d, the money spent on free quarter totalled £21 2s 0d. The parliamentary commissioners agreed that the parish had already paid more than was due (for other examples see Chapter 3). This amicable system, however, did not always prevail. No such allowance was made for the inhabitants of Portishead and Weston, who had quartered 60 men for two weeks during the same siege, 'whereof only ten paid for their quarters'. Similarly, although the village of Portbury had 'quartered Lieutenant-General Cromwell's own regiment at the siege of Bristol', they had received neither tax credit nor payment and were therefore out of pocket to the tune of £143 3s 3d. (6)

Pressure to pay in cash

Nevertheless, a real effort was being made by the generals of the New Model Army to establish good relationships with local people. Colonel John Lilburne, in addressing the Commons in the summer of 1645 on their successful campaign in the western counties, emphasised that the key to winning over country villagers in future lay in a policy of regular pay for the troops. This would ensure that the soldiers would 'constantly be able to pay their quarters', which would endear them to householders and put them in a favourable light when compared with their royalist opponents. The latter, it was claimed, had cruelly oppressed inhabitants partly by demanding the very best free accommodation and partly by insisting (with threats of plunder) that 'a day's pay be laid under their trenchers'. Lilburne went on to recall that, on some occasions when the New Model had been ready to move on in Somerset, the soldiers had asked their hosts how much they owed for their quarters. This allegedly provoked a response of total amazement. 'The people wondered at us, what kind of men we were, or what we meant by such a question; divers of them telling us that they never knew what it was to finger soldiers' money; so that I am confidently persuaded that the readiest way to make the people yours is to enable the soldiers to pay their quarters'. Although Lilburne's claims could well have contained an element of truth in relation to some parts of the county, there is firm evidence to suggest that some of the villagers in the area around Bristol at the time of the siege in 1645 would not have been so complimentary in their comments (see below).(7)

Sadly, the aim of maintaining the pay of the troops proved impossible to achieve. In spite of the fact that parliament had issued a firm order for its new professional army in May 1645 ('that no quarter or provisions for man or horse in any quarters be taken without payment of ready money'), they had also added a rider that this regulation would only operate if 'pay continued unto the army'. That was the problem. Therefore, although some people in the Somerset countryside (if by no means the majority) had reason to be pleased with the army's policy towards free quarter in 1645, the inhabitants of Westbury in Wiltshire viewed things quite differently when the army was quartered there in February 1647 (a few months after the ending of the war). In a petition to its Commander-in-Chief, Sir Thomas Fairfax, the mayor and population of the town complained most bitterly that the constant burden of free quarter (on top of the regular taxes) had thrown them into a state of great distress. Nor had the reputation of the army for fairness been justified. For instance, they argued, 'whereas the rumour of the soldiers paying for their quarters may appear to the world to be something, yet we find it in effect nothing'. They were currently suffering the presence of one hundred dragoons, who had already been in the town for thirty days. Although the soldiers had promised that they would settle their debts as soon as they received their pay, this did not happen in reality. Indeed, when the pay had finally arrived, householders had only been given a fifth 'of what the charge of quartering amounts to'. The petition concluded with a strong plea that they should be freed from long spells of free quarter, 'unless it be upon a march for a night or two'. (8)

The Cost to Parishes and Individuals

Therefore, in spite of occasional attempts to create a more acceptable system, the general picture in the western counties throughout the war was one of severe hardship inflicted on the local population by this means. An analysis of expenditure on the war effort in the hundred of Keynsham, during the two years of occupation by parliamentary forces (1642-3, 1645-6), reveals that no less than 34 per cent was spent on free quarter alone. Out of a total sum of £2,812 claimed in compensation (which also included the cost of the Propositions, the weekly assessment, requisition, plunder etc), £956 was attributed to the billeting of soldiers. Within the hundred, the actual impact varied greatly from village to village. Some places, such as Thrubwell and Charlton, escaped completely from this kind of imposition. Others were hit regularly and hard, including Belluton (74 per cent of their total bill), Marksbury (63 per cent), Farmborough (56 per cent) and Publow (51 per cent). Exactly the same sort of situation prevailed in the hundred of Wellow, where again 34 per cent of the expenditure went on free quarter, 24 per cent on tax and 42 per cent on plunder, requisitions, forced labour and other elements. Indeed, throughout the country as a whole, the major economic cost to local communities stemmed from this one single item of war expenditure - free quarter. (9)

Some villages suffered much more heavily than others from this threat. Their fate depended partly on luck and partly on their exact location - their proximity to a garrison, a town of strategic importance, the site of a battle or a major thoroughfare used by armies on the march. This was the lot of the small village of Twerton, near the garrisons of both Bath and Bristol and on the main artery which linked the two. The inhabitants were therefore easy prey throughout the entire war - to a company of Waller's own regiment, to two hundred of Captain Abbot's cavalry 'when they marched against Bristol', to forty-seven men of Sir Thomas Fairfax's own Lifeguards, to thirty-one soldiers from the Bath garrison (who stayed for over six weeks), to ten New Model Army troopers from Cromwell's regiment and finally to '800 soldiers of Colonel Montague's regiment, when they marched from Bristol to Devizes for one night with 30 horse and 18 oxen'. In between, they had also accommodated thirty-one of 'Sir Thomas Fairfax's soldiers being sick men, some a week, some a fortnight and some a month'. They were not paid for their efforts. (10)

It was much the same story in the town of Chard, which lay on Somerset's border with Devon at a key point on the western road. The inhabitants were, therefore, constantly at the mercy of major armies passing through on their way to crucial campaigns in Cornwall, Devon, Somerset and Dorset. Sir Ralph Hopton and the Marquis of Hertford rendezvoused there with 6,500 royalist troops on their way to fight the Battle of Lansdown in 1643. In the following year, the king with some 10,000 men stayed in or around Chard twice, first in pursuit of the Earl of Essex into Devon and then, after his victory at Lostwithiel, on his return. In December 1644, royalist forces besieging Taunton withdrew to Chard as a parliamentarian force approached to relieve that town for the first time, while in May 1645 it was the turn of the parliamentarians to stay in Chard as they marched to break up the second siege there. In October, Sir Thomas Fairfax visited Chard on his way to Exeter with 9,000 men from the New Model Army, to be followed a few days later by Oliver Cromwell with another force. (11)

Other towns suffered from free quarter in a different way. Cirencester in Gloucestershire was not so much oppressed by the constant arrival of large field armies marching through on their way to campaigns (although this did happen briefly in 1643 at the time of the siege of Gloucester). It was, however, greatly afflicted in March 1643 by the plight of severe over-quartering at the hands of local forces. The county's royalist commissioners wrote in dismay to the king pointing out that, in addition to the 1,000 garrison soldiers, the town was also now expected to quarter Prince Maurice's regiment of horse and (on the orders of Prince Rupert) a regiment of dragoons, two troops of horse and 200 unattached men. The problem was largely one of unco-ordinated planning in the early months of the war with commanders left largely to take their own decisions. This situation placed enormous demands on the local inhabitants, especially those living inside the town. As the commissioners pointed out, the countryside around was unable to support such a considerable strain - the area between Bristol and Gloucester was unproductive because it was under enemy control, while other areas had either been 'lately plundered and pillaged by His Majesty's forces' or had endured 'great pressure of late by the free quarter that His Majesty's army hath had'. Commanders were to find out through bitter experience that there was a limit to how much ordinary people could provide. (12)

The arrival of the New Model Army in north Somerset in the summer of 1645 for the siege of Bristol witnessed a period of acute suffering for local people in the villages around. Sir Thomas Fairfax brought with him an army of around 10,000 men, all of whom needed accommodation at various points during the campaign. This meant that inhabitants of the surrounding area endured three months of intensive activity by quartermasters out in search of billets. The village of Wellow, for instance, had fourteen visits from Fairfax's army in quick succession between July and September, including Colonel Waldron's foot regiment of 2,000 men for one night - an overall total of three thousand troops, costing £282 to a farming community of no more than thirty-two houses. The hamlet of Edmondscott in the parish of Milverton twice faced up to a terrifying ordeal during the same period in 1645. First, four infantry regiments consisting of about 2,000 soldiers arrived 'when they came from the Naseby fight', staying over one weekend with villagers and consuming seven hogsheads of beer in the process. Shortly afterwards, some 1,500 Scottish cavalry demanded quarter on more than one occasion. Quite apart from the accommodation, these unwelcome visitors cost the hamlet ten hogsheads of beer (as well as meat and other provisions), two meadows of grass eaten by horses and five acres of oats and barley ruined by soldiers' boots. Total losses sustained amounted to £84.

In the the village of Publow, forty-two out of the sixty-two households quartered between them 1,381 men spread out over that three-month period (averaging 32.8 men per household) and 511 horses (averaging 12.1 each). Although few individuals were inflicted with impossible numbers for one night's stay, Lyson Hopkins had a hundred to contend with on one occasion and Widow Jennings fifty. For most, however, the effect was cumulative, as fresh soldiers arrived almost daily in a village which became increasingly devastated. Uncertainty as to what each day held in store contributed more than anything to the stress of this situation.

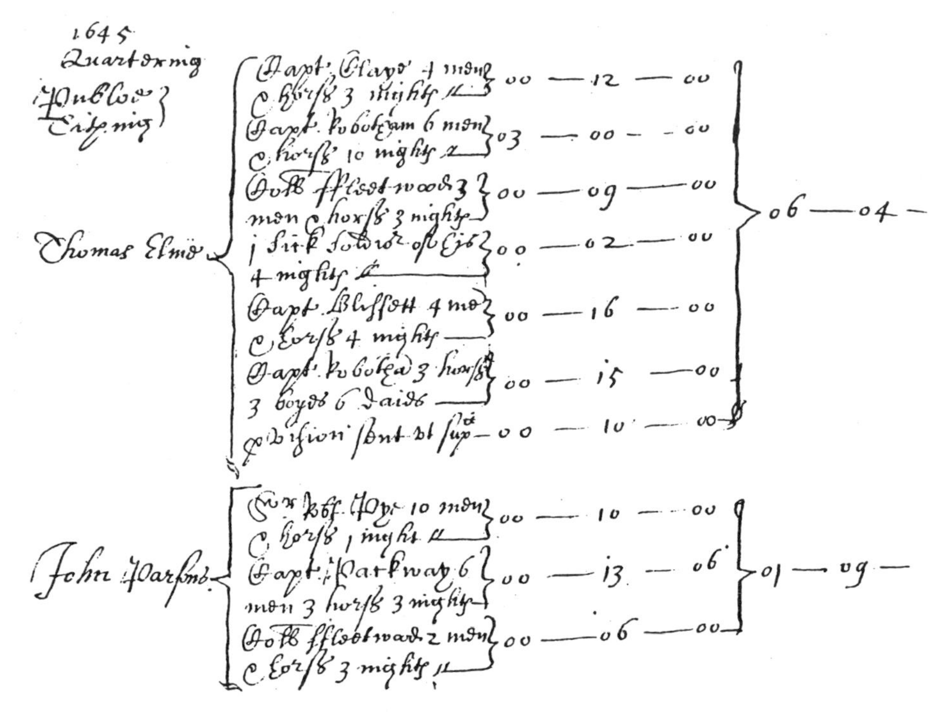
1645
Quartering
Publow Tithing

Thomas Elme
00 — 12 — 00
03 — 00 — 00
00 — 09 — 00
00 — 02 — 00
00 — 16 — 00
00 — 15 — 00
00 — 10 — 00
06 — 04 —

John Parsons
00 — 10 — 00
00 — 13 — 06
00 — 06 — 00
01 — 09 —

Compensation claims submitted by Thomas Elme and John Parsons of Publow for the quartering of men and horses from the New Model Army in 1645. (By courtesy of the Public Record Office - SP28.175)

Alexander Gage, churchwarden, was visited on no fewer than ten occasions; but perhaps John Hedges had the most varied experience of all. The seven demands for billets he received included one from the General's gunsmith, who brought along his wife and boy, and one from a sick soldier, who stayed for thirty-five nights! Hedges, like others in the village, found himself forced not only to stock up one group with provisions to consume during their duty at the siege of Bristol, but also to suffer the galling sight of Colonel Fleetwood's men carrying away '3 wain loads' of his oats at the end of their stay. Another villager, Nicholas Martin, had the unenviable task of looking after 140 oxen from the artillery train for a total of three nights.

Combe Hay, which had suffered greatly in 1643 from the daily rendezvous of Waller's army before the Battle of Lansdown (see Chapter 6), did not escape in 1645. The village had no fewer than eight visitations between July 1645 and January 1646. Their first intruders seemed innocent enough (twenty-five officers and men from the New Model Army, who were part of the reconnaissance party which frightened the Bath garrison into surrender), until they demanded on departure 'beer, flesh, beer, bread' for four hundred men at the rendezvous on Bathampton Down. But worse was to follow. After a whole regiment of eight hundred infantry had descended on the village, 'moving from Bristol to Devizes' for one night in September, they were followed hard at heel next day by 'one company more of thirteen hundred...which company spoiled and killed 80 sheep'. Plunder all too often was the bed-fellow of free quarter. The village of Whittoymeade perhaps felt that they had been let off lightly, when only thirteen men arrived for billets on one occasion in 1645 - that is, until they realised that the troops had 'killed and carried away 7 sheep' at a cost of £5 8s 2d. But what inhabitants of the western counties found most difficult to handle (as at Combe Hay) was the lack of time for recovery

Sir Thomas Fairfax (1612-1671), commander of the New Model Army. Engraving by Engleheart after Bower. (By courtesy of the York City Art Gallery)

between one nightmare experience and another. Demands for free quarter were irregular and unpredictable; they could appear in clusters or they could not appear at all. Local people therefore lived with nerves continually on edge. (13)

By the time the siege of Bristol was over and the bulk of the New Model Army had departed for service elsewhere, the villages and towns in north Somerset and south Gloucestershire were in a state of acute depression. In November 1645, the parliamentary commissioners in Bristol (Colonel Martin Pinder and Harcourt Leighton) wrote to the Speaker of the Commons outlining the dire situation in which the countrymen found themselves. They were owed an enormous sum of money for the twin cost of free quarter and requisitions, money which they were 'in daily expectation to receive'; but sadly, the army treasurer could not possible sanction 'such a large allowance of arrears as these adjacent parts have justly due to them'. At the same time, the very same victims were still being oppressed by continued demands for both free quarter and tax contributions 'without any consideration of their present and past sufferings'. In January 1646, the commissioners again wrote to the Speaker from Bristol. 'The accounts of the free quarter during the siege', they reported, 'have been taken, which amounts to so great a sum that without your honourable encouragement of the poor country, they will be undone'. This plea for at least some reimbursement of the money owed was made partly out of genuine concern for the local community and partly for the good of the Bristol garrison which had remained behind. 'The garrison of this city cannot subsist unless it be bounded with contributions from the hundreds round about it' - and those contributions could hardly be made by people who were in a state of bankruptcy. (14)

The Countryman's Experience of Billeting Troops

The sheer terror of free quarter is well illustrated by the experiences of Sir Humphrey Mildmay, a royalist sympathiser, who lived at Queen Camel in Somerset at the very moment, in 1644, when the armies of both the king and the Earl of Essex were crossing and recrossing the county on their Cornwall campaign. He was to suffer from friend and foe alike, as forces from both sides demanded free quarter without discrimination. He recorded in his diary that the vicar had already fled the town by 7th July 'for fear of the cannon balls'. By the 17th of the month, Mildmay was billeting some of the royalist soldiers who had arrived in the village, including Captain Wigmore who spent the day 'at dice' in his home. He endured the anxiety and inconvenience for a while and was still 'at home in health, but much in want' a fortnight later. However, with the arrival of Middleton's parliamentary forces on 13th August, he decided to escape to the comparative safety of the Bridgwater garrison. He returned on 9th September, but the presence of so many disorderly soldiers forced him 'to hide a time'. Disgusted and terrified by the 'rude and most ungodly soldiers' who crowded both town and countryside, he lived in constant dread of their next move. His worst fears were soon to be realised. 'The villains came for me and had me', he recalled, 'but I made escape and fled to Yeovilton to bed'. By the spring of 1645, he was back at home - only to find that the situation not improved in the slightest. As one group of soldiers departed leaving their devastation behind them, they were simply replaced by another. He recorded in his diary: 'I was preparing for church, but the soldiers interrupted. All the houses are full; all in disorder...The soldiers marched. I came to my Camel, where I saw the ruins of my house'. (15)

Other individuals in the three western counties recorded similar experiences of free quarter, which aroused feelings of fear, loathing and disgust. John Turberville, a Somerset man, wrote these words to a relative shortly after the ending of the war: 'My house is, and hath been, full of soldiers for a fortnight; such uncivil drinkers and thirsty souls, that a barrel of good beer trembles at the sight of them, and the whole house nothing but a rendezvous of tobacco and spitting'. William Sadler, another resident of Somerset, apologised to the Clerk of the Quarter Sessions for his inability to attend, fearing the dire consequences if he left his unwelcome guests unattended: 'Excuse my absence at this time', he wrote,

Villagers experience the horrors of free quarter as troops commandeer the use of their living space. (Line drawing by Stephen Beck)

'for we have with us a troop of soldiers and those none of the civilest that I have seen, which makes me unwilling to be from home at this instant'. In the aftermath of the war, Mrs Wheatley of Glympton in Oxfordshire expressed to her husband her fear of what lay in store for some unlucky householders in Gloucestershire. A regiment of unruly soldiers, some of whom had been billeted on her, were heading their way. 'They were', she wrote, 'as very rogues as can be, swearing and cursing like their father the devil - a wicked company'. When their captain complained that she was too stern with his men, she had replied that she 'had not been bred to discourse' with such rough soldiers as that. On hearing his indignant response that he himself was a gentleman, she had told him 'so may be he was', but as yet she could not see it! Charles Steynings of Holnicote in Somerset described how his house continued to be 'infested with billeting and quartering of soldiers' long after the war was over - so much so that 'our poor country is like to be exhausted'. Indeed, such was the extent of his growing poverty that he feared that he would be eating 'hay with our horse ere winter overpass'.(16)

Other individuals suffered from bullying and the threats of violence - especially if they were suspected of favouring the enemy. When the king quartered his army at Chard in September 1644, some of the troops, who were billeted with 'an ancient, honest, poor man', found themselves served with boiled meat and broth to which they objected. Their quartermaster, a man called Grimes, poured a torrent of abuse on the host, calling out 'You old rogue, do you give us your hog's wash; we will have roast meat'. In April of the same year, when Colonel Mynne's Irish troops entered Newent in Gloucestershire in search of free quarter, they were greeted by Sir Edward Clark, a prominent supporter of the royalist cause. Although Clark had issued firm instructions to all local residents that they were to take their share of billeting, some of them objected on the grounds that these particular soldiers were catholics. Determined to make an example, he strode up to the house of one such objector (William Hill, a yeoman) and, 'with sword in hand, said that if he did know of anyone in the town that would not open his doors to Colonel Mynne's soldiers, he would break it open'. (17)

Although many soldiers at village level in the western counties were accused of unruliness, uncouthness and violence, few were apparently accused of rape. There were such strong feelings of suspicion in many villages against soldiers that girls were actively discouraged from developing relationships. This is not to say that liaisons did not take place, but they were quickly condemned on grounds which were religious (the puritan influence was extremely strong in many areas), social (there was a deep-seated fear of disease) and financial (there was a concern that any bastard child would become chargeable on the parish). Girls, therefore, who were seen 'keeping company with soldiers', were strongly suspected of having sex outside marriage - like the servant in Somerset, who was spotted by her employer entering a barn with a soldier. She was later ducked in the local stream by incensed villagers. When, in 1645, a group of 'very rude' royalist cavalry entered the Somerset village of Doulting in search of billets, they demanded that a woman should be provided for them as cook. However, it was later noticed that Joan Eaton, who had quickly volunteered for the job, had 'remained there with the soldiers all day and night'. Previously suspected of 'entertaining' troops in the past, she was henceforth treated as an outcast in the village. A farmer from North Petherton, who was quartering soldiers from the New Model Army, discovered that some of them had accompanied his maid 'when she went a-milking'. Furious at her behaviour, he immediately dismissed her from employment, because 'he would not keep such a slut in his house'. He was also concerned that he would have to support mother and child, if the worst happened. (18)

The Townsman's Experience of Garrison Troops

Town dwellers suffered just as much as country folk, especially if they were forced to be hosts to a garrison. Under those circumstances, responsibility for the free quarter system was usually undertaken by the town corporation rather by individuals. The Chamberlain of the borough of Chippenham, for instance, charged a local rate in October 1644 'for the quartering of soldiers'. In Gloucester, faced with the arrival of Massey's regiment in February 1643, councillors agreed to accommodate these 1,500 new residents by allocating six soldiers to each alderman, five to each sheriff, four to each councillor and the remainder to the citizens in proportion. Similarly, the Chamberlain of Devizes made a payment of 10s 0d in 1646 'for soldiers quartered at The Lamb', while the landlord of The Bell in Gloucester submitted a bill for £6 4s 8d for the cost of billeting and feeding a number of troops over a long weekend in January 1644. This included the use of his 'three chambers', wine, a shoulder of mutton, a 'piece of beef and cabbage', fruit and cheese, 'a loin of veal', bread and beer and '7 horses at hay'. Inns, of course, were often commandeered by the military for this purpose - as were other places with spacious accommodation. Abraham Hale, for example, was the keeper of the house of correction (or workhouse) in Devizes, who had been forced to feed and accommodate a large group of pressed soldiers. The bill came to £15 7s 0d and, although he had been promised full payment by the Chamberlain, he had only received £4 10s 0d. When he subsequently petitioned the Quarter Sessions for relief, he made the plea that this had been a crippling loss, because he was 'a very poor man'. (19)

The alarming extent of free quarter in garrison towns is illustrated by the plight of eleven innkeepers from Bristol, who submitted a joint claim for compensation in March 1646. They detailed the money owed to them as a result of demands for accommodation and food made by soldiers at various times during the war from December 1642, money which together mounted to the incredible sum of £988 11s 5d. Many of the items concerned 'diet and horsemeat' for troopers and their horses; 'hay and provender for horses'; or the quartering of men at a rate of 8d per day. Some of the innkeepers, however, had particularly trying situations to face, such as Roger Pillorne of The Lamb in Turk Street, who was not only forced to feed and board '150 men and horses of Sr William Waller's brigade after his defeat near the Devizes', but also to sacrifice ' 3 butts of sack taken into the castle by order of Col. Nathaniel Fiennes [the Governor]'; and Arthur Sturt of The White Horse in Redcliffe Street, who lost 'a barn of hay, which Col. Fiennes caused to be set on fire' (presumably as part of a policy to remove buildings which could give cover to the enemy). Sturt apparently suffered far more than the others, claiming over £324 in compensation.

Quartering of cavalry troops often meant allowing their horses to feed off your meadow, as John Osborne of The Bear in Redcliffe Street found to his cost when Alexander Popham arrived back from the bloody skirmish on the Mendips in June 1643 with 90 horses, who were put 'at grass' for several nights; or as John Love of The Rose outside the Temple Gate discovered in 1643 when his newly-cut hay, neatly made up into a large cock, 'was eaten up by the horse of Col. Fiennes his troop as they attended the service at the line [i.e the line of earthwork defences around the city] during the siege'. Quite apart from these eleven innkeepers, however, there was at least one other who suffered from free quarter losses in Bristol at this time. In the careful accounts he maintained for his cavalry troop, Colonel John Fiennes (brother of the Governor) listed the money he owed to a number of Bristol traders - debts which could not now be settled, because Bristol had fallen to the royalists and he was no longer there. Included in the list was James Hall of The Horse and Crown in St Giles 'for the quartering of divers of my troopers with their horses after they came up to Bristol' until the troop finally broke up after the fall of the city; and 'for quartering the several horses, who lay sorely wounded at Bristol',

It: there is owinge to James Hall of the Horse & crown in St Giles for the quarteringe of diverse of my troopers with their horses after they came up from Bristolle till they were dismissed, and disposed of into other troopes (the perticulers are expressed in his bill) for which I am alsoe ingaged, the summe of — 18 · 1 · 3

It: there is owinge to the sayd Mr Hall for quarteringe the severall horses (who lay sorely wounded att Bristolle) for which I am ingaged — 1 · 5 · 8

It: There is alsoe owinge to John Lord Inkeeper of the crowne without Lawfords gate in Bristolle from 28, of my troopers expressed by name in his bill, for quarteringe — 6 · 15 · 9

Accounts of Colonel Fiennes reveal the cost of quartering to James Hall of the Horse and Crown, Bristol. (By courtesy of the Public Record Office - SP28.147)

and had been left behind by troopers caught in the heat of the battle. Hall's total loss was over twenty pounds. (20)

Even after the New Model Army had recaptured the western counties in the late summer of 1645, the problem of free quarter in towns did not go away. Garrisons were still needed to ensure that the West continued to remain in parliament's hands; and the counties were alive with the constant movement of the field army in search of surviving groups of armed royalists. These soldiers, with no local loyalty and little human sympathy, descended on west country towns with monotonous regularity for temporary shelter and sustenance. By the end of 1645, local townsfolk had had enough. The borough of Chippenham first sent a messenger to Major-General Skippon, Governor of Bristol, urging him 'to remove soldiers'; then, hearing that Sir Thomas Fairfax (commander of the New Model Army) was in Bath, hired a horse for Adam Gouldnye to ride there 'to speak with the Lord General for the removing the soldiers from hence'. It was all to no avail. Shortly afterwards, the Chamberlain again imposed a rate on the town 'for quartering of soldiers'. (21)

In February 1646, Bath Corporation, meeting to discuss the situation, decided as a first step 'that a petition shall be preferred to the Houses of Parliament for release of free quarter'. Two of the councillors made the journey to London to deliver the petition by hand. The Mayor of Bath, John Biggs, also took the precaution of writing to John Harington of Kelston, a good friend to the locality, imploring him to persuade his son, Captain Harington, to use his influence in the army on behalf of the city. In particular, he was asked to ensure that no further financial levies were imposed in view of the city's terrible distress. Visits by previous troops had caused terrible devastation in private houses, as soldiers on the rampage had indulged in looting and wanton destruction. 'Our houses are emptied of all useful furniture, and much broken and disfigured; our poor suffer for want of victuals', complained Biggs. 'We have now 400 in the town and many more coming; God protect us from pillage'. Captain Harington responded by bringing his own company to Bath so that he could keep an eye on their behaviour to protect local people.

The move clearly worked. The mayor's subsequent letter of gratitude to Captain Harington gives a graphic picture of the horrors of free quarter and its associated terror of plunder, even though Harington's presence had prevented the worst excesses 'as doth often happen under soldier-like quarterings'. On the arrival of the troops, a financial levy was demanded of the citizens backed by the threat of pillage to those citizens who 'had not monies ready'. Although the city was spared the usual demand for conscripts, it was nevertheless required to produce eighteen horses for the army's use. There was little plunder as such, 'excepting in liquors and bedding', but food set aside by families for the day's meal was taken at will by a troop from Marlborough (though 'they restored it again to many of the poorer sort'). The discomfort endured by local people in a tightly confined city seething with disreputable humanity cannot be overstated.

Troops billeting in Bath Abbey. (Line drawing by Stephen Beck)

Family life was disrupted ('our beds they occupied entirely'); city administration was disrupted ('the Town House was filled with troops'); and religious worship was disrupted ('the churches are full of troops, furniture and bedding'). And this was a friendly troop! People lived in a state of fear and suspicion. Even the mayor was obliged to find a poor man to smuggle his letter to Harington: 'I dare not send a man on purpose on horseback, as the horse would be taken', he wrote. 'God preserve our kingdom from these sad troubles much longer'. (22)

The sheer disgust felt by householders in Bristol at the loathsome behaviour of the royalist soldiers billeted on them is vividly described in a contemporary pamphlet. 'They fill the ears of the inhabitants with their blasphemous, filthy and ungodly language;...they fill their houses with swearing and cursing insomuch that they corrupt men's servants and children;...and on the sabbath, these guests or rather these beasts spend their time in dicing, drinking, carding and other such abominations'. Sometimes twenty or thirty soldiers were packed into a house, 'causing men, women and children to lay upon boards, while the cavaliers possess their beds, which they fill with lice'. (23)

THE HORRORS OF WAR 4

TERRORISED

BY QUARTERING SOLDIERS, 1648

The worst extremes of quartering were told later by William Prynne, who lived in the little village of Swainswick on the edge of Bath. He had gained national fame during the 1630s through his attacks on the bishops and the court in a series of hard-hitting pamphlets. An ardent puritan in religion, he had supported the cause of parliament in the Civil War, but had gradually become disillusioned by the high-handed attitude of the army. After the ending of the war in 1646, he not only worked with the 'peace party' in an attempt to bring about a settlement with the king, but also launched a scathing attack on the military. The army awaited the opportunity to teach Prynne a lesson - and the moment finally arrived in May, 1648, when Prynne received a visitation. He later wrote:

William Prynne (1600-1669).
By courtesy of the Treasurer and Masters of the Bench of Lincoln's Inn

Some thirty of them came to my house shouting and hollowing in a rude manner...climbed over my walls, forced my doors, beat my servants and workmen without any provocation, drew their swords on me ....and using many high provoking speeches, brake some of my windows, forced my strong beer cellar door and took the key from my servant, ransacked some of my chambers under the pretext to search for arms, taking away my servants' clothes, shirts, stockings, bands, cuffs, handkerchiefs and picking the money out of one of their pockets; hollowed, roared, stamped, beat the tables with their swords and muskets like so many bedlams, swearing, cursing and blaspheming at every word; brake the tankards, cups, dishes wherein they fetched strong beer against the ground, abused my maidservants, throwing beef and other good provisions against their heads and casting it to the dogs; they continued drinking before, at and after supper till most of them were mad drunk, and some of them dead drunk under the table. They then must have 14 beds provided for them (for they would lie but two in a bed) and all their linen washed; my sister answering them that there were not so many beds in the house, and they must be content as other soldiers had been with such beds as could be spared; they thereupon threatened to force open her chamber door, and to pull her and her children out of their beds, unless she would give them three shillings apiece for their beds and next days quarters.

Source: William Prynne, *A Legal Vindication of the Liberties of England against Illegal Taxes* (1649), pp 24-26

CHAPTER 6

Forced to Yield:
Requisitions, Plunder and Wanton Damage

To see one or two houses ruined in a place had been no great matter; but all the way we marched from Okington to Taunton...such devastation of houses, nay depopulations in many places;...rich pastures, but no cattle left to eat them. (Officer in the New Model Army, 1645)

The Loss of Horses

Although free quarter did much to damage the livelihood and morale of the rural community, the economy was much more seriously undermined by the common practice of requisitioning food, animals, equipment and farm labour. Sadly for ordinary local people, free quarter and requisitions frequently hit them at one and the same time (i.e. at the moment when armies were marching through the county and in need of both accommodation and supplies). Tensions then ran high at village level, as friction developed between uncouth soldiers and their reluctant hosts. It was at this point that the line between official requisitions and blatant plunder became somewhat blurred.

The greatest setback of all was for a farmer to lose his horse, which was vital not only for personal transport, but more particularly for work on the fields and transport of goods to market. Horses, however, were equally vital to the war effort - and they were always in short supply. From the very start of hostilities, therefore, the armies of both sides adopted the practice of requisitioning them. In London, for example, no fewer than 3,757 horses were taken during the first year for parliament's service at an estimated cost of over £54,000. As early as the autumn of 1642, the king authorised the commanders of his field armies to take by compulsory purchase as many horses from villages as they needed, though payment did not always materialise. Furthermore, he decreed that owners, who later attempted to recover their animals by force, were to be subject to the death penalty. (1)

In spite of this threat, some farmers felt so passionately about the matter that they often took the law into their own hands. This was sometimes made easier for them if the requisitioned horse had been sold to a civilian by a plundering soldier intent on making private profit. William Beeny, a yeoman from Portbury in Somerset, had had his white mare seized by the king's soldiers in 1644, 'there being a great many horses and mares then taken away in that county about that time' (as he said subsequently in evidence). Two years later, he spotted the mare at a cattle market in Bristol, where Thomas Witherley's wife had brought it to be sold. Without waiting to ask questions or argue his case, he quickly impounded it, 'knowing it to be his own goods'. He was supported in this action by William Eames, who had originally sold the animal to him. Bartholomew Allen, a Bristol grocer had a similar experience. His brown bay mare had been seized by soldiers, while it was wintering at his father's house at East Chinnock. Some time later, however, he saw the mare being driven to Bristol by Nicholas Edwards, a carrier from Warminster, and forcibly recovered it. These two men were fortunate, but normally it was impossible to identify or reclaim stolen horses.

Other owners tried hard to recover their horses by bribery. In 1643, Sir William Russell, the royalist Governor of Tewkesbury in Gloucestershire, had sent his men out to scour the countryside for horses. One of their victims was Robert Haynes of Appersley, who lost four horses in these raids. Next morning, in a state of great distress, he sought help from Richard Dowdswell of Bushley, an influential local man and a royalist activist. Knowing that Haynes was a member of the trained bands, Dowdswell promised to 'help him to his horses' on condition that he 'fetched his arms' to the Town Hall in Tewkesbury for use by the garrison. Haynes meekly complied, only to find to his dismay that Dowdswell had tricked him and reneged on his promise. Sometimes owners were helped in the recovery of their horses by troops of the other side. In September 1644,

Farm horses seized by soldiers. (Line drawing by Stephen Beck)

for example, the inhabitants of the area around Farleigh Castle in Somerset complained most bitterly about the number of horses stolen by the royalist garrison there. Hearing this, Major Dowett (a parliamentarian officer based at West Dean, near Salisbury) rode with a troop of horse across the county to Farleigh to seek redress. He arrived and (according to the newsbook, *Perfect Occurrences*), 'took the inmates so completely by surprise, that he carried off sixty horses from beneath the very walls'. (2)

Given these experiences, it is hardly surprising that more complaints were made after the war about the theft of horses than about any other aspects of violence or plunder by soldiers. Compensation claims abound in the Somerset parish accounts for horses seized during the conflict at a nominal value of roughly £6 0s 0d each. The hundred of Wellow lost a total of twenty-nine horses, including seven from Claverton and ten from the village of Wellow itself. The inhabitants of Midsomer Norton claimed £67 0s 0d for ten horses taken by parliament, whereas the small hamlet of Edmondscott in the parish of Milverton had fifteen horses seized, including two young horses which died as a result of being 'chased by soldiers'. The parish officials at Bruton did not mince words in their compensation claim but, discounting the niceties of official terminology, simply entered a new heading on their sheet - 'plundering'. Under it they listed, among other

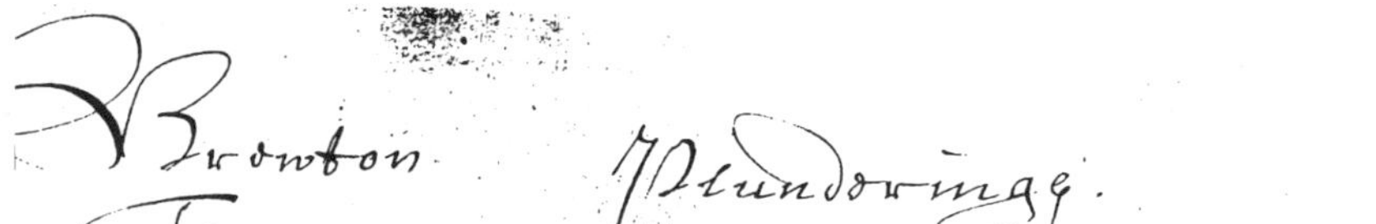
Brouton Towne. Plunderinge.
Taken from Maurice Stevens by Coll. Endlowes men, 1 horse and other goods att one tyme to ye value of 15-00-0
From Jeffery Johnsone by Maior Wansly, goods to ye value of 08-00-0
From Wm Coleborne by Maior Mansey 1 horse and other goods to ye value of 07-00-0
From Edward Morris by one Thos: Saundery a troop under Coll. Cole a nagge wth rost 07-00-0

Part of the compensation claim submitted by the town of Bruton (1646), listing horses and other goods lost by Maurice Stevens, Jeffrey Johnson, Wm. Coleborne and Edward Morris. (By courtesy of the Public Record Office - SP28.175)

items, 8 horses and 45 beasts. It was a similar story elsewhere. In 1643, as Waller's army was awaiting the advance of Hopton's royalists from Cornwall, they seized on eighty sheep from the village of Combe Hay and pressed Elizabeth Bailey's mare into service 'to carry ammunition after the army of Sir William Waller'. Sometimes such property was 'borrowed' rather than permanently requisitioned. Indeed, in January 1643, Deputy Lieutenants in Wiltshire and Somerset were specifically authorised by parliament 'to take horses... as often as they shall find it necessary for the carrying of soldiers from place to place' - on condition that, once the particular task had been accomplished, the horses should be 'restored to their owners' or compensation given for any horses lost or 'spoiled'. Later in the same year and on the strength of this edict, claims were made for two horses from Corston, which had been 'pressed by Sir William Waller's warrant and left at Devizes' and two horses from Norton St Philip, which had been loaned to Waller 'to carry ammunition from Bath and never returned'. (3)

Local people were incensed. Animals, unlike furniture and equipment, could not quickly be repaired or replaced, and could scarcely be hidden. Parliament, in an attempt to silence the growing volume of complaints, passed an Ordinance in May, 1643 'to redress the abuses', which were causing country people to be 'distasted and discouraged'. They felt that it was unacceptable for officers, who knew nothing of previous contributions made by a community, suddenly to seize animals in this way. In order to regulate the system, therefore, officers in future would first be required to gain permission from the County Committee or Deputy Lieutenants; and then to mark the horses, before entering full details of the number taken on official lists. Horses seized from those people, who were 'well-affected' to parliament's cause, were also to be valued for later payment. It had little lasting effect. Front-line commanders continued to take the law into their own hands as necessity demanded. (4)

Theft of horses could occur in various circumstances. Villagers were particularly vulnerable after an army had been billeted on them for the night and had time to investigate possibilities. Following their capture of Cirencester in January 1643, for instance, the royalist troops (according to an eye-witness) went out 'to their night quarters in the villages round about, where they did eat up all their provision of victuals and spoiled much corn and hay; when they went away, they took with them all the horses of the villages round about'. On the other hand, individuals were even more vulnerable when they were out riding in the country. In 1643, William Orwell, a 16-year old husbandman from Barton Regis in Gloucestershire, was asked by William Tiler to help him to ride his two horses to Bristol. On the way, Orwell found himself some distance ahead of Tiler, when he was accosted by six troopers. These men first accused him of being in possession of a stolen horse and then violently knocked him to the ground, before making off with their prize. (5)

Damage to Crops

The immediate harvest could also be ruined - and with it a substantial part of the farmer's income - by the thoughtless or deliberate actions of a visiting regiment. One of the worst incidents occurred in Combe Hay in the summer of 1643, when the inhabitants discovered that their village had become the daily meeting point for the whole of parliament's army. Waller had camped on Claverton Down, just outside Bath, for the three weeks immediately prior to the Battle of Lansdown. The unfortunate villagers were therefore forced to endure 'ye daily concourse of ye whole army to our village, during Sir William Waller's being about Bath Downs and Odd Down'. This caused considerable damage as the soldiers trampled their way across the fields, 'spoiling our grounds ready for mowing'. Troop commanders could also requisition a meadow, thus depriving the farmer of valuable fodder for his own animals. During that same period, Captain Butler's troop of horse did 'eat up a mead of grass belonging to Gyles Parsons' in Hinton Charterhouse, before moving on to Englishcombe, where they 'had free quarter in one meadow of John Clement for one whole day about mowing time'. Not too far away, John Lanes of Clutton was claiming compensation of £10 16s 0d for the fact that a close of his oats was 'eaten up by some of the parliamentary horse'; and John Rosewell of Twerton £8 0s 0d for Colonel Strode's decision to quarter on his meadows 'three score and ten horses a little before [the] Lansdown fight, which remained with him for a fortnight and upwards'. Just after the war, Cromwell's troops from the New Model Army visited Chippenham in Wiltshire, where four hundred horses were put into the West Mead, totally ruining the crop of hay. Nor were parliamentarians the only culprits. As the siege of Gloucester was beginning in 1643, the king arrived at Tredworth Field with 6,000 of his troops. According to tradition, the land there was covered with standing corn when the army entered it that morning. By evening, the horses were knee-deep in mud. (6)

The Temporary Loss of Labourers, Carts and Teams

Seed-time and harvest alike could equally be wrecked by a sudden demand from a local garrison for labourers and ploughs to work on fortifications, especially when the value of this service was not set against the weekly assessment. In Somerset, the village of Norton St Philip was called upon three times to to provide a plough for three or four days to labour on the earthworks at Bristol, whereas Whitchurch was expected to maintain two men over a period of eight weeks 'for raising of the bulwarks of Bristol'. Both Dunkerton and Englishcombe, however, opted to pay money instead of releasing further workers in this manner from their already depleted land force. John Pope and William Teggs of Norton Malreward, on the other hand, were twice summoned to bring their four oxen to the assistance of the New Model Army. On the first occasion, they were required to carry 'one load of straw for the siege of Bristol' and 'one load of faggots'. Later, their task was to help in moving the artillery train from Bristol to Keynsham - 'and from thence we carried the train to Devizes five days', they recalled. In doing so, they lost valuable time on their own fields. When the New Model Army took Nunney Castle in 1645, Lieutenant Frin was left with the task of collecting together all the goods and provisions, which had been stored inside, and dispatching them to Bristol. He therefore commandeered all the parish ploughs, wagons and teams of oxen to transport 'loads of beef, bacon, butter, cheese, household stuff, lead from the castle and all the ammunition and parish arms'. (7)

Nor were such sacrifices limited to the communities in north Somerset. After Colonel Edward Massey (the parliamentary Governor of Gloucester) had captured Tewkesbury on 4th June 1644, he immediately set about the task of strengthening the fortifications. Orders were therefore issued to local officials to supply 25 inhabitants each day to assist with this labour. A rota system was quickly devised, which meant that the men living in the High Street would work on Tuesdays, Wednesdays and Thursdays, while those from Church Street worked on Fridays and Saturdays and those from Barton Street on Mondays. Later that month, Massey shifted his campaign to Wiltshire, where he occupied Devizes. Determined to prevent the town from again becoming the base for a royalist garrison, he instructed the High Constable of the hundred of Potterne and Cannings 'to summon in all the able-bodied men for work...with such spades, shovels, pickaxes and other tools as they have for the present demolishing and throwing down of all such works and fortifications as are now standing about Devizes'. Seven months later, however, after the town had been recaptured by the royalists, the same High Constable received (on 10th January 1645) a warrant from the new Governor there, Charles Lloyd, to send '200 able men with spades, mattocks and shovels, and provision for one whole week' to help rebuild the same fortifications! Six carts with ox teams were also required to carry timber for the defences. Furthermore, the men would not be permitted to go home without licence, but were to stay for the period in question in the town, where barns or billets would be provided for them.

Over the next two days, further orders were made for one horse team and two more ox teams to carry timber, cannon baskets and faggots from Potterne Woods into the town. On 25th February, the Governor demanded another workforce of 100 men with their tools for a whole month, plus no fewer than five horse teams with their carts. Lloyd's aim was to transform the partially-ruined castle into a fortress, a task which was to take him three months to achieve (January - March 1645). During this period, the inhabitants of the Potterne and Cannings hundred faced repeated demands for labourers, carts and teams - demands which they attempted to resist by means of delays to deadlines and desertions under the cover of darkness from their work in the trenches. The High Constables (John Forest and Michael Paradise) had a thankless task and were constantly subjected to high-handed threats, bullying tactics and personal abuse from Lloyd. Such was the tension that Paradise was finally murdered in a most brutal manner by troopers from the Devizes garrison. (8)

Major operations, such as strengthening defences or preparing for a major assault, always put extra strain on the resources of the local community. In August 1643, as the king was preparing for the siege of Gloucester, he issued orders from his court at Matson to Sir Baynham Throckmorton, his High Sheriff for Gloucestershire. Warrants were to be despatched throughout the county to ensure that all workmen and materials vital for the success of the siege were assembled. These included 40 miners from the Forest of Dean, who were 'to repair to our Train of Artillery before Gloucester by tomorrow night with such tools as they use' (i.e. for undermining the city's fortifications); a smith 'with an anvil, bellows, fitting instruments to work and a proportion of coals'; and 30 woodworkers with their tools to work 'in the making of faggots and such other materials' (i.e. for filling in the wet ditches around the walls). The High Sheriff was also to commandeer 80 three-inch planks, 900 one-inch boards and 20 'small flat boats' - all by the next night! The men selected for duty were given no choice, but were to report 'on pain of death'. (9)

As the war progressed, military commanders faced growing resistance from local communities to the requisitioning of their men, animals and equipment, a policy which brought serious disruption to the farming operation. Both sides, therefore, sought opportunities to reassure local people or to regulate the practice as far as possible. In January 1644, for instance, reports reached Sir Ralph Hopton in Bristol of rumours, which were spreading throughout the surrounding area, that labourers sent in to work on the fortifications were not only left unpaid, but were also likely to be conscripted as soldiers. Hopton therefore instructed the High Constable of the Grumbaldash hundred, in sending out warrants to the villages for a total of 60 labourers 'with good and serviceable spades and pickaxes' to work on the Fort Royal on Brandon Hill, to emphasise that the work would only last for four days and that they would be paid their wages out of the contribution money.

Parliament, too, tried to ensure that those commandeered for service did not lose out financially. In August 1644, with the establishment of the Association of the Western Counties (including Somerset and Wiltshire), county commissioners were authorised to requisition carts, carriages and horse for military service, on condition that they paid their owners 12 pence per mile for the outward journey for a cart with five horses and 2 pence per mile for a single horse. The men who had escorted the carts and teams to their destination, of course, always ran the risk of being plundered on their return journey. To overcome this problem, John Payne (Waggon-Master-General to Prince Maurice) adopted the practice of issuing safe conduct passes to those involved. In October 1644, for example, 23 men with 66 oxen and 3 horses (who had been pressed for service in transporting items for the royalist army, but who were now discharged) were issued with a pass entitling them to a safe and quiet journey with their cattle 'to their several dwelling places'. (10)

The Loss of Crops, Animals and Other Produce

Much as the farmers resented all this interruption to the growing and harvesting of their crops, their worst problems actually arose once the harvest had been gathered in. A hungry troop could quickly sniff out their much-needed supplies. Newton St Loe in Somerset suffered in this way just before the Battle of Lansdown when five loads of hay were taken for Sir William Waller's troops, two for Sir Arthur Haselrig's cavalry and 'one load for Mr Ashe's own horse'. Widow Hales of Littleton lost corn valued at £1 16s 0d to Waller's men, while on the same occasion the village of Whittoymead forcibly supplied 'two horse loads' of provisions for the army rendezvous on Bathampton Down. Thomas Stibbins, who rented the rabbit warren at Stoke Gifford on the Mendips, was compelled to

The plundering of a private house, 1642. (An original painting by Angus McBride - by courtesy of © Osprey Publishing Ltd.)

deliver 205 pairs of rabbits for use by local parliamentary forces, thus losing the £12 9s 8d which he would have received for them at Bristol market.

In Wiltshire, Colonel Lloyd, the new royalist Governor of Devizes, not only pressurised the neighbourhood into assisting with the task of fortifying the castle (see above), but also made a number of demands for supplies of food and cattle fodder - one in late December 1644, ordering the hundred of Potterne and Cannings to send 40 cartloads of hay and straw, and two more in the following March. The first of these requested all the hundred's wagons 'laden with straw', while the second ordered the instant dispatch of large quantities of butter, cheese, bacon, wheat, barley and peas. Farm produce therefore remained vulnerable for as long as it was stored on the farm. On the other hand, there was no greater guarantee of safety if it was taken to market. In 1643, Colonel Nathaniel Fiennes, the parliamentary Governor of Bristol, sent Quartermaster Longbotham out in search of supplies for the garrison. Arriving at the market in Wrington, he saw a large quantity of oats and beans which Mrs Avery, Richard Grimstead and Thomas Hillman had brought for sale from their homes in Yatton. Longbotham duly seized the lot without payment. Sometimes more unusual items were requisitioned from local villagers. In October 1643, George Maxwell, the royalist Governor of Berkeley Castle in Gloucestershire, was fearful of being subjected to an imminent siege. Determined to make his stay as comfortable as possible, he ordered the Constable of the village of Berkeley to supply him with a bed, one mat, a bolster, two blankets and a coverlet. (11)

Most of the above incidents were the result of spontaneous demands by troops, who happened to be in the area at the time or were simply passing through. It was not until the latter stages of the war that armies developed a better organised and more systematic commissariat to cater for the needs of soldiers on campaign. This was particularly true of parliament's New Model Army, which was established in 1645, but it was also true of the king's own army in the latter months of 1644. As it neared Marlborough, the king sent Chief Commissary Pickney on ahead to organise the supply chain. By the time of the arrival of the main force on 12th November, Pickney had conducted an accurate survey of the ability of the town and its immediate vicinity to sustain an army for a period of days. The questionnaire he used, which still survives, required detailed statistics on the number of mills, ovens and carriages in the town and how much wheat, cheese, malt and salt was stored there. Armed with this information, he was in a position to report to the king that the seven mills were able to grind 37 quarters of wheat in twenty-four hours and that the five bakers in town could bake 30 quarters of bread in the same time *[a quarter of corn measured 8 bushels or 64 gallons]*. Pickney therefore quickly set the bakers to work, placing sentries on the doors of their houses 'that they may not be intercepted in the service', and then sent out a warrant to the Mayor of Salisbury to make up the shortfall in bread (some £200 worth in total). He also reported that Marlborough could in addition provide 8 cwt of cheese and 2 tons of salt.

At the same time as he was dealing with the town itself, Pickney and his assistants were also busy sending out warrants to the High Constables of six neighbouring hundreds for a whole range of other commodities. The High Constable of Kingsbridge, for instance (who was threatened with a £500 fine for his lack of urgency), was instructed to provide 2 oxen, 20 sheep, 5 calves, 24 pigs, 60 chickens, 10 dozen pigeons, 24 ducks, 12 turkeys, 12 geese, 12 dozen rabbits, 5 quarters of wheat, 20 cwt *[a hundredweight measured 112 lbs]* of cheese, 40 lbs of butter, 6 dozen eggs, 5 quarters of malt, 20 quarters of oats, 3 quarters of beans, 10 loads of hay, 4 flitches of bacon, 2 bushels of salt and two large candles - all within forty-eight hours! In similar fashion, the High Constable of Ramsbury's list included 22 cwt of bread, 12 cwt of cheese, 3 fat 'beefs', 10 sheep, 4 dozen chickens, 40 bushels of beans and peas and eight teams with their carts.

Pickney's reach, however, extended far beyond the Marlborough area. He also sent warrants to the king's commissioners in Somerset, ordering them to deliver 'all the clothes, shoes and stockings that have been provided in the western parts for our army'; and to Francis Hawley at Bristol, asking him to admit his officers who had been sent to receive 'clothes and other provisions'. Nor did his meticulous forward planning neglect one other area vital to military welfare. In a warrant to Humphrey Panter, the army surgeon was instructed 'to take up such medicines, both of physic and chirugery as you shall think fit for the use of our army'. Through careful attention to detail and determined action, the Chief Commissary had therefore managed to ensure that the army was well cared for during its five-day stay in Marlborough. The cost of this efficiency to the population in the surrounding area was, however, considerable. (12)

Although many parts of the three western counties managed to escape this concentrated type of oppression, it is nevertheless true to say that the suffering experienced in the area around Marlborough was by no means unique. Parliament's Grand Committee, meeting in Gloucester in 1644 to investigate wartime abuses in the county, discovered that hardly a village in the Inshire Division around the city of Gloucester remained unscathed from the effects of plunder (much of it relating, of course, to the period of the siege). They also reported that the situation was particularly severe in the area around Tewkesbury, which had been ravaged on numerous occasions by armies of both sides. In January 1644, for instance, Prince Rupert based himself on the town and duly plundered the inhabitants of surrounding villages. According to the newsbook, *Perfect Occurrences*, the Commons was informed of 'the intolerable oppressions of the Duke of Plunderland and his plundering cavaliers, lately come into these parts about Tewkesbury; and that he sends about his cruel warrants, threatening fire and sword to all those that shall carry away any victuals or any provisions to the garrison at Gloucester'.

A year earlier, he had similarly terrorised the area around Cirencester, after taking the parliamentary garrison there by storm (2nd February 1643). Eye-witnesses reported that his men 'went into the country and took away all the horses, sheep, oxen and other cattle of the well-affected' and that he subsequently 'sent at least 200 cart loads of plunder to Oxford'. But that was only the start of his violent campaign. On 1st February, the king had advised him by letter that 'at Cirencester, Stroud, Minchinhampton, Tetbury, Dursley, Wotton-under-Edge and Chipping

The pillaging soldier of 1642 caricatured with an artichoke for a sword, a cooking pot with duck for a hat, a dripping pan for a shield, a spit with goose for a musket and wine bottles for powder cartridges.
(By permission of The British Library - ref: 669F (12) - 'The English Irish Soldier)

Sodbury great quantities of cloth, canvas and buckrams were to be had' for the urgent task of making soldiers' 'suits'. He therefore instructed Rupert to visit those places with 'a competent body of horse' and to bring all the available cloth to Cirencester, having first made detailed lists of what was taken and having issued receipts to the owners. Each clothier was to be assured that, 'upon his repair to Oxford', he would receive recompense for his goods. In anticipation, the king had already dispatched three of his master-tailors to make up the cloth. What, however, was intended to be a well-organised and civilised act of requisitioning was transformed by Rupert into a violent and merciless act of plundering. An eye-witness noted that, two days after the capture of the town, 'they took away cloth, wool and yarn, besides other goods from the clothiers about Stroudwater, to their utter undoing, not only of them and theirs, but of thousands of poor people, whose livelihood depends on that trade'. Many were ruined in consequence. (13)

The result of all this oppression was that certain areas became so totally impoverished through plunder and requisitions that they were unable to pay their taxes. In April 1645, Colonel Massey complained on the arrival in Gloucester of a troop of horse from Newport that he would be unable to support them: 'We have very little meat for man or horse, the country being spoiled and ruined round about us'. In the same month, the Mayor of Gloucester wrote to the Committee of Safety in London on a similar theme. As a result of the heavy demands of war on the local populace, he argued, the countryside around 'was so extremely exhausted and miserably destroyed that it was even ready to give up the ghost'. This in turn meant that they could no longer generate enough cash to maintain sufficient forces for the protection of outlying districts. In consequence, marauding royalist troops had seized their opportunity and 'miserably plundered our country on every side of what is left'. Such was the state of anxiety in the villages that John Guise of Elmore in Gloucestershire wrote to his Steward in 1644, advising him of the need to take urgent precautions. 'I heard that the king's army are like to fall down suddenly', he warned. 'Fearing the worst lest there should be plundering and taking away of cattle upon their coming down, I think it good that you get all my cattle as near the house as may be'. He then gave him instructions that, on receiving news of an imminent royalist raid, he was to 'put them all in the wood yard for a day or two till we can come to secure you'. (14)

The Plundering of Salisbury

One of the most dramatic accounts of plunder at the hands of rampaging troops is contained in the compensation claims submitted by the Mayor of Salisbury in December 1644. Earlier in the month, a force of parliamentarians had surprised and dislodged Colonel Francis Cook's garrison force in the town, a task made easier by the fact that Salisbury lacked strong fortifications and was largely defenceless against determined attack. Several of his men were killed and many captured. But although the town was quickly taken over by Colonel Ludlow for parliament, it was not long before he, too, was surprised by a counter-attack led by Sir Marmaduke Langdale. Ludlow was routed with considerable losses on 31st December. The royalist soldiers, as if in revenge for their earlier

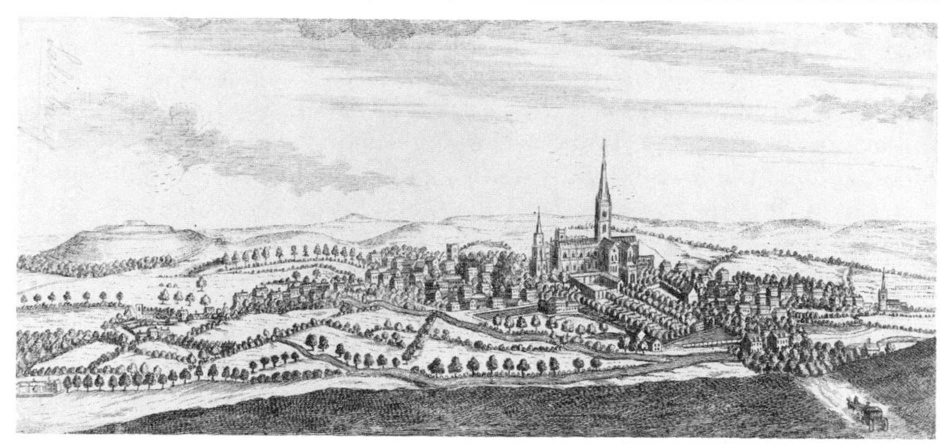

The unfortified town of Salisbury in 1723. (By permission of The British Library - ref: K43, Stukeley View of Salisbury, vol. 39, page A)

humiliation, then proceeded to vent their spite on the townsfolk by subjecting them to three days of sustained terror. Once their raids on property had ended, the Mayor drew up a list of the damage sustained, providing graphic detail of the outrage. It is the story of acute human suffering.

John Jeffreys lost property to the value of £17 5s 0d, including money, two cloaks, various items of clothing, a silver spoon and three horses, all 'taken by force'. Thomas Lawes was even worse off. Not only did he suffer the theft of 'linen and other things to the value of £50 and wine to the value of £20', he also lost a box of silver plate, which had been given for safe keeping to the Mayor's wife (presumably because she had a secure hiding place). William Autram was forced to endure a whole series of visits on the same day by marauding soldiers, 'being at his house six separate times', during which they seized much of his 'wearing apparel and linen'. William Phillips was also the subject of multiple raids. The soldiers first humiliated him in the street by taking the hat from his head; then then visited him at home and virtually left him without any clothes, taking all his 'wearing apparel both linen and woollen'. When, however, they arrived on the third occasion, he was ready for them with a bribe: 'They came again afterward and had a plundered again, but that I gave them ten shillings'.

Thomas Kynton was not so lucky. His house was plundered and stripped of virtually all he possessed - a grey carpet, a table cloth, a pair of sheets, a pair of blankets, a collared suit, two grey suits, a coat and a cloak. Old Myles the cobbler lost five shillings 'out of our purses', three pieces of leather, six pairs of shoes and several items of clothing worth £6 5s 0d in total, an enormous sum for an ordinary worker to forfeit. Of the many remaining claims on the Mayor's list, two are particularly heart-rending. Widow Ranlington was an old, sick woman in need of permanent care and frequent bandaging. But she, too, was visited: 'Taken away from the Widow Ranlington and the woman that tends her by the troopers in hot water, linen cloth...£4 10s 0d'. That was bad enough, but for James Sadwa, a leather worker, the plundering was the last straw. He had already 'been much oppressed' by having to quarter seven men for three days, 'being a poor man as I am and saving {i.e. without} a groat'. Now he faced a bill for four pounds to replace vital stock and materials of his trade. (15)

Newly-arrived soldiers in a town often found that the billets they had ear-marked for the night had already been stripped by previous soldiers on the march. Richard Atkyns, a cavalry captain in the Marquis of Hertford's army in 1643, recalled one such incident in his diary: 'That day I went to my quarters at Glastonbury, where there was a handsome case of a house, but totally plundered, and neither had bread or beer in it; but only part of a cheddar cheese, which looking blue, I found my foot-boy giving to my greyhounds, and reproving him for it; he cried, saying there was nothing else to give them'. On another occasion, however, his luck changed when an item of plunder unexpectedly fell into his hands: 'Myself and some of my officers went to seek for arms; of which we found many; and observing a hole in an elder hedge, I put in my hand and took out a bag of money'. The fear of plunder often caused ordinary people to hide their valuables at the first hint of troops in the area (see also Chapter 9). (16)

Attempts to control plunder

Almost from the very start of the war, both sides realised the importance of controlling the scale of unauthorised plunder. Troops were easily tempted to go on the rampage for many different reasons - a need to compensate the lack of regular pay, a sense of power over unarmed civilians, a desire to seek revenge on enemy sympathisers and a basic instinct to loot as part of the mob (especially after the elation of victory). Officers often struggled in vain to maintain discipline. 'A very great licence broke into the army', commented the Earl of Clarendon after the royalists had taken Bristol by storm in 1643. Nevertheless, royalist and parliamentarian commanders alike knew only too well that merciless pillaging of the countryside would result not only in the alienation and hostility of the local community, but also in their inability to pay the weekly assessment through sheer impoverishment.

In March 1643, for example, the royalist commissioners in Gloucestershire wrote to the king outlining their extreme difficulty in collecting the tax in the hundreds around Cirencester, which were 'very much impoverished' since the arrival of the royalist garrison. A major cause of the trouble was the seizure of between 200 and 300 horses from local villages, which had 'utterly disabled them' from sowing in the fields. The land, therefore, was lying waste, the end result of which would be the people would suffer 'a dearth in these parts' and the commissioners would suffer a shortfall in taxation. They ended their letter with a heartfelt plea to the king to secure the county from further 'plunderings'. (17)

In fact both king and parliament had already made an attempt, in November 1642, to regulate such abuses. A parliamentary Ordinance ordered the restitution of goods, which had been plundered or pillaged, and authorised the owners, on spotting the stolen property, to reclaim it with the help of a constable. The king's proclamation stipulated that army officers were forbidden to seize money or goods 'without a warrant declaring the cause'. These measures, however, were largely ineffective and generally ignored by front-line troops. Realising that the situation had deteriorated, the king issued a much stiffer edict in March 1643, stating that anyone taking horses, money or goods without a warrant was 'to be hanged without mercy'. At the same time, however, villages were to supply victuals to forces stationed there on presentation of an official warrant; in return, they would receive 'tickets' or receipts, which would be paid 'when God enables us'. In December of the same year, he went on to deal with a related problem, namely that of the 'straggling soldier' (i.e. a person who followed the army, pretending to be a soldier, but whose real purpose was to plunder and rob ordinary subjects). The king therefore ordered the arrest and punishment of all persons who could nor produce a pass signed by an officer. (18)

In spite of these official orders, however, the practice of plundering continued almost unabated throughout the war. Much was left in reality to the consciences of individual commanders, who on occasions at least imposed a limited control over their troops. The Marquis of Hertford, for instance, did his best to discourage his troops from plundering local inhabitants as they marched northwards through Somerset in June 1643. When his army reached Taunton, he instructed his Provost-Marshal-General to hand-pick a number of cavalry to deal with 'any plundering in the houses or goods of His Majesty's subjects'. They were to arrest any officer or soldier caught in the act and, 'without any further dispute or examination, cause him immediately to be executed'. Richard Symonds recalls in his diary the firm action taken by commanders in the king's army in 1644 on their march through Gloucestershire, Somerset and Wiltshire. At Badminton, two foot soldiers were 'hanged on trees in the hedgerow for pillaging of the country villages'; then, on the journey between Bath to Wells, two more were 'hanged for plundering'; and finally, near Great Shefford, 'a soldier was hanged for plunder, but the rope broke'.

Parliament's New Model Army also succeeded in imposing a much tighter discipline. A commander, who took part in the expedition to relieve Taunton in 1645, described the success of this much tougher approach. He recalled that when a proclamation was made threatening the death penalty for acts of plunder, the veteran members of the dragoons (with guilty consciences born of past misdemeanours) voiced their whole-hearted approval - on condition that their wages were actually paid! Nevertheless, he continued, the edict had 'caused so much good order in our march' that he had not heard of any villager complain of losing so much as an egg. The only exception was that, on a hard march in hot weather over the plain, soldiers did help themselves to water as they passed through the villages. (See also 'Post-Siege Plunder' in Chapter 9) (19)

Commanders were particularly sensitive to the feelings of the country population, when their continuing support was vital to the success of a campaign. At the siege of Gloucester in 1643, for example, the king was furious that his officers were issuing vast numbers of warrants for food supplies on their own initiative. In a proclamation to be published throughout the army, he explained that, as he relied on the co-operation of local people to supply them with food throughout the siege, proper controls were needed to ensure that the burden on subjects was both eased and spread. In future, therefore, no officer should 'presume to send out any warrants' without a signature from either the king, the High Sheriff or the commissaries. In November 1643, Prince Rupert also showed a much more sympathetic attitude to the inhabitants of Wiltshire, after they had agreed to pay him £1,200 a week for four weeks in support of the royalist forces. He consequently issued instructions banning officers from requisitioning horses, cattle, provisions or goods. In future, they were to pay for all food supplies (at a rate of 1s 6d a bushel for oats, 2s 0d a bushel for peas and beans, 5d a day for horses on hay and 2s 6d a week for horses on grass) and that compensation was to be paid to 'the party suffering' for any loss or damage. (20)

Protection Orders

In certain circumstances, communities or individuals could secure their protection from plundering, either by paying a sum of money or by seeking the assistance of influential friends. In August 1643, for example, the king - having dined in Tetbury on his way to the siege of Gloucester - issued an order to all his officers that they should 'neither plunder the houses nor take away any of the goods held within the houses or grounds of any of our loving subjects of the town and parish of Tetbury'. This protection was probably in response to the town's agreement to support his new garrison there. Its effectiveness, however, scarcely lasted a month. Sir Samuel Luke noted in his diary for 12th September that, following an insulting remark made to a royalist captain by a carrier from Tetbury, a party of cavalry from the Cirencester garrison rode over to teach the town a lesson. Arriving there with the full intention of plundering the houses, they were again 'bought off' when 'the townsmen agreed to pay them £300...to secure themselves and their goods'. (21)

Samuel Webb, a wealthy clothier from Nether Lyppiatt in Gloucestershire (a man who had much to lose from plundering), purchased two separate protections in 1643 - one from Prince Maurice in February and the other from Prince Rupert in August, both promising security for his family, goods, animals and houses. Sir Arthur Aston, who was helping to besiege Gloucester at the time, wrote to Prince Rupert in total amazement

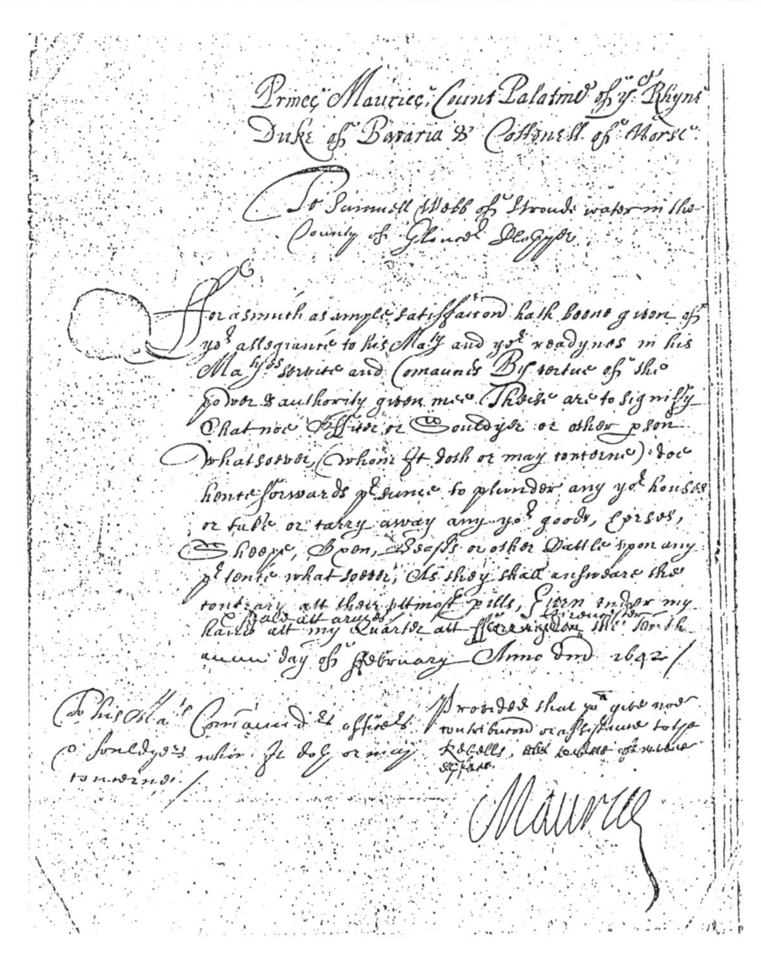

Prince Maurice, Count Palatine of ye Rhyne Duke of Bavaria & Collonell of Horse.

To Samuell Webb of Stroud water in the County of Gloucester.

Forasmuch as ample satisfaction hath beene given of yor allegiance to his Maty and yor readynes in his Maties service and Comaunds By vertue of the power & authority given mee These are to signify That noe Officer or Souldyer or other pson whatsoever (whom itt doth or may concerne) doe henceforwards presume to plunder any yor houses or table or carry away any yor goods, horses, Sheepe, Oxen, Beasts or other Cattle upon any pretence whatsoever; As they shall answeare the contrary att their uttmost perills, Given under my hand & seale att [illegible] att my Quarter att [illegible] this [illegible] day of February Anno Dom 1642/

To his Maties Comaunders officers & Souldyers whom itt doth or may concerne./

Provided that you give noe contribucon or assistance to the Rebells, else to bee of noe value.

Maurice

Samuel Webb's protection order from Prince Maurice instructing that no officer or soldier should plunder his 'house or table' or seize his 'goods, horses, sheep, oxen, beasts or other cattle'. (By kind permission of Gloucestershire County Council - Record Office ref: D745/X4)

at this generosity. 'Here is one Samuel Webb, a clothier, who doth assist the parliament against the king and yet, by what means I know not, he has obtained a protection from His Highness, Prince Maurice'. He said that he had so far managed to restrain his soldiers and 'would not let any man meddle with him', but he looked with covetous eyes at the 'good quantity of scarlet and other cloth in his house'. At the very moment when Rupert received Aston's letter, he was in the process of issuing another protection order to Robert Taylor of Upton St Leonard, presumably again for cash. (22)

Foresight was an important element in the search for protection. Prior to the siege of Gloucester in 1643, a group of sixteen citizens there with royalist sympathies sent a petition to the king seeking protection from plunder, if his armies managed to capture the city. They pleaded with him to instruct his commanders 'that, upon entrance into the city, they forbear to plunder any house until the loyal therein be distinguished from the disloyal'. In return, they agreed to hand over 'a reasonable proportion in money' for their own indemnity and the soldiers' satisfaction. A list was drawn up shortly afterwards of 104 citizens of Gloucester, who were loyal to the king. (23)

Parliament, meanwhile, had been issuing protection orders of its own. In February 1643, two Wiltshire royalists benefited, namely James Long of Draycott Cerne and James Montague of Lacock. Sadly, however, a protection order in itself was no absolute guarantee of protection. In 1642, for instance, Godfrey Goodman, the former Bishop of Gloucester, felt secure on receiving a promise of protection from the parliamentary committee and had therefore failed to conceal his property. Before long he was subjected to the most ruthless plundering both 'by soldiers and the rude multitude', in consequence of which he had been left 'very poor' with his stock 'utterly exhausted'. The whole concept of the protection order also provided an opportunity for ruthless individuals to make extra profit from the war. In 1643, a Mr Wyatt of Tewkesbury was on active service for parliament as part of the Gloucester garrison. This put at serious risk his property in Tewkesbury, a town which was then garrisoned for the king by Sir William Russell. Giving evidence later, Wyatt's sister (Mrs Merson) described how she had been approached by William Allen (a royalist agent), who urged her to 'pay some money to preserve her brother Mr Wyatt's house from plundering'. Under this pressure, she paid Allen £20 'for the use of the king's army'. (24)

Individuals, who were denied the chance to purchase a protection order, could nevertheless resort to bribery as a way of reducing the impact of requisitions or threatened plunderings. The bailiff responsible for running the Marquess of Salisbury's estates at Marston and Pebworth in Gloucestershire calculated that he had paid out a total of £453 7s 6d in response to the demands made by various armies from 1643 to 1646. These included the provisions sent to the garrisons at Sudeley and Chipping Campden as well as to the king's army at Gloucester, Esam and Evesham; the quartering of numerous troops, both royalist and parliamentarian; the requisitioning of horses and carts; and the payment of taxes to both sides. This sum, however, would undoubtedly have been greater had it not been for the shrewd tactics employed by the bailiff, when faced by groups of menacing soldiers. Armed only with a pot of ready cash, he was quick to offer bribes in return for more lenient treatment. Thus he gave 10s 0d to Sir William Waller's quartermaster 'to prevent quarter'; 17s 0d to Colonel Bennett's quartermaster 'to prevent a warrant for £6 17s 0d' (i. e. a tax demand); 10s 0d to Colonel Walgrave's quartermaster 'to prevent the sending of £4 worth of veal, mutton and lamb'; and £1 5s 0d to Captain Fisher's Cornet 'for his courtesies' (unspecified). He also anticipated trouble (and the likely threat of plunder) by slipping 3s 0d as a sweetener into the hands of the 12 parliamentary soldiers 'when they fetched the money imposed on the parish'; and 5s 0d to 'the foot soldiers that came to the house daily, when the king lay at Evesham'. (25)

Communities of impoverished farmers, who could afford neither to buy a protection order nor to offer a bribe, increasingly resorted to joint measures of passive defiance, armed resistance or violent counter-attacks in what Ian Roy terms as 'guerrilla warfare'. This was particularly true in those areas that had suffered almost to breaking point from the brutal methods employed by soldiers in robbing them of their property and their livelihood. When, therefore, in 1643 royalist troops used strong-arm tactics to collect the weekly tax in Padworth, near Gloucester, the townsmen collected together 300 men in arms from neighbouring villages, sallied forth against the soldiers and drove them away. Realising, however, that another attack would almost certainly be made with heavy reinforcements next day, they 'took advantage of the night and loaded all their provisions and goods and carried the same away with their wives and children to Gloucester, and left the town to the cavaliers; who next day came... but found nothing but old lumber, not worth their carrying away'.

Elsewhere in Gloucestershire, groups of armed villagers patrolled the country areas, protecting their property. The royalist Governor of Berkeley Castle complained to Prince Rupert that he could not send foot soldiers out to requisition supplies, because the country people would simply 'knock them down'. Furthermore, he said, they had even mounted a combined attack on a troop of royalist cavalry and 'killed six of them'. The miners of the Forest of Dean, on the other hand, preferred the tactic of passive resistance, when summoned to give their services at the siege of Gloucester. The High Sheriff of the county (Sir Baynham Throckmorton) wrote in despair to Lord Percy, General of Ordinance. 'Last night the miners were here and this morning most of them are gone home without ever acquainting me with it'. He instructed Percy to send troops after them to bring them back by force - and 'to burn the homes of those that resist or refuse instantly to come with them'. He concluded on a note of sheer exasperation - 'Never man had such rogues to deal with'. He was eventually forced to recruit replacements from South Wales, a tribute to the effectiveness and power of the country people, when once organised into resistance. (26)

A Somerset Labourer's Complaint

A popular ballad of the time vividly illustrates the frustration and anger of country people. Entitled *A Somerset Man's Complaint*, it tells of a poor farm labourer who, having witnessed the easy pickings gained by marauding soldiers, vows that he too 'will a plundering' go. He will sell his cart and plough and buy a sword; then, all he will need is a warrant from a captain to give him authority 'to steal a horse without disgrace, and beat the owner, too'. He continues his lament:

I had six oxen the other day
And them the Roundheads stole away,
A mischief be their speed.
I had six horse left me whole,
And them the Cavaliers have stole.
God's sores, they are both agreed.

How I do labour, toil and sweat
Endure the cold, hot, dry and wet,
But what dost think I get?
Have just my labour for my pain
These garrisons have all my gain *[i.e through requisitions]*

There goes my corn, my beans and peas,
I do not dare them to displease,
They do so swear and vapour.
Then to the Governor I come
And pray him to discharge the sum *[i.e. pay the money]*
But nought can get but paper. *[i.e. a receipt]* (27)

The Plundering of Enemy Sympathisers

If an area was overrun by one side in the war, the property of all those who had shown any sympathy towards their opponents was immediately vulnerable to attack. Indeed, some of the most vicious and heartless acts of plunder occurred when soldiers ran amok, seeking revenge on real or imaginary supporters of the enemy. Commanders on both sides had great difficulty in controlling the behaviour of their troops in such circumstances. Sir William Waller admitted: 'Our soldiers plunder malignants, do what we can, and embezzle their goods; there is no way to prevent it'. His words were echoed by the Earl of Clarendon, who said that royalist troops regarded the 'malignity' of an area as an 'excuse for the exercise of any rapine or severity among the inhabitants'. (28)

Edward Hyde, Earl of Clarendon; adviser to the Prince of Wales in Bristol, 1645. (By kind permission of Bristol Central Library)

Examples abound. In September 1643, 150 parliamentary soldiers from Gloucester and Tewkesbury, under Captain Scriven (son of a rich ironmonger from Gloucester), went to

Castlemorton to plunder the house of a known catholic, Rowland Bartlett. Taking advantage of the fact that the local people were all at the Ledbury Fair, they seized his watch, broke open a chest and took £600 in money and £60 worth of linen, not to mention silver plate, jewels and bracelets. 'In their strict search, they met with Mrs Bartlett's sweetmeats; but these they scattered on the ground, not daring to taste them for fear of poison'. Bartlett's house was subsequently plundered on a further four or five occasions. In March 1644, Colonel Massey found himself short of fuel for the Gloucester garrison, largely because supplies from the countryside had been intercepted by royalist troops. In an act of revenge, he instructed Giles Hicks to take a team of workmen 'to fell and cut down the woods, trees and coppices of Sir Richard Ducie and Sir Ralph Dutton' (both of whom had been declared royalist delinquents). In May of the same year, John Nicholas of Winterbourne Earls in Wiltshire (and father of the king's Secretary of State) wrote to his grandson. He explained that he had been termed a delinquent and was now in hiding, not daring to stay in his own house after the plundering of his horses and goods by parliamentarian soldiers. 'My house was plundered thrice in a week', he complained, 'and my very wearing apparel taken away by base fellows, whom we could not resist, being so many of them'. (29)

Although Nicholas was clearly a convicted royalist, many of the people who were plundered by parliamentarian soldiers were still in the 'suspect' category and some of them were actually loyal to parliament. This mattered little to troops, whose only real motivation was personal gain. Colonel Massey, for instance, sent Captain Backhouse in February 1644 to raid Sir Ralph Dutton's fields and barns at Standish and Holcombe in Gloucestershire. There was no doubting Dutton's delinquency, for he was Adjutant to the royalist Governor of Oxford. The mission was accomplished and Backhouse later reported his success, proudly claiming that the Gloucester garrison's granary had been filled to last for six months, 'for the corn of Master Guise, Sir Ralph Dutton and others, whom we call malignants, was brought in - indeed by myself'. The only problem was that 'Master Guise' (unlike Dutton) was a man who had supported parliament faithfully and, although he was on the list of suspects, he was eventually cleared of all charges of delinquency (see The Horrors of War 6). Another member of the Gloucester garrison, Captain Matthews, launched further raids on 'suspects' in May 1644 (although both of his victims mentioned below were later released by Massey without charge). Mr Humphreys was attacked by soldiers 'broke open his house and plundered him and his servants of all the wearing clothes they could lay hands on'. His neighbour, Mr Arden, later described how Matthews came to his house with 100 soldiers 'and did take away from him almost all the goods they could carry to the value of near £40'. He was escorted prisoner to Gloucester, where an apologetic Colonel Massey explained that Matthews 'would never leave plundering and that it was his course wheresoever he went'. (30)

One of the worst examples of the plundering of enemy sympathisers involved the inhabitants of Longleat in Wiltshire. They suffered one night of terror in April 1643, when Captain Jones (a member of Sir Edward Hungerford's Wiltshire forces) raided Longleat, breaking open wardrobes and cupboards and carrying off dresses, plumes of feathers, velvet saddles and other luxury goods. According to a newsbook published at the time, this incident was part of a more general round of reprisals organised by Hungerford's force of 700 horse and foot on his return to the county and just before his attack on Wardour Castle. The report claimed that 'their soldiers seized upon Master Arundel's cattle and killed most of his goats on Horningsham Common, and they also got into the park at Longleat and killed some of Sir James Thynne's fallow deer'. Later, after Hungerford had gained the surrender of Wardour from Lady Arundel, his soldiers apparently ran amok inside the castle, destroying a beautiful chimney-piece 'with their pole-axes' and, 'in a wild fury', tearing to pieces a number of rare pictures. Outside, 'they burnt all the out-houses', let loose the two herds of deer, cut down many mature oak and elm trees and dug up the heads of twelve large fish ponds, destroying the fish in the process. Their last act of wanton destruction was to sever the two-mile pipe, which brought fresh water to the house, cutting it up and selling it at six pence a yard. (31)

This sort of conduct was by no means limited to the forces of parliament. An inhabitant of Blakemore Forest, under the shadow of the royalist garrison at Devizes, wrote to her cousin in London in June 1645, describing the 'miserable distracted times' in which they lived. 'I have thought fit to give you a touch of the miserable sad condition of our poor county of Wiltshire; being almost all over distressed with continual vexation of plundering by soldiers of the king's forces. I can hardly express our sad condition...And to add further misery to our country, Colonel Lloyd [Governor of Devizes] with a party of horse and foot...came to Bromham, when they utterly destroyed by fire one of the famousest buildings in these western parts, Sir Edward Baynton's house, a member of parliament; it being a stately fabric of stone, with great store of very rich furniture. Nothing now is left standing but walls and chimneys. I suppose fifty or three-score thousand pounds cannot repair the loss; it is a great grief to our neighbours. When these troubles of quartering, billeting and plundering will cease, I know not'. (32)

At a slightly lower level, royalists forces in Wiltshire began a policy in the spring of 1643 of plundering those who had made financial contributions to parliament. They raided Mr Jenner of Widdell, for instance, and took away from him '16 fat oxen, some horses, 100 sheep, plundered his house, spoiled and carried away his hay, corn, wood and other goods to the value of £800'. Bristol merchant, Richard Locke, had given assistance to the parliamentary garrison during the 1643 siege. When, later, he moved to Bedminster in Somerset with his family for the period of the royalist occupation, royalist troops seized the opportunity to raid his property. Colonel Slingsby's men fired his house and 'burned down his barn and other houses full of corn'. This, together with the cost of plundered goods and household equipment, meant that he sustained a total loss of at least £250. (33)

Quite apart from these perceived enemies, who suffered from spontaneous attacks by troops out in search of plunder, there was another category of sufferers, who lost heavily during the war. These were the 'notorious delinquents' (or major supporters) of both sides, whose estates were duly sequestrated (or confiscated), if they happened to lie within the bounds of enemy territory. County sequestrators were then given the power to sell all their farm produce, equipment and personal effects and to collect the rents from tenants, with the proceeds devoted to the maintenance of local forces (see Chapter 10 for a full description of the system). Although the official sequestrators of both sides usually took their responsibilities seriously, the system was wide open to corruption and abuse by minor officials and army officers, tempted to embezzle goods for their own personal use.

This is well illustrated by one notorious case. Sir John Berkeley of Bruton in Somerset, who had fought actively for the king in the west, was high on parliament's wanted list when they regained control of the area in 1645. His estates were duly sequestrated. However, before the official sequestrators could take action, a certain Mr Foy visited one of the Berkeley farms run for Sir John by Mr Rington. Foy duly seized 20 sheep, 67 'lesser sheep', 8 young beasts, 6 bacon hogs, 4 suckling pigs and other animals at an estimated total value of £192. In his compensation claim, submitted later, Rington also listed: 'all the wool in me loft, which I guess to be 20 weight but cannot confirm, because I do not weigh it till it be sold; but by the number of fleeces which we layed in it before, I believe I lost 20 weight... value £30'. To add to the suspicion, Foy drove hurriedly away with his haul 'without appraising it at all'. It was sometime later that the official sequestrators of the Bruton hundred, Mr Bord and Mr Tibbet, arrived and proceeded to take away 40 loads of wheat, 10 loads of peas, 12 loads of barley, various other foodstuffs and a sum of money, all worth £245 in total. Although Foy's identity is not revealed, it is more than likely that he was sent by parliamentary forces operating in the area. (For a similar incident, see the case of Sir James Long in Chapter 10) (34)

George Trevelyan of Nettlecombe suffered in like fashion. A keen and active supporter of the royalist war effort in Somerset, he was duly sequestrated for his delinquency, but allowed to pay a composition fine of £1,000 in January 1645 to recover his real estate. Thereupon, he was granted 'a protection' of his property by the Somerset Committee to free him from further plunderings. In spite of this, however, he was raided by soldiers shortly afterwards, who 'took away divers of his goods and drove away twelve plough oxen, two fat oxen, one hundred sheep and two horses'. He immediately appealed in desperation to the Committee, who (in March) granted him the authority 'to search for seize and take away the same goods and cattle' with the assistance of local constables in the area.

Sadly, in spite of a prolonged search, he was unable to trace even one of the items which had been plundered or to gain any form of compensation. (35)

Goring's Campaign of Terror

These experiences of people living in the western counties were not unique. Donald Pennington and Ronald Hutton have both drawn attention to the plight suffered by communities throughout the entire country from plundering parliamentarian and royalist troops alike. John Morrill also found evidence of 'systematic plundering' in thirty counties and petitions against the behaviour of soldiers in twenty-two. Certain commanders, including Prince Rupert (see above), gained a reputation for the brutality and extent of outrages committed by their troops. Colonel Nicholas Mynne had landed at Bristol in December 1643 with a regiment of royalist infantry from Ireland. During the next seven or so months, he terrorised the inhabitants wherever he went, 'did rob the country about Stroudwater' and 'plundered to the bare walls' elsewhere. Just before he was killed, fighting Massey's forces at Ridmarley, he was planning to devastate the villages around Gloucester 'with fire and plunder' and 'to burn up the corn on the ground, it being then near harvest'.

In Wiltshire, as the war was ending in 1646, Colonel Massey's brigade of troops ran amok as they awaited disbandment. Bulstrode Whitelocke recalled that, in August, great complaints had been made about his soldiers 'killing men, robbing others and forcing the countrymen, where they quartered, to give them money; and they would then go to other places and do the like there'. Fairfax wrote to the Speaker of the Commons, reporting that the burden on the people there had become intolerable. 'They not only tax the country, but by plunder, robbery and other insolences, do so dishearten and affright the people that it is feared many will quit their habitations, if timely remedy be not applied'. Under this pressure, parliament was stung into voting £6,000 to be rid of them, Fairfax and Ireton going down to Devizes in October to disband the troops with six weeks back pay. (36)

Nevertheless, some of the worst excesses of the war were committed in Somerset in the spring of 1645 by royalist troops under the command of Lord George Goring. On 4th March, the king had sent the young Charles, Prince of Wales, to Bristol as General of the Western Association to co-ordinate the royalist effort. Goring, who had initially based himself on the Somerset/Dorset border with 4,500 troops at Chard and Crewkerne, was eventually appointed overall commander of the king's forces in the west. Although he was by nature an instinctively brilliant general, he was also unreliable, irresponsible and ruthlessly ambitious. Furthermore, he was a massive alcoholic - a point made by Sir Richard Bulstrode, a fervent supporter of the royalist cause: 'After all that can be said in General Goring's behalf, he had likewise his blind side, for he strangely loved the

Lord George Goring, appointed Lieutenant-General of Horse in the king's army in 1644, campaigned in the West in 1645. Portrait from the studio of van Dyke. (By courtesy of Lord Clarendon)

bottle, was much given to his pleasures, and a great debauchee'. To make matters worse, when he was in the west country, he apparently had two chief assistants 'who fed his wild humour and debauch'. This, in consequence, made him 'turn his wantonness into riot and his riot into madness'. The troops followed the example of their leader, who made little attempt to control their behaviour. (37)

Wherever Goring's soldiers went, the villagers and townsfolk lived in a state of perpetual fear. From Chard and Crewkerne in March, his army moved on to assist in the siege of Taunton; in April, his cavalry was based first at Bruton, but later withdrew to Glastonbury and Wells; then, after a brief return to the king in Oxford, they camped at Ilminster in May, before suffering their final defeat at Langport on 10th July at the hands of the New Model Army. For four months, therefore, they terrorised the county. The historian, John Oldmixon, writing ninety years after the event, observed that Goring's forces 'committed so many acts of cruelty and rapine, that his name is infamous there to this day, especially about Taunton, which town he besieged; and during the siege, his soldiers made themselves terrible by continual butcheries, rapes and robberies, insomuch that the name of Goring's Crew is even now remembered with abhorrence'. (38)

When parliament's New Model Army arrived in Somerset they saw with their own eyes the desolation which Goring's men had created. A commander in that army recorded his feelings as they marched towards Taunton in May 1645: 'To see one or two houses ruined in a place had been no great matter; but all the way we marched from Okingham to Taunton , [there was] no place...but you might track the devil by his cloven foot; such devastation of houses, nay depopulations in many places; and those fields, pastures, plains, formerly beautified and enriched with flocks and herds. You may pass ten miles and scarce discern anything: rich pastures, but no cattle left to eat them. You would suppose the great Turk, his Janissaries and armies, rather than their native prince, his soldiers, had been there...The poor people come from all parts, rejoicing,

Charles, Prince of Wales, aged 14 years, at the time when he was appointed commander of the king's western forces with his headquarters in Bristol. Portrait by William Dobson. (By courtesy of the Scottish National Portrait Gallery)

praising God, and thanking us from delivering them from those beasts of prey.' (39)

Sir Edward Hyde, later Earl of Clarendon, was a member of Prince Charles's council in Bristol and therefore witnessed the events of this period at first hand. He recalled in his *History of the Rebellion* that the king's commissioners in Somerset brought in daily complaints against 'the riots and insolences of the Lord Goring's soldiers'. Clarendon emphasised that these terrible disorders simply 'alienated the hearts of those who were best affected to the king's service'. He went on to relate the occasion when, on 2nd June at Wells, a petition was submitted to the prince from 6,000 Somerset Clubmen, who had assembled in protest at Marshal's Elm, near Street. The stated reason for their rising, he said, 'was the intolerable oppression, rapine and violence exercised by the Lord Goring's horse'.

The prince did his best to take Goring to task over this matter, advising him 'to suppress and reform the crying disorders of the army by good discipline and severity upon enormous transgressors'. In a letter to Goring, dated 15th June, the prince outlined the 'great complaints' he had received from the inhabitants on a visit to Dunster, concerning 'the insolencies and injuries' they had sustained from Goring's men. He particularly urged him to check, as a matter of urgency, how many local people still remained as prisoners in the hands of his soldiers, men who had been taken from their homes 'for no reason, but to compel them to redeem themselves for money'. It was all to no avail. According to Bulstrode, the general had no money to pay his troops, so he 'connived at the licence they took'. (40)

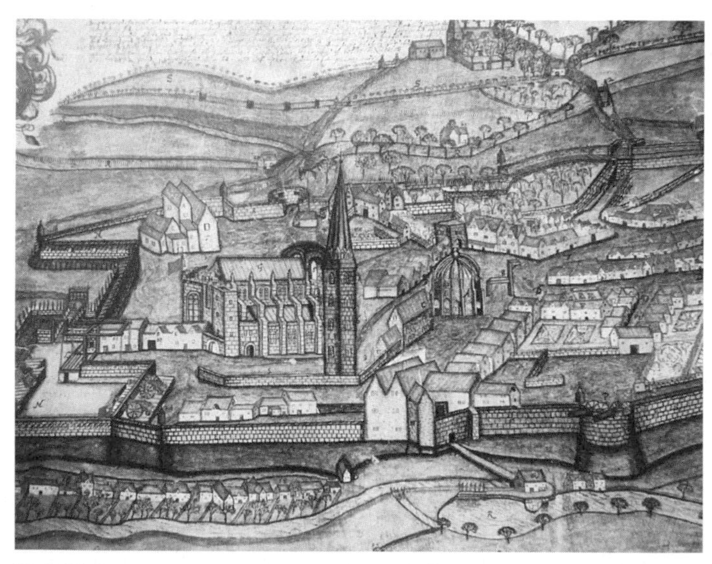

Detail from a contemporary view of the garrison of Malmesbury on 23rd October 1646, the day before the fortifications were demolished - see Chapter 4. (By courtesy of the Warden and Freemen of Malmesbury)

THE HORRORS OF WAR 5

RAMPAGING TROOPS

IN SOUTH BRENT, 1645

On 24th March 1645, a force of sixty royalist cavalry under Colonel Ayscough arrived in South Brent [now Brent Knoll] in Somerset in search of quarters. They stayed there for eleven days, during which time they committed a number of serious atrocities and ruthlessly plundered the inhabitants. They broke into private houses, stealing twenty-five shillings from John Jones and seizing twelve bushels of malt and six yards of cloth from Steven Cock, as well as breaking open all his chests and locks. Worse still, they completely wrecked the contents of Maude Blake's home as they stole quantities of cloth and linen.

Out in the street, three of the soldiers, who were quartering with Henry Simons, spotted a fat bullock being driven into the village by an employee of John Grabhams, who had just bought the beast at Axbridge fair. They immediately seized it and handed it over to Henry Simons's servant (Phillips), ordering him 'to look after it at his peril'. During the night, however, the owner (Grabhams) successfully retrieved the animal. Discovering their loss, the soldiers, in a wild fury, savagely beat up Phillips and 'set a sword to the breast of the said Simons's wife and threatened to run her through, if she would not fetch a rope to hang her man'. The noose was duly tightened around the neck of the terrified Phillips and only released when Henry Simons produced twenty shillings 'to appease their fury'.

Their reign of terror quickly spread to neighbouring villages. They seized twenty horses from the villages of South Brent, East Brent and Burnham; robbed and killed a farm labourer on the highway near Axbridge; plundered John Gilling, a butcher, on his way home from the market; threatened the inhabitants of Lympsham that, when they quartered there, the villagers should lie on straw while the soldiers took their beds; and smashed up William Lush's house in Berrow, threatening to kill his wife and burn his home, if he obstructed the progress of their theft. In Burnham, they not only plundered the house of the tithingman, but also ordered him to produce from the village a large quantity of beans and oats 'on pain of plunder'. Although he hurriedly gathered together what he could, his efforts were greeted with scorn and they threatened 'to tie his neck and heels together, if he brought them not 40s 0d the next morning'.

The local people were so incensed at all this scandalous behaviour that they took part in a spontaneous uprising against Ayscough's men on 4th April. Inspired by John Somerset, a much respected inhabitant of South Brent, the villagers armed themselves with pikes, staves and muskets and launched a surprise assault on their tormentors. Although no life was lost, several soldiers were wounded, including Lieutenant Brown, who was hit in the thigh 'with one musket shot and several smaller shot'. Badly hurt, he sought refuge in the house of Thomas Gilling in South Brent 'from the violence of the mutinous and tumultuous people'. Gilling, however, shut the door in his face, calling out 'be gone, be gone!'

Somerset and Gilling were arrested and imprisoned for several weeks in Bristol. Although they were eventually released after a mass petition from the villagers, additional troops had already been sent to the area to conduct a series of reprisals against the community. A new round of plundering and violence, therefore, took place. In a petition to the king's county commissioners, no fewer than eighty-one inhabitants from the villages of South Brent, Berrow, Burnham and Lympsham listed losses and damage sustained *after* the uprising, estimated at over £687 in value. These items included the theft of money, clothes, animals, household goods and silver plate, as well as damage to property when houses were 'broken up'.

Sources: Collected documents relating to the episode in Henry Symonds (ed.), 'A By-Path of the Civil War', *SANHS*, vol. 65, pt. 2 (Taunton, 1919) pp 49-75; David Underdown, *Somerset in the Civil War and Interregnum* (Newton Abbot, 1973), pp 90-1

The memorial in St Michael's Church, Brent Knoll, to John Somerset (d. 1663). It is thought that he is flanked by his first and second wives. (Author's collection)

CHAPTER 7

Forced to Improvise: The Disruption of Trade

No man dares travel. The country is so full of soldiers. God send a speedy end to these troubles. (John Nicholas of Winterborne Earls, Wiltshire, 1644)

Disruption of shopkeepers in towns

War-time suffering was by no means confined to those living in the countryside. Although farmers tended to be natural targets for troops out in search of supplies and horses, town dwellers also found that their livelihood could quickly be disrupted or even destroyed by the sudden intrusion of war.

Shopkeepers were often the first to suffer when a town was taken by assault. The eye-witness account of the capture of Marlborough by royalists in December 1642 (see The Horrors of War 8) provides a graphic description of the wanton destruction of food and books belonging to specialist dealers in the town. Nor was this an isolated example. Traders in Salisbury experienced a similar fate in December 1644, when royalist forces raided the city and ran amok through the streets. Many lost their entire stock, which was almost impossible to replace, including Ambrose West, draper, whose shop was 'broken up by the soldiers' with estimated losses worth £80; Richard Banks, draper, £200 worth; Mr Rowland, tailor, £30 worth; Robert Johnson, shoemaker, £5 worth in leather boots and 36 pairs of shoes; Peter Williams, mercer, £85 worth; Robert Hartford, innkeeper, over £10 worth in oats, peas, 5 barrels of beer and his 'provision of diet, both dressed and raw'; and Edward Penny, butcher, £2 10s 0d worth 'plundered from me in meats and

The east wall of the Cathedral Close at Salisbury. The remainder of the city was open to attack. (Author's collection)

sheep'. Some craftsmen lost their raw materials, like John Fussell, cobbler, who had a quantity of 'white leather' seized; others the special orders they were completing for customers, like Richard Taylor, whose 'suit of clothes being not quite finished' was snatched from under his nose; and others their implements of trade, like John Page, who was devastated when a soldier carried off all his 'working tools'. (1)

Business life inevitably suffered severe disruption during the course of a siege, and the preparations which took place internally before it. This was due in part to the obligation imposed on all citizens to take their turn in working on the fortifications; and in part to the fear which led many shopkeepers to flee the city before their businesses were subjected to the horrors of rampaging troops. This was certainly the situation in Bristol in July 1643, as the parliamentary garrison awaited the arrival of the royalist army fresh from its success at the Battle of Roundway Down. According to one newspaper reporter: 'The tradesmen and other inhabitants are summoned in by tickets set up in several places to shut up their shops and go forth every Monday, Tuesday and Thursday for the raising of new fortifications...There are at no time but few shops open in the city, for the most part but one in ten, the rest are gone away'. In 1644, it was estimated that so many houses and shops had been abandoned that the Corporation had 'utterly lost' over £200 in rents. (2)

Nevertheless, shopkeepers did not always suffer in this way. When the military situation was more stable (as we shall see later), traders could actually do quite well out of the war. Army quartermasters, who never relied simply on requisitions to supply their needs, were always ready to buy food and clothing for their troops whenever sufficient cash had been generated for them through the taxation system. From the detailed accounts maintained by Colonel John Fiennes, who was captain of a cavalry troop and colonel of an infantry regiment within the Bristol garrison in the summer of 1643, we know that he spent generously with local businessmen. However, such was the changing fortune of war that traders could suddenly be caught out by unpaid debts. Fiennes had authorised the fifty-eight members of his cavalry troop to purchase cloth for new uniforms from six drapers and mercers in the city, together with other necessary items. The goods, which totalled over £180, were bought on credit. Unfortunately, a few days after the soldiers had collected their purchases, Prince Rupert took Bristol by storm. In the resulting confusion, the debts remained unpaid. Fiennes himself was honest enough to list these items for future possible action under a heading of 'money owed to Bristol traders'. Such debts, however, were seldom honoured. Even as late as 1662, John Russell, a butcher in Bath, was still petitioning the city corporation for reimbursement. His complaint was that 'in the last late wars, upon the coming of the King's army into this city, he delivered by the order of the then Mayor and Justices so much beef unto the Constables of this city for provision of the said army as came to the value of three pounds and 15 shillings'. William Thurman, a shopkeeper in Devizes, suffered in a similar manner through the non-payment of debts. Long after the war was over, there were 'several persons' in the county who still owed him 'for the many parcels of wares sold them', totalling £200 in all. At least half of these, however, were incapable of paying, so desperate was their plight 'by reason of these troubles'. (3)

Disruption of Cross-Country Trade

The plight of individual shopkeepers in many towns throughout the West was an inevitable consequence of civil war. Of even greater importance to the economy of the western counties, however, was the severe dislocation of trade across the area caused by military activity. Trade along the Severn Valley to Bristol and Exeter could be cut at will by the Gloucester garrison (held by parliament throughout the war). Similarly, traders journeying to London from the West could easily be intercepted for much of the war by royalist garrisons along the Upper Thames Valley, including Reading and Wallingford. This situation presented both king and parliament with something of a dilemma. On the one hand, each wished to prevent the enemy from gaining valuable supplies from traders (particularly weapons of war). On the other hand, the economy of the locality from which the merchants were drawn was greatly dependent on the successful maintenance of trade. Any substantial decline would result in widespread unemployment, which would seriously affect the capacity of local people to pay their war-time taxes. Both sides therefore hesitated initially to disrupt commercial activity, apart from a blockade of ports by parliament to prevent the supply of arms to the king. Indeed, on 8th December 1642, Charles issued a proclamation deploring the fact that west countrymen travelling to London with cloth had been stopped - an action which he feared would penalise those loyal to his cause, as well as those more hostile. He therefore ruled that merchants in future were to have 'free and uninterrupted passage'. (4)

Official policy, however, was not always implemented by garrison commanders, who often viewed the merchants' convoy as something of a soft target. West country clothiers probably suffered more than most as they headed across hotly disputed territory in Wiltshire and Berkshire to their main markets in London. On 16th March 1643, for instance, one such convoy of 8 cart loads and 24 horse loads of broad cloth (amounting to 380 cloths in all), organised by John Ashe of Freshford in North Somerset, was seized by Sir Arthur Aston, the royalist Governor of Reading. He alleged that Ashe was attempting to smuggle weapons of war to the capital, for a search had uncovered a number of items used by musketeers secreted inside the packs. Parliament immediately protested to the king's committee in Oxford and demanded the return of the cloth. Charles complied by ordering the release of all the goods seized by the Reading garrison to their owners, except those belonging to Ashe (who was by now marked out as a leading figure in the rebellion in the West). (5)

From 'The Groot Boeck' of accounts kept by the Ashe firm in London between April 1640 and February 1643, we know that trade from north Somerset was certainly disrupted during the early months of the war. Whereas John Ashe had regularly sent a convoy up to London once a week until the end of October 1642, there were no deliveries at all from Freshford in November, only one in December and two in February. There is also an indication that the problem he faced was with delivery rather than production because, whereas he had been dispatching an average of fourteen cloths a week from his own workshops, he suddenly sent fifty in one batch in December followed by a further forty-eight in the January consignment. He had clearly been stock-piling until the situation improved. The 380 cloths which were seized by the Reading garrison in March were not all owned by Ashe himself. He was the organiser of this weekly convoy to his brother's shop in London, a convoy which also catered for neighbouring clothiers among his family and friends. There is little doubt that the disruption experienced by Ashe in November 1642 was the result of the king's abortive attempt to regain London. The Thames Valley suddenly became alive with military activity. Advancing with his army from Oxford, Charles reached Reading on 4th November before sending Prince Rupert out to take Brentford by storm eight days later. After the Earl of Essex had blocked his advance at Turnham Green, the king withdrew to Reading on 19th November before establishing winter quarters in Oxford. The route from London to Somerset, which was far too perilous for traders to use during those four frantic weeks, continued to be fraught with difficulty until the royalist garrison finally abandoned Reading on 18th May 1644. (6)

As the war progressed, both sides gradually reversed their policy over freedom of movement for traders. In January 1643, parliament prohibited carriers from taking their goods to Oxford or elsewhere 'without special licence'. The king retaliated in July by stipulating that trade with London was prohibited, although subjects would still have the freedom to trade elsewhere. A further proclamation in October, however, extended the ban to Gloucester as well as London, warning of the severest penalties for those who disobeyed. Loyal subjects were encouraged to seize goods transported in contravention of this order, offering a reward of one-third of the value. (7)

These measures seriously hit the livelihood of west country clothiers, who had traditionally relied on the market at Backwell Hall in London as an outlet for most of their goods. Such was their distress that the Gloucestershire clothiers sent a petition to the king in August 1643, outlining their situation. On the one hand, the war had caused the loss of much of their property; on the other, the ban on travel to London prevented them not only from finding a market for their cloth, but also from reclaiming stocks of cloth and money held for them there by London merchants. In reply, the king agreed to let 'the well-affected' travel to London to bring back their property. Furthermore, he would make arrangements for the sale of their cloth elsewhere by negotiating with Bristol merchants to export goods on their behalf and ordering the treasury to buy up as much of the Gloucestershire cloth as possible.

These ideas did little in practice to relieve their distress. In May 1644, a delegation of west country clothiers put forward their case to the king and his council in Oxford. Charles, however, rejected their compromise proposal for a 'free market' to be set up in Reading, where they could sell their cloths to the merchants of London. He urged them instead to concentrate their trade on 'the western parts', which he controlled (and where he could, of course, benefit from the lucrative new excise tax, imposed on the sale of goods). In spite of their lack of enthusiasm for this plan, he ordered that 'the cities of Exeter and Bristol should be appointed by proclamation to be from henceforth the public mart towns for cloth and other woollen manufactures'. The mayors of those cities were to make all the necessary practical arrangements and his army commanders were to ensure that clothiers were unmolested as they transported their goods there.

The plan failed miserably, due in part to the fact that the Gloucester garrison, parliamentarian throughout the war, continued to block trade along the Severn valley. As a result, the clothiers maintained their pressure on the king, who eventually gave way by agreeing to issue special licences to individual traders in cases of particular suffering. This relaxing of restrictions therefore opened up again the possibility of renewed trade with London, a hope which became much more of a reality with the fall of both Beverstone Castle and Malmesbury to parliament in May 1644. According to John Corbet, the fall of Beverstone (brought about after the Governor, Captain Oglethorpe, had been captured 'in a private house, courting his mistress') resulted in the great benefit of freeing 'the clothiers of Stroudwater from the bondage and terror' of the castle's garrison, thus releasing them to trade more confidently. A contemporary observer noted that the taking of Malmesbury was a serious setback to the king's plans, partly because it put a serious block on trade between the West and Oxford and partly because 'the trade of clothing [was] opened from those parts to London'.

Beverstone Castle; garrisoned by the king in 1642, but captured by Massey's Gloucester garrison in 1644. (Author's collection)

Indeed, he had heard a report that 'there are upon the way now coming out of Wiltshire towards London thirteen wains laden with woollen cloth, which will be welcome to the merchants and drapers here, and other wares and commodities will be sent and returned from London into the country'. (8)

However, even when officials turned a blind eye and trade began to flow again, merchants were still obliged to contend with the individual whims of local garrison commanders as they made their way along the hazardous route to the capital. The Earl of Clarendon admitted in his *History of the Rebellion* that the king's policy was frequently undermined by 'particular governors, who, having garrisons near great roads, received large tolls for their safe conducts and protection, and sometimes very great seizures of such goods as thought to have escaped their attention'. The truth of this was experienced only too well by several convoys of west country merchants bound for London in 1645. One such group from Gloucestershire, escorted along side roads by over sixty parliamentarian cavalry from the Gloucester garrison, was intercepted in March by royalist troops from Banbury, losing 72 wool packs in the process. In another incident during the spring of that year, a large company of Wiltshire clothiers had taken the precaution of making a prior agreement about their safe conduct to London with Sir John Boys, royalist Governor of Donnington Castle. In return for a payment of three pounds per wagon, he guaranteed that they would be unmolested. However, as they approached Marlborough, they were intercepted and captured by a group of cavalry from the garrison at Basing House. When news of this reached General Massey, Governor of Gloucester, he immediately despatched a force of two hundred cavalry, who secured the release of the unfortunate clothiers.

Probably the worst example of extortion of this kind, however, occurred in May 1645 when a party of merchants set out from Devizes in Wiltshire. They had made an agreement with the royalist Governor, Sir Charles Lloyd, that they would pay a sum of over £400 in excise duty once they had sold their cloth in London and had returned safely with their teams. Passing safely through Marlborough, they were suddenly halted just outside Newbury by Sir John Boys with troops from the garrison at Donnington Castle. He brushed aside their protests and the agreement they had already reached in Devizes, insisting that he had just as much right as Lloyd to collect the excise duty and that he required the tax immediately. The clothiers were therefore forced to borrow the money from their friends in Newbury, before they were allowed to proceed on their journey. Their troubles, however, were by no means ended. No sooner had they left Newbury, than they were seized by royalist troops under Colonel Blake, Governor of Wallingford Castle, who immediately impounded their cargo and detained them for several days. Furthermore, 'the troopers searched the clothiers' pockets and took from them every penny they had'. Their release was only secured by the promise of a further £10 on each pack of cloth. When eventually they reached London, they estimated that

Sir John Boys (1607-64), royalist governor of Donnington Castle in 1645. (By courtesy of the Ashmolean Museum, Oxford. Photograph: Photographic Survey, Courtauld Institute of Art)

they had lost a third of the total value of their goods. (9)

The cloth trade as a whole was badly hit in the western counties by the disruption of war. Crippling taxation, heavy tolls, perilous trade routes, irregular markets and the departure of workers to the wars all played their part in plunging the industry into a state of severe depression by 1647. Even when the war finally ended, the ancient weavers of Westbury and Devizes in Wiltshire were to find that new attitudes threatened the very heart of their operation. In a petition to the magistrates, they complained that apprentices returning from the wars no longer felt obliged to heed the statutes which regulated the trade. They observed that many apprentices had 'in these disordered times and contrary to their duty, forsaken their parents and masters under the colour of following the wars'; furthermore, now that the war was over, they had not only refused to complete their apprenticeships, but had also proceeded to get married even before the age of twenty and had had the audacity to set themselves up with their own looms. Such were the unsettling effects of war. (10)

Nor were clothiers the only traders to suffer dislocation as a result of the conflict. In May 1644, Colonel Massey's troops, operating near Chippenham in Wiltshire, seized 'seven wains or wagons laden with sack and other wines, going from Bristol to Oxford'. Then, in January 1645, some more of his soldiers intercepted a convoy of carriages in the Forest of Dean 'and took from them two wagons laden with cider'. In 1643, Sir Samuel Luke noted in his diary that the king's garrison in Marlborough had 'stayed all the wains that shall come that way out of the west country with cheese and other things and have taken away all their commodities'. He also recorded that 'two wagons of salt and two of wine', which were destined for the king in Oxford (where salt was exceptionally scarce) were seized by parliamentarian troops in Wiltshire.

Even if their cargo was of no interest to the soldiers, carriers were always in grave danger of losing their animals, an enormous blow to their livelihood. Luke highlighted an incident in March 1643, for instance, when royalist forces 'took away 30 carriers' horses going into Wiltshire and three wains with 18 head of cattle and carried them into Reading'. The perilous situation in the western counties in 1644 is best summed up by comments made in letters written by men on the spot. 'The times have been dangerous for travelling in these parts', complained Richard Green in

Troops intercept a convoy of clothiers' goods. (Line drawing by Stephen Beck)

a letter to Sir Edward Nicholas. John Nicholas was even more pessimistic when writing to his grandson. Communication of all kind was difficult, he said, 'all passages being stopped...No man dares travel, the county is so full of soldiers. God for his great mercy, send a speedy end to these troubles'. (11)

Disruption of Overseas Trade and River Traffic

Although most farm produce and manufactured goods travelled to market by road, merchants in the western counties were also heavily involved in overseas trade through the ports of Bristol, Gloucester, Minehead, Bridgwater and Dunster. This, too, was liable to severe disruption throughout the Civil War. The Society of Merchant Venturers in Bristol, which had been established in 1552, had received a new charter from Charles I in 1639. A wealthy and influential group, which dominated membership of the city's Corporation, it petitioned both king and parliament in 1642, expressing alarm at the disastrous consequences of war on its trade: 'Our ships now lie rotting in the harbour without any mariners or freight or trade into foreign parts, by reason of our home-bred distractions, being grown so contemptible and despised there, that our credit is of no value'. (12)

Parliament controlled the navy and with it the seas. In December 1643, in an attempt to prevent merchant vessels trading with royalist ports, an Ordinance was issued empowering an individual to 'equip and man a private vessel of war at his own expense' and then to seize any ship which was sailing from or to a port in enemy hands. These so-called 'adventurers' were granted the right, once the case against the impounded ship had been proved, to retain both ship and contents for their own profit. 'The Tiger', bound for Marseilles in February 1644, was one such vessel to fall prey to this system. Its cargo, organised by Henry Gough of Bristol (the factor), consisted of goods supplied by two merchants, Giles Dunster (22 bales of calf skins and 36 pigs of lead, valued at £503) and John Holworth (37 barrels of calf skins, 22 casks of tallow and 84 pigs and 24 bars of lead, valued at £190). The ship sailed out of the port of Bristol, then under the control of a royalist garrison, and was almost immediately seized by adventurers in the Severn estuary. Its entire cargo was confiscated and sold in accordance with the Ordinance. (13)

Adventurers, however, were not alone responsible for the decline in overseas trade, which was reflected in the sharp decline in customs revenue collected at the port of Bristol in 1644. The plight of Richard Locke, a member of the Society of Merchant Adventurers, illustrates vividly the range of misfortunes that could strike a ship owner, undermining not only his own livelihood, but also the livelihoods of all those who produced, transported and supplied his cargo. His ship, 'The Reformation', with twenty pieces of ordnance on board, was twice requisitioned in 1643 by Colonel Fiennes (parliamentary Governor of Bristol) to patrol the Severn

Sir John Pennington, Royalist Admiral, who assembled a fleet of captured ships at Bristol. (By courtesy of Bristol Central Library)

estuary and protect the harbour against a predicted attack by royalist troops. Later in the year, after Bristol had fallen to the king, Locke's ship was again requisitioned by the royalist Admiral, Sir John Pennington (who was in the process of building up a new royalist fleet based on Bristol), to transport soldiers from Dublin to Liverpool. These serious interruptions to his work, all undertaken at his own expense, cost him £700 in cash and eight months in trading time. To compound his misery, in the following year, he chartered his ship (valued at £1,000) to a Bristol merchant for trade with the West Indies, only to hear that it had been seized *en route*, confiscated and sold by royalist leaders.

Having lost his own vessel, 'The Reformation', Locke then became an adventurer in 1644, using other merchants' ships. He first traded in 'The Marigold' between Bristol and Cadiz, but 'was surprised in the River Severn by some of the parliament's frigates', losing his entire cargo of wine and tobacco. He then switched to 'The James', but again 'going down the River of Severn, was taken by the parliament's ships, where he lost in Newfoundland fish above £250'. Given the opportunity, he was clearly happy to deal in a wide range of goods. However, his substantial trade in tobacco was badly hit, not just by seizure on the high seas, but by what he called 'that unhappy monopoly of Lord Goring's practices'. Locke, on landing his tobacco in Bristol, had apparently been forbidden to sell it on the open market. Instead, he had been forced to supply it exclusively at fixed cut-price rates to officers in Goring's royalist army. Locke estimated that this has cost him over £4,000 in profit. (14)

Merchant shipping, which was usually well armed for its own protection, was always vulnerable to the covetous desires of garrison commanders and city councils. In December 1642, Bristol Corporation, seeking to build up the city's defences, authorised its water bailiffs to seize the ordnance from all the ships in the river. This was followed two months later by another order, instructing all owners of ships in the port to bring their ordnance into the city. In December 1643, after royalist forces had seized control, Shershaw Cary, a Bristol merchant, arrived in the port with his ship, 'The Elephant and Castle', packed with goods from St. Lucia. However, before he could unload, 'the ship and all belonging to her was seized upon by the king's party... and eight of her best guns taken from her and were placed about the [earth]works of the city in several places'. His ship, which was used by the garrison to patrol the estuary, was not returned to him for nine months, even though he went over to Bath in person 'to solicit His Majesty about it'. (15)

In addition to roads and seas, traders also made considerable use of the river Severn as a main thoroughfare linking Bristol with Gloucester, Tewkesbury, South Wales, Worcester and Warwickshire. Although large vessels could not sail up the river beyond Bristol, goods of all kinds were transported in flat-bottomed barges (or trows). Needless to say, this route was just as liable to blockage or attack as the roads and the seas. From his stronghold in Gloucester, Colonel Massey could easily control the passage of produce and materials up and down the river, especially to deprive the garrison at Bristol after its fall to the royalists in 1643. Similarly, Sir John Winter, from his royalist bases in the Dean Forest at Lydney and Beachley, could make life difficult for the Gloucester garrison in maintaining its supplies. In February 1644, he put forward half the cost of 'a pinnace of his to be employed for guarding the River of Severn'. The Society of Merchant Venturers and Bristol Corporation together made up the rest of the money, a clear sign that trade in and out of Bristol via the river was of vital importance to their livelihood. This move by Winter was almost certainly in response to the fact that Massey had already launched a 'frigate' on the river in the previous year to protect his supplies. The treasurer of the Gloucester garrison had paid out a total of £11 12s 6d to carpenters, sawyers, blacksmiths and nailors 'employed in building the frigate on the Governor's orders'.

Earlier in 1643, Massey had attempted to strike a remarkable deal with Sir William Russell, the royalist Governor of Worcester, who had put an embargo on the movement of all goods by river between Worcester and Gloucester, including some that were already stuck in a trow in Worcester waiting for permission to sail. Massey had therefore written to Russell suggesting an agreement between them that 'there might be free commerce and trade (ammunition excepted)' along the Severn and that he would let their boats pass, if Russell would adopt a similar policy. Nothing, however, came of the proposal. Nevertheless, Massey was still able to maintain a valuable trade along the river in 1643 between Gloucester and both Tewkesbury and Bristol (i.e. before its fall to the royalists). The treasurer of his garrison made frequent payments for 'sixteen boatmen that were employed on service to Tewkesbury', 'weighing and stacking of coals that came from Tewkesbury', 'the boatmen for bringing the ordnance from Bristol', 'boatmen that brought corn and salt from Tewkesbury', 'the 16 boatmen that brought hay from Mr Freeman's of Bushby', 'the bargemen and watermen that brought a barge laden with glass from Tewkesbury' and 'another barge laden with corn for the garrison from Tewkesbury'. (16)

Benefits of War to the Local Economy

Not all businessmen and traders, however, lost out as a result of the war. There is clear evidence that some craftsmen and manufacturers, for instance, reaped substantial rewards during these years as armies moved around the west country in search of uniforms, equipment and weapons. In Bristol, the Council submitted to the king's demand in September 1644 by providing 1,500 pairs of shoes and stockings from local craftsmen, even though they were paid for by means of a weekly levy on the populace. Similarly, the city of Wells was ordered in July 1644 to stand the cost of a supply of horse-shoes, made by local smiths for the king's artillery train; and, two months later, 500 pairs of shoes and stockings, which were to be stored in the Town Hall ready for collection.

The metal workers in Bristol quickly adapted to the needs of war and the city therefore became a valuable centre for arms manufacture. Richard Marsh, keeper of the king's stores of ordnance there in 1645, realised the enormous potential of the situation. In a letter to Sir Edward Nicholas, the Secretary of State, he emphasised that there was no lack of either materials or skilled workmen to produce a vast store of weapons: 'If constant payment were settled, I would undertake to arm for His Majesty 20,000 men a year, viz. 15,000 muskets and bandoliers, and 5,000 pikes'. Only lack of regular finance prevented him from achieving this objective. Although, at that moment in time, the Bristol craftsmen were owed a total of £1,200, there is nevertheless evidence to suggest that they gained handsomely from the needs of war over the period as a whole. At the beginning of 1644, for instance, Marsh wrote a letter to the General of His Majesty's Train of Artillery, in which he described how he had contracted one of six gunsmiths resident in the city to manufacture 200 muskets and 200 sets of bandoliers a week at a cost of £210. He had also made agreements with other suppliers in both Wells and Bristol to make up to 15 barrels of gunpowder a week at £5 per barrel (each barrel containing 100 lbs of powder) and to produce drums at £1 3s 0d each. Furthermore, a plumber had undertaken 'to cast one ton [of musket shot] by Thursday next' at the rate of £16 per ton. The workers who benefited from these contracts were only too happy to be provided with work. Most could not afford the luxury of political scruples and were therefore prepared to work for either king or parliament when opportunity arose. (17)

Indeed, according to an account prepared by Alderman Richard Aldworth, the local armaments industry had already supplied the parliamentary garrison with major resources in five months at the start of 1643. These included 120 barrels of gunpowder, 90 corslets, 148 swords, 149 belts, 100 pikes, 388 muskets, 201 pairs of bandoliers and musket rests, 72 hundredweight of musket bullets, plus panniers, spades and pickaxes for use on the fortifications. The total paid by the Council for all these items was £1,469 3s 5d, a most welcome addition to the income of local people. Other workers, too, benefited from the war effort at a time when the city was anxious to improve its defences. Carpenters, smiths, plumbers, masons, turf-layers and labourers were all called upon to provide expertise in strengthening walls and building earthworks - and were paid for doing so. Scouts and spies were also recruited to gain intelligence of enemy movements. All-in-all, a sum of over £3,000 was injected into the local economy during this five-month period - a considerable boost to a community suffering from the pressures of taxation and free quarter. Similar benefits were also experienced by the local workforce in Gloucester both before and after the siege (see Chapter 8). [18]

When the royalists took Bristol in the summer of 1643, the king himself issued two warrants from the city in August to Francis Walker, an ironmaster from Gloucestershire. Walker, who had previously supplied the royalist armies with munitions, was now commissioned to supply 'a considerable number of pieces of artillery' for the better defence of Bristol. He was urged to use his forges to cast '10 culverin, 10 demi-culverin and 10 sakers very well fortified' and to send them down the river Severn. He was also instructed to provide 'such quantities of round iron shot' as he could produce in different sizes for the cannon and to dispatch them to 'the offices of our ordnance' in Bristol. 'Full and speedy payment' was promised.

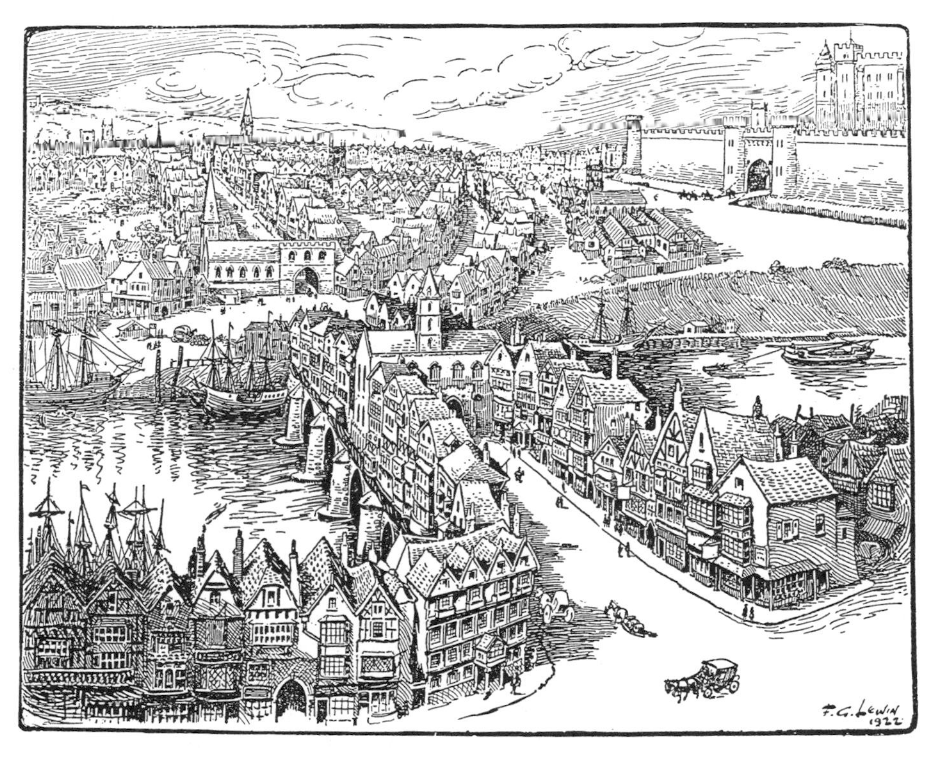

Bristol Bridge in the 17th century, giving access from the south to the inner, walled area and castle. The river Avon was always busy with trading vessels. A drawing by F.G. Lewin (1922). (By courtesy of the Bristol Central Library)

The iron used in this task almost certainly came from the Forest of Dean, where sixteen foundries, many of them owned by Sir John Winter of Lydney, produced high-quality pig iron of the type needed in the manufacture of armaments. Much of it was sent up the Severn to the forges and workshops of Warwickshire and Worcestershire, although some forges had also been set up in the Forest. Indeed, at the siege of Gloucester, the royalist army was supplied with 400 cannon balls produced at the Sowdley furnace. This contribution to the war effort gave a most welcome fillip to the employment of miners, foresters, metal workers and carriers in an area which was generally impoverished.

During the years of royalist occupation (1643-45), Bristol also became a major centre for the collection and storage of armaments manufactured alsewhere in the West, as well as those imported from France; and for their subsequent distribution to other garrisons held by the king's forces, including Oxford. Furthermore, the city was in addition established as an important administrative centre, which witnessed the setting up of a mint by Thomas Bushell (with authority to coin £100 a week); a printing press by Christopher Baker (with the task of producing books, pamphlets and official documents); and a tax office to deal with the growing list of taxes, including customs and excise duties. Each of these new areas of activity demanded a team of clerks, assistants, storekeepers, messengers and carters - many of whom would have been recruited from the local community. (19)

Exactly the same sort of benefits and opportunities presented themselves to people living outside the major garrison towns. For instance, the villages in rural Wiltshire in the area surrounding Chalfield Manor were also called upon to provide services and supplies for the parliamentarian garrison in residence there during six months in 1645. Quite apart from the taxes they paid in kind (i.e. by sending in foodstuffs or contributing labour on the fortifications in lieu of cash payments - see Chapter 4), local craftsmen, farmers and labourers were also paid for specific items or hired to assist the garrison in various ways. Indeed, out of total tax collection of £547 received *in cash*, the Collector (William Tarrant) actually ploughed back almost a quarter of it (£130) into the local economy. Half of this sum was spent on buying in additional food from individual villagers, including capons, pigeons, codfish, eggs, butter, oats, beer, fruit, salads, tobacco, spices, mustard, vinegar and malt.

Money was additionally spent on a whole range of materials from outside dealers, including a large supply of paper 'to make cartridges', pitch and tar ('to mend the boat to fish the moat'), 'Venice glasses' for the Governor and shrouds for those who died. Large numbers of craftsmen were brought in to place their expertise at the garrison's service - glaziers, coopers, tinkers, saddlers, brewers, tilers, plumbers, joiners and basket workers ('to make the cannon and musket baskets'). Perhaps the greatest demand, however, was for gunsmiths and metal workers to fix '25 muskets bought of country men', to supply pistols, to mend the drawbridge and to repair 'the cook's jack' or 'boiling furnace'. Men were employed 'to watch and fodder the oxen', to look after the sheep, 'to see to the hay and keep it from spoiling', to labour on the fortifications and 'to bury the garbage about the house'. Women were taken on to cook in the kitchen, to wash the table linen and to nurse sick soldiers. A local surgeon was also brought in regularly, receiving fees for his consultations and cash for his medicines. In addition to all this, both men and women were used on a regular basis to act as messengers, guides and spies, including one man who 'sought out cattle and gave intelligence of them' (presumably in a royalist controlled area). Garrison forces, therefore, did not simply plunder the countryside at will, living off the land at the sole expense of the inhabitants. Where taxes had been paid and money was available, governors were usually quite content to purchase their requirements from local tradesmen, patronise neighbouring markets and employ village craftsmen. When this happened, the community benefited greatly. (20)

Armies on the march also depended in part on the willingness of local people to offer their services for reward. When Colonel Massey, for instance, made sorties from Gloucester to Ross-on-Wye and Malmesbury, he relied heavily on paid labour from the villages he passed through. His accounts for May 1644 list, among many, payments for 'those that watched the draught horses', 'watching the ammunition wagon 2 nights', 'shoeing the draught horses', 'a carpenter for helping the wheelwright', 'one that brought hemp', 'the plough drivers which carried the hemp', 'the wagon hauliers and drawers' and 'the ox drawers, which helped to draw the piece' [i.e. the large cannon]. Quite apart from these farm labourers, carpenters, blacksmiths and carriers, Massey also bought from a local shopkeeper '11 quire of paper to make cartridges' [i.e. for the musketeers] and '6 ounces of thread', at the same time supplying 'drink for those that made the cartridges'. He was always very quick to reward his helpers with alcohol - the carpenter and the wheelwright were given 'fresh liquor', while those who had hauled the large cannon were given a celebratory drink 'at their parting'. Army officers, therefore, did not always resort to plundering the local community on their travels. (21)

Bath's Booming Health Trade

Those who became adaptable to changing circumstances were often able to survive or even to boost their income. This was certainly true for those involved in the health trade in Bath, where the hot water springs, recently refurbished by the Corporation, had already revived the city's reputation as a first-class resort by the outbreak of war in 1642. Business, however, was hit badly once hostilities had commenced, partly because many of its regular clients had already joined the king in York. A newspaper reporter commented: 'The inhabitants of Bath express great griefs that they have had little company this summer...The poor guides are now necessitate to guide one another to the ale-house, lest they should lose their practice. The

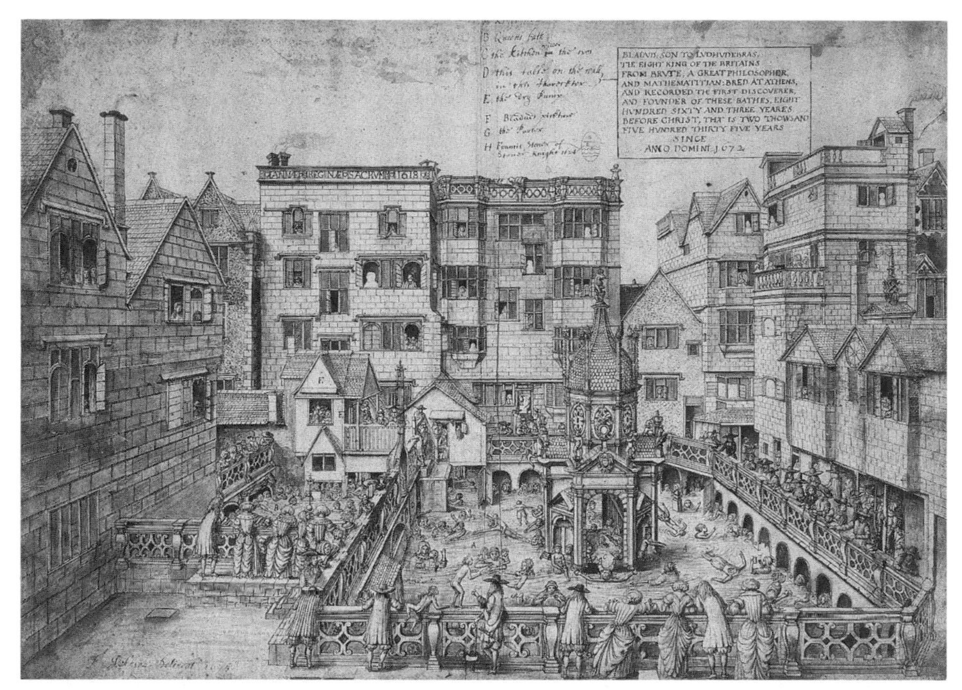

The King's Bath in Bath, a drawing by Thomas Johnson (1675). The vigorous social life depicted here lay at the heart of Bath's success as a flourishing health resort, served by the many lodging houses which surrounded the baths.
(© The British Museum)

ladies that are there are fallen into a lethargy for want of stirring cavaliers to keep them awake...The poor fiddlers are ready to hang themselves in their strings for a pastime for want of other employments'. (22)

In spite of this initial setback, however, business quickly revived as the city began to adjust to changing circumstances by catering for a different type of clientele. Those who now flocked into the city included wounded soldiers looking for a cure for their mutilated limbs. For instance, Lord George Goring arrived for a few days in April 1645 in the hope of curing 'his lameness'. However, perhaps the best example of this is the case of Sir Gervase Scrope in April 1644. The king felt so strongly that only the waters of Bath could revive his valiant servant, who then lay wounded in enemy hands, that he even arranged to send a hostage to gain his temporary release while treatment was given. 'His Majesty is informed from London', wrote one correspondent, 'that Sir Gervase Scrope's extreme indisposition of body, occasioned by his wounds is such, as according to his physicians, in probability nothing but the present use of the Bath can relieve him'. The king therefore offered Scroope's son as a hostage to gain a permit for his wounded friend through enemy lines unhindered. (23)

Bath also gained heavily as a health resort from the large number political and military leaders who chose to be based there, rather than in

Bristol (even though the latter was established as the military headquarters for both sides in turn). Unlike Bath, which had abundant supplies of fresh spring water piped into the city from the surrounding hills, Bristol was regarded as an unpleasant and unhealthy place - with good reason! During the time of royalist occupation, refuse was left to accumulate in the streets with ever-increasing stench. 'The city itself is now so nasty and filthy', wrote one observer, 'that a traveller that comes out of the fresh air can scarce endure it'. Epidemics thrived in these conditions, especially when drinking water was pumped up out of the river during time of drought. Both King Charles and his son, therefore, preferred the purer air of Bath, where at least the water was uncontaminated. In 1645, for instance, a report reached London from Bristol that ' the sickness increases fearfully in this city...[so that] the Prince is resolved to remove upon Monday to Bath'. Sir Thomas Fairfax, Major-General Skippon and General Cromwell were all to follow in his footsteps later in the year and were duly honoured on arrival by the Council with gifts of wine and sugar. Bath's exceptional fortune in remaining an essentially healthy city throughout the period of the war was enormously beneficial to its prosperity as a spa. Many places, including Bristol, suffered frequently from the scourge of the bubonic plague, which devastated the population and ruined trade. Bristol in fact had already lost a sixth of its population on three separate occasions between 1565 and 1603 from major epidemics. (24)

Bath therefore remained a bustling and vigorous centre, attracting a large number of distinguished guests in its inns and lodging houses. The fortifications remained intact; buildings were not burnt down on the pretext of military necessity (as at Marlborough, Bristol, Gloucester and Cirencester); and there was little evidence of wanton vandalism. Charles Paman, visiting Bath in 1646, commented on the fact that it had survived the war pretty well unscathed: 'For Mars made it not his house, but thoroughfare, and rather baited than dwelt here'. Under these favourable conditions, its shopkeepers and craftsmen thrived as they continued to cater for an ever-increasing consumer society. The markets also remained open throughout the war - a sure sign of stable economic activity. The Council was most punctilious about appointing its ale-tasters and supervisors of fish and meat on a regular basis; the market house was kept in good repair; the common was tightly regulated, enabling cattle to graze and hay to be gathered. All-in-all, the citizens of Bath would certainly have concurred with the advice given to the Mayor of Chester in 1644 urging him 'to have a special eye to the preservation of the market'. They were only too well aware that their existence depended upon it. (25)

The Disruption of Markets

Not all places were as fortunate as Bath. Markets and fairs were often disrupted through sieges, sudden attacks or the transit of troops in search of plunder. Unstable market conditions were particularly to be found in those towns which frequently changed hands during the war (like Malmesbury); the 'open' towns which lacked strong defences (like Marlborough or Chippenham); or those which lay on the main route across a county (like Devizes in Wiltshire). In Bristol, for instance, the St James's tide fair, a great annual event, was not held at all in 1644, thus depriving the Sheriffs of their traditional rents from booths and stalls. The Corporation therefore granted them £50 'in respect of their great loss'. Revenues from lettings at fairs in Stow-on-the-Wold also fell dramatically during the war. Whereas John Chamberlayne had received £77 from these in 1641, total income slumped to a mere £1 0s 6d in 1643 - and the fair of 1644 was cancelled due to an outbreak of plague spread by soldiers. Even by 1645, the takings had only reached a modest £5 10s 7d.

Markets were affected in exactly the same way as fairs. In 1646, for example, Tobias Allen, who had rented space in the market at Devizes in Wiltshire for the sale of yarn and wool, complained to the Corporation 'that by reason of the unnatural war', which had occurred during the time of his tenancy, 'the market was much unfrequented and thereby he was disabled to make up his rent out of the profits'. Saturday markets in Marlborough, which provided a vital outlet for the goods of local farmers, were seriously disrupted in June 1645. Major Dowett's royalist cavalry regiment, based on Devizes, adopted the despicable practice of lying in wait on the downs throughout the previous night, so that they were well-placed to intercept the produce of countryfolk on their way to market. (26)

The case of Thomas Hannyball of Mere in Wiltshire indicates the alarming vulnerability of all those who travelled with their goods to market. A mason by trade, he had found himself unemployed 'by reason of this present war'. However, showing great initiative in an attempt to support his family, he had set himself up as a trader in cheese, buying it at one market and selling it on at another. All went well until on one occasion, as he set out for market, he was accosted by the two constables of Mere, who seized from him 'two hundred of ordinary cheese at the price of 16s a hundred'. He had in fact bought the cheese on credit with a promise to pay the suppliers after he had sold it at market. The constables (who had clearly received an instant demand for supplies from royalist forces) ordered him to take the cheese with three horses to the king's garrison at Faringdon. In a petition to the Quarter Sessions, Hannyball complained that he had never been paid for the cheese, the loss of eight days work (caused by the journey to Faringdon) or the cost of feeding the three horses *en route*. As a result, he was totally impoverished. (27)

Garrison commanders lived in dread that country markets would be closed down, thus depriving them of a vital supply of additional produce of the type so greatly appreciated at Chalfield. Market traders, in constant fear of being ambushed, could easily be discouraged from visiting the markets at all or terrorised into not supplying the enemy. Furthermore, if they lived in an area under the firm control of either king or parliament, the markets themselves would also be controlled and denied to the opposition. Colonel Edward Massey, Governor of Gloucester, expressed these fears in October 1643 in a letter to the Earl of Essex. The royalists, he said, had not only occupied Tewkesbury and Sudeley, but also intended 'to lie at' Stroud, Painswick, Cheltenham, Newnham, Mitcheldean and Newent. This would have the effect of strangling his own garrison's source of supply. 'The country already dare not or will not look upon us', he complained, 'being also likely to lose our markets, since we are not able to defend them from the enemy's seizure'. According to John Corbet, immediately after they had survived the siege in 1643, 'the enemy actually lay at our doors, commerce was clean taken away, and we a far distance from the fountain of our future supplies'. Massey did his best to release this stranglehold by sending out 'strong parties to maintain our markets and encourage that part of the country which is yet clear'. He only managed, however, to extend his command to a band of no more than three to seven miles around the city. (28)

In order to overcome the problem being experienced by Massey, some commanders of garrisons and field armies adopted active policies to encourage farmers to supply them with their produce. In February 1643, for instance, the king issued a proclamation in which he guaranteed 'free and safe resort to the markets of Cirencester', which would be held every Monday, Wednesday and Friday. Officers and soldiers were warned not to interfere in any way with this trade, from which the newly-established garrison there would benefit. The problem of maintaining food supplies was even greater in Bristol with a much larger garrison to support. In June 1644, therefore, the Governor (Sir Ralph Hopton) came up with a novel idea, which would assist local farmers in selling their surplus goods, as well as ensuring that his own troops were fed. Warrants were sent out to the High Constables of seven hundreds in south Gloucestershire 'commanding all the inhabitants, which have the best store of hay, butter, cheese and bacon...or any other sort of provisions' (above what was required for their own families), to transport the same to Bristol. There they would find storehouses provided for their use under the control of people whom they could trust. The garrison would then draw food from the storehouses as required, buying it in 'at the market price for ready money', which would be handed over on the spot to those in charge. (29)

Large field armies in transit experienced just the same problem of supply. This was particularly the case in August 1643, when the king assembled an army of 30,000 men for the siege of Gloucester. In order to ensure that his troops were properly fed, he ordered (in a proclamation issued from Painswick) the setting up of daily markets at Matson, 'where our soldiers may provide themselves of all manner of victuals for their relief, paying reasonably for the same'. Realising only too well the extent of unlawful plunder inflicted by soldiers, he went out of his way to reassure farmers from neighbouring villages that they would be protected. He therefore stipulated that, if any soldier did 'rob, spoil or take away from any person coming to market to our camp any of their goods or victuals', he would be 'forthwith apprehended and hanged without mercy'. Markets did in fact survive at various times and in various places throughout the war, even though they were always liable to disruption in proportion to the amount of military activity in the area. (30)

THE HORRORS OF WAR 6

A VICTIM OF INTRIGUE:

THE CASE OF WILLIAM GUISE

William Guise of Elmore in Gloucestershire had been deemed a 'delinquent' by the County Committee and his estates rendered liable to sequestration (or confiscation). His appeal (in which he was represented by his son, Christopher) was heard by the Commissioners for Sequestrations in March 1648. The witnesses, who gave evidence, told an amazing story of conspiracy, intrigue and corruption, which had created a nightmare situation for Guise to endure.

There was no doubt in people's minds that he had supported parliament loyally at the start of the war by providing loans, horses and weapons, putting sixty or so of his tenants in Elsmore 'in a posture of defence' and sending provisions to Sir William Waller when he fought at Highnam. In 1642, he had also voluntarily agreed to pay £40 in Proposition money (see Chapter 3) but, not knowing where to pay it, had sent his minister to the Mayor of Gloucester to say that it was ready for collection. However, in February 1643, the Council of War there, noting that the money had not been paid, authorised the Governor to collect it.

The officers deputed to visit Guise, Captain Matthews and Captain West, were unscrupulous plunderers intent on seizing every opportunity for personal gain. According to eye-witnesses, they arrived at the house with over sixty horse and knocked with such violence at the door that Guise's wife and mother-in-law ('a very ancient gentlewoman') ran 'in great fear and amazement to the windows, not daring to open the door'. The soldiers, however, quickly forced entry and waited for Guise to return home. As soon as he arrived, they put into practice their deceitful conspiracy by pretending that they were Prince Rupert's men out in search of quarters. Guise, not recognising any of them as local troops from the Gloucester garrison and realising that the royalist cavalry were 'very thick on the hills' round about, believed them. They then forced him to drink the health of Prince Rupert, 'presenting their pistols to his breast', and demanded of him which parts of Gloucester's defences were weakest. Although he replied to this question, he provided false information.

It was at this point, when they felt that had enough incriminating evidence against him, that they revealed their true identity as 'the parliament's men'. Totally ignoring their original mission of collecting the Proposition money, they now told him that, as an obvious supporter of the king, his possessions would be confiscated. If he resisted, 'they had the power to torture him'. Placing him under arrest, they therefore 'rifled his house of linen, wearing apparel, money, plate, arms and horse' to the value of £200. He was then taken prisoner to Gloucester, where he was held for two days. When, however, the Governor (Colonel Massey) heard about this, he sent for Guise and apologised 'that a person of quality should be so abused', saying that Matthews and West had had no authority for their actions. The latter were eventually reprimanded, but were only able to make restitution of a few small items, the rest having already been disposed of.

After this terrifying episode, Guise became the victim of circumstances, which heightened the feeling in some that he might be a royalist sympathiser after all. In the autumn of 1643, he left his home, because 'he was much oppressed by the king's army' and feared further plundering. The garrison soldiers took his departure 'in the worst sense' (i.e. that he had deserted to the royalists) and plundered his home in consequence, taking 80 loads of corn and hay. Suspicions increased when it was known that he had gone to stay with his brother in Monmouth (a royalist garrison). Although he had only intended to stay for a fortnight, he fell down the stairs and was incapacitated for fourteen weeks. He then went to convalesce in Bath (a health resort, but also another royalist garrison), where he was issued with a demand to lend the king £200. On refusing to pay this, he was summoned to explain himself in Oxford (where the king was based) but managed to escape under cover of darkness without lending the money.

At the end of the hearing the Commissioners ruled in Guise's favour and dismissed the charges against him - thanks in part to the skilful advocacy of his son. They undoubtedly realised that he had been the victim partly of intrigue, partly of unfortunate circumstances and partly of his own naivety.

Sources: GRO, D 128, Guise of Elmore Papers; G. Davies (ed.), *Memoirs of the Family of Guise of Elmore, Gloucestershire* (Camden 3rd Series, vol. 28, 1917), pp 87, 123-6, 166-77

Line drawing by Stephen Beck

CHAPTER 8

Forced to Defend:
The Siege of Gloucester, 1643

The enemy...daily acted to the terror of the inhabitants, shooting grenadoes, fire-balls and great stones out of their mortar pieces...Then in one night, they shot above twenty fiery melting hot bullets...which were seen to fly through the air like the shooting of a star. (John Corbet, chaplain to the garrison governor, 1643)

The Importance of Gloucester

All the demands and the horrors of war, described individually in the previous chapters, were brought together with increased intensity during time of siege. Trapped within the narrow confines of a town's medieval walls, the inhabitants were often subjected to the combined threats of deprivation, destruction, plunder, free quarter, starvation, disease, injury and sheer terror. Such was the lot of the citizens of Gloucester during the twenty-seven-day siege by royalist forces in 1643.

At the time of the Civil War, the city itself contained about 4,500 inhabitants with a further five thousand living outside in the surrounding districts (known as the Inshire Division). The City Council, which consisted of a mayor, 12 aldermen and 28 councillors, was therefore responsible for an area of some forty-five square miles. Once the war had started in August 1642, it established a Committee of Defence to co-ordinate the war effort and later a Council of War to liaise with the garrison force.

The city, which was largely puritan in religion and parliamentarian in sympathy, was a centre of considerable economic and strategic importance in the Civil War. It dominated a region rich in agricultural and other natural resources, including iron from the Forest of Dean, which was vital for munitions; it effectively blocked access between the king's headquarters in Oxford and his supply grounds in Wales; and it controlled trading routes both along the Severn Valley and between the west country and the capital.

Both king and parliament viewed Gloucester with covetous eyes. When, therefore, Bristol fell to royalist forces after a short siege in July 1643, it quickly became apparent that their next target would be Gloucester. Successful occupation of that city would give them total control of the West. On 10th August, with the local citizens braced for the inevitable, the king arrived with an army estimated at 30,000 in strength. Ranged against them was a meagre parliamentary garrison of just 1,400 men under the command of Lieutenant-Colonel Edward Massey and supported by the voluntary effort of the inhabitants. Once the king's summons to surrender had been rejected, the siege began in earnest. The impact of the siege and its preliminaries on the ordinary inhabitants is vividly described in two eye-witness accounts given by John Corbet, domestic chaplain to the governor, and John Dorney, the Town Clerk of Gloucester. Their material, which is supplemented by a wealth of other documentary evidence, enables us to recreate life during the siege and to identify the various ways in which the citizens became involved.

Citizen Soldiers

Some residents quickly became active as soldiers in a determined effort to defend their city. As the storm clouds of war began to gather in the spring of 1642, the trained bands of Gloucester were mustered in readiness under the command of Captain Scriven, whose father was a local ironmonger and a former mayor. The Corporation had re-equipped this force in February of that year with sixty new muskets and bandoliers, purchased from suppliers in both London and Bristol. At the same time, the city Council decided that all its members were to arm themselves with weapons - the aldermen being expected to purchase four sets, the sheriffs three and the councillors two. They were subsequently each entrusted with a stock of gunpowder and match (for the matchlock muskets) for speedy issue to other citizens in time of emergency.

John Corbet was somewhat dismissive of the effectiveness of this citizens' army as being 'effeminate in courage and incapable of discipline, because their whole course of life was alienated from warlike employment'. Nevertheless, Scriven's men were given a baptism of fire in September 1642, when they were involved in a fierce skirmish near Worcester on an expedition to assist parliamentary forces under Colonel Nathaniel Fiennes. By the time of this engagement, the trained bands had been joined by a company of 'volunteers', established in July. Corbet was again pessimistic about committing the defence of the city, let alone the county, to volunteers who were 'as a cake not turned, a kind of soldiers not wholly drawn off from the plough or domestic employments'. In spite of his criticism, however, the trained bands and volunteers, fighting as the 'Blue Regiment' under the mayor of Gloucester (lawyer, Dennis Wise), distinguished themselves in March 1643 when they helped Sir William Waller to rout a royalist force of 2,000 Welshmen under Lord Herbert at Highnam, two miles west of the city. In the process, they experienced the sheer horror of war (500 royalists were killed), the exhilaration of capturing 1,500 prisoners and the excitement of boosting their own arsenal by 1,600 weapons seized.

Shortly afterwards, in April 1643, the trained bands and volunteers were amalgamated into an enlarged Town Regiment of five hundred infantry. This was initially commanded by Colonel Henry Stephens, but later (following his capture in June) by the governor of Gloucester himself,

Colonel Edward Massey. It was entirely officered, however, by local citizens, including Thomas Pury, senior (Member of Parliament and lawyer) and Thomas Pury, junior (Member of Parliament and trainee barrister), together with a number of councillors - William Singleton, Luke Nurse, John Nelme, John Evans and Robert Stevenson. Whereas (according to Corbet) the initial task of this regiment was 'to defend the city only within the walls', it was not long before they bore 'the full duty of soldiers'. During the siege, this was to include not only the tiresome chore of patrolling the defences, but also the exciting task of making night-time sorties into enemy trenches outside the walls with the aim of nailing their guns or plundering their weapons and tools. During one such raid out of the North Gate, described by Dorney, 'a little boy of Captain Nelme's company, having shot away all his bullets, charged his musket with a pebble stone and killed a commander therewith'. For that youngster at least, the game of 'playing at soldiers' would never be quite the same again.

The local inhabitants, of course, were not the only ones responsible for defending the city on the front line. They had been joined in November 1642 by a parliamentary garrison, which was initially under the command of Colonel Thomas Essex. In the following month, however, he was succeeded as governor by the Earl of Stamford, who quickly left Lieutenant-Colonel Edward Massey (thirty-eight years of age) in charge as deputy governor, backed by an infantry regiment and two troops of horse as garrison. From the outset, Massey was actually governor in all but name, in spite of the fact that he was not finally accorded that title until April 1643. Although the arrival of regular troops in Gloucester was undoubtedly welcome, their presence was bought at considerable cost to the residents, especially with the arrival of reinforcements in March 1643. By the time of the siege, something in the region of 1,400 troops were based in Gloucester with high expectation of wholehearted support from the local population.

Col. Edward Massey, deputy governor (1642) then governor (1643) of Gloucester; later Major-General of the Western Association (1645). (By courtesy of the National Portrait Gallery, London)

This partly meant that all those living inside the city walls became jointly responsible for accommodating the soldiers. The Corporation therefore ruled, on 7th February 1643, that all citizens were to offer lodgings at a theoretical cost to the soldier of three shillings a week.

Aldermen were each expected to take in six soldiers, councillors four and ordinary citizens 'in some proportionable manner' as their means would allow. Detailed instructions were issued to individuals, such as these sent to Mrs Hayward: 'You are to receive these three soldiers to diet them for a month, at three shillings per week apiece, to be repaid you out of the soldiers' pay'. In practice, of course, householders were not paid at the time, but simply given signed tickets indicating the number of soldiers accommodated, all in the vain hope that settlement would be made at a later date. It is estimated that the inhabitants paid out something in excess of £4,000 towards the cost of this free quarter during a five-month period in 1643. After constant grumbling and regular requests for repayment, the Council finally agreed to partial reimbursement of inhabitants at the rate of 4s 6d in the pound.

The root of the problem lay in the fact that the soldiers themselves were invariably unpaid for long periods, which caused such resentment that mutinous feelings simmered perpetually just below the surface. In spite of the fact that parliament had voted £1,000 towards the pay of the garrison in November 1642, the cash was not actually delivered to Gloucester until almost two years later. The Corporation was therefore obliged, in an attempt to head off serious mutiny, to raise loans at 20 per cent interest and sell off valuable items from the city's silver plate. This meant that the soldiers could be paid at least in part whenever the situation became threatening. Thomas Blayney, treasurer of the Gloucester garrison, made two emergency *ad hoc* payments in the spring of 1643, for instance, one of £10 to Captain Evans 'when his company was ready to disband for want of pay' and the other of £5 to Captain Tanner for similar reasons. John Corbet summed up the worsening situation inside the city, which saw the soldiers 'mutinous and desperate', a situation aggravated by the fact that 'no monies came from the state' to relieve the financial crisis and the local citizens had already contributed far beyond their means. The governor was therefore forced into humiliating negotiations even with 'the vilest mutineers' and to use his diplomatic skill 'in keeping together malcontented soldiers'. (2)

Working on the Defences

From the outset of civil war in August 1642, the citizens of Gloucester were actively involved in strengthening the city's defences against all threats from outside both real and imaginary. The old medieval walls were in a state of terrible decay, presenting (in the words of John Corbet) 'no considerable defence'. One broken-down section by the North Gate, for instance, actually had a tree growing in the middle of the rubble. The only solid part of the fortifications lay on the eastern side, stretching from a point just above the East Gate down as far as the South Gate with a wet ditch outside the walls. Given the strategic importance of Gloucester, the Corporation was confronted with a situation of grave urgency.

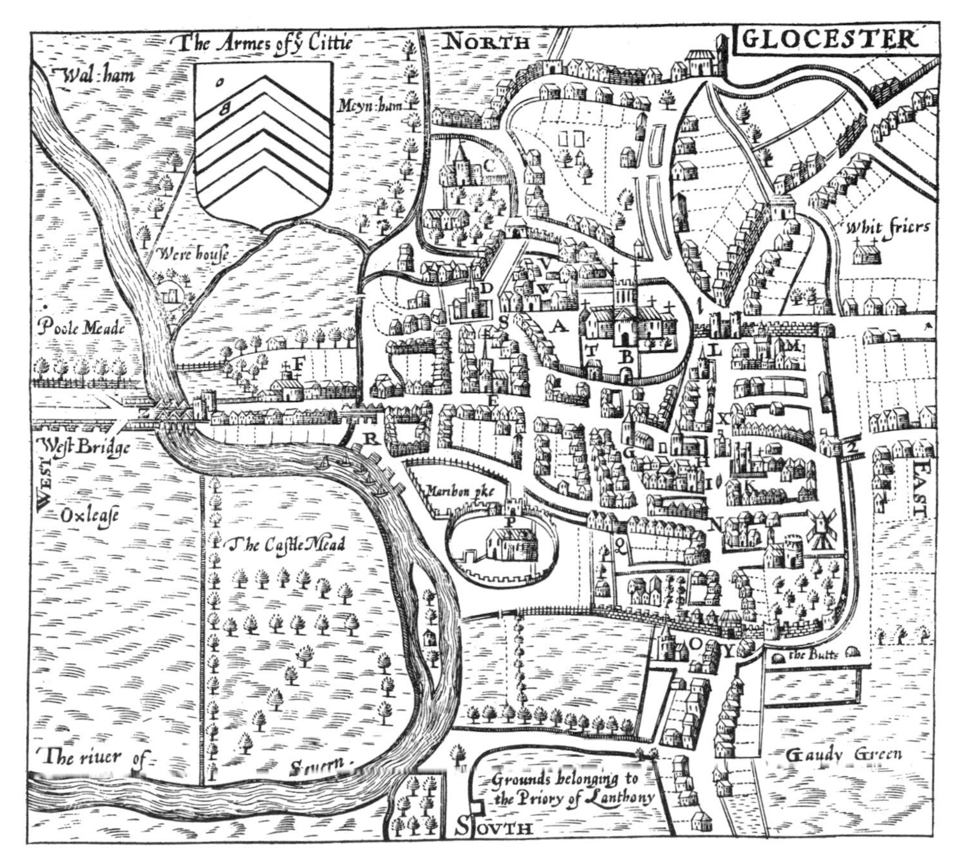

John Speed's map of Gloucester in 1610, showing the city's remaining fortifications. Key points marked on the map (which are also mentioned in this text) are: B = the Cathedral; D = St Mary de Lode's Church; E = St Nicholas's Church; I = All Soints' Church; N = St Mary de Crypt's Church (with Greyfriars alongside); O = St Owen's Church; V = the Bishop's Palace; Y = Southgate; Z = Westgate; 1 = inner Northgate; 2 = Eastgate. (Author's collection)

Therefore, on 5th August 1642 (which was over two weeks before the king raised his standard at Nottingham), the city's ruling body decided to establish a Committee of Defence to co-ordinate the task of strengthening the defences. Consisting of four aldermen, eight councillors and two stewards, it was given responsibility for planning, financing and raising the fortifications and doing 'anything else that in their discretion it shall consider may concern the defence and welfare of the city'. They set about their work with vigour, ordering iron chains for the gates and turn-pikes as obstacles to be constructed on roads leading into the city. In particular, however, they commenced a period of frantic activity in repairing the old city walls, strengthening them by lining them with banks of earth, building lines of earthworks to plug the gaps in the walls, constructing sconces outside on which to mount their cannon and digging ditches by the gates to prevent any cavalry charging through. The committee invested heavily in spades, shovels, pickaxes and wheelbarrows to assist the work and appointed Samuel Baldwin, a local mason, as surveyor of the defences. Money to cover the cost of the operation was raised through the sale of corporation plate (including four old maces and an old mayoral seal, producing in total £46 4s 6d), the taking out of loans from local people at 20 per cent interest (raising £930 in all) and the personal contributions donated by individual members of the Corporation (with aldermen giving 16s 8d each, sheriffs 13s 4d and councillors 10s 0d). All that was lacking was a large band of labourers to complete the task.

The local inhabitants responded willingly and with great commitment to the challenge. According to Corbet, 'the citizens did mainly show their care and affection in fortifying the town, a work both expensive and tedious, being of great compass and raised from the ground'. It is true that much of the initial work in the autumn of 1642 and spring of 1643 was undertaken by local craftsmen and labourers who were paid for their efforts and therefore benefited financially from the war situation. The Chamberlain's accounts detail a whole list of charges entailed in stocking the armoury ('two barrels of powder', 'setting the muskets straight', 'mending the locks', 'lead for bullets', 'casting the bullets', 'weighing and placing up of four packs of match', 'making up of powder'), preparing the magazines ('making clean of All Saints' Church to put powder in', 'a new key for the lock at Christ Church, where the powder is put'), equipping and maintaining the horses, which were on standby duty and repairing the fortifications ('workmen at the Beareland ditch', masons at the North Gate, rehanging the Alvin Gate, 'labourers at Dockham', carpenters 'for work at the several gates', '2 ton and a half of timber' and paviours 'for paving about the posts at the several gates').

These payments by the Chamberlain to inhabitants all related to the city's own agreed responsibility for repairing the fortifications and maintaining its regiments of trained bands and volunteers. In addition, however, the treasurer of the garrison force itself (Thomas Blayney) also drew heavily on the expertise of local citizens in supplying its wartime requirements - citizens who showed enormous flexibility and ingenuity in adapting their peacetime skills to the needs of the crisis. Throughout the months leading up to the siege in 1643, therefore, Blayney made lavish payments for services, all of which helped to sustain the livelihood of local people and their ability to pay their wartime taxes. Amongst the many to benefit in this way were Edward Hooker (gunsmith) for mending muskets and supplying weapons; Caesar Goodwin (smith) 'for his work in making carriages for the ordinance'; John Palmer (cooper) 'for work done about the saltpetre tubs and powder barrels'; John Aubrey (coalman) for 'three tons of coal for the powder works'; Simon baker (bell-founder) 'for the casting of 238lbs of musket bullets'; Mr Jordan (bookbinder) 'for paper for the public service' (i.e used in making up charges of powder); Thomas Barnes (saltpetre maker) 'for a fortnight in the siege for making saltpetre'; Thomas

Davis (powder maker) for his work 'in the siege'; Edward Chambers and John Wasstred (blacksmiths) for making pikes; Mr Hulford (farmer) for supplying provender for the horses; John Williams (roper) for '90lbs of match' used by the musketeers; John Barbard (bell-founder) for 'casting grenadoes'; Thomas Smith (plumber) 'for casting of 529lbs of pistol bullets'; and Mr Harris (shoemaker) for supplying boots. In addition, there were all the 'carpenters, sawyers, blacksmiths and nailers' employed in building a frigate for use on the river; the workmen used in 'pulling down the houses' outside the fortifications; the labourers 'employed on the fortifications'; the masons who built the drawbridges; the woodcutters who supplied the fuel for the guards at night; the miners 'for their service at the siege' and the scouts who brought in intelligence - including Walter Taylor, who received an extra £3 'for the salt wherein he carried his letters, when he came from London'.

Quite apart from those hired for their specific skills, however, ordinary people were increasingly used as volunteers. This was particularly true in the days immediately prior to the arrival of the king's army in August 1643 and during the siege itself. On Sunday 6th August, five days before the city was formally summoned to surrender, John Dorney wrote in his diary: 'This day we wrought hard in the amending and repairing of our bulwarks'. As members of a devout puritan community, the local people had apparently decided to split their duties on Sundays and Saints' Days. Thus, two weeks later, Dorney observed that 'some of ours, whilst others went to church to implore divine assistance, wrought at our works within the city'. It could sometimes be far more worrying for those at prayer in church, as explosions from mortar shells rocked the very foundations of the building. Nerves were constantly on edge. When on 3rd September, for instance, news reached the church of an imminent attack on the East Gate, the minister 'dismissed the congregation without any sermon'. Four days earlier, on the other hand, two fast-day sermons had been successfully preached at St Nicholas's Church without any interruption, 'only a musket bullet fell into the church, but did no harm'. All-in-all, the inhabitants were able to combine their religious worship and their defence duties without much conflict.

On weekdays, all the inhabitants worked furiously without interruption. Dorney greatly admired 'the cheerful readiness of young and old of both sexes, as well of the better as inferior sort of people by day and night, to labour in the fortification of our city'. He was especially full of praise for the 'women and maids' who worked almost daily in the Little Mead (which lay outside the line of the defences), 'fetching in turf for the repairing of our works'. This was often done under the very noses of the enemy and in the face of persistent gunfire. Once the royalists had commenced their bombardment, the remainder of the townsfolk were called upon to undertake various emergency tasks. According to Corbet, the East and South Gates were 'dammed up and rammed with a thickness of earth' to make them 'cannon proof', while the walls 'from port to port were

The citizens of Gloucester at work on strengthening the defences under the supervision of aldermen and councillors. (Line drawing by Stephen Beck)

lined to the battlements'. This earth reinforcement helped the defences to absorb the impact of the cannon balls as they thudded against the walls. When breaches were made in the stonework, they were rapidly plugged by teams of citizens on stand-by duty. For instance, after a severe battering on 14th August, Dorney recorded that they 'quickly made up the breach with wool-sacks and cannon baskets'. Then, on 3rd September, in anticipation of a major assault on the East Gate, the inhabitants were called upon to dig breastworks and trenches inside the walls across Southgate Street and to line the walls of houses nearby with earth for protection. In the period leading up to the siege, the councillors themselves (on a rota system in groups of three) were responsible each day for organising teams of citizens (with their spades, shovels and baskets) to assist with the building of earthworks and inspecting the quality of the work undertaken.

The councillors were also responsible for organising the nightly watch of the city by the citizens themselves. As early as November 1641, the Council had given instructions, 'by reason the times are dangerous', that twelve men were to keep watch and ward 'for the apprehending of all suspicious persons' during the hours of darkness. This number was doubled in August 1642, when guards were established at each of the four main gates, which were locked between 9.00 pm and dawn and the keys delivered to the mayor for safety. Initially, it was left to the constables to 'provide and appoint able householders to watch', drawn in rotation from inhabitants within each sector of the city. By October, however, it had been decided that one member of the Council should keep watch alongside the appointed citizens at each of the gates 'for the more safety thereof'. By April 1643, the responsibility of these duty councillors was increased when they were styled 'Captains of the Watch', with duties commencing much earlier at 5.00 pm. Citizens who failed to turn up for their allocated stint were to be fined ten shillings or given 48 hours imprisonment. A reserve force of guards was based at the Wheat Market in Southgate Street, so that help could be dispatched urgently to reinforce the guard at any point of attack; and six horses were maintained in readiness for scouts to be sent out on vital reconnaissance missions 'to see and prevent such dangers as are now to be feared'. (3)

The Demolition of Homes

Although all the citizens of Gloucester were called upon to make sacrifices of time and energy in strengthening the defences against siege, some were required to make one of the greatest sacrifices of all for the sake of the community - namely, the total loss of their homes. Even before the start of the siege, the reconstruction of the city's defences had resulted in the demolition of some properties in the suburbs, which were situated near the line. This was due to the need partly to extend or realign the works and partly to clear a wide corridor outside the ditch so that defenders had clear visibility. The Chamberlain's Accounts, therefore, make reference to houses being 'taken down by order', 'digged up for the fortifications' and 'taken into the works'. Whole streets were destroyed in this way, particularly in the area outside the South Gate. This, however, was only the beginning.

In June 1643, as the prospect of siege loomed ever closer, the Council had devised a contingency plan for use in case of large-scale attack. They considered it vital, under those circumstances, to clear away all the houses which lay in the suburbs outside the walls and which, otherwise, would provide convenient cover for the enemy during their assault. It had therefore decided in advance to demolish a total of 241 houses (amounting to a third of the entire property in Gloucester), if need should arise and, in the meantime, to appoint a committee 'to consider where such persons whose houses are to be pulled down in the suburbs, may be conveniently placed in houses within the city'. In doing this, the Council not only showed commendable skills in organisation and forward-planning, but also displayed genuine understanding and compassion towards these refugees. The people themselves reluctantly agreed.

Once the siege started in earnest on 10th August, the plan was put into immediate action. John Dorney described, in his day-by-day account of the siege, the fatal moment when the city had rejected the king's terms for surrender: 'We had, after the return of our messengers, fired all our suburbs on the north, east and south parts, as being those that could and would have done us most harm'. He went on to say that, after this burning of the houses, the city was like 'a garment without skirts, which we were willing to part withal, lest our enemies should sit upon them'. The 241 houses were duly destroyed, causing instant poverty and enormous anguish to a large number of people. When in October 1646, after the end of the war, the citizens of Gloucester submitted a compensation claim for the losses sustained in this episode, they estimated the total cost at £28,720. This included a sum of £4,000 for personal possessions lost in the fire, which was in addition to the value of the barns, stables, gardens and orchards. In all, seventy-five owners were listed as claimants, many of whom rented out cheap accommodation to poorer people, such as Thomas Dennis and his mother, who rented out fifty properties in the South Ward at a total value of £350. Not all the houses were sub-standard, however. Mrs Evans owned seven houses together valued at £1500, whereas Mr Mitchell's personal dwelling alone was worth £500, Alderman Powell's £340 and Mr Terrett's £200.

Compensation for their losses was extremely slow to materialise. Finally, in September 1653, parliament decided to resolve the matter by granting the city land in Ireland, which had been confiscated from catholic rebels. Initially, £10,000 of such land was released, the rent from which was to be used to compensate owners. However, as the rent proved difficult to collect and the land inadequate in size, negotiations with parliament rumbled on to 1659, by which time most of the affected owners had

Aldermen and councillors supervise the demolition of houses in the Gloucester suburbs. (Line drawing by Stephen Beck)

probably received some measure of compensation. Meanwhile, the Council itself had occasionally taken steps to relieve those who were suffering acute distress, such as Edward May, whose home at Kingsholm 'was in the time of the siege of this city burnt down'. In view of the fact that he was therefore 'destitute of a habitation', they granted him (in January 1645) the use of 'a pigeon house...for him and his family to dwell in' with permission to build a chimney on the adjoining land.

Quite apart from losses sustained in the fire, certain meadows around the city were flooded in order to make the task of the besiegers that more difficult. This, too, proved costly for the farmers concerned. The parish of Kingsholm, for instance, claimed no less than £2,000 damages for 'the Little Mead and Meanham and other grounds being drowned from the beginning of the wars'. The petition, which accompanied all these claims, stressed the great sacrifice made by the people involved, who had 'demonstrated their good affections' by surrendering their houses in the common cause. By the end of the war they were 'extremely impoverished' through 'the grievous losses' they had sustained. (4)

Nights of Terror

Although the owners of property in the suburbs were the first to suffer loss, they were quickly joined in their anguish by those living inside the city walls. On Saturday 12th August, John Dorney noticed the enemy making great preparations in Gawdy Green in readiness for a bombardment of the fortifications. Three cannons were drawn up there, along with a number of mortars, and were later strengthened by three more in Friar's Orchard and two in a battery near the East Gate - all 'within less than a pistol shot of the town wall'. The inhabitants looked on helplessly, bracing themselves for the terror to come. The bombardment started in earnest that night, when the silence was suddenly broken by the royalists who 'shot several great grenadoes out of their mortar pieces'. Although these explosive devices apparently 'all brake, but did no harm', they were clearly sent to give the inhabitants a foretaste of what lay in store.

Next day, the besiegers launched their first bombardment on the wall itself, firing shots each weighing between fifteen and twenty-three pounds. Dorney recalled how they 'began to batter the wall and the brick house over against Rignall Stile'. Over the next two weeks, the same formula was adopted by the royalists - grenades and other missiles fired into the town itself by night (in order to frighten the inhabitants), followed by a bombardment of the defences during the day (in order to make breaches through which to storm the town).

This night-time terror, which partly ensured that the citizens never slept, was vividly described by both Dorney and Corbet. The enemy, they recalled, 'daily acted to the terror of the inhabitants by shooting grenades, fire-balls and great stones out of their mortar-pieces...In one night, they shot above twenty fiery, melting hot bullets, some eighteen pound weight...which were seen to fly through the air like the shooting of a star. They passed through stables and ricks of hay, where the fire, by the swiftness of the motion, did not catch; and falling on the tops of houses, presently melted the leads and sank through; but all the skill and the industry of the enemy could not set one house on fire'. Indeed, during the siege, Gloucester was remarkably spared from fire damage within the walls, unlike the towns of Hull, Lyme and Bridgwater. Sometimes potential fire hazards were effectively dealt with by quick-thinking residents. On one occasion, for instance, a grenade 'fell into the street near the South Gate, but a woman coming with a pale of water, threw the water there and extinguished the fuse thereof'. This prevented the explosion, enabling curious by-standers to lift up the entire device and ascertain its weight - namely, sixty pounds!

Nevertheless, some damage was done to property by these missiles, as Corbet admitted: '...[the grenades] falling upon the houses did rend and tear the buildings, when the people within were preserved'. One grenade 'fell in at the top of Mr Hathway's house into his chamber over the kitchen'. From there, it apparently crashed through the end wall of the room, before exploding in the courtyard below. On its way, one piece of it 'fell in the kitchen chimney, where three women were sitting by the fire'. They escaped unhurt. Many people, of course, had narrow and frightening experiences like this. Once a 'fiery, melting hot iron bullet', weighing eighteen pounds, 'came through three houses and fell into a chamber of Mr Comelin, the apothecary'. This was spotted in time, however, and dowsed heavily with water.

Meanwhile, the bombardment of the walls continued with increased vigour. Corbet recalled how, on 19th August, the enemy guns 'began a most furious battery upon the corner point and made over an hundred and fifty great shot against it, whereby the stones were sorely battered but the works stood firm'. Nevertheless, the resolve and courage of the inhabitants remained undiminished. They were apparently 'not daunted at the noise of the cannon' - indeed, they showed such contempt for its ineffectiveness that,

Greyfriars, a medieval friary, used by Massey as a command post to control the defence of the East and South Gates. Badly damaged during a bombardment, August 1643. (Author's collection)

while the guns were still blazing away, 'women and children wrought hard, lining the walls and repairing the breaches'. When a cannon ball missed its target, of course, it tended to fly over the wall and into the town, where it could cause unintentional damage. This did in fact happen from time to time, although fate often seemed to intervene on behalf of the inhabitants in unusual ways. On one occasion, a twenty pound shot 'came through a chamber of the inn called The Crown, carried a bolster before it into the window and there slept in it'. Later in the siege, 'a cannon bullet, its force almost spent, struck down a pig, which our soldiers ate and afterwards jeered the enemy therewith'. Some buildings, not mentioned by Dorney and Corbet, were also damaged - including St Katherine's Church (which was destroyed); the South Gate (which was later demolished because of its battered state); St Nicholas's Church (which lost part of its steeple); and St Owen's Church in the suburbs (which was demolished during the clearance of buildings prior to the siege). But all-in-all, in spite of the noise and the terror, comparatively little damage was inflicted inside the town.

Casualties were also surprisingly light. Corbet in fact claimed that only fifty people died within the city - and certainly there is no indication in the parish registers of extensive burials during this period. Dorney recalled just a few injuries, including 'a man and a maid hurt' in the great bombardment of 19th August; a woman 'mortally wounded' after the fall of a grenade in Southgate Street; and 'two or three hurt a little by the flying of stones of the wall' during cannon-fire. Sergeant Foster, who arrived with parliament's relief army, reported that the inhabitants put the total of those killed during the siege as low as 30 or 40. The majority of these had apparently lost their lives when natural curiosity had got the better of them, causing them to 'peep' out at the enemy from their cover - including a boy and a girl who, 'through their indiscretion', were 'gazing over the walls'; Captain James Harcus who, at the time, was 'too venturously looking' to see what damage his grenade had inflicted; and a civilian, hit at a house near the wall, where 'he was peeping' at the spectacular cannon bombardment from Gaudy Green. There were of course other casualties, some of whom later received relief from a fund established by the Council in October 1643 to assist those who had been wounded. John Assard, for instance, 'who did good service at the time of the siege and is now in misery' was granted £1 10s 0d in aid, while Jane Heard received £1 0s 0d for wounds sustained. (5)

The Threat of Starvation and Disease

Long before the siege started, the city Council had shown great foresight and wisdom by building up stocks of food for use in emergency. The citizens were expected to play a full part in these contingency plans. As early as January 1643, it had decided that 'for the provision of victuals in this city...every inhabitant that contributeth to the relief of the poor shall within fourteen days provide so many bushels of peas as he or she is rated to pay weekly pence for the poor, upon pain of 20 shillings apiece'. In April, a similar decision was taken for the building up of stocks of corn. Furthermore, the Council itself, realising that the city was 'threatened with siege', adopted a policy of stockpiling emergency rations by buying in supplies under the direction of a specially-appointed committee. The commissioners were empowered 'to contract with any person for anything that may serve for victuals...and receive any fat cattle, corn or other provision to be kept and employed...for the use of the inhabitants and soldiers here'.

The result of all this planning was that the inhabitants survived comfortably during the siege itself. There was, however, one moment of crisis at the very outset, when the royalists (according to Dorney) 'cut the pipes that conveyed our water from Robinshood Hill to our conduits, and diverted the course of the water that drove our corn-mills, so that we were forced to content ourselves with pump and Severn water, and to grind our corn with horse-mills'. Indeed, the besieging army had managed not only to divert the stream from Upton St Leonard, which normally fed the corn mills, but also to burn down many of the mills themselves. Nevertheless, the inhabitants successfully managed to improvise by resorting to traditional horse-power for grinding their corn.

A potentially much more serious situation, however, arose out the loss of their pure water supply, piped down to drinking fountains inside the city from neighbouring springs. Although some of their emergency supply was pumped up from wells within the city, the remainder came from the polluted waters of the Severn. This constituted a serious health hazard, as other cities such as Bristol had found to their cost. Water-borne diseases, such as typhoid, could spread rapidly in such circumstances within the narrow confines of a city packed with humanity for the siege. Gloucester, however, survived this threat surprisingly well and the population remained in reasonable health throughout. It helped, of course, that the weather during the assault was good - it was high summer and, according to Dorney, it only rained once.

The inhabitants showed great inventiveness and courage in maximising their food supply. Several times, apparently, some of the men 'would go forth out of the works and fetch hay out of Walham' [which lay to the north-west of the city]. The royalists retaliated by setting on fire some of the cocks of hay. Similarly, with considerable audacity, the citizens ensured that their cattle remained healthy and well-nourished. On Wednesday 30th August, Dorney recalled: 'This day we turned out our cattle to graze in the Little Mead, and so continued afterwards, guarded by some musketeers, taking them in at night'. They even constructed 'a bridge of ladders' over the earthworks so that the cattle could cross. In his summing up, Dorney highlighted as one of the garrison's greatest achievements 'the plenty and store of provisions we had in the town of all sorts, so that we turned out, even to the very last hour they [the enemy] stayed before us, above two hundred head of cattle over our works to graze in the very noses of them, besides others we kept in the town upon hay'.

Supplies of a different kind were equally vital to the garrison - namely, gunpowder and musket bullets. At the start of the siege, they had a stock of just forty barrels of gunpowder, but these were supplemented by an on-going supply manufactured within the city. Dorney commented: 'We kept two powder mills going, and with them made three barrels a week'. One of the mills was situated in outbuildings at the cathedral, the other at the quay. Bullets were made from lead, which had been removed from the roof of the former bishop's ruined palace, The Vineyards, at Over. As already discussed, local craftsmen contributed readily to the cause of war by adapting their skills. Bell-founders turned their hands to making grenades; blacksmiths constructed pikeheads and plumbers made bullets. Periodically during the siege, the town crier, acting on orders from the mayor, announced the next distribution of powder, bullets and match from the magazine in the church of St Mary de Crypt. (6)

St Mary de Crypt's Church, used by Massey during the siege as an ammunition store. (Author's collection)

Psychological Warfare

The citizens of Gloucester were by no means limited in their suffering to physical hardship and personal injury. In the months prior to the siege and during the siege itself, they were subjected to a great deal of anxiety and psychological stress, which rapidly undermined their morale. John Corbet noted that, even before the Civil War had started, the inhabitants had been made anxious by 'the rumours of war', realising, as they did, that the city would be a prime target for attack in view of its strategic importance. Once hostilities commenced, rumours multiplied and 'quickly filled the ears and tongues of the people'.

As the autumn of 1642 gave way to winter, Gloucester's small parliamentary garrison under Colonel Thomas Essex was withdrawn. The inhabitants suddenly felt isolated as the city, in Corbet's words, 'was again left naked'. They could see the net tightening around them as they were 'cast into the midst of an enraged enemy', encircled by the king's forces in Oxford, Herefordshire, Worcestershire and Wales. Although a garrison was eventually restored to Gloucester under Lieutenant-Colonel Massey's command in December 1642, the loss of Cirencester to Prince Rupert and Tewkesbury to Sir William Russell in February 1643 provided a shattering blow to morale - especially when Rupert followed this up by issuing a summons to Gloucester to surrender as well. 'The summons', wrote Corbet, 'found the people extremely dashed at the strange turn of things...The hearts of many sunk very low and began to lie flat'. Gradually Massey was forced to abandon his small satellite garrisons at such places as Sudeley and Berkeley, giving the royalists free reign to control and terrorise the countryside around. A distinct atmosphere of gloom prevailed within Gloucester. 'The clouds gathered round the city', commented Corbet, 'our men were confined to the town walls'. The royalists worked hard to increase the sense of gloom by putting psychological pressure on the citizens in every possible way. 'The enemy breathed out threatenings; many false friends sought cunningly to make us afraid'. This was not difficult, because the city's fortifications were still unfinished, the soldiers were mutinous, none of the promised subsidies had been received from parliament and supplies from the countryside around had largely been choked by the enemy.

The loss of Sudeley Castle early in 1643 threatened Massey's hold on Gloucester. It was recaptured in 1644 and later slighted. (Author's collection)

Then in July 1643, came two mortal blows. First, the defeat of Sir William Waller's western army at the Battle of Roundway Down, in Corbet's words, 'cast these parts of the kingdom into a miserable plight'. The king was now total master of the field in the West. His forces, completely unbridled in the county, 'came up to our gates and, by threats, would seem to shake the walls of the city'. But worse was to follow. The fall of Bristol later in the month meant that the king's territory now extended in the west from Cornwall northwards almost to Scotland. 'Gloucester did stand alone without help and hope', lamented Corbet. News of Bristol's surrender 'brought forth a dark and gloomy day to the city of Gloucester...Many became crest-fallen'. Matters were made even worse by the fact that the support of the people in the countryside around, previously loyal to Gloucester's stand, gradually crumbled. The royalists locally had systematically weakened their resolve, partly through a reign of terror and partly through dire warnings of the consequences of a prolonged siege to the surrounding community. The result, complained Corbet, was that 'the whole country forsook us', urging them to make peace. They argued that 'the standing out of Gloucester', however advantageous to parliament, would only bring them misery; because, with the arrival of a great army in the vicinity, they expected 'a destruction of corn and cattle'.

Charles I and his secretary, Sir Edward Walker. (By courtesy of the National Portrait Gallery, London)

The inhabitants of Gloucester, therefore, felt totally isolated as they, with a small garrison of 1,400, faced up to the approach of an army of 30,000 men. They had already suffered an enormous amount of anxiety and stress over the previous months as the enemy gradually closed in. But now came the greatest test of all. The royalist forces were led by the king in person so the 'the terror of his presence might prevail with some and the person of the king amaze the simple'. As the citizens of Gloucester saw the king with their own eyes, questions of loyalty and treason were no doubt uppermost in their minds. The pressure on them mounted further when the king's summons on Thursday 10th August was delivered. His terms were tempting. 'If they [the inhabitants and soldiers] shall immediately submit themselves and deliver this city to us, we are contented freely and absolutely to pardon everyone of them, without exception; and do assure them, in the word of a king, that they nor any of them shall receive the least damage or prejudice by our army in their persons or estates'. His threats, on the other hand, were frightening. 'But if they shall reject this offer of grace and favour and compel us by the power of the army to reduce that place...they must thank themselves for all the calamities and miseries that must befall them'.

In view of these attempts to lower their morale and weaken their resolve, how did the citizens of Gloucester survive? A clue is to be found, perhaps, in their reaction to another example of the psychological warfare waged by the royalists against the people themselves (i.e. as opposed to the soldiers). This occurred on Sunday 3rd September, when the siege was at its height. Dorney recalled: 'In the afternoon, a paper was shot upon an arrow into the town, the content whereof was this: these are to let you understand that your God, Waller, hath forsaken you and hath retired himself to the Tower of London; Essex is beaten like a dog; yield to the king's mercy in time, otherwise if we enter perforce, no quarter for such obstinate traitorly rogues. From a well-wisher'. Their reaction was instant. A defiant reply was penned in verse and fired back into the enemy camp by the same arrow. It concluded thus:

'...But for our cabbages which you have eaten
Be sure ere long ye shall be soundly beaten'.

Throughout the hostilities over a twelve-month period since the start of the war, the inhabitants had been strengthened in their resistance by three major factors. First, their deep-seated puritan faith, which led them to believe passionately in the justness of their cause. Corbet noticed that 'those stuck most to the business, who were held up by the deep sense of religion'. The regular services held in church throughout the siege were vital to their determination and spirit. John Dorney, Town Clerk, concluded his own account with heartfelt praise to the Lord for His 'gracious acts of divine providence...who has gone out with our hosts, whose eye hath watched over us and whose strong hand was with us. He made us a city of refuge to others and hath now been a refuge to us in the time of our distress'.

Secondly, they were strengthened by the steely resolve of the city Council, which never wavered under the defiant leadership of Thomas Pury, senior. They refused to sue for peace; they worked hard to bond the entire community together and to ensure that there was no wastage of its valuable economic resources. No resident freeman, for instance, was allowed to absent himself from the city once it had become a garrison on pain of disfranchisement (thus keeping all major tax-payers within the walls); 'money, plate, valuable goods of any kind or riches were not suffered to pass the gates, but to rest as in a safe treasury' (thus retaining all its financial assets). They realised only too well that seepage of this kind would have had a devastating effect on morale. Furthermore, the councillors were always active in planning, organising and supervising the defences, setting a personal example by always paying more in contributions or taking more soldiers for free quarter than the ordinary citizens. Corbet noticed that the weaker spirits and waverers were 'born up by the zeal of the rest and the soldiers' power'. Spirits gradually rose. 'No cross show or doubtful resolve did hinder the business; all suspended their private cares; and the women and children acted their parts in making up the defects of the fortifications'. By keeping everyone actively employed, the Council brought unity of purpose to those trapped behind the confines of the walls.

Confidence was further increased by the efficient and determined manner in which they maintained essential services for the community throughout the crisis from spring to summer in 1643. Law and order were maintained; the city's accounts were rigorously controlled so that cash was always available for crucial tasks unrelated to the war ; the four hospitals for the aged poor continued to function; money from charitable trusts was distributed as normal and the poor rate was collected by parishes with meticulous care. On 7th March, the Council ordered parish official within the city to 'take a special care to provide for the relief of the poor by making new rates according to the present necessity'. Later, during the siege, a double rate was in fact levied so that those working as volunteers on the fortifications could be provided with the means to support their families and relief could also be given 'to such impotent persons as are not able to work'. Even during these moments of extreme danger, the Council continued to care for its citizens in a most responsible manner.

Thirdly, they were inspired by the imaginative and forceful leadership of the governor, Colonel Massey. He and his garrison forces 'vowed never to see within the gates the face of a conquering enemy'. The governor himself 'appeared in public, rode from place to place with a cheerful aspect', encouraging individuals and lifting spirits'. He also lifted spirits by ensuring that the garrison forces made 'a perpetual noise'. According to Corbet, whenever the enemy's cannon had been silent for a while, 'one or two of our guns gave fire to disturb the calm and signify to the country that we were yet alive'. Furthermore, Massey also realised the importance of activity for those involved. Before the siege actually started, he organised a series of sorties into enemy territory to boost morale. When, for instance, Welsh forces occupied Highnam House, two miles from the city in March 1643, Massey successfully brought his garrison out in a joint attack with Waller. The resulting capture of 1,500 Welshmen did wonders for the spirit inside Gloucester. As Dorney wryly remarked: 'an inveterate hatred derived from fabulous tradition, had passed between the Welshmen and the citizens of Gloucester'. The Civil War sometimes gave the opportunity to settle old scores!

Massey continued the policy of active defence, even when the city was finally besieged. The accounts of Corbet and Dorney make frequent references to raids on enemy trenches outside the walls, sorties to nail the enemy cannon and attacks to frustrate attempts to undermine the East Gate. At the height of the siege, for instance, Captain Harcus led two sorties from the Southgate to attack the royalist trenches in Gaudy Green (trenches which were designed to provide cover near the walls for undermining operations and a final assault). Harcus's men skilfully crossed the moat using ladders and caught the enemy totally by surprise, seizing many of their shovels and pickaxes in the process. Another such attack was led at night by a citizen soldier in Thomas Pury's own company. They emerged from a hole dug in the dungeon of the gatehouse and crept forward to the entrance to the mine. Throwing grenades into the mine shaft, they waited for the panic-stricken miners to emerge, 'our four musketeers playing at them as they ran out'. Four royalists were killed and others wounded. This action in itself did little to win the siege, but it made a major contribution to victory in the psychological war which had been taking place. Dorney was rightly proud of 'the constancy of resolution in citizens and soldiers in the midst of so many temptations by reason of promises, threats, delay of succour and want of intelligence, even to the very end'. (7)

Gloucester was finally relieved on 8th September 1643, when the Earl of Essex reached the city with an army of 15,000 troops drawn mainly from London. The king, hearing of the approach of this large force, had already lifted the siege two days earlier and had withdrawn to Sudeley Castle.

THE HORRORS OF WAR 7

INCARCERATED

IN OXFORD CASTLE, 1642-3

The hundred or more prisoners, who were taken by the royalists at Marlborough in December 1642, had already suffered much misery during the horrors of the assault (see The Horrors of War 8). Worse, however, was to follow. Locked up overnight in a barn, they were bound next day and dragged in terrible weather conditions through mud and ice to Oxford Castle. There they came face-to-face with William Smith, Provost Marshal-General of the king's army and the man responsible for organising prisoners. His reputation for savagery was already legendary. 'That bloody Marshal Smith', wrote one observer; 'that monster of iniquity', commented another; 'this serpent Smith', echoed a third.

The Reverend Edward Wirley, a prisoner in the castle for fourteen months, witnessed with his own eyes the dreadful hardship and vile treatment endured by the Marlborough contingent. Even the gentlemen who had been captured there (including John Franklin, MP, and Lieutenant-Colonel Ramsey) arrived having been 'stripped of their clothes and put into old filthy rags'. Many were forced to sleep 'on the bare boards' in a small room packed with some forty people, who at times were 'up to their ankles in their own excrements'. There they became 'close prisoners', being denied all human contact and kept 'without the benefit of converse with the living or dead, men or books'.

According to Wirley, the ordinary soldiers were even more roughly treated. 'There were nine score persons brought from Marlborough, wet and very dirty, who, after their cords were taken off, were put up into a high tower and lodged upon the boards. The rooms were so stuffed with them that they could not lie down one by another...On these poor souls did the viper Smith exercise his more than savage cruelties. He allowed them but five farthings a day, so that many of them grew very sick, all very weak...Now there began to be a great cry among them for bread and water; but Smith and his officers denied them both, though a river ran below the castle walls'. So desperate were they for water, that if ever they were brought out for cross-examination, they seized the opportunity to drink 'the water wherein most of the gentlemen had washed their hands' or rainwater from the courtyard. More than one story circulated at the time of prisoners driven in total desperation to the point of drinking their own urine.

Medical help was always refused to Smith's cries of 'the devil take them'. Although any money or food sent in by relatives was normally seized, sometimes the guards were successfully evaded. Food smuggled in to the Marlborough men apparently saved their lives. Truculent prisoners were singled out for special treatment. 'Some hath he tied neck and heels together for the space of forty-four hours', noted Wirley, 'not suffering them to have one bit of bread or drop of water'. Another poor wretch was savagely beaten with a cane before being locked in dungeon without light or water for forty-eight hours. Those who tried to escape were submitted to the torture of horrid burns inflicted by the smouldering match of a musketeer.

Part of Smith's objective in conducting this reign of terror was to force the prisoners to yield to the king's mercy. Release could be gained by first taking the Protestation (i.e swearing to support the king and church against the Earl of Essex) and then paying money to buy their freedom. Mr Bailey from Marlborough paid £200 to gain freedom in this way for himself and his son. The son, however, refused to take the Protestation and therefore continued in prison. The Marlborough constable, Mr Dunden, on the other hand, took the Protestation, but refused to pay the £59 fee demanded.

Eventually, in March 1643, Wirtley and others managed to escape from the castle through a hole in the wall, lying low in a baker's yard before swimming the river to safety. Their vivid description of their conditions (which were 'below the grave') and Smith's violent and disgraceful methods created a sensation in London and the Commons. Indeed, such was the outcry against him that he was even discarded by the king's own parliament, which had him arrested and then pilloried in the streets of Oxford.

Sources: BL, 93 (23), *The Prisoners' Report or a True Relation of the Cruel Usage of the Prisoners in Oxford* (1643); BL, E89(13), *A True and Most Sad Relation of the the Hard Usage and Extreme Cruelty on Captain Wingate*, 9th February, 1643; BL, E105(16), *Intelligence from the Army...with a Relation of Captain Wingate's Escape from Oxford*, 8th June 1643; Charles Carlton, *Going to the Wars* (1992), 249-50

St George's Tower, part of the derelict medieval castle, which was used as a prison in Oxford during the war. (Author's collection)

CHAPTER 9

Forced to Share: Living in the Shadow of a Garrison

You may read it in the ruins of this place...her heaps of rubbish, her consumed houses, a multitude of which are raked in their own ashes. Here a poor forsaken chimney, and there a little fragment of a wall that have escaped to tell what barbarous and monstrous wretches there have been.
(George Newton, Minister at Taunton, 1646)

The Strategic Use of Garrisons

In many counties in England, the nearest ordinary people came to personal involvement in military affairs was through the activity of a local garrison. Indeed, large numbers of soldiers spent the entire war serving as members of garrisons and never actually took part in open-field battles. By the summer of 1645, almost half the royalist forces (which totalled something over 40,000 men in all) had been spread thinly between garrisons dotted around the country. Sir Ralph Hopton, for instance, was alone responsible for 40 garrisons when he commanded the west of England for the king, while in the final months of the war no fewer than 81 royalist garrisons nationwide surrendered with some 23,000 troops. (1)

Each garrison, whether royalist or parliamentarian, became responsible for controlling a specific area. Within that area, its tasks included subduing the local community, if hostile, by placing it under martial law; guarding vital routes for armies and traders, centres of economic importance and supply lines; collecting taxes to support the war effort in general and the garrison in particular; strengthening its force by recruiting soldiers through local impressment; housing a central armoury and powder magazine for the area; protecting the local community from attacks by enemy patrols and providing a refuge for them in times of danger; offering security for the goods and valuables of local people under threat of imminent attack; and requisitioning food and other supplies to support the garrison, especially when taxes failed or wages remained unpaid. In view of the fact that garrisons could become virtually self-sufficient, it was tempting to both sides to establish more and more such garrisons simply in order to ensure that troops were fed. This policy, however, undermined the strength of field armies - a point made by parliamentarians, who often taunted royalist commanders for preferring to have a garrison 'at every five miles and not to fight so often in the field'. This proliferation of garrisons inevitably put an enormous amount of strain not only upon the inhabitants of the towns or villages concerned, but on the surrounding area, which effectively became a military zone.

There were several types of garrison. In the west country, the major ones were situated either in defendable towns such as Gloucester, Bristol, Bath, Taunton, Bridgwater and Malmesbury (i.e. towns which were protected to a greater or lesser degree by medieval walls, major earthworks or deep moats); or strong medieval castles, such as Sudeley, Berkeley, Beverstone, Nunney, Farleigh, Dunster and Wardour. Other garrisons were posted in towns of strategic importance on major

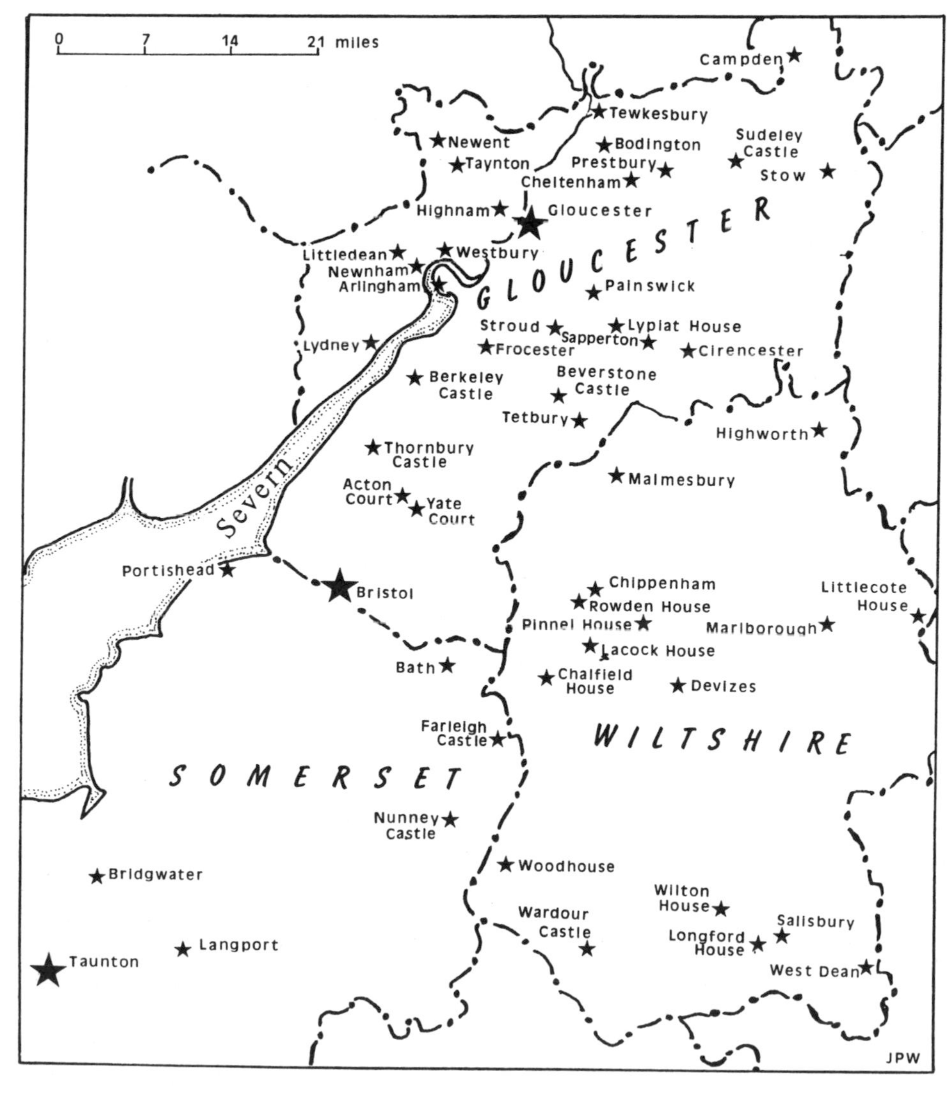

Map showing the location of important garrisons in the three western counties

routes, but which lacked formal defences and were therefore 'open' to frequent attack. Relying heavily on barricades and minor earthworks, these included Tewkesbury, Cirencester, Stow-on-the-Wold, Wells, Langport, Minehead, Salisbury, Chippenham, Marlborough and Devizes. They therefore tended to change hands in fairly rapid succession. Major garrisons with a large area to patrol often needed the support of smaller outposts or satellites placed in a network at strategic points. These minor strongholds could be situated either in large country houses, suitably strengthened with earthwork defences, such as (in Wiltshire) Chalfield House, Longleat House, Woodhouse, Rowden House, Littlecote House, Wilton House, Longford House, West Dean, Lacock Abbey, Pinnel House, (in Gloucestershire) Yate House, Acton Court, Highnam Manor, Huntley House, Lypiatt House, High Meadow, Prestbury Priory, Campden House, Hartbury Court, Eastington Manor, Lydney House, Boddington House, Miserden Park, (in Somerset) Wellington House and Sydenham House; or in solid medieval churches, where the tower provided a strong point for defence, such as the churches at Highworth in Wiltshire, Burrow Bridge in Somerset and Painswick, Westbury and Newnham-on-Severn in Gloucestershire. (2)

Although some of these garrisons saw little action throughout the entire war (for example, Miserden Park, Chalfield House and Littlecote House), others found themselves in the thick of fierce fighting during times of siege. It has been estimated that, out of 645 engagements during the course of the three Civil Wars (1642-6, 1648, 1650-1), no fewer than 31 per cent of them were sieges accounting for over 20,000 deaths. Sieges (which could last for several weeks or even months) were much more gruelling and dangerous to endure than open-field battles (which only lasted one day) - and, by their very nature, caught up far more ordinary people in their wake. The experiences of local townsfolk and villagers are vividly illustrated by the major sieges which took place in the three western counties (Bristol, Gloucester, Wardour Castle, Taunton and Bridgwater), as well as by events which occurred in the minor garrisons. (3)

The degree to which communities were oppressed depended largely on the character and background of those appointed to be governors of garrisons and commanders of armies. In the first year or so of the war, both sides relied heavily on the leadership of well-established county families to spearhead the war effort. For parliament, direction was exercised in Gloucestershire by Thomas Pury, Sir Robert Cook and Nathaniel Stephens; in Somerset, by Alexander Popham, John Horner and William Strode; and in Wiltshire, by Sir Edward Baynton, Sir John Evelyn and Sir Edward Hungerford. For the king, control was in the hands of such men of local stature as Sir John Stawell, Edmund Wyndham, Sir John Poulett, Sir John Berkeley, Sir Ralph Hopton, Lord Chandos and Sir James Long. Although their commitment to the chosen cause was beyond reproach, they also retained a deep sense of loyalty and understanding towards their neighbours within the county. This helped to ensure that countryfolk were more justly treated as the demands of war grew. Later in the conflict, however, these local leaders were deliberately sidelined and their role as governors and commanders delegated instead to carefully-chosen outsiders. They were trusted and experienced soldiers, who had no family or friendship ties with the local populace and who therefore had no compunction in collecting taxes and requisitioning supplies without compassion. Colonel Edward Massey, Sir Henry Bard, Colonel Nathaniel Fiennes, Prince Rupert, Prince Maurice, Sir Charles Lucas and Sir Jacob Astley viewed their military needs with far greater objectivity and pursued their ends with a far more determination and ruthlessness. Put bluntly, their task was to extract from the countryside as much as they could for the cause they served, irrespective of the methods used. (4)

Stripping the Countryside

In the area immediately around a garrison, ordinary everyday life became virtually paralysed as the threat of attack increased. Quite apart from the growing demands placed on them for free quarter as the besieging army assembled (see Chapter 5), local people also faced the total loss of their produce as the garrison hurriedly built up stocks for the siege and, at the same time, swept the locality clear of anything that would benefit their attackers. In the spring of 1645, for example, Colonel Robert Blake, the parliamentary Governor of Taunton, managed (in the nick of time) to take in three months supplies from the surrounding districts, just before Sir Richard Grenvile's royalists arrived to commence the siege. In an earlier assault on the same garrison in October 1644, Colonel Edmund Wyndham had succeeded in capturing the poorly fortified town, but had still to tackle the castle, where Blake's forces were firmly secure. In a desperate attempt to starve the garrison into surrender, Wyndham issued an order forbidding the townsfolk from buying in any provisions from the countryside, lest they should manage to smuggle them into the castle. According to the *Parliament Scout*, it was 'like starving all Somerset to make Taunton Castle yield'. Exactly the same policies were adopted when Sir Thomas Fairfax brought the New Model Army to lay siege to Bridgwater in July 1645. Camping on Weston Moor two miles from the town, he spent two days scouring the countryside around for supplies and clearing it of enemy outposts planted by the Governor, Colonel Wyndham. These included Sydenham House (where 100 prisoners were taken) and the church at Burrow Bridge (which yielded 150 more). Suddenly the whole area had become a no-go battle zone. Country people living inside that zone often found themselves being conscripted against their will into the besieging army (as at Taunton, where Lord George Goring had ruthlessly forced many villagers to join the ranks), though large numbers of these inevitably deserted at the first opportunity (as at Bridgwater where 300 men, taken prisoner by Fairfax in the early stages of the assault, promptly volunteered to fight for him instead). In such terrifying circumstances, some villagers sought refuge with their valuables inside the garrison (as at Taunton); some co-operated with the attacking force by helping them to make scaling ladders or brush faggots for the assault (as at Bridgwater); and some simply went into hiding. Bulstrode Whitelocke commented that, at the siege of Taunton in 1645, 'the country thereabouts was much unpeopled by the besiegers'. (5)

Not all garrison commanders, however, requisitioned or plundered their requirements at will. Colonel Edmund Ludlow, Governor of Wardour Castle during its three-month siege in the winter of 1643-4, made it a

Edmund Ludlow was commissioned as cavalry captain in Wiltshire by parliament in 1643, acting as governor of Wardour Castle (May 1643 - March 1644); appointed High Sheriff of the county (May 1644), he was promoted to colonel of a Wiltshire cavalry regiment under Massey (July 1644). (By courtesy of the Ashmolean Museum, Oxford)

point of principle that he 'always paid the country people' for whatever he took from them. Although desperately short of ready cash at the time, he 'suddenly made a seasonable discovery of money, plate and jewels to the value of about twelve hundred pounds', which had been hidden in the castle by its actual owners. He was able to use this, therefore, to build up his stocks for the siege, even though the royalist forces were already moving into the villages around to stifle his supplies. He recalled in his *Memoirs*: 'We ventured one morning, knowing it to be market day, to draw out between forty and fifty pikes and firelocks, with which we went about a quarter of a mile from the castle upon the road that leads to Shaftesbury. According to our expectation, the market people came with carts and horses loaded with corn and other provisions, which we seized and sent to the castle, paying for it the market price, at which they were not a little surprised. By this means we furnished ourselves with three months more provisions than we had before; which we had no sooner taken in, when the enemy drew round the castle and, from that time, blocked us up more closely'. (6)

One of the best examples of the countryside around a garrison being stripped of all its essentials is provided by a compensation claim submitted by Richard Aldworth, the former Mayor of Bristol. Here was a man who had already given generously to parliament's cause in the early months of the war, contributing no less than £1,200 out of his own pocket in 1643 to pay the soldiers in Colonel Thomas Essex's original garrison force. When, however, the New Model Army arrived outside the city in the summer of 1645 to commence the siege, a large part of the force quartered upon his land at Ashley. They not only stripped his meadows of turf (presumably to line their siege works), but also took all the hay crop from his other fields, valued at fifty pounds. This was apparently 'eaten by all the horses in general'. Furthermore, the soldiers pulled down two of his houses (valued at forty pounds) so that they could use the timber to build a series of huts. As a result of all this intrusion, his tenants at Ashley stopped paying their rent, because of 'the damage they have suffered in grass'.

It was much the same in other villages round Bristol. As it prepared to take the city by storm, the besieging army found itself in great need of wood for the construction of scaling ladders, bridges and pike staves. They therefore instructed the inhabitants of Abbot's Leigh to cut down 'young timber trees' in Mr Norton's wood, to deliver '300 deal boards' and supply '4 masts for the making of the bridge at Bristol', plus a good quantity of ladders and pikes. Portbury, Backwell and Wraxall were all called upon to supply ladders and pikes, while the latter was ordered in addition to provide four men and ten oxen for a period of three days to haul timber to Bristol. From Norton Malreward they requisitioned a load of straw (often used for the protection of gun emplacements) and a load of faggots (used for filling in the ditch prior to an assault). Such was the distress in Bedminster caused by excessive demands during this period, that the parliamentary commissioners wrote in great concern to Sir Thomas Fairfax, alerting him to the fact that the inhabitants had 'suffered in the eating and spoiling of their hay, grass and corn to the sum of 400 loads', at an estimated cost of over £266. They urged him to provide urgent payment to all the owners out of the weekly assessment. (7)

Protection and Burning Money

There was an expectation that the garrison, drawing its resources from the locality to which it had been assigned, would treat the inhabitants with the sort of respect shown by Ludlow and protect them from enemy attacks. Sometimes, however, bribes were required to make the system work. In 1644, for instance, the royalist governor of Langport (Sir Francis Mackworth) promised protection for the estates of the Cote brothers from Curry Rivel, but only after they had sent him cattle for the use of the garrison. On the other hand, if villagers refused the demands of the local garrison for supplies, some of the more ruthless governors would not hesitate to send in troops to demand 'burning money'. This amounted in reality to protection money to save their houses from being burnt to the ground. The worst exponent of this tactic was undoubtedly Sir Henry Bard, the royalist governor of Campden House in Gloucestershire, who terrorised the locality with his brutal threats. Even the royalist Earl of Clarendon thought fit to comment that Bard's garrison 'had brought no other benefit to the public than the enriching the licentious governor thereof, who exercised an illimited tyranny over the whole country'. After leaving Campden, Bard issued a characteristic statement to the inhabitants of South Worcestershire (who had been under his control when at Campden) demanding unpaid tax arrears within a week. Failure to comply would mean that 'you are to expect an unsanctified body of horse among you, from which if you hide yourselves (as I believe each of you hath his hole) they shall fire your houses without mercy, hang up your bodies wherever they find them and scare your ghosts into your drabbling garrisons'. (8)

The Jacobean lodges, gateway and stables are all that remain of Campden manor house, garrisoned for the king by Sir Henry Bard but deliberately burnt down on his departure in 1645. (Author's collection)

In April 1645, Bard launched one of his many raids on the local population as part of a reign of terror, an incident reported in *The London Post*: 'A party from Campden marched from thence to Winchcombe and plundered the whole town, drove away the cattle and left the poor people not so much as a clean shirt for Easter Day'. His oppressive regime was also felt at Marston and Pebworth, where the bailiff of the Marquess of Salisbury received frequent visits from Bard's officers demanding money and provisions. It is significant that, although numerous payments were made to various commanders of both sides over a period of many months, by far the greatest single sum went to Bard (£100). The suggestion that violent pressure might have been used on occasions is perhaps confirmed by two other entries in the bailiff's accounts. First, an indication that, when the local parliamentary committee sent Captain Roberts to collect their tax arrears, they accepted a token sum of £5 after 'taking into consideration the miserable sufferings I had by Colonel Bard'; and secondly, the sum of two shillings, which was a legal fee 'for taking my oath for the abuses by Colonel Bard and recording it' (i.e. a sworn statement to be used later in evidence against Bard's 'war crimes'). (9)

Other commanders, too, followed Bard's example of ruthless behaviour towards local people, especially when an area was suspected of complicity with the enemy or was actually under enemy control. In 1645, for instance, Lord George Goring fired houses on this pretext in the Somerset towns Minehead and Bampton. It has to be said that Prince Rupert had already set the example when campaigning in Northamptonshire. He issued warrants to the inhabitants of Wimmersley, demanding supplies and the services of labourers on pain of 'the total plundering and burning of your houses and what other mischiefs the licensed and hungry soldiers can inflict upon you'. (10)

Some communities certainly felt that they were nor getting the protection they had expected from their local garrison. These feelings were eloquently expressed in a petition from people 'dwelling near unto the garrison of Malmesbury' in Wiltshire at the beginning of 1645. Their complaint was that people residing in the neighbourhood had gone to enormous lengths to support the parliamentarian garrison by providing both free quarter for the soldiers and plough teams 'to carry stone and timber and other materials for the fortifications, and to carry hay, wood and coals for other uses of the said garrison, without any payment for the same'. Furthermore, local gentry had run up huge debts in providing ammunition, arms and horses not just for the garrison, but for the defence of the county as a whole. In return for all this, the petitioners had hoped 'to have been protected in some measure from violence and rapine', yet they had found themselves continually at the mercy of royalist raiding parties who had not only demanded taxes, but had 'plundered and spoiled' the petitioners. The garrison troops had totally failed to take any action, but had 'rather applied themselves to excessive drinking, profane swearing and vicious and riotous living'. This neglect of duty had meant that the enemy had always managed to surprise the garrison troops and thus 'to ruin us'. (11)

Clearing Houses in the Line of Fire

Survival of the neighbouring community became an increasingly vital issue with the approach of enemy forces intent on launching either a siege or an assault of the garrison in question. Malmesbury, for instance, changed hands six times during the war, putting local villages in a constant state of jeopardy, for it was no longer simply a question of yielding to a demand for taxes and supplies. Their very homes, barns and churches were now at stake as the garrison sought to establish an area of clear, open ground immediately outside their line of defences. This was essential for a number of reasons - to provide an unobstructed line of fire from their protective walls and earthworks; to deny the attackers any possible cover for their sharp-shooters as they moved in for the assault; to ensure that no cottages or sheds remained which could be used as billets for shelter or lodging; and to remove any materials (such as wood and stone), which might be useful to the enemy in building huts or maintaining fires.

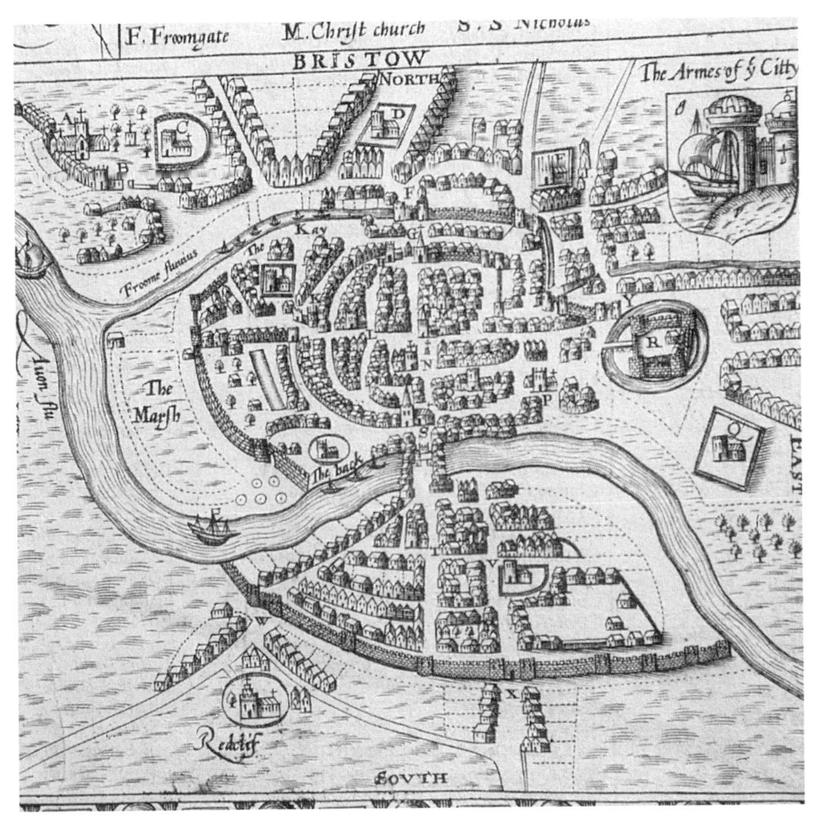

John Speed's map of Bristol (1610), showing the city walls and castle. (By courtesy of the Bristol Central Library)

Military necessity, therefore, often resulted in a 'scorched earth' policy around the garrison as suburbs outside the walls were razed to the ground. There were exceptions - the royalist garrison in Bath failed to do this in 1645 on the approach of the New Model Army, just as successive garrisons in Malmesbury (both royalist and parliamentarian) rejected that option throughout the entire war. Elsewhere, however, it was very different. The City Council in Gloucester, for instance, ordered the demolition of 241 houses in the suburbs as the siege of Gloucester commenced in 1643 (see Chapter 8). In Bristol, as early as October 1642, the Corporation had given instructions that the little cottages or hovels, which had been packed into the area around the old castle walls, should be removed to enable the moat to be reopened and platforms erected for the cannon. Later in August 1645, the royalist Governor (Prince Rupert), faced with the approach of the New Model Army, ordered the destruction of villages outside the long line of earthworks, which protected the city itself. He was only partly successful, because Sir Thomas Fairfax had anticipated his actions by sending out a party of horse ahead of the main force 'to prevent the burning of the towns and villages adjacent'. They arrived in the nick of time and managed to save places like Stapleton, Keynsham and Hanham from destruction, even though Rupert had actually despatched 'parties of horse with fire-balls to set them on fire'. Sadly, however, Fairfax's men were too late to save Bedminster to the south and Clifton, Redland and Westbury-on-Trym to the north, which were duly 'consumed with fire'.

At Bedminster, many homes were burnt to the ground, together with St John's Church (the rebuilding of which was estimated at a cost of £3,500 in 1653). The old medieval college at Westbury-on-Trym, which had been transformed into a manor house by Ralph Sadleir, was badly damaged by fire, along with several chests of records. In September 1646, his tenants in Westbury submitted claims totalling £2,000 for damage sustained to their property, while those in Redland claimed £460 for the destruction there. In Clifton, tenants put in a bill for £845 for fire damage to their houses, which also left the manor house in ruins and the church devastated to such an extent that it needed total reconstruction in 1654. The flimsy wooden structures, which provided homes for ordinary village farmers, were easy to demolish. It was much more difficult to remove the solid stone churches which served these parishes - yet the task was doubly vital, because churches could provide a strong forward base for the attack on the garrison, with the nave being used as a powder store and the tower as a look-out post. St Owen's Church in Gloucester, for instance, which stood outside the South Gate of the city, was demolished prior to the siege of 1643 - though its valuable fittings and materials (particularly lead and stone) were carefully removed for future use elsewhere. (12)

The importance of removing houses and other substantial buildings from this clearance zone was highlighted during the siege of Bridgwater in July 1645. The royalist garrison had been partly thwarted in this task by the obstructive attitude of the lord of the manor, Henry Harvey, whose home stood by the bridge just outside the main fortifications. In spite of an order for its destruction, Harvey, through 'much strong influence', managed to secure its preservation. However, when the house was eventually captured during the assault of the town, the New Model Army quickly converted it into a forward base for its guns, which were then turned onto the royalist's earthworks in the market place (much to the anger of the garrison). Harvey, a major property owner in Bridgwater, later claimed that, as a result of action taken by the royalist governor in preparing for the assault of the town, he had lost 20 houses and 30 gardens 'pulled down and laid waste', a pigeon house, a barn and two stables 'burnt to the ground by him upon the storming of the town'; and, as a result of the capture of the town by parliament's forces, 3 or 4 other houses and all his 'household stuff, wearing apparel, books and money', so that he had ' not a bed left to him to lie on'. (13)

Houses could also be destroyed by the garrison for a completely different purpose as they prepared to face up to an assault. Defensive earthwork structures were often required in towns either to supplement the old medieval walls or, where these were lacking, to provide a least a modicum of protection. The building of these inevitably caused the removal of many houses on the edge of the town. Archaeologists have in recent years uncovered massive civil war ditches at Taunton (built by Blake in 1645 and over sixteen feet wide), Devizes, Bridgwater (thirty feet wide) and Gloucester (over seventeen feet wide in Southgate Street and over thirty-two feet wide outside the South Gate). In Chipping Campden in Gloucestershire, 'near half the houses in the town' were pulled down when Campden House was fortified with earthworks. Furthermore, such earthworks were usually topped with freshly-cut turves from the local meadows - another form of destruction which robbed the local community of important grazing land for several years to come. (14)

Every Street a Battleground

If the experiences of countryfolk outside a garrison were sometimes frightening, the experiences of the civilian population inside were always horrendous once the assault had been launched. As a prelude to the storm, the attackers often mounted a day-and-night bombardment to terrorise the inhabitants and break their morale through tiredness. This happened, for instance, at both Bridgwater in July 1645 and Taunton in July of the same year, where, according to an eye-witness, it felt as if they were being 'besieged by a wall of fire'. This terror was accompanied by threats issued by the assailants that they would 'hang up every man, woman or child that came out'. Once the assault started, the civilian population could only cower in corners as troops devastated their property in bitter house-to-house fighting. Some of the garrisoned 'open' towns possessed only flimsy defences of earthworks, barricades and turnpikes. These were quickly penetrated by a determined force, so that private property then became the battleground for brutal combat. Even in Langport, which saw far less street fighting than some Somerset towns, all the main structures (the market house, town hall, market cross, Hanging Chapel and bridges) suffered severe damage during the battle in 1645. (15)

When Prince Rupert's forces took the Gloucestershire town of Cirencester in February 1643, he found 'the gardens and backsides' of many householders used as breastworks, the streets 'barricaded up with chains, harrows and wagons of risebushes', the market place set up as a mount for cannon and four large private mansions equipped with artillery as strong points for defence. The Spittalgate, he noticed, was defended by houses 'whose eaves were lined with musketeers'. This concentration of defence within the town itself meant inevitably that ordinary homes took the full brunt of the attack. One eye-witness recorded: 'About twelve o'clock, two or three regiments of foot...began a furious assault on the Barton, a great farm which lay not far from the town westward [and one of the fortified strong points], where they were valiantly entertained by some hundred musketeers that lay under the garden wall. So there continued at the Barton a very hot fight for some two hours, our men lying under the shelter of the wall'. Eventually, the royalist pikemen under Colonel Usser gained access to the grounds of the house from the rear. The colonel himself, 'with a fire-pike in his hand', set fire to the house and some hay stacks alongside. His soldiers did the same to other stacks, 'which made the place too hot and smoky for the enemy' so that they quickly fled, choking on the fumes. Once this breakthrough had been made, the royalists burst into the town crying 'the town is ours, follow, follow', leaving the farm and its contents in ruins. The garrison forces were hotly pursued from street to street, before making a last stand for over an hour in the market place, where surrounding houses were turned into mini garrisons. (16)

Lord George Digby had fought at Edgehill in 1642, before helping to lead the attack on Marlborough. By 1645, he was a general and a member of the king's council of war. (By courtesy of Bristol Central Library)

Marlborough in Wiltshire was also a town which lacked formal defences. When, therefore, a royalist force under the Lords Wilmot, Grandison and Digby launched an attack in December 1642, they soon broke through the hastily erected earthworks and barricades. A large dwelling house just behind the front line, which had been turned into a stronghold by the small garrison, was quickly fired by an exploding grenade. The resulting panic, as defenders deserted their posts, encouraged the royalists to surge forward into the town itself, crying out 'a town, a town for King Charles'. According to one eye-witness, they burst through the streets with drawn swords, 'cutting and slashing those men they met with, whether soldiers or not'. They also caused an enormous amount of damage (estimated at £53,000) as the soldiers ran amok, destroying 53 houses in the process (see The Horrors of War 8). (17)

In spite of the fact that Malmesbury in Wiltshire was a walled town with strong natural defences provided by steep cliffs and two rivers, the immediate suburbs had not been demolished in preparation for possible siege. The town's situation meant that any attacking force was limited to an approach along a narrow neck of land known as Abbey Row and leading to the West Port. Although the medieval walls and gates were still largely intact, the old Westport Gate had long since been demolished. In its place, by 1642, stood the West Bar, a heavy spar of wood with iron spikes protruding, which in turn was protected by earthworks and trenches on each side. Assaults on Malmesbury, therefore, were exclusively directed at this one point, standing as it did at the head of a narrow lane (Abbey Row) lined with the houses of the town's overspill population. These houses inevitably suffered considerable damage from the heavy hand-to-hand fighting, which took place on most of the six occasions when the town was captured during the war. In March 1643, after Sir William Waller had retaken it from the royalists, he described his advance along Abbey Row in a letter to the Earl of Essex: 'We fell to work with the town, which is the strongest in land situation that ever I saw; in the [out]skirts of the town, there were gardens walled in with dry stone wall, from whence the enemy played on us as we came on, but within half an hour we beat them out of those strengths...We fell on the West Port, wherein they had cast up a breast work and planted a piece of ordinance: the street so narrow at the upper end next the work, that not above four could march in abreast...As we fell on, our musketeers possessed themselves of some houses near the port, from whence we galled the enemy very much'. Eventually, Waller captured the town after a surprisingly meek surrender by the garrison.

Although the royalists recaptured Malmesbury in the following month, Colonel Edward Massey (the Governor of Gloucester) managed to restore the parliamentary garrison in May 1644 after another fierce battle along Abbey Row. In a letter to parliament, he described how his infantry and artillery pushed their way into the suburbs. 'The foot broke their way through the houses till they came almost up to the [earth]works and the only place of entrance into the town'. Here he erected a barrier across the street, so that his artillery could draw up within range, and captured 'the houses within pistol shot of the works' in readiness for the assault. The attack took place at night in pouring rain, as Massey's men launched a furious attack with muskets blazing and grenades exploding. The earthworks were quickly captured and the town taken. The cost of all this war-time activity to the residents of Abbey Row, however, had yet to be calculated. Three years later, in 1647, they and the other inhabitants of the parish of West Port submitted a heart-rending petition for urgent relief to the Wiltshire Quarter Sessions. 'Our parish is grown very poor and much decayed', they complained, 'and a great part of our houses and our church being pulled down and utterly destroyed'. The flimsy structure of their cottages had been no match for for rough treatment of troops, the explosions of powder (which had totally removed one row of houses), the close-quarter damage of musket fire and the destructive power of cannon balls fired from small pieces of artillery on the roof of the Abbey. The petition also gives a clue as to the reason why successive Governors of the town had resisted the temptation to demolish these cottages prior to a siege, in spite of the cover they repeatedly gave to the attacking force. It was apparently most convenient to have such accommodation close at hand for the benefit of friendly troops arriving at the town after the curfew had been sounded for the night. The residents therefore attributed some of their distress to the fact that their location right next to the town meant that they had 'suffered and sustained more than ordinary losses in regard of the abundance of soldiers that came continually to the garrison in the evening, when the gates were shut up and could not be admitted to enter the garrison'. They had therefore been forced to entertain both them and their horses. (18)

Taunton, unlike Malmesbury, was a town with few permanent defensive features, although it did boast a strong medieval castle, which was still capable of defying a siege. Garrisoned by the royalists for fourteen months from May 1643, it was retaken in July 1644 for parliament and placed under the governorship of Colonel Robert Blake. Surviving a three-month siege mounted by Sir Edward Wyndham later that year, it was again threatened by royalist forces in March 1645, culminating in a close siege from mid-April. During the slight respite, Blake had worked hard to strengthen the defences by building earthworks across each entrance to the town and blocking all the streets with solid barricades. This meant that the town could only be taken piecemeal, a situation which condemned the

Taunton Castle survived two sustained royalist sieges in 1644 and 1645. (Author's collection)

houses of many citizens to certain destruction. Sir Ralph Hopton finally launched a series of royalist assaults over a period of five days, commencing on 6th May. Faced by determined resistance, with each hedge and bank fiercely defended, the royalist forces eventually gained a foothold on the eastern side of the town, where about a hundred houses were fired in an attempt to terrorise the inhabitants. 'We will not leave a house standing, if you do not yield' was the cry, as yet another furious attack was started and sustained over an eight-hour period. So violent was the storm of musket fire that, according to one observer, 'nothing was heard but thunder and nothing was seen but fire'. Another onlooker reported: 'they played with their grenadoes and mortar pieces so hot and long, that they fired the town; so that I believe the one half of the town, which was two long streets of the suburbs, be burnt to the ground'. The defenders were

Colonel Robert Blake fought for parliament at the siege of Bristol (1643), before capturing and, as governor, twice defending Taunton from royalist attack. After the Civil War, he was appointed admiral and commander of the fleet. (By courtesy of the Ashmolean Museum, Oxford)

gradually pushed back through the town, fighting from house to house, until they reached the market place where cover was provided by earthworks, which ran between the castle and St Mary's Church. These were in fact the only remaining strong points in their possession. Much of the rest of the town lay in ruins. Blake's garrison, however, had miraculously survived. On 11th May, Hopton, hearing of the approach of a relief force from the New Model Army, hurriedly withdrew. (19)

Churches as Strongholds

Towns like Taunton, which were more open to attack, always relied on one or two strong points where last-ditch stands could be made. Medieval castles within the precincts of a town were particularly valuable, wherever they existed, as at Bristol, Taunton, Bridgwater and Dunster. Although the castle at Devizes lay partly in ruins even before the Civil War, its gatehouse was still sufficiently strong to provide a last refuge for the royalist garrison when Cromwell captured the town in September 1645. Churches, too, were ideal for the same purpose, providing as they did solid walls and strong towers. Many churches were therefore fortified during the war, causing major and lasting disruption to the religious life of the community. In Gloucestershire, the Abbey Church at Malmesbury, with pieces of light artillery mounted on its roof, provided a major strong point near the West Port. It therefore bore the brunt of fire from besieging armies as they attacked along Abbey Row, a fact testified by its outer walls, which are heavily pitted with the marks of musket balls. The church of St Peter, St Paul and St Mary in Westbury-on-Severn and the neighbouring manor house were together garrisoned and fortified throughout much of the war. In May 1644, Colonel Edward Massey arrived with a large force of horse and foot in an attempt to recapture the stronghold from royalist Colonel Winter. According to eye-witnesses, Massey's men brought up stools and ladders to the church, which enabled them not only to fire their pistols through the windows at the garrison, but also to throw in grenades. The subsequent fire caused the enemy to rush out in panic, before eventually surrendering. Massey then moved on to Newnham, where St Peter's Church had also

Musket bullet marks on the west wall of Malmesbury Abbey testify to the fierce fighting which took place during frequent attacks on the town. (Author's collection)

been garrisoned and strengthened by earthwork defences. According to John Corbet, the royalists were quickly driven from their outer fortifications, before making something of a stampede for the safety of the church. Massey's men, however, 'were too nimble...and rushed upon them', so that both friend and foe 'tumbled into the church altogether'. Although Winter's men then cried for quarter, one of his old servants (not wishing to face the shame of surrender) apparently 'gave fire to a barrel of powder, intending to destroy himself and all the rest'. The powder blast, which 'blew many out of the church and sorely singed a great number', so enraged Massey's troops that they 'fell among them and, in the heat of blood, slew nearly twenty'. (20)

St Michael's Church at Highworth in Wiltshire was fortified and garrisoned by the royalists in 1644. The garrison, however, was confronted in June 1645 by a detachment of the New Model Army under Oliver Cromwell, who immediately summoned it to surrender. When the Governor, Major Henn, refused to comply, Cromwell brought up his artillery as a prelude to the storming of the church. The warning shots, which were fired at the tower (judging by the scars which remain), were nevertheless sufficient to bring about a surrender. According to Joshua Sprigge, 'the soldiers had good booty in the church, took seventy prisoners and eighty arms'. The tower of St John's Church in Devizes (Wiltshire), which also carries the scars of war, was used as a look-out by the royalist garrison during Sir William Waller's siege of the town in July 1643, as was that of the neighbouring St Mary's. The lead from the roofs of both churches was plundered during the same episode for the manufacture of musket balls. During the siege of Bristol in 1643, Rupert occupied Clifton Church as a look-out post from where he could view the city. Guarded by Colonel Washington with 200 muskets, 100 pikes and two cannons, it was inevitably subjected to attack by garrison forces. The churches of St Mary's in Marlborough (Wiltshire) and St Michael's at Eastington (Gloucestershire) provide other examples of buildings used in the war effort and pitted with the marks of cannon or musket fire. Sometimes churches were used as magazines for the safe storage of gunpowder. During the siege of Gloucester in 1643, the church of St Mary

The deep scar to the left of the west door of St Michael's Church, Highworth, was reputedly made by a cannon ball fired by the New Model Army in 1645. (Author's collection)

de Crypt inside the town was requisitioned for this purpose by parliament, while the nearby church at Matson was used in similar fashion by the besieging royalists.

The very strength and security of these buildings also made them suitable as prisons. The churches of St Mary de Lode and Trinity in Gloucester, for instance, were both commandeered to house the 1,500 Welsh prisoners who surrendered when Highnam Court was seized by Massey's forces in March 1643. Similarly, the 1,000 parliamentarians who were captured in Prince Rupert's raid on Cirencester in February 1643 were imprisoned in St John the Baptist's Church; while St Edward's Church at Stow-on-the-Wold became a temporary prison in 1646 for 1,000 members of Sir Jacob Astley's royalist army, which surrendered there in the last battle of the war. St Mary's Church in Painswick, Gloucestershire, saw service in March 1644 as both a stronghold and a prison. Colonel Massey, Governor of Gloucester, had established an outpost there, which consisted of the church itself and the adjoining manor house (Court House), suitably encompassed by earthworks. Attacked by royalist forces under Sir William Vavasour, the small garrison withdrew into the church, which then suffered a fierce bombardment by two small cannons, before entry was finally gained by firing the doors and throwing in grenades. Forty defenders and a number of civilian volunteers were killed in the fighting. The walls of the church still bear the scars of battle, which saw the tower and east end damaged and the north aisle gutted by fire. The church then became a temporary home for the parliamentarian prisoners, one of whom (Richard Foot) carved a heartfelt inscription onto one of the pillars - a quotation adapted from Spencer's *Fairie Queen*: 'Be bold, be bold, but not too bold'. (21)

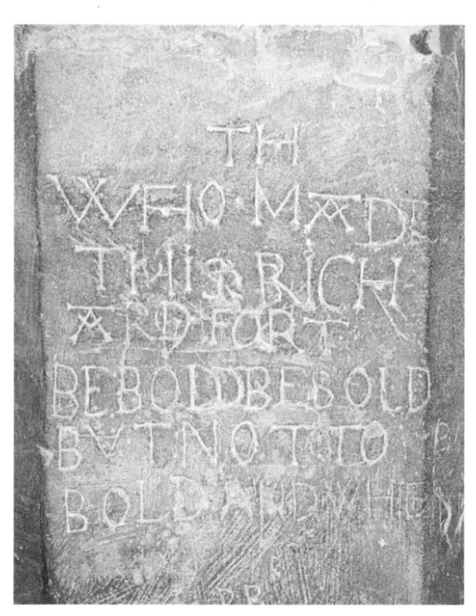

The inscription carved by Richard Foot on a pillar inside St Mary's Church, Painswick (see left). (Author's collection)

In Salisbury (Wiltshire), another town which lacked strong outer defences, the Cathedral Close was regarded by both sides in the war as the vital area to garrison. Surrounded by medieval walls and strong gates, it proved an ideal refuge for royalist troops under Colonel Francis Cook in December 1644, when they were surprised in the town by a detachment of Colonel Ludlow's Wiltshire horse. Cook's men fled, barricading themselves first in the Close (until the parliamentarians forced two of the gates) and then in two local inns, the Angel and the George (until these were set on fire by their pursuers). According to the parliamentarian writer, John Vicars, once the fire had taken in the buildings, forcing the royalists to surrender, Ludlow's troops actually 'helped to quench the fire'. Ludlow, of course, had every intention of establishing his own garrison in the town and therefore did not wish to generate unnecessary hostility among the local population. He subsequently strengthened the Close and set up his own headquarters in the massive structure of the Belfry, a medieval tower standing two hundred feet high near the cathedral. A few days later, however, nine hundred royalist troops, led by Sir Marmaduke Langdale, returned to Salisbury under the cover of darkness and caught Ludlow's garrison totally by surprise, many of the troopers having retired to bed in their billets around the town. After fierce fighting in the streets and about the market square, the royalists quickly gained the upper hand, causing their heavily-outnumbered opponents (who totalled no more than 450) to flee for their lives. (22)

Ordeal by Fire

The use of fire to destroy buildings or force out defenders during an assault has already been mentioned in connection with Cirencester, Marlborough, Taunton, Westbury-on-Severn, Newnham, Highworth and Salisbury. At Langport in Somerset, Mackworth's royalist garrison, which fled from Fairfax's pursuing troops after the rout of Goring's army in the battle on Ham Down, fired about twenty houses in Bow Street, partly to create a smokescreen to cover their flight and partly to put burning obstacles in the path of the enemy. At Bristol, in 1645, Prince Rupert fired the city in three places, after the New Model Army had successfully stormed its outer defences, in order to impede its progress. According to Joshua Sprigge, who was with the army, the fire proved difficult to extinguish, which 'begot a great trouble in the general and all of us, fearing to see so famous a city burnt to ashes before our faces'. Soldiers also claimed the right to set alight any building from which snipers were directing their fire. For instance, during the siege of Bristol in 1643, royalist forces, having breached the outer fortifications, 'marched directly into the suburbs, where the streets being narrow, many soldiers and officers were killed from the windows and tops of houses, which stopped their advance'. Colonel Gerard therefore issued a general warning 'talking loud to the people of firing the town, if they did not forbear shooting out of the windows'.

In all instances where buildings were to be burnt, several methods of firing were used. Individual soldiers could be sent in with a tinderbox (if time permitted) or a 'fire-pike', which consisted of a shortened pike with an inflammable bundle attached to the end. The artillery could also target thatched houses with heated shot, thus causing fire to spread, or mortars could be used with their explosive grenades to achieve the same effect. The fire-pikes could also be used to terrorise the enemy. When Colonel

Wentworth managed to breach the outer defences in the siege of Bristol in 1643, he sent an officer to ride 'along the inside of the line with a fire-pike'. This apparently 'quite cleared the place of the defendants, some of them crying, *wildfire* '. When, after the breach, the parliamentary horse staged a counter-attack, Wentworth quickly despatched them by sending some of his men to run at them with fire-pikes. 'Neither men nor horses were able to endure it;' reported one observer, 'these fire-pikes did the feat'. (23)

The siege of Bridgwater in Somerset by the New Model Army in July 1645 provides probably the most dramatic example of the destructive use of fire. After Sir Thomas Fairfax's troops had successfully stormed and captured the eastern part of the town (Eastover), the royalist troops withdrew across the River Parrett, which divided the town, into the safety of the castle area. From there Colonel Edmund Wyndham, the Governor, ordered a fire bombardment of Eastover. A parliamentary eyewitness recalled: 'Our forces had not been two hours in the first town [i.e Eastover], but the enemy shot grenadoes and slugs of hot iron and fired it on both sides, which by the next morning burnt that part of the town (of goodly buildings) down to the ground, except three or four houses'.

Fairfax therefore decided on an immediate assault of the western part of the town, using similar tactics in retaliation. 'Our cannon played fiercely into the town, grenadoes were shot and slugs of hot iron in abundance, whereby several houses in the town were fired, and the wind being high increased the flame'. Soon the town was burning in twenty places, including Cornhill, St Mary's Street and High Street. The people who suffered most, however, were the ordinary inhabitants. 'The townsmen within were in great distraction, every man employed how to save his house and goods...All that night they employed themselves to quench the fire in the town'. Fire-fighting equipment, however, was often in short supply during the Civil War, mainly because supplies of the copper-riveted leather buckets, which were manufactured in London, became virtually impossible. The number of buckets for use in Gloucester, for instance, slumped to thirty-two in 1645 from over two hundred at the start of the war. The fires, therefore, continued to rage in Bridgwater, where about one hundred-and-twenty houses in all were destroyed out of a total of approximately four hundred. (24)

Spies, Saboteurs and Conspirators

Both sides in the Civil War made good use of intelligence provided by either local people or prisoners. The parliamentarian garrison at Chalfield, for instance, employed a number of countrymen in this way and listed them quite openly in their accounts as 'spies' (see Chapter 7). In May 1645, as he mounted his operation to relieve Taunton from siege, Sir Thomas Fairfax sent spies into the town to let the garrison know that the signal for his approach would be the firing of ten pieces of artillery from the hills ten miles distant. Two months later, as he prepared for the assault on Bridgwater, he himself gained information from royalist prisoners that the garrison there was well provisioned for a siege and only lacked mills to grind their food within the fortifications. At the same time, however, he gathered far more encouraging intelligence from the villagers around that the inhabitants of the town were 'godly people', who would assist him in his attack. Events were to prove the accuracy of this prediction. After Fairfax had suddenly captured the eastern part of the town and commenced the bombardment of the western side, some of the townsmen apparently turned saboteurs to undermine the garrison's resistance. As the flames spread from the 'slugs of hot iron' launched in the bombardment, several additional fires were started deliberately in Silver Street, Friar Street and Pig's Cross to speed up the inevitable surrender. (25)

This, of course, was a highly dangerous tactic for ordinary citizens to adopt, however deep their loyalties to one side or the other. If it succeeded and was followed by a speedy surrender (as at Bridgwater), the garrison forces had little time to unveil the culprits. If, however, the plot failed, then retribution was swift at hand. This was the case in Taunton in May 1645, when Sir Ralph Hopton's royalist forces were besieging the parliamentarian garrison of Colonel Robert Blake. In a furious attack, Hopton had already seized most of the town and the outer fortifications, leaving Blake's men penned inside a few remaining strong points (i.e the castle, the church, the Maiden's Fort and the market place). At this moment, a group of pro-royalist civilians inside the town tried to spread fires in those parts which were still held by the garrison. Unfortunately for them, two of their number were caught in the act and lynched by an angry mob; another was cut to pieces by the soldiers; and a female accomplice was, according to an eye-witness, given a 'quick dispatch' by a crowd of women. Altogether some fifty people (who allegedly had been promised £10 each for their work) were implicated, several of whom were later hanged. (26)

Two of the most interesting examples of espionage at work, described by Colonel Edmund Ludlow in his *Memoirs*, took place during the siege of Wardour Castle in Wiltshire in 1643. As the royalist forces were gathering prior to the commencement of the siege, they sent a spy into the garrison in the form of a twelve-year-old boy. When the youth arrived at the castle, begging to be given menial employment as a turner of the garrison spit, Ludlow agreed to the request being deceived by his tender years. However, after a gun had mysteriously exploded as it was being fired, the guards on duty that night became highly suspicious of the boy. After rigorous cross-examination, they threatened to hang him immediately unless he would confess the truth. To frighten him further, they 'tied a piece of match about his neck and began to pull him up on a halberd'. A confession was quickly extracted in return for his life. He had been sent to ascertain the strength of the garrison, poison the water supply and the beer, blow up the ammunition and 'poison' the cannon (including the one that had exploded).

Wardour Castle, captured by parliament in 1643, was then held by Edmund Ludlow, who withstood a three-month siege until his surrender in March 1644. (Author's collection)

For his pains, he was to be paid half a crown.

Ludlow himself was not averse to the idea of infiltrating the enemy camp. Just before the siege of the castle had started in earnest, he had managed to send a civilian spy out into the countryside 'to inform us the the state of affairs'. This agent happened to meet 'at an honest man's house not far from the castle', a royalist soldier who had been reluctantly pressed into service. The man agreed to gather information on behalf of Ludlow, while remaining a member of the royalist forces. For instance, as soon as he heard of the approach of parliamentarian forces to relieve the castle, he was to 'appear with a white cap on his head and blow his nose on his handkerchief' (or, failing that, on his sleeve!). Some days later, this newly-recruited spy did indeed manage to signal messages across to the garrison from inside the besieging army, warning in particular of royalist plans to undermine the castle walls. (27)

Both sides frequently recruited spies on the spur of the moment to suit a particularly urgent need. Royalist sympathisers in Bridgwater, for instance, employed someone who was least likely to arouse suspicion to convey a message to the advancing royalist army in June 1643. 'The next morning', recalled Hopton, 'came a cripple on horseback...to advertise that the enemy had quitted that town; so a party was presently sent to seize it, which they did'. As the war progressed, however, proper intelligence networks were established by army commanders, while at the same time retaining the services of ordinary local people. Edward Clarke of Newent, for example, gathered together a team of messengers and spies, including cloth carriers, in the Forest of Dean to provide information on the movement of enemy forces and the location of parliamentary sympathisers suitable for plundering. Sir Samuel Luke, Scoutmaster General to the Earl of Essex, received no fewer than 261 reports from his scouts between February 1644 and April 1645 at his base in Newport Pagnell in Buckinghamshire. These agents, some of whom were based in towns throughout the western counties, provided valuable information (based partly on rumour and local gossip) about military activity. (28)

Nor did army commanders simply rely on official scouts and spies for intelligence. Almost from the outset of the war, the king expected all loyal subjects to pass on vital knowledge concerning the location of enemy forces to the nearest official or officer. His proclamation of 9th December 1642 stipulated that the inhabitants of Gloucestershire (and other counties) were to give immediate notice of any movements by Essex's troops to the constable of the parish. The declaration of the Gloucestershire royal commissioners on 11th January 1643 went even further in an attempt to prevent Massey's incursions into the countryside around Gloucester. Any inhabitants failing to report the arrival of 'such rebels' in their village or town would risk the confiscation of their estates. Similarly, ordinary citizens were under obligation to report those who 'entertain or harbour any of the enemy's scouts, spies or intelligencers'. This sort of pressure sometimes led to individuals being wrongly accused of spying. Christopher Dale of Salisbury was arrested 'upon suspicion of being a spy', as he was returning home from Wincanton with a party of butchers. He denied under cross examination that the had purposely 'gone out of his way to view the army'. The army, he claimed, had marched across his path and he had merely continued to ride in a straight line through it! In Gloucester, however, there was no doubt in the mind of the Council about the subversive practices of one inhabitant. William Garrett was duly fined forty shillings, in October 1643, 'he being taken for a spy'. Such was the level of anxiety in that city, fed by endless gossip and rumour, that the Council decided, in September 1645, to take action. 'To prevent clamours and false reports', it ruled, church bells should not be tolled 'for the death of any person whatsoever, before sunrising nor after sunset' - nor should they be rung at any funeral. (29)

In most occupied towns the citizens were content to concentrate their energies on maintaining the flow of everyday life whatever their own political sympathies. In Bath, for instance, the City Council met regularly throughout the entire war with those favouring the king sitting amicably alongside both the neutrals and those supporting parliament. Although Bath was largely puritan in religion and parliamentarian in persuasion, the townsfolk limited their opposition to the royalist garrison (which was installed between July 1643 and July 1645) to the slow payment of taxes, the withholding of traditional gifts to eminent royalist visitors and the sudden revival of celebrations marking Gunpowder Treason Day (5th November) and Crown Nation Day (the anniversary of Queen Elizabeth I's accession). These anti-catholic occasions gave local puritans the opportunity to reaffirm their protestant faith, while at the same time 'thumbing their noses' at the garrison. There was no underground resistance movement, no sabotage and no acts of heroic defiance. They concentrated instead on farming their fields, weaving their cloths and keeping open their markets. They submitted to the occupation with sullen acceptance, biding their time for the fortunes of war to turn. (30)

This was not always the case in Bristol, a city which lacked Bath's firm commitment to parliament's cause. By the spring of 1643, Bristol was firmly under the control of a parliamentarian garrison commanded by Colonel Nathaniel Fiennes, although the fall of Cirencester to Prince Rupert's forces in February had sent warning signals of possible threats ahead. It had also stimulated a group of royalist sympathisers inside Bristol to launch an audacious plot to seize control of the city. The leader of these conspirators was Robert Yeatman, a prominent merchant who had previously held the position of sheriff, assisted by George Bowcher, another highly respected merchant. Their force included some of the officers and soldiers inside the garrison, who were disgruntled at the sacking of the former Governor, Colonel Thomas Essex; a group of slaughtermen; and a motley collection of sailors. The rising, which was timed to take place on 7th March, had the backing of the king and Prince Rupert, who was to appear at the appropriate moment with reinforcements.

Colonel Nathaniel Fiennes, parliamentary governor of Bristol during the siege in 1643. (By courtesy of Bristol Central Library)

The plan in brief was that the conspirators would assemble in four houses, including those of Yeatman and Bowcher, where weapons had already been stored; the garrison officers, who had defected, would use their authority to seize the Guard House and the Frome Gate; and Prince Rupert would enter the city on the agreed signal, which was the ringing of bells in two of the churches. Sadly for them, Governor Fiennes had already gained intelligence of the plot, thanks largely to Yeatman's own indiscretions in The Rose tavern. His troops made lightening raids on the houses where the rendezvous was taking place, seizing a large stock of arms and around sixty prisoners, including several merchants, a barrister, a brewer, a soap-boiler, a goldsmith, a hatter and two Oxford scholars. Although some of these were later heavily fined through loss of their estates and most of the poorer sort were released after a spell in prison, the two ringleaders were tried and condemned to death. On 29th May, therefore, Robert Yeatman and George Bowcher were hanged from a scaffold erected in Wine Street, immediately outside Yeatman's own house. They left between them sixteen children and a warning to others that it did not behove ordinary citizens to meddle in the war. (31)

Fears of Starvation

Within the confines of a garrison under siege, citizens and soldiers alike were always subject to the fear of starvation, if supplies ran out. Everything depended on the efficient forward-planning of the Governor, as well as on the length of the siege itself. Colonel Massey at Gloucester in 1643, Colonel Wyndham at Bridgwater in 1645 and Prince Rupert at Bristol in 1645 had all managed to stock-pile adequate provisions as they prepared for the siege. Rupert in fact ordered all the inhabitants to provide themselves with enough food to last for at least six months. After a survey, however, it was discovered that, out of the 2,500 families remaining in the city, some 1,500 were too poor to provide for themselves in this way. He therefore introduced emergency plans to compensate for this shortfall. Cattle from the countryside around were seized and taken inside the walls, while 2,500 bushels of corn were imported from Wales. When the city was finally taken by Fairfax's forces, it was discovered that the Fort Royal contained almost eleven months' provisions for 150 men, whereas the castle itself contained about half that quantity in addition. (32)

The danger was, however, that if a siege became too prolonged, foodstocks would inevitably run short. Colonel Ludlow, for instance, had made careful plans to make adequate arrangements for his parliamentarian garrison at Wardour Castle. A well had been sunk in the keep to provide fresh water; provisions had been bought from local farmers to last for a good three months. Nevertheless, the siege, which commenced in December 1643 and lasted until the following March, put enormous strain on supplies long before the castle surrendered; as Ludlow recalled in his *Memoirs*: 'Our beer was much spent, our corn much diminished, and we had no other drink but the water of our well which, though we drunk dry by day, yet was sufficiently supplied every night'. In an attempt to conserve remaining supplies, he sent away his troop of horse (partly because he lacked sufficient provender) and introduced a strict system of rationing. 'Three pecks and a half of wheat one day and a bushel of barley another served near one hundred men, which was all our force...This allowance was so short that I allowed one of the horse we had taken to be killed, which the soldiers eat up in two days'. As the siege neared its end, the situation became desperate. 'Our provision of corn which, at the rate we lived, would have lasted three weeks longer, was blown up with part of the ammunition; but our provision of flesh, being about four days, was preserved'. (33)

In such circumstances, some garrison commanders tried to conceal their dire state from the enemy by subterfuge. Colonel Richard Pater, the royalist Governor of Nunney Castle in Somerset, allegedly arranged for their one remaining pig to be so badly tortured that its agonising squeals would convey the impression that an entire herd was being killed for a feast. There is also a tradition that, during the siege of 1644, the garrison of Taunton was also reduced to its last pig. They therefore whipped this

Nunney Castle, which formed part of the Bristol garrison, was held for the king from 1643-45 by Richard Prater, a catholic. It was captured by a detachment of the New Model Army in August 1645, after cannon-fire had breached the walls. (Author's collection)

half-starved animal around the castle walls, making it cry in different places to deceive the attackers into a belief that fresh supplies had been smuggled in. Ludlow, too, attempted a similar form of deception during the siege at Wardour, when he received a visit from the king's emissary offering terms for surrender. Ludlow later recalled how he had permitted him to enter so that he would report back favourably to the enemy on the state of the garrison's provisions. The soldiers had been carefully briefed to create the impression that their empty hogsheads were full of beer and to spread out their slender stocks of beef, pork and corn on the top of empty barrels so that 'everything appeared double to them to what it was'. (34)

Sometimes, of course, a garrison found itself virtually at the end of its resources with the threat of starvation becoming more and more of a reality. By December 1644, the town of Taunton was in a desperate condition. Closely besieged by royalist forces under Colonel Edmund Wyndham for almost three months, the civilian population as well as Blake's garrison soldiers were in a constant state of hunger. Fortunately, a relief force under the command of Major-General James Holborne arrived just in time, forcing the royalists to break up the siege. In a letter to Prince Rupert, Wyndham stated how he had 'reduced them to that misery that it was impossible for them to have held out a week longer'. He illustrated this further by describing how Blake's troops had sallied out of the town to give chase to the royalists as they pulled away, but that they 'were so hungry' that they were unable to pass by any house without first stopping to search for bread. This not only enabled Wyndham's men to make good their own escape, but also to ambush the parliamentarians as they came out of the houses, killing them 'with the bread in their mouths'. Many ordinary citizens, however, had been saved from starvation by the timely appearance of the relief party. Joshua Sprigge recalled how the soldiers had found on arrival 'a sad spectacle of a flourishing town almost ruined by fire, and the people well nigh famished for want of food'. (35)

Bringing Pressure to Bear on the Garrison

Civilians who found themselves caught up inside a garrison for the duration of a siege did not always remain passively submissive as they awaited their fate. On numerous occasions they made significant contributions to the outcome of events by putting concerted pressure on the garrison forces. In July 1645, for instance, as the New Model Army marched into Somerset, Prince Rupert (the royalist Governor of Bristol) decided to strengthen his outlying garrison in Bath by sending a detachment of Welsh cavalry. However, when they arrived in the city, they were met by a noisy street demonstration. 'The town cried out as one man all against the Welsh: No Welsh, No Welsh!'. Such was the hostility of their reception by the citizens 'that the officers and horse would not stay to dispute it', but returned sullenly to Bristol. The inhabitants had reacted in this way not merely because of a dislike of the Welsh, but largely because of a genuine anxiety about admitting 'soldiers from infected Bristol', which apparently was 'so much infected that it was more like to take an army that be taken by it'. In Bridgwater, too, the royalist Governor (Colonel Wyndham), who had just rejected a generous offer of surrender terms, found himself pressurised by the townsfolk to negotiate with Fairfax's besieging army. With their homes burning about their ears as the New Model Army continued its fire offensive, the inhabitants cried out as one man: 'Mercy, for the Lord's sake'. Wyndham gave way and sent out hostages so that the negotiations could commence. (36)

In Bristol, terrifying news reached the walled city that royalist forces had breached the outer line of defences during the siege of July 1643. On hearing this, Mrs Dorothy Hazzard, a devout puritan who was not at all impressed with the lack of dynamism displayed by the Governor (Colonel Fiennes), gathered together two hundred women. They hurried to the vital Frome Gate of the city, where they worked furiously to strengthen it by blocking up the entrance with earth and woolsacks. She then sought out the Governor himself, urging him to stand firm in the defence of the city and promising him the active support of her body of Amazons, who, with children in arms, would provide a human shield against the enemy 'to keep off the shot from the soldiers, if they were afraid'. Although her pleas fell largely on deaf ears, the presence of her female task force alongside the soldiers at the Frome Gate certainly helped to strengthen their resolve. (37)

Meanwhile, further pressure was being mounted on the Governor from other quarters within the city. The very same news about the breach in the fortifications, which had stirred Mrs Hazzard into action, had provoked an entirely different response in other inhabitants. According to the Earl of Clarendon: '...the confusion in the town was very great and the apprehension that the army was already entered and that they should all be made a prey to the soldiers, if there were no articles made and conditions obtained for them, made the people so clamorous that the Governor yielded to their importunities and sent a trumpet to the prince to treat upon surrender'. However, the native population was not always such a benefit to those launching an assault upon a town. Indeed, the very presence of women and children inside a garrison could sometimes act as an inhibiting factor to the attacking force, especially where the inhabitants were known to be sympathetic to the cause. At Bridgwater, Fairfax actually delayed his final assault on the western part of the city (where Governor Wyndham and the garrison had taken refuge) to enable the women and children to leave. They were given two hours in which to depart lest, as Fairfax stated, 'the innocent should suffer with the nocent'. To his undying credit, Wyndham rejected the idea of keeping them as a human shield and permitted some eight hundred people in all to leave, including Mrs Wyndham. (38)

There is no doubting the power of ordinary citizens to influence the course of events, when they were united in fear. In 1644, a force of 1,500 soldiers from Ireland under Lord Inchiquin disembarked at Bristol for service in the royal army. This caused a wave of protest in the parliamentarian press concerning the presence of 'papists' in Bristol. When, therefore, three more shiploads of troops arrived from Ireland two months later, the pilots at Pill rose in mutiny and refused to allow them to sail up the Severn. Furthermore, Alderman Hooke called a meeting of sixty leading citizens in support of the pilots and warned the Governor that any attempt to force the 'papists' on the city would result in a rising by the trained bands. The ships were quickly diverted to Bridgwater! Earlier, in June 1643, Edward Popham, commander of parliament's forces in west Somerset, viewed the

This thirteenth-century gateway to Taunton Castle was one of the few parts of the civil war defences to survive. (Author's collection)

approach of Hopton's army with a deep sense of alarm. He therefore instructed all his remaining forces in Taunton to withdraw, bringing with them all their weapons and ammunition and throwing the ordinance into the castle moat. 'Upon this', noted Popham in a letter to Colonel Fiennes, 'the townsmen rose upon the soldiers, kept the guards and would not suffer them to march away'. In the middle of this 'mutiny' by the townsfolk, the royalists arrived, captured 1,000 weapons, 22 barrels of powder and eight cannons. Popham was understandably furious with the inhabitants of Taunton. (39)

Personal pressure from outside the garrison could also be crucial in the context of a civil war, which had split families asunder. During the siege of Wardour Castle in 1643-4, Colonel Ludlow was visited separately by two 'kinsmen', who each tried to persuade him to surrender the castle. He also received a letter from Sir Francis Dodington, the commander of the besieging forces, 'wherein taking notice of the relation between our families, he expressed himself ready to do me any friendly office and advised me to a timely delivery of the castle'. Pressure was increased even further as the siege reached its climax by the growing amount of fraternisation that took place between the garrison forces and the besiegers. They were already in close proximity and the breaches made in the fortifications made exchanges of conversation easy. Ludlow later recalled that the enemy had continued 'discoursing with my soldiers most of the night, promising them liberty to march away, if they would deliver Mr Balsum, our minister, or myself to them. Next morning, many of them came up to one of the breaches to persuade us to surrender'. Many of the common soldiers on both sides were, of course, drawn from the locality and knew each other well. (40)

Post-Siege Plunder

The citizens of a besieged city undoubtedly breathed a huge sigh of relief once the siege was over and the guns were silent. At the same time, however, they braced themselves for the inevitable sequel, namely the terror of violent plundering by troops, who regarded it as the rightful perk of victory. In drawing up the terms of surrender, the commanders of both sides normally tried to ensure that the lives and property of innocent inhabitants were protected. They did not always succeed. For instance, after the capture of Taunton by the royalists in June 1643, Hopton had drawn up a highly satisfactory agreement with the town council for a ransom payment of £8,000, aimed at preserving them from looting and damage. Amicable relationships were vital to the royalists, if they were to take advantage of the willingness of the country people around to provide them with free quarter, if 'soberly taken'. Although he and his generals were therefore 'very desirous' of establishing a firm discipline among the troops, they found themselves totally unable 'to repress the extravagant disorder of the horse', which completely ruined all his attempts to gain local confidence. It was a similar story in Bristol in July 1643. At the end of the siege, Colonel Nathaniel Fiennes (the Governor) and Prince Rupert agreed that 'all the inhabitants of the city shall be secured in their persons, families and estates, free from plundering and all other violence and array whatsoever'. The officers and soldiers of the garrison were to be escorted unmolested out of the city as far as Warminster; all gentlemen, who had taken refuge in the city, were 'if they please, with their goods, wives and families, bag and baggage, [to] have free liberty to return to their own homes or elsewhere, and there to rest in safety'. (41)

Sadly, all these terms were broken in a most shameful fashion. An eye-witness reported: 'When they came in, they ran like a company of savage wolves into men's houses and fell to plundering all sorts without distinction'. According to the royalist writer, the Earl of Clarendon, many of Rupert's troops were hungry for revenge, having been themselves badly plundered by parliamentarian forces after the siege of Reading the previous April. In consequence, some eight hundred of the Bristol garrison (including Fiennes himself) were seriously plundered as they left the city, many stripped of their clothes as well as their possessions. Ordinary householders, too, suffered considerable losses as their homes were ransacked. Various shopkeepers tried to salvage their goods by paying what amounted to protection money, only to find that the promises made by some soldiers were immediately broken by others. They were therefore forced to endure the galling experience of seeing their stock sold off openly in the streets. Certain inhabitants were targeted for special treatment, after a number of defectors in the garrison force had pointed a finger in the direction of those most disaffected to the royalist cause. The result was 'that one whole street upon the bridge, the inhabitants whereof lay under some brand of malignity, though no doubt there were many honest men amongst them, was almost totally plundered'. Two days after the fall of Bristol, the city Council tried in vain to halt the atrocities by granting £10,000 to the king as a sign of the 'love and good affection' of the city. It was all to no avail. (42)

According to Sir Bernard de Gomme (the royalist military engineer, who had worked on the fortifications of Bristol), this plundering was the work of 'stragglers and sharks that follow armies merely for spoil and booty'. He described how Prince Rupert did his level best to tackle a situation which was rapidly becoming out of control. Riding up to his rampaging troops, he 'was so passionately offended at the disorder, that some of them felt how sharp his sword was'. Even Nathaniel Fiennes, in a speech to the House of Commons, lavished praise on both Rupert and Maurice for the attempts they had made to quell the rioters. 'I must do this right to the Princes, contrary to what I find in a printed pamphlet, that they were so far from sitting on their horse, triumphing and rejoicing at these disorders, that they did ride among the plunderers with their swords, hacking and slashing at them, and that Prince Rupert did excuse it to me in a very fair way, and with expression as if he were much troubled with it'. Part of the problem was that the soldiers felt that it was their right to take plunder after the successful storm of a town, a fact confirmed by Sir John Byron in a letter to Rupert. He had been sent back to Oxford after the victory with his two brigades, only to find that many of his men had deserted in an attempt to remain in Bristol. The reason for this, he said, was their anger at the thought that they had been deliberately sent away to deprive them of 'their share in the pillage of Bristol'. They wanted guarantees that they would have their fair proportion 'as well as the others'. (43)

Cirencester, of course, had been one of the very first towns to experience the horrors of post-siege plunder, when Rupert took it by storm in February 1643. There, too, the violence had been indiscriminate. 'They

Sir John Byron (created Lord Byron in October 1643) was one of the first to join the king in York at the start of the war. He later served as colonel of his own regiment of cavalry at Edgehill, Roundway Down, Bristol (in 1643), Newbury and Marston Moor. (By courtesy of the Ashmolean Museum, Oxford)

spared not to plunder their best friends', wrote one observer; 'for I can assure you, some of the most notorious delinquents were the most notably plundered of all the town'. Nevertheless, royalist troops made a point of searching out some of the main parliamentary sympathisers by 'burning some particular men's houses, which were purposely set on fire after the town was won'. All-in-all, he noted, 'the value of the pillage is uncertain, but very great, to the utter ruin of many hundred families'.(44)

In view of the high risk that property would be lost, burnt or plundered during a civil war siege, it is hardly surprising that many citizens attempted to secure their valuables in one way or another. Some quite literally dug a hole in their garden and buried their cash until the danger had passed. A few, caught up subsequently in the turmoil of war, never returned to reclaim it. A number of these civil war coin hoards have been unearthed in recent years during building operations. In 1980, one such hoard was located in East Street, Taunton, just inside the old East Gate to the city. This was the area that suffered extensive damage by fire during fierce fighting in the sieges of 1644 and 1645. The hoard, which had been buried in an earthenware vessel in the ground behind the house, consisted of 275 silver coins (mostly shillings) with a total value of £14. 8s. 0d. - although another part of the hoard had clearly been scattered by the bulldozer before discovery. The latest date represented on the coins was 1644, a clear indication of their loss during the Civil War.

Another hoard was discovered in 1935 buried in a farmyard at Ashbrook, Ampney St Mary, near Cirencester. Stored in an earthenware vessel, it it consisted of 347 silver coins (the latest one struck in 1645-6). In 1981, a further discovery was made under the floorboards of a converted old barn in Weston-sub-Edge, also in Gloucestershire. A total of 307 silver and two gold coins (the latest dated 1642) had been secreted in a specially-constructed lead pipe, along with a scrap of paper on which was written, 'Ye hoard is £18'. Elsewhere, twelve silver spoons (with an estimated date of 1637-8) were found in 1963 beneath the floorboards of a house in West Market Place in Cirencester.(45)

While coins could be hidden in the garden, larger items of value were less easy to conceal. Many inhabitants, therefore, decided to store these for safe keeping in the castle or similar strong point within the garrison. In Bristol, the 1643 terms of surrender had clearly stated that all those who had carried any goods into the castle for safety during the siege were to 'have free liberty to carry the same forth'. Some writers at the time estimated that as much as £100,000 worth of property had been secured there in this way. Much of this was also plundered, as troops broke their way into the castle, although some owners managed to redeem their own items by paying fines. After the siege of Bridgwater in 1645, Fairfax's men discovered a large amount of property which eminent royalists (including Lord Goring and Colonel Wyndham) had stored there for safety. Although this was not in fact plundered by the troops, the parliamentary commissioners ordered it to be seized and sold in the streets. With the money raised, they were able to pay five shillings a man to the common soldiers as a reward for their work and to deter them from plunder. In fact, the articles of surrender were scrupulously observed, the soldiers refraining from violence and conducting themselves 'very gallantly' towards both inhabitants and prisoners alike. Later, in writing to the Speaker of the Commons, Fairfax requested a further financial bonus for the troops in recognition of their disciplined behaviour: 'I am very desirous to give some encouragement to the Army for their many services and especially for their honest and sober demeanour this day towards the prisoners and town, in refraining that violence and injury which hath often times brought dishonour upon most of the armies of this kingdom'. Parliament responded by sending down a sum of £5,000 to the army. (46)

The New Model Army had certainly established a growing reputation for honest conduct, as further witnessed by their self-restraint after the siege of Bristol in 1645. The terms of surrender stated that all citizens residing in the city or suburbs 'shall be saved from all plunder and violence, and be secured in their persons and estates from the violence of the soldier'. On this occasion, the terms were scrupulously observed. Other parliamentarian commanders had also established high standards of behaviour for their soldiers in victory, including Colonel Edward Massey, the Governor of Gloucester. His chaplain, John Corbet, recalled the capture of Malmesbury in May 1644: 'Upon the first entrance, Colonel Massey preserved the town from plunder, nor at any time did he suffer his soldiers to ransack any place that he took by storm, giving this reason, that he could judge no part of England enemy's country, nor an English town capable of devastation by English soldiers'. Sadly, when he operated as a field commander in Wiltshire in the dying stages of the war, the control he exerted over his marauding troops was far less impressive (see Chapter 6). (47)

The Devastation of Siege Warfare

In spite of Massey's own generous sentiments, many English soldiers were quite capable of devastating an English community, as witnessed by the inhabitants of Taunton in 1645. When the New Model Army's relief force entered the town on 11th May, after a siege which had lasted some 94 days, they were greeted by an appalling sight - the townsfolk in a state of starvation, with two-thirds of their houses burnt almost to cinders; and 150 of the garrison soldiers dead, with a further 200 badly wounded. Of the homes that remained standing, most had been stripped of their thatch to feed the horses and their bedcords to provide match for the musketeers. Next day, the terrified country people from the area around cautiously left their hiding places in the woods and made their way into the town out of sheer curiosity. An observer noticed their 'broad eyes of wonder' as the viewed the indescribable scene. On the first anniversary of the town's relief, George Newton, their puritan minister, asked the congregation to imagine what the situation *would* have been like if the town had actually been captured, by looking at the extent damage sustained in the *unsuccessful* assaults. 'You may read it in the ruins of this place', he said. 'Look about her and tell her heaps of rubbish, her consumed houses, a multitude of which are raked in their own ashes. Here a poor forsaken chimney, and there a little fragment of a wall that have escaped to tell what barbarous and monstrous wretches there have been'. (48)

THE HORRORS OF WAR 8

TAKEN BY STORM

AT MARLBOROUGH, 1642

Under threat of imminent royalist attack, Sir Neville Pool, MP for Marlborough, fortified the town in late November 1642 with 150 militia under the command of a Scotsman named Ramsey. These were reinforced by countryfolk visiting the town for market day, who suddenly found themselves enlisted with muskets thrust into their hands! The royalist raid a few days later, by 7000 horse and foot from Oxford under Lord Wilmot, is vividly described in a contemporary pamphlet entitled, *Marleborowes Miseries - written by those who suffered.* After somewhat flimsy resistance by inexperienced defenders, a general assault of the town took place, the attackers allegedly running through the streets 'with their drawn swords, cutting and slashing those men they met with, whether soldiers or not'. The town was totally surrounded. None escaped. The sequel was horrific.

The royalists now *'set fire in two other places of the town with their hands, of set purpose and malice, the fire raging and consuming house after house, without any stop or hindrance, or any man to help quench the flames. Thus we had four great fires at one time flaming, a fearful and very sad spectacle to behold: and at the same time, the soldiers breaking up of the shops and houses, and taking away all sorts of goods: breaking of trunks, chests, boxes, cabinets, bedsteads, chambers, closets, cupboards, coffers - they would break and dash them all to pieces: and carried away all kinds of wearing apparel... all sorts of sheets, beds, bolster cases, cutting up the cases and scattering the feathers in the very streets to be trampled on by horses and men: also searching men and women's pockets for money, and threatening them with pistols and swords to shoot or run them through, if they would not give them money: by which means, compelling many men to lead them to the very places where they had hid the money in the ground...*

Besides this, the spoil they did among men's goods was as much as their loss which they carried away - as in letting out whole hogsheads of oil and vessels full of vinegar, treacle, spice and fruit: and all this thrown about the shops, cellars and houses: besides the taking away and burning of books, for in one of our bookseller's houses they maintained a great fire for five hours together with nothing but books and papers. ...They brake up the town house and there they brake the chests and coffers that the records were in; and carried them away and brake off the seals and rent the writings in pieces. And the town's Great Charter they also carried away - so that we thought that Jack Straw and Wat Tyler's days had been come again'.

According to this source, they took in all about 100 prisoners; 7 barns full of corn and 53 houses were burnt down, leaving 195 people homeless. 600 families (c 2000 people) were subsequently in need of relief. An estimated £50,000 worth of damage was done to goods and property.

How far can this colourful account be believed? Is it, in fact, no more than political propaganda designed to rouse passionate feelings against the royalists? The story was in part substantiated by the Venetian ambassador, who wrote home with the news of Wilmot's attack on Marlborough: 'He half destroyed the place by fire, routed the parliamentary troops and sacked the houses of the disloyal people, carrying off several prisoners'. The royalist historian, the Earl of Clarendon, also confirmed many of the details:

When the king's soldiers fell on, after a volley or two, they [the townsfolk] *threw down their arms and ran into the town...The streets were in many places barricaded, which were obstinately defended by some soldiers and townsmen, who killed many men out of the windows of the houses...Ramsey, the governor, was himself retired into the church with some officers, and from thence did some hurt; upon this, there being so many killed out of the windows, fire was put to the next houses, so that a good part of the town was burned, and then the soldiers entered, doing less execution than could reasonable be expected; but what they spared in blood they took in pillage, the soldiers enquiring little who were friends or foes.*

Sources:
BL, E248(8), *Marleborowes Miseries: or England Turned Ireland, Written by those who Suffered* (1643); Edward, Earl of Clarendon, *The History of the Rebellion and Civil Wars in England,* vol.6, pp 156-7 (1888); CSPV, 1642-43, p 219

St Mary's Church, Marlborough, where parliamentarian leaders made a last-ditch stand against the royalist assault. Marks on the church walls are attributed to musket fire. (Author's collection)

CHAPTER 10

Forced to Endure:
The Lingering Effects of War

Nothing appears to our sight but ruin. Families ruined; congregations ruined; sumptuous structures ruined; cities ruined; court ruined; kingdoms ruined. Who weeps not when all these bleed?
(Richard Baxter, 'Saint's Everlasting Rest', 1649)

Sickness and Plague

It has been estimated that almost 85,000 men were killed in England during the Civil Wars, that slightly more than this were wounded in the fighting and that about 100,000 soldiers and civilians died from disease as a result of their involvement in military activity. Life, for instance, was extremely precarious for the inhabitants of any town or castle under siege, especially if their fresh water supply had been cut off (as at Gloucester in 1643) or their food stocks largely exhausted (as at Wardour Castle in 1644 or Taunton in 1645). It has been calculated that even small town garrisons could reckon on losing at least ten per cent of their population from disease during the war. Water-borne diseases, such as typhoid, quickly spread through the narrow confines of a packed city once drinking water had been taken from the polluted waters of the neighbouring river. Many sea-ports had also suffered from the scourge of the bubonic plague. spread by rats from the ships. Bristol, for instance, had lost a sixth of its population in this way on three occasions between 1565 and 1603, whereas in Newcastle the epidemic of 1636-7 carried away over thirty per cent of the population. The exhausted and hungry residents of a city under siege, living in crowded and unhygienic conditions, were easy prey to sickness of all kinds. (1)

The city of Bristol, so vital as a garrison throughout the war, suffered greatly from diseases as citizens and soldiers crowded into the narrow confines of the protected area. 'The new disease is very hot in that city', commented one visitor to Bristol in 1643, 'and near 200 die weekly thereof'. A year later, the plague again struck in a most devastating manner. For twelve months from October 1644 the population was ravaged, in spite of the Council's efforts to establish pesthouses. When the infection was first spotted in the area around the castle, an order was issued to remove all sufferers 'from out of the infected houses' to Knowle House or some other safe place outside the line of the defences. Seven months later, in June 1645, the regulations were further tightened against the worsening situation, which was described in a letter to Sir Samuel

Luke by one of his scouts. 'Bristol is extremely empty at present of soldiers and grievously oppressed with pestilence, which sweeps away 100 and sometimes 140 a week'. Henceforward, those infected were to be sent to a pesthouse complex of nineteen huts, but they would be allowed to return home after thirty days, if they stayed in good health. They would then remain in quarantine for a further fifteen days with no visitors permitted, using their time 'to wash their clothes and houses to avoid further infection'. It is estimated that this particular outbreak claimed as many as 3,000 lives.

The wealthier and more important inhabitants did their best to escape this threat to their lives by fleeing the city, not always realising that the plague had already spread to neighbouring areas. The Prince of Wales, commander of the king's western army, slipped away to Dunster in May 1645, where he was horrified to discover that eighty people had died of the disease in the previous month. Such was the general fear that the inhabitants of one street in the town had apparently knocked small holes into the party walls of their houses 'to avoid all necessity of going into the open street, whose air was considered dangerous to life', while at the same time maintaining contact with their neighbours.

By the summer of 1645, the situation was just as worrying to Sir Thomas Fairfax and the New Model Army as it was to the court of the Prince of Wales. As they left Sherborne on their way to besiege Bristol, Fairfax's concern was that of exposing his troops to the risk of catching the plague. His chaplain, Joshua Sprigge, noted at the time that it was impossible to quarter their forces 'in any town or village, but the sickness was in it'. Fairfax himself commented that 'the soldiers...run daily into infected houses...they must quarter where the sickness is very rife'. Nevertheless, in spite of all the risks, the troops were apparently spared. 'Not one officer or soldier in our army died of the plague that we could hear of', declared Sprigge. (2)

Parliamentarian Pensions: Maimed Soldiers and Widows

Large numbers of people were therefore caught up, one way or another, in the experience of war, but the suffering they endured was by no means confined to the four years of military action. The 653 battles, sieges and skirmishes reported between 1642 and 1646 left in their wake an untold amount of human misery for destitute widows, abandoned orphans, maimed soldiers and sick survivors. In theory, at least, help was at hand for many of these unfortunate wretches. As early as 24th October 1642, parliament had passed an Ordinance authorising maintenance to be given to maimed soldiers and the dependents of those who were killed. In doing so, they expressed their desire at every opportunity to 'let their children and posterity know the respect they bear to the memory of those who have spent their lives in the service of the church and commonwealth'. The plan in short was to encourage individual parishes to fund pensions from the local poor rates, allocating four shillings a week to those who qualified after authentication of injury or death had been received from the soldier's commanding officer.

This system of funding, of course, imposed yet another financial burden on local people, already groaning under the oppression of weekly assessments, free quarter, requisitions and plunder. Gradually, the government injected further cash of its own, granting a sum of £45,000 after the ending of the war, which enabled something in the region of 6,000 pensions to be awarded. Each county also became responsible for appointing a treasurer to collect money raised for the pensions fund by means of a maimed soldiers' rate charged on parishes. Nevertheless, the number of claims was so great and the shortage of cash so acute that a comprehensive solution was never possible. The system itself badly creaked. In 1646, the Somerset magistrates in Quarter Sessions noted that, because no treasurer for maimed soldiers had been appointed over the last year, no money had been collected - and there was 'a great want thereof, both to satisfy the pensions formerly granted and relieve others that have been maimed in the parliament's service'. Little wonder, therefore, that this question featured regularly in the lists of grievances submitted by both the army and the Levellers during the period 1646-1648. But in spite of their campaigns, the backlog of payments nationally was so great that, even as late as 1659, some 6,500 would-be pensioners were petitioning Lord Fairfax for relief. (3)

Nevertheless, some people were lucky. The petitions they submitted to the county Quarter Sessions for pensions provide a graphic view of their plight, the nature of their wounds and the levels of relief offered. Inevitably, in a civil war situation, there were some who were barred from even applying. All those suspected of royalist sympathies were struck off the lists, including some who had managed to slip through the net when royalist forces had been in control of the west country. The Somerset magistrates in 1646, therefore, warned in advance 'that several persons disaffected to the parliament receive pensions within this county as maimed soldiers', ordered the immediate ending of their payments. On the other hand, those who had fought for parliament received favourable consideration.

Out of a sample of twenty-eight petitions submitted to the Somerset Quarter Sessions between 1647 and 1659, eight related to the claims of widows. These included Christian Marks of South Petherton whose husband, Lieutenant Francis Marks, had been killed in action in Cornwall, leaving her with three small children 'and nothing to maintain them'. She was granted a gratuity of £4.00 'for the present from the treasurer for maimed soldiers, followed by a further sum of £3.00 in the following year. Maud Cope from Wellington, on the other hand, was granted twelve pence a week from the parish poor fund to support her and her two children, after the death of her husband at the storming of Wellington House had left her destitute. She continued to petition over the

Maimed soldiers and widows begging outside a church in the post-war years. (Line drawing by Stephen Beck)

following years, receiving several small sums in addition. One of the saddest cases, however, was that of Joan Burt of Durlenge. Owing to her 'great age', she was unable to support the children of her son, Jeffrey, who had been 'cruelly hanged' at Taunton after imprisonment, or the two children of her daughter (who had died) and her son-in-law, John Abbott (who had been killed at the siege of Bridgwater). The magistrates referred the case to the village overseers of the poor for action. Equally sad, was the petition of Alice Dramond of Horningsham to the Wiltshire Quarter Sessions in 1646. The loss of her husband, fighting for Colonel Edmund Ludlow at the siege of Wardour Castle, was only the start of her misery. Left with three small children and 'nothing to keep them', she was subsequently 'plundered by the adverse party of that little she had'. The whole family was then struck down with leprosy, so that they were now likely to perish 'for want of food and be turned out of door naked for want of house room'. Her case, too, was referred to the parish overseers of the poor for relief. (4)

An even more positive response was given to a petition submitted in July 1644 to Colonel Edward Massey, Governor of Gloucester. Joan Harris had been servant to Colonel Thomas Essex (a previous governor there), while her husband had fought for parliament in the garrison at Tewkesbury (where his pay arrears had risen to £15) and had subsequently been killed in Waller's army at the Battle of Roundway Down. Meanwhile, Joan had not only fallen on hard times, but had become so lame in one of her legs that she was 'like to lose her limb for want of a good surgeon'. Although her request to be given free treatment by one of the garrison's own surgeons was rejected, Massey did authorise an immediate payment of fifteen shillings. (5)

Long-Term Suffering: Stress, Accidents and Injuries

The men who survived the war, but in a sick or maimed condition, suffered from all kinds of problems not necessarily inflicted by enemy weapons. Some suffered from what was called 'camp fever', a type of malaria, brought about by a combination of exhaustion, polluted drinking water, inadequate diet and endless nights spent camping rough in sodden fields. For instance, James Tutt, a fuller from Taunton, had been struck down by 'a great and tedious sickness' on his last march to Worcester. At the time of his petition, he had been sick for sixteen weeks and was now 'under the surgeon's hands to the utter undoing of his poor wife and child'. This condition, which was well known in the army, was often fatal and always frightening. Richard Baxter, a chaplain in parliament's army at the siege of Bristol in 1645, suddenly found himself afflicted by the disease. Wisely, he rode with haste in the direction of Bath, which was famed as a health resort, where soldiers could find their cures, and sought out the most distinguished physician in town, Dr Thomas Venner (who had already published a book, *The Baths of Bath*, on the healing powers of its waters). Baxter suffered misery for a fortnight, after which 'the fever ended in a crisis of sweat and urine', though he was unfit for duty for several weeks. (6)

'Camp fever' was partly the result of stress on active duty. Some civilians too suffered in the post-war years from stress brought about by prolonged exposure to nights of terror during a siege or cumulative tension brought about by repeated visits from tax collectors, soldiers on free quarter and plunderers. One such sufferer was Lady Jordan, who sadly went out of her mind. According to John Aubrey, she was at Cirencester when it was besieged and 'was so terrified with the shooting that her understanding was spoiled, [so] that she became a tiny child'. Her friends therefore took pity on her and made baby dolls with which she could play. The combination of stress and tiredness could also cause terrible accidents on the field of battle through sheer carelessness. One royalist officer wryly commented: 'we bury more toes and fingers than we do men'. Sometimes, however, the human damage was far greater than toes and fingers. After the Battle of Lansdown, for instance, Sir Ralph Hopton was busy interviewing prisoners on the slopes of Tog Hill. According to Captain Richard Atkyns, who was with him at the time, some of the prisoners were 'carried upon a cart wherein was our ammunition - and had match to light their tobacco'. Suddenly, 'the ammunition was blown up and the prisoners in the cart with it, together with the Lord Hopton, Major Sheldon and Cornet Washnage...The hurt men made lamentable screeches'. Hopton had suffered terrible powder burns, his head swollen 'as big as two heads and his eyes near burnt out'. He was left temporarily blinded and was seriously ill for many days. Major Sheldon, too, was badly burnt. Atkyns, who found him 'complaining that the fire was got within his breeches', was horrified at the sight facing him - 'from as long a flaxen head of hair as ever I saw, in the twinkling of an eye, his head was like that of a blackamore'. (7)

Hopton at least recovered to fight another day. He had the means and the power to ensure that he received the best medical attention available at the time from the regimental surgeon. Not everyone involved in battlefield accidents was as lucky. Nicholas Small of Taunton was injured in this way while on active service for parliament at the siege of Oxford. He was in the process of cleaning his musket, which he had been ordered to do, when it went off by accident, causing an horrific injury to his hand. He was so badly maimed that, at the time of his petition some years later, he was 'in a very distressed condition' and altogether disabled from work. When Small first applied for a pension to the Somerset Quarter Sessions in 1652, he was not successful because his wounds 'had yet to be seen'. It was a strict rule that an applicant needed, first, to gain supporting evidence of the fact of injury from the officers responsible for him at the time (which Small had done) and, secondly, to be subjected to a personal examination of the wounds to ascertain whether the disability would be permanent. By the time that Small's petition was given a second hearing later in the year, the magistrates were satisfied on both counts and he was awarded a yearly pension of £4 0s 0d. (8)

A similar procedure was adopted for pension claims resulting from battlefield injuries inflicted by the enemy. These could affect almost any part of the body, for many soldiers wore little or no armour. Out of thirteen wounds precisely identified in the sample of claims to the Somerset magistrates, no fewer than six were related to the hands (e.g. 'right hand shot away' in the siege of Taunton) and the others spread evenly between the throat, body, shoulder, arm, eye and thigh. Cuts from swords, gunpowder burns, broken limbs and deep wounds from the thrust of pikes were all familiar hazards for both cavalry and infantry alike. The worst wounds were often those inflicted by musket fire, where the ball had torn the flesh apart both on entry and on exit or smashed the bone, causing serious internal damage from floating fragments. Infection quickly spread in these circumstances, especially when bullets had been deliberately doctored with contaminated horse-hair (as was claimed at the siege of Rowden House in Wiltshire in 1645) or 'poisoned' (as was blamed for royalist fatalities at the capture of Cirencester in 1643). (9)

Thorough examination of wounds and speedy treatment were always important to counter any risk of such infection. Colonel Ludlow, for

Colonel John Belasyse (created Lord Belasyse, January 1645) joined the king at York at the start of the war and raised six regiments of horse and foot at his own cost; he fought in many major battles, including Edgehill, Newbury, Naseby and the siege of Bristol (1643), being wounded in the latter. (By courtesy of the National Portrait Gallery, London)

instance, described how one of his officers was 'shot through the body and into the thigh' during the siege of Wardour Castle in 1644. After being taken to Southampton, 'where his wounds were searched', it was discovered that 'the bullet that went in at his belly' had lodged 'at the chine of his back with a piece of the waistband of his breeches; which, being cut out, he wonderfully recovered'. A few individuals survived even the worst injuries. Lord Belasyse, for instance, lived on for forty-three years after the siege of Bristol, during which a piece of musket bullet had lodged in his head. Lord Grandison, on the other hand, was also wounded in the same siege with a musket shot in the leg, 'of which, although he was carried to Oxford and thought past danger, he died two months after'. A third casualty there, Sir Nicholas Slanning, 'was brought off the field, his thigh broken with a musket bullet, of which he died a fortnight after'. Injuries sustained from musket fire were at the root of most claims submitted for pensions. They tended to cause far more lasting disablement, whereas wounds by the sword could heal quite quickly, if they were treated properly at the start. (10)

The Somerset list of pensioners provides examples of a wide range of injuries and the relief offered by magistrates. Richard Hillier of Taunton had 'endured much misery in Taunton during the sieges, there having had his body much bruised; and, having received many wounds, is very lame and deformed in his body to the great hindrance of his livelihood'. Although he had a wife and three small children to support, the magistrates were not convinced by the generalised description of his injuries. 'Let him get a certificate about his wounding in the service and that he is maimed', read their endorsement. Only then would they be prepared to consider it. On the other hand, they were perfectly satisfied with the 'very sad condition' of Richard Ballard of Taunton, who had received 'a shot from the enemy in the throat' at the siege. They ruled that he should be granted twelve pence a week by his parish for the support of his wife and three children.

Nor did they have any hesitation about awarding an annual pension of twenty shillings to John Middlewick, who had been wounded at the Battle of Cropredy Bridge in 1644 and was now totally incapacitated by his horrific injuries. 'He had received a cut from the enemy throughout the face; and had had his bowels trod out by a horse; and was then run through with a Turk [a scimitar] to the unparalleled hazard of his life'. Perhaps the strangest case the magistrates dealt with, however, was that of Richard Parker from Wellington, who had experienced a miraculous escape from the jaws of death. He had been a member of the garrison at Wellington House, where he had been taken prisoner. Attempting to escape, he had been recaptured and condemned to be hanged. His captors, in executing the sentence, had placed him on a ladder with a rope around his neck and had actually 'cast him off the ladder'. The rope, however, had snapped. Nevertheless, enough damage had been done to him by his fall that, in an unconscious state, he had been taken for dead (he 'lying a long time dead in the place'). Although he had eventually revived, he remained in a very weak condition and was consequently awarded a pension of eight pence a week from his parish. (11)

Pensions of course, were in very short supply. Many maimed soldiers, therefore, first sought assistance from their family and friends, though some were more successful in this than others. In 1648, the Wiltshire magistrates heard the sad case of James Swann, who had been a soldier in parliament's army and had lost the use of both his right hand and left arm at the siege of Marlborough in 1642. He had therefore travelled to Blandford in Dorset, hoping that his old friends, who lived there, would come to his aid. Unbeknown to him, however, they had already given their support to the royalist cause. They, therefore, 'by reason of their disaffection to ye parliament', refused point-blank to provide their former friend with any relief. Such were the divisions brought about by the war! He returned home in a miserable state and was totally impoverished 'by reason of ye charges and expense of lying under the surgeon's hands'. Fortunately, his claim was supported by Colonel Edmund Ludlow and his pension was granted. (12)

The Restoration and the Granting of Royalist Pensions

With the coming of the Restoration in 1660, it was the turn of the royalist ex-soldiers to gain some relief for the scars of battle. Even as early as May 1643, Charles I had indicated his intention to grant proper pensions to those maimed or widowed as a result of service in his army. Officials in parishes under royalist control were therefore instructed to raise local rates for their support or to use local almshouses for their relief. It was not, however, until the Restoration that money was made available on a national scale and some proper relief provided. In 1662, parliament agreed that maimed royalist soldiers should be granted pensions up to a maximum of £20 a year and that a special fund of £60,000 should be set up to support loyal cavalier officers who were impoverished. Some seven thousand applications were received for the latter! On the local level, too, ordinary soldiers wasted no time in making the most of their new opportunities. William Stokes of Shepton Mallet, for instance, had been a long-serving campaigner for the royalist cause throughout the entire war. First wounded at Babylon Hill, near Sherborne in 1642, he had fought at Edgehill, Reading, the sieges of both Bristol and Gloucester, Bolton Bridge, Liverpool, Marston Moor (where he had received 'many dangerous hurts') and Naseby in 1645, where he was taken prisoner. He had then escaped to London, where he had 'languished fourteen weeks'. At the time of his petition to the Somerset Quarter Sessions in April 1661, he was 'a very poor man' with a wife and six children to support, but 'unable to work, having lost the use of his limbs'. He had endured sixteen years of misery after his war service without any support. The magistrates therefore granted him a pension of forty shillings a year, which in fact became the standard pension for ex-soldiers in Somerset after the Restoration, to be paid on a quarterly basis. (13)

With the coming of a more generous regime in 1660, the floodgates seemed to open in Somerset as more and more pensions were granted. Whereas a list of pensioners for the county in 1647 indicated that there were just 35 ex-soldiers receiving relief, by 1668 this figure had rocketed to a peak of 359. Thereafter, the numbers gradually declined to 314 in 1672, 298 in 1674, 269 in 1676, 224 in 1678 and 212 in 1680. The decline was caused partly by natural wastage, as pensioners died off, and partly by an increasing watchfulness on the part of county officials, who became alarmed at escalating costs. From the outset of the Restoration period, they had tried to work on a notional maximum, simply replacing those who died by worthy applicants from the waiting list. For example, an order dated October 1666 read: 'It appears that James George, lately a pensioner within this county, is dead; this court doth order that Robert Smith be admitted a pensioner in the place and room of the said James George...'.

In spite of this plan, however, the numbers continued to increase so rapidly that the magistrates resolved in April 1670 'that for the future, no new pensioners be admitted until the number of pensioners be reduced unto the old proportions hereunto admitted'. Although the numbers were gradually brought under control, the magistrates had a sneaking feeling that the system was being abused by pensioners who did not fall into the 'needy' or deserving' category. They therefore set up a committee in January 1677 to investigate which people were 'unfit to have their pensions continued'. By October, the list was being pruned. James Stagg of Keynsham, for instance, was discovered to have 'now become of ability to maintain himself without any help of a pension' and was therefore 'discharged'. The full list of royalist pensioners published in 1678 indicates that the greatest numbers were living in the hundreds of Williton and Freemanors (17), Bruton (16), Whitley (14), Keynsham (12), Bathforum (11), Hawthorne (11) and Taunton (11). The lowest numbers came from the hundreds of Hunstpill and Puriton (1), Martock (1), Stone (10, Whitstone (1), Andersfield (2), Hartcliffe and Bedminster (2), Kingsbury East (2) and South Petherton (2). (14)

Homelessness

The lingering effects of war were by no means limited to the physical scars of battle endured by old soldiers and their dependants. Civilians, too, continued to suffer from the ravages of war long after official hostilities had ceased in 1646. Some of the most unfortunate victims were those whose houses had been deliberately burnt down by soldiers anxious to remove all possible cover which might benefit the enemy during a siege or storm of a town. After the war, the village of Twyford petitioned the Wiltshire Quarter Sessions for relief. They claimed that they were much impoverished by the virtue of the fact that the village had been 'a frontier guard betwixt the king and parliament' for several winters. Their vital position in the war zone had therefore made them extremely vulnerable to attack and, in consequence, the village was 'barbarously burned by that cruel instrument, Sir Jacob Astley'. The position of Beachley, at the mouth of the Wye in Gloucestershire, also meant that it was central to the war zone in that it commanded river traffic between Bristol and south Wales via the Severn. In view of the fact the the royalists had attempted to establish a fortified garrison there, Colonel Massey sought approval from parliament in October 1644 to demolish all its buildings. 'There are', he said, 'about 16 or 17 dwelling houses in Beachley, which being destroyed or fired, there will be no shelter for the soldiers this winter'. This was duly accomplished.

The royalists themselves adopted a similar practice in the Forest of Dean in an attempt to deprive Massey of quarters for his troops, when they were besieging Lydney House. In April 1645, therefore, Prince Rupert and Prince Maurice raided two or three parishes, looting property and burning every building (mostly humble cottages) that could give shelter to a soldier. The inhabitants fled in terror and hid in the mines. All-in-all, it is estimated that, in the country at large, over 150 towns and 50 villages suffered deliberate damage to property during the war and that over 11,000 houses were destroyed, making 55,000 people homeless. Most victims found the cost of rebuilding well beyond their means (with expenses running at £10 for a humble cottage and £40-£60 for a farmhouse) and therefore remained homeless long after the war had ended. (15)

The problem of homelessness for those who were displaced in this manner was not a problem that could easily or quickly be resolved - as witnessed by one group of poor people from Bridgwater. When, at the siege

Prince Maurice, the king's nephew and Prince Rupert's brother, fought at Cirencester, Lansdown, Roundway Down and the siege of Bristol (1643); he was later appointed lieutenant-general of the king's western forces, before operating on the Welsh borders. (By courtesy of the Ashmolean Museum, Oxford)

of the town in 1645, soldiers (acting on the instructions of the Governor, Colonel Wyndham) had fired their houses in West Street and North Street, 'they were sent to the parish of Wembdon...to be provided for'. They were still there four years later in 1650, when the case was brought to the Somerset Quarter Sessions, having been moved constantly from one house to another. The parish, which was a mile from Bridgwater, complained bitterly at the extra burden placed on their finances by the arrival of these people in need of long-term relief and urged the magistrates to move them back instantly to Bridgwater. When the Corporation of Bridgwater objected, those displaced persons had suddenly become unwanted refugees through no fault of their own. (16)

To be fair, the Corporation found itself in a desperate situation of its own, following war-time devastation, which had seen the destruction of one-third of its houses. Such was the town's total impoverishment that Sir Thomas Fairfax had written personally to the Somerset Commissioners urging them to be extremely lenient on them when imposing taxes. Even as late as December 1656, it had proved impossible to launch a rebuilding programme. 'We have no help towards repairing 120 dwelling houses consumed in the late war', wrote Henry Miles, Mayor of Bridgwater to Lord John Desborough, Member of Parliament and General of the West. He therefore pleaded to be allowed to salvage stones from a small sconce by the bridge and a wall by the castle, both of which had been built by the former garrison but were now derelict. The Corporation, in an attempt to solve the problem of homelessness, wished to use the masonry to rebuild the old almshouses, which had been 'utterly demolished' during the war. 'Many poor shall bless you for them', he concluded. Desborough readily agreed to the request without charge. (17)

Meanwhile, a similar problem was being experienced by a group of parishioners from Taunton St James, whose houses were burnt in the final siege of that town in 1645. Rendered homeless by the exigencies of war, they were ordered to live in two large houses (three miles to the north) belonging respectively to Mr Warr and Sir William Portman. They had continued to live there after the war, 'not knowing where to go', in spite of an order from the County Committee in 1646 that they should 'return home'. In view of the fact that their homes had been burnt down, this was not easy! They not only defied that order, but also two subsequent ones from the county magistrates. Their petition to the Quarter Sessions in 1649 requested that they should be temporarily rehoused until more permanent dwellings could be provided for them. The response was harsh. The magistrates gave them one month to move, threatening gaol for any who refused. Their ultimate fate is unknown.

Even more affluent people could be permanently ruined by the deliberate firing of buildings. Joan Goulding, from Devizes in Wiltshire, had made a comfortable living from her malt mill before the war. Unfortunately, this was situated directly opposite the castle in the town, which was occupied for much of the war by a royalist garrison. On the approach of parliamentary forces in 1643, the garrison troops, in an attempt to remove nearby cover, burnt to the ground 'her dwelling house and all her goods and household stuff therein, with a mill house and malt mill, and all her outhouses to the value of £220'. In one fell swoop, she had lost all her wealth together with her entire livelihood. A widow with four children to support, she was now faced with a life of poverty. In view of her negligible resources, the prospect of rebuilding the malt house was totally out of the question. The Wiltshire magistrates granted her an immediate sum of five pounds. Sometimes the suffering caused by arson affected a whole community, as was the case in Bedminster (Somerset) when, faced with the approach of the New Model Army in July 1645, the royalist governor of Bristol had ordered the destruction of villages in the vicinity (see Chapter 9). The minister and inhabitants described in their petition of 1653 how 'their parish church was, by soldiers under the command of Prince Rupert, burnt down and was therefore become unserviceable for the public meeting of the said parish, consisting of eight hundred souls'. Repairs were estimated at £3,500, which the inhabitants were quite unable to afford in view of the impoverishment of many by the war. Indeed, royalist troops had also burnt to the ground 'a great number of their houses' in the same episode which had devastated the church. The parishioners now sought permission to launch a nationwide collection for the rebuilding of their church, having been without one for over seven years. (18)

Needless to say, there were some who tried to exploit personal disaster through acts of opportunism. Richard Netheway, a Bristol brewer, petitioned the Commons in December 1645 alleging that royalist troops, in retaliation for the support he gave to parliament, had ruined him by burning down his valuable property near the Pithay Gate. He and his family were therefore in a distressed condition and in need of urgent relief. The Commons not only ordered the immediate payment of £500 in compensation, but also instructed their local commissioners to relocate him in any suitable house confiscated from local royalists and to find a sum of £500 in further compensation. This seemed a just settlement, at least until Netheway had the gall to present a second petition twenty years later to the restored Charles II, outlining a totally different story. He alleged that he had been a loyal supporter of the king throughout the war, supplying Prince Rupert's garrison with £120 worth of beer. Furthermore, he had readily agreed to their suggestion that they should burn down his property at the Pithay Gate, lest the parliamentarians should use it as valuable cover in their attack on the city. In view of the resulting poverty from which he still suffered, he pleaded either for compensation or for a post in the customs service. The king's response is not known!

Another case of shameless opportunism involved Laurence Chislett of Taunton, who petitioned Protector Oliver Cromwell for relief in 1657. He pleaded that he and his two sons had served parliament as volunteers, but that his sons had lost their lives in the war and that he had lost £500 'by plunder and fire' to his 'utter ruin'. He had been imprisoned for 20 weeks in Taunton Castle by Sir John Stawell, but had escaped and had acted as scout to conduct parliament's forces into the town, when it was captured. He was now old and homeless, having lost all his estates, and had only received £5 in relief all those years. Cromwell ordered and investigation. The evidence, however, in the subsequent report was damning - Chislett was an 'implacable and incorrigible person', whose sons 'lived some years after the war, and got good estates and offices'. His petition was refused. (19)

The Cumulative Effects of War

Communities continued to be affected in the post-war period by what can best be described as the delayed impact of unrelenting oppression experienced at the hands of soldiers between 1642 and 1646. Ordinary people in seventeenth-century England were well accustomed to dealing with natural disasters beyond their control, including harvest failure, epidemics, roaring inflation, unemployment and clothing industry depression. In isolation, they probably viewed the ravages of the Civil War as just one further setback to be endured. Such, however, was the drain on their limited resources during these years that, when the war was over, they had little resistance to offer as further disaster struck. Their in-built resilience had been broken. Wiltshire villages in 1646, therefore, pleaded with the magistrates for extra relief. The inhabitants of Cricklade, for instance, already 'much impoverished by the unnatural war', had suddenly been afflicted by a deadly plague, which had closed the markets and cut off all local trade. They had therefore been forced to maintain for seven months over one thousand sick people, who were already 'destitute of bread, money and employment'. The village of Twyford had been 'much impoverished', because it had been a 'frontier town' in the war and had suffered extensive burning at the hands of Sir Jacob Astley's royalist troops. That in itself was bad enough, but now it had 'groaned under God's heavy judgment of the plague for at least five months'. They had no resources left to cope with this latest disaster. 'Twyford is much exhausted', was their heartfelt cry. People living in the small hamlets near Roundway Down (the scene of a royalist victory in 1643) had also been infected by the plague, which had spread from Devizes. For them, too, it was the final straw. Their cottages were already packed with 'poor people...disabled by being so much plundered at the business of Roundway Hill' (i.e. as the rival armies had camped and manoeuvred before the battle). (20)

Individuals often found, as Joan Goulding had done with her malt mill in Devizes, that a single action undertaken by soldiers during the war could affect them for the rest of their lives. Many examples have already been given of the plundering of ordinary people in town and country alike. Although the victims were outraged at the time, with little hope of redress or compensation, most managed eventually to recover from their ordeal, gradually replacing stolen cattle or mending broken furniture. This was not easy, however, when the plunderers had seized all you possessed. In April 1645, royalist troops under Sir Richard Grenvile, on their way to besiege Taunton, had taken by storm Wellington House (owned by parliamentarian commander, Colonel Alexander Popham). Some of the local inhabitants, fearing an attack on the town itself, had taken refuge with all their belongings in the house for security. These included Anne Martyn, a widow, who suffered the total loss of her cattle and household goods to the value of £175, together with cash amounting to £22. The list of plundered items (submitted as evidence with her petition for relief in 1650) included 'several kine, one heifer, ten young cattle, three calves, five colts, a mare and a horse, forty sheep, five beds with their furniture, bacon, butter, cheese, wool, linen, corn of all sorts, pewter, brass and other goods'. In addition, she lost her eldest son, who was killed in the raid. It took another five years after her petition before, in an impoverished state, she was granted ten shillings relief by the Somerset magistrates, followed by a further twenty shillings in 1656. (21)

There was also the problem of displacement from normal prewar life, which individuals wrestled hard to re-establish. Samuel Stevens had served an apprenticeship to a tailor in Bishops Lydeard in Somerset and had subsequently lived there for seven years. He had then fought in parliament's army for four years, before returning to Bishops Lydeard to rent a house and pursue his trade. Much to his horror, he found himself 'disturbed by the inhabitants of the same parish', who presumably rejected him either as a threat to other tailors or as a possible charge to their poor rate fund. Fortunately for him, the magistrates found in his favour and authorised his settlement in the town. Roger Taunton from West Monkton had been displaced in a different manner. A poor, impotent, blind man, he had been an inmate of the local hospital (or almshouse) for several years 'before the late troubles'. However, at the time of the sieges of Taunton, the hospital had been occupied by royalist forces and Roger Taunton had been ejected. He had still failed to gain his former place, even as late as 1653. (22)

Broken Bridges, Damaged Hospitals and Neglected Fields

By the end of the war, many of the ancient hospitals (which had catered for the impotent poor) and bridewells or houses of correction (which had set the able-bodied poor to work) had been put out of action. The bridewell at Ilchester in Somerset had been fortified by the royalists, but deliberately fired as Fairfax advanced with the New Model Army in 1646. Those at Taunton and Shepton Mallet had suffered considerable damage in the war, while that at Devizes in Wiltshire had been used to billet soldiers. The Somerset magistrates in 1646 noted that 'the hospitals and spittals within this county have been of late, by reason of the present distraction, much neglected to the great aggrievance of the poor people'. Although they did their best to revive the system, it all took time. Fortunately for county and parish officials struggling with severe levels of poverty, there was no mass demobilisation of the army in 1646 to flood the labour market. Indeed, the New Model Army actually increased in size, reaching a peak of over 53,000 by December 1649 - a total made possible by the recruitment of ex-royalist soldiers. There is therefore no evidence of a serious crime wave sweeping through English towns and villages, prompted by marauding gangs of unemployed veterans out again in search of plunder. (23)

Nevertheless, poverty remained a problem, partly because another by-product of the war hindered rapid recovery and the growth of employment. Roads and bridges had been left in such a bad state of repair throughout the west country that trade and farming activity were seriously hampered. In November 1644, for instance, Colonel Massey, who was shadowing the march of Colonel Gerard's royalist troops from Wales, had pulled down all the bridges on the Avon in order to cut off Gerard's retreat and break his supply chain. This type of destruction, brought on by the necessities of war, caused endless suffering to local communities throughout the western counties. As a result, the officers of several Somerset villages carried their grievances to the Quarter Sessions in 1646 and 1647. Those from Huish, for instance, reported that royalist forces had broken down the village bridge. This was proving disastrous to some of the local farmers, who relied on the bridge to reach their land. As there was no other way across the river, their fields remained 'unmanured to their great prejudice'. The situation was even more serious in Luccombe, where the bridge had deteriorated so badly during the war that several people had died trying to cross it.

Various other places throughout the county complained 'of the defect of several bridges, occasioned by the marching of armies to and fro'. This meant, they said, that country folk could not move their goods to market 'but by and through unusual ways' and with great hazard to their lives. Nor was it easy for local parishioners to repair such damage without assistance. The inhabitants of Bedminster were concerned not only that 'their highways were much impaired and decayed by reason of the great carriage towards Bristol' during the war, but also that they only possessed four ploughs between them, yet had 'five road ways to repair'. It was even worse in Widcombe, where the residents were responsible for three main roads, which provided links to the markets in both Bristol and London. 'Since these unhappy wars', they stated, ' by reason of the often passage of armies and carriages...the ways are grown so ruinous that the inhabitants, being for the most part very poor and eaten out with free quarter, taxes, contributions and billeting of soldiers...are not able sufficiently to repair them without some competent contribution...' (24)

The difficulty of finding resources to undertake necessary repairs was a problem faced by many impoverished country parishes. The tithing *[or*

Bridges, broken down during the war, often lay unrepaired for years afterwards, causing severe difficulties to farmers. (Line drawing by Stephen Beck)

hamlet] of Milbourne, just outside Malmesbury in Wiltshire, for instance, reported to the county magistrates that several highways and two bridges there were 'completely decayed' as a result of 'the great and heavy carriage to and from the late garrison of Malmesbury'. Furthermore, another bridge had been completely 'pulled down by the garrison' during an emergency. Bearing in mind that they possessed very few ploughs between them, they requested permission to impose a rate of two pence in the pound on the tithing. Sometimes, however, the task of rebuilding was completely beyond the means of a small hamlet. The inhabitants of Castle Eaton in Wiltshire explained how their bridge over the Isis was in good repair at the start of 'the last unhappy war', but that Lieutenant-Colonel Carr, to protect his garrison at Cirencester from royalist attack, 'pulled down the whole bridge in the night and threw all the timber thereof down the river'. The tithing was small, the bridge was 70 yards long, the original timber had been lost and the stone arches had been damaged. The magistrates, estimating that repairs would cost £100, ruled that the charge should be borne by the whole parish and not just the tithing. (25)

Nor were these problems limited to the countryside. Bristol City Council expressed concern in 1646 for the condition of the streets of the city and

Part of the walled defences on the northern side of the inner city at Bristol with old houses situated alongside the river Frome. (By courtesy of Bristol Central Library)

the rivers which ran through it. The war in general and the siege in particular had caused such neglect that the streets were currently 'full of dirt and other noisome soil and filth'. A year earlier Joshua Sprigge had commented, at the time of the city's capture by the New Model Army, that the streets were 'so noisome and the houses so nasty as that they were unfit to receive friends or freemen till they were cleansed'. This clearly represented a health hazard, which would increase the risk of sickness and infection. The churchwardens of each parish were therefore ordered to organise a large-scale cleaning up operation and to ensure that the streets in future were kept 'sweet and clean'. The Council also noted that the rivers had lately 'been very much choked with dung and other trash and filth' to the detriment of navigation. They therefore ordered that in future 'no stone, coal, ashes, soil, dung or rubble shall be thrown or cast out of any man's house into the River of Avon or Fromc' on pain of a £5 fine. (26)

Another problem, facing local farmers in 1646 was the harm brought to previously-cultivated land through sheer neglect during the war years. In many parts of thc western counties, endless attacks by plundering soldiers and thoughtless damage inflicted on crops by the trampling of boots had combined to discourage a country population already weary of the conflict. Fields were therefore abandoned and rents unpaid. In Gloucestershire, it was estimated that, by 1648, the annual rental value of estates had slumped most dramatically from their prewar levels, including those belonging to Anthony Arnold of Westbury (from £100 to £40), Thomas Rogers of King's Stanley (£40 to £10), Thomas Buck of Winterbourne (£160 to £50), Thomas Veal of Alveston (£120 to £40), Sir William Whitmore of Pucklechurch (£120 to £90) and Thomas Jeyne of Tewkesbury (£38 to £16). In Somerset, the sequestration commissioners, who investigated the extent of royalist estates in the Brent hundred in 1645, had great difficulty in assessing the current value of the land. They complained, for example, that eleven acres of land in South Brent with a value 'in the best times' of £2 13s 4d was now worthless, because 'since these times, it hath laid common'. The parsonage there, worth £60 'in the best times', had fallen to

£40 in rental since hostilities began, while the 60 acres farmed by Robert Sheppard had been devalued from £32 to £28. These losses, of course, not only affected the landowner, but the whole livelihood of the local community. (27)

Richard Dowdswell, agent to the Earl of Middlesex for his estates at Forthampton, near Gloucester, found rents increasingly hard to collect, as tenants were squeezed dry by both sides in the conflict. 'In truth', wrote Dowdeswell in 1644, 'if things continue much longer at this pass, no money will be had, neither for soldier nor landlord, for indeed the lands will lie unmanured and untenanted...and if a speedy end of these sad times happen not, it will be worse undoubtedly'. As he predicted, there was a dramatic fall in annual rents with only £80 collected out of a possible £600. Those leasing Forthampton House abandoned it completely; other tenants demanded substantial reductions in rent to compensate for damage inflicted by troops. Such was his plight that Dowdeswell gloomily feared that the cost of free quarter and weekly taxes would soon 'devour the whole revenue'. Worse still was the lasting harm done to the farming community and its lands. (28)

The sheer desperation of those forced to abandon their land is reflected in the heartfelt cry of Hugh Wolcott, writing from Wellington in Somerset in March 1643 to his cousin: 'It has pleased God to set a great destruction amongst us here in our land; men have almost been at their wit's end, for no Turkish slavery can be worse than hath been inflicted over us. We have been robbed and stripped of all our goods, both within doors and without, and led away captive from house to harbour, and like to suffer death'. Wolcott and his wife had been forced to flee from his own home to seek refuge with his parents. He asked his cousin to try and sell his property on his behalf, but was not optimistic of success: 'Estates do go at very low value than formerly they have been', he complained, thanks to the fact that no farmer had been 'able to make good' the losses and damage sustained in the war. This meant that 'one hundred pounds in the purse' was now worth far more than two hundred pounds per annum in theoretical rent for land, much of which had been laid waste or abandoned. (29)

The Disruption of Religious Life

In many parishes throughout the western counties, the religious life of ordinary people was seriously affected by the war. This was partly due to the fact that church buildings themselves were sometimes damaged or destroyed in the fighting. Many had been used as garrison strongholds, prisons, lookout posts, barracks or magazines (see Chapter 9) and had therefore been in the front line of military conflict. Others had been subjected to deliberate destruction inflicted by puritan soldiers on stained glass, altars, organs, statues, vestments and other fittings which could be conceived as being idolatrous. The war presented some with the ideal

Throughout the country puritan soldiers burnt or destroyed any 'popish' symbols they discovered in churches, including religious pictures and books. (By courtesy of the Ashmolean Museum, Oxford)

opportunity of continuing the work of purification of churches from any remaining trappings of the Roman Catholic religion - a process which had started in the previous century.

In Gloucestershire, for instance, Colonel Massey stripped the churches 'with more than ordinary enthusiasm, selling the communion plate and tearing the prayer books, while his soldiers wore the surplices over their arms'. In Bristol, monuments on the tombs were vandalised in St. Mary's, Redcliffe, where the organ was also dismantled by troops, who took the pipes into the streets and used them as trumpets. In Somerset, the church of South Petherton suffered twice, once in September 1644, when the monuments and organs (installed only eight years earlier) were 'torn down' by cavalry of the Earl of Essex's army; and later, in July 1645, when Colonel Fleetwood's cavalry from the New Model Army smashed the stained glass windows. They went on to do exactly the same thing at Martock, before visiting the church at Tintinhull, where they seized the surplices and cut them to pieces. Organs were particularly vulnerable. Over the border in Devon, for instance, the soldiers 'brake down the organs and, taking two or three hundred pipes with them in a most scornful and contemptuous manner, went up and down the streets piping with them'. With this sort of background, the Dean and Chapter of Salisbury Cathedral decided in 1643 to avoid the risk of destruction by dismantling the organ and storing its 200 pipes safely until the arrival of 'better times', while the churchwardens at Warminster in Wiltshire hid the organ pipes under the floor of the tower. Salisbury did not escape completely, however. In July 1644, troops commanded by Lieutenant-General Middleton plundered the cathedral, seizing and selling its plate, vestments, cushions and soft furnishings. In Gloucester Cathedral, the cloisters were used as stables by Scottish troops under General Leslie in 1645. (30)

The cloisters at Gloucester Cathedral were turned into stables in 1645. (Author's collection)

Taynton church in Gloucestershire suffered more than most. Shortly after the siege of Gloucester had ended in 1643, Colonel Massey led his troops out of the city on a sortie against royalist strongholds. They were, however, intercepted by Prince Rupert's forces and driven into Taynton, where they took refuge in the church. According to a royalist source, they quickly turned the chancel into a stable for their horses and tore out sheets from the prayer books to light their pipes, which they duly smoked 'on the high altar'. It was also alleged that some of them, mockingly, put on the surplices over their armour. The moated church, however, was soon to become a fortress, as it came under a sustained attack from a party of royalists led by Captain Whiffin. Although the besiegers successfully fired the church - despite the efforts of the puritan minister, who took pot shots at them from the rectory window - Massey's men escaped with both their lives and the communion plate. The church lay in ruins and was not rebuilt (on another site) until 1647.

Taynton Church, which stood inside a frontier war zone, was destroyed in the incident described opposite. It was rebuilt on a new site in 1647 by the puritan, Thomas Pury, as a presbyterian chapel on a north-south axis. (Author's collection)

Wells Cathedral suffered a number of violent attacks from local troops drawn from the north-eastern sector of Somerset, where puritanism was rife. They deeply resented the High Church policies of the Bishop of Bath and Wells, William Piers, which had undermined their puritan culture during the 1630s. As early as August 1642, after a great rendezvous of parliament's supporters on the Mendips, Alexander Popham led his trained bands down into Wells, crying out how they had vanquished the papists. They then proceeded to tear down all the stained glass in the cathedral and sacked the Bishop's palace, destroying all the organs and pictures. According to one eye-witness, a portrait of the Virgin Mary was 'put on a spear and carried about in contempt and derision'. Nor was this attack on Wells an isolated instance. The Wells Chapter Library Book records that, in the following year, Popham's Bath Regiment returned to the city and 'broke down divers pictures and crucifixes in the church and Our Lady Chapels. Likewise they did plunder the Bishop's palace and broke all such monuments and pictures they espied'. A month later, they were back again - 'Mr Alexander Popham's soldiers...after dinner rushed into the church, broke down the windows, organs, fonts, seats in the choir and the Bishop's seat, besides many other villainies'. Nor were soldiers the only culprits. In 1643, Richard Allen, the newly-appointed puritan minister of Batcombe, came to the cathedral for his induction service, accompanied by his brother (another clergyman) and a friend from London. The latter, spotting a crucifix behind the choir, 'most maliciously threw a stone at it

A contemporary print which depicts puritan soldiers ransacking a church to destroy altars and crucifixes. (By courtesy of the Ashmolean Museum, Oxford)

and broke it', while the other two kept guard. (31)

The Abbey Church in Bath, on the other hand, escaped lightly during the war - partly because it was in itself the product of the puritan revolution, built at the turn of the century as a place in which 'to hear sermons'. Whereas some cathedrals (like Hereford) were actually dismantled, some (like Durham) were used as prisons and other (like St. Paul's) served a dual role with the nave used as stables and the cloisters turned into a shopping arcade, Bath Abbey received protection from local families, both royalist and parliamentarian, who had contributed to its construction. Even so, prior to the Battle of Lansdown, Sir William Waller had been constrained to quarter troops there - virtually alongside his wife's own grave. Nevertheless, the organ and the small amount of stained glass survived unscathed, although the figure of Bishop Peter on the west façade lost its mitre and the angel next to him lost its head. The worst vandalism in fact was committed by royalist troops, who were billeted in the Abbey during the two years of occupation. Spotting Waller's effigy of on his first wife's tomb and remembering his part in the Battle of Lansdown, they spitefully hacked off both his nose and his sword hand. (32)

Perhaps the worst desecration of all took place in January 1643 in the

Royalist soldiers, billeted in Bath Abbey, deface the effigies of Sir William and Lady Waller. (Line drawing by Stephen Beck)

chapel of Sudeley Castle in Gloucestershire. According to Sir William Dugdale, parliamentarian soldiers 'broke down the monuments; made the body of the church a stable for their horses and the chancel their slaughterhouse. To the pulpit, they fastened pegs on which they hanged the carcasses of sheep. Of the communion table, they made a dresser or chopping board to cut their meat. Into the vault, where lay the bodies of those noble people, they cast the guts and garbage of the sheep; leaving in every corner of the church their own loathsome excrements'. (33)

Damage sustained in attacks like these took many years to repair. When William Schellinks toured the western counties in the summer of 1662, for instance, he noted in his diary that the damage inflicted in 'the recent war' was still highly visible in cathedrals at Gloucester, Salisbury (especially in 'the bishop's house') and Wells (particularly on the west front and in the bishop's palace). Repairs were only just under way and 'a very large organ' was still awaiting installation at Wells. From the ordinary person's point of view, the spoliation of church fabric in this way inevitably resulted in frequent and sustained disruption of church services both during and after the war.

This, however, was only part of their problem. From the summer of 1643, an Assembly of Divines at Westminster had been working on a radical reform of church organisation and worship. By 1646, bishops had been abolished, a new Directory of Worship had replaced the Anglican Prayer Book and parliament had ordered the establishment of a Presbyterian system of church government. At the same time, County Committees were instructed to report all clergy who were immoral, unsuitable or royalist to the Committee for Plundered Ministers in London, so that they could be ejected from their livings and replaced by godly puritan divines. From March 1643, royalist clergy were also subjected to the 'sequestration' or confiscation of their estates and property, although they were later able to 'compound' for the return of these estates on payment of a fine. (34)

In north-east Somerset, eighteen 'malignant' or 'scandalous' clergy were ejected in all. Although this only amounted to some 20 per cent of the total clergy in that area, it nevertheless represented a great loss for the parishioners concerned - especially when, as it transpired, it proved difficult to replace them. A letter from Somerset, written in the summer of 1646, emphasised how desperate the situation had become: 'Ministers we have very few; our churches are interrupted. You talk at London of getting maintenance for them, but where are the men that must do the works?' As late as January 1648, William Prynne complained in a letter to the Somerset Committee that they had removed his own chaplain from Swainswick, thus leaving 'three parishes together like sheep without a shepherd, quite destitute of all spiritual food for their souls, in such a barren place, where there are ten parishes more adjoining without any settled minister to instruct them'. The city of Bath fared no better after the Rector, James Masters, had been ejected in September 1645 'for joining the royal forces'. It took over three years before a permanent replacement had been found. Further south in Somerset, Richard Hooper (the minister at Beaminster) wrote to George Trevelyan in August 1643, apologising for his absence from a friend's funeral. He explained that he was overworked with many extra duties 'by reason of the absence of my neighbouring ministers'. He could not afford to be away for even one day, having both Netherbury and Beaminster temporarily under his care. (34)

County Committees, who relied heavily on incriminating evidence supplied by local villagers against their clergy, moved quickly to evict their victims by force and without mercy. The plight of these ordinary and often humble members of the Anglican ministry is vividly told by John Walker in his *Sufferings of the Clergy*, published in 1714. Many were condemned for continuing to use the Book of Common Prayer, including Henry Fowler, Rector of Minchinhampton, and Humphrey Jasper, Vicar of South Cerney (both in Gloucestershire). Fowler was subjected to a great deal of violence when he was visited by troops on New Year's Day in 1643. These ruffians 'came to his house and, finding him by the fire, seized him as their prisoner; [one] took him by the throat and held the point of his sword to his breast; two more presented their pistols to him, another shook his pole-axe over his head, calling him mass-priest'. Such was his prolonged beating that he was left both deaf and incontinent. Jasper, who was initially 'plundered of all that he had', fled from his vicarage in South Cerney, but returned after Cirencester had been captured by royalist troops. He was, nevertheless, so terrorised by parliamentarian soldiers over the coming months that he was frightened to sleep at home. Instead, he took 'straw-ricks and hay-ricks for his lodging' or lay on the chancel floor of the church 'to be out of the way'. He did not even dare to be seen by his own parishioners in the street, 'for the generality of them were for the parliamentary party'. Samuel Broad, the Rector of Rendcomb in Gloucestershire, suffered in much the same way. He was so harassed by groups of marauding soldiers that he was 'forced to keep himself in a chamber, where there was a trapdoor, concealed with a heap of apples on it, through which he was let down'.

The negative and sometimes hostile attitude of members of the local congregation towards their ejected minister, born partly out of fear for themselves, added to their suffering. Henry Collier, Rector of Steeple Langford in Wiltshire, was ejected from his comfortable living, which had been worth well over £300 per annum. According to his grandson: 'at the time of his ejectment, he had eleven children who, with his wife, were turned out in a very deep snow and forced to stand, not a little while, in the open street before any neighbours would or dare admit them into their houses'. This, however, was just the beginning of their ordeal and humiliation. They were then 'forced to lie six nights in a barn', before eventually they found a cottage 'as mean as any in the village'. The status and comfort of their previous life had been shattered, emphasised by the fact that Collier was forced to send his children out daily into a neighbouring wood 'for dry wood, which they brought back in bundles upon their shoulders'.

This sheer degradation of being ejected with total loss of earnings was also experienced by William Piers, Rector of Kingsbury in Somerset. As son of the Bishop of Bath and Wells, he came from a much more affluent family and therefore felt the humiliation much more deeply. His daughter later described how he was therefore forced 'to marry an ordinary woman with a small estate', just in order to gain some means of subsistence. The value of the holding was, however, so small that, from being Archdeacon of Taunton and Rector of Kingsbury, he was forced to be a 'day labourer', to 'thresh in the barn for his livelihood and to go to market himself to sell cheese'. Witnesses recalled that he had often been seen at Ilminster 'sitting in the market with a cheese upon his knees' or travelling the countryside 'with a little paltry horse' to sell tobacco. His daughter added that she had seen her father and other local clergy, whose estates had been sequestrated, sitting together 'eating bread and salt and drinking water', none of them 'having a penny to buy beer'.

The very suddenness with which the ejectors could swoop was terrifying in itself, as three ministers discovered to their cost in Somerset. Mr Gooden, Rector of Lydeard St. Lawrence, 'was outraged in the church, being dragged out of the pulpit'. Later, in a destitute condition, he begged for help from his successor, whose wife told him 'to take his flail and thresh'. William Holway, Rector of North Cheriton, 'was seized on in the time of his sermon by some fellows, who presented their pistols at him and carried him away before the Committee'. William Kemp, Rector of Puddimore, 'was forced from his home with eleven children who, together with his goods, were thrown into the streets; some of his children were naked to their shifts and shoes'. (36)

Those who suffered in this way often suffered very greatly. Nevertheless, in spite of the turmoil experienced in parts of the western counties, it is true to say that many isolated country parishes (some 60 per cent in Somerset) muddled on quietly throughout these years and were largely undisturbed by traumatic changes elsewhere. Many ministers passively stayed put, content to keep a low profile until the return of better times. The majority of parishes clung on to the Prayer Book and continued to worship along traditional lines of the Anglican Church. Their task was made easier by the fact that parliament's reforms in church government were often ineffective; that distribution of the new Directory of Worship was largely inefficient and that godly puritan clergy (as replacements for the 'malignant' and the 'scandalous') were in short supply. The towns, too, were far more likely to be visited by radical sectarian preachers, often drawn from the ranks of the army chaplains. Wells, Taunton and Bridgwater felt the impact of the Baptists during the post-war years, while Bristol, Bath, Keynsham, Warminster and Salisbury all had encounters with the Quakers. Over much of the area, however, religious life went on as normal with both clergy and congregations content to let the revolution slip quietly by. The pull of what David Underdown has called 'the comfortable certainties of the old religion' proved too much for most. (37)

Punishment of Royalists

The task of punishing all 'delinquents' (i.e. all those guilty of papacy or assisting the king in the war) commenced shortly after the start of hostilities and continued well into the 1650s. In March 1643, parliament established Sequestration Committees in each county (to work alongside the County Committees and often consisting of an identical membership) to begin the 'sequestration' (or nationalisation without compensation) of royalist or papist property. From September 1644, a central committee in London (the Committee for Compounding under Somerset clothier, John Ashe) met at the Goldsmiths' Hall to arrange for those charged to 'compound' for the return of their estates (i.e. to pay a fine, which was nominally one-tenth, one-sixth or one-third of the value of their estates, but could extend to two-thirds). Although this composition fine was payable only to the Committee for Compounding, the revenue generated locally during the period of sequestration while the fine was being calculated, was enjoyed by the County Committee. It is not surprising, therefore, that the Sequestration Committees showed great enthusiasm in tracking down as many delinquents as possible or that sequestration proceedings were often long drawn out.

The Sequestration Committee appointed sub-committees to operate within the various hundreds of the county, each with its own team of sequestrators, assessors, treasurers, agents, collectors and informers. These were normally all local men with first-hand knowledge of their neighbours' property, men of comparatively humble birth, who acted with a great amount of zeal and a certain degree of ruthlessness. Frequent complaints were made about their unreasonable and high-handed approach. When necessary, troops were employed from the local militia to give them protection or to guard confiscated property. Their task was to identify delinquents within their area, to organise the valuation and sale of personal property, to estimate the annual value of real estate, to rent out some of the land, to manage the remainder and to allocate profits. Both the central committee and the sub-committees usually met at least once a week to investigate new cases and receive revenue. (38)

In all, 303 delinquents were referred to the Committee of Compounding from Somerset. Although the largest fines were inevitably paid by the county magnates, including Sir William Portman (£4,600), George Speke (£2,390) and George Trevelyan (£1,500), many men of more modest means were also caught in the process. Some were those who had fought actively for the king and therefore had little excuse, like Thomas Gibbs of Bath, who was charged with 'adhering to the forces raised against the parliament' and taking away arms from the well-affected around Bath. He was fined £48. Others had voluntarily assisted royalist forces in the war effort, like Robert Fisher of Bath, who had supplied them with food and was fined £57 2s 0d. Quite often, however, individuals found themselves charged with delinquency and sequestration on technical grounds, having fallen victim to circumstances. William Cogan, clothier, was charged with deserting his home in Chard to join the royalist garrison in Exeter. In justification, he explained that his house had been rendered uninhabitable by the constant plundering of troops from both sides, so much so in fact that 'he scarce had a bed left to lie on'. Having friends in Exeter willing to help him, he therefore went to live with them until the garrison surrendered. He had never taken up arms against parliament, but had willingly given them money under the Propositions and had endured great losses.

John Harvey, also from Chard, was charged with contributing to the maintenance of the king's forces. In fact, when Hopton's army had camped in the town on its march from Cornwall in 1643, Harvey and three others had been ordered to collect a local rate for the army's use - 'which they refused to do; whereupon they were threatened to be plundered, sent to prison and tied head and heels together'. Under pressure of this kind they had reluctantly organised the rate. Harvey was fined £170. John Question, a surgeon from Dunster, had originally accepted a commission as a captain in the king's army, but had had second thoughts, deserting before his service had actually begun. He had later suffered the loss of £400 in the siege of Dunster Castle, when many of his houses had been burnt, but had nevertheless contributed £40 to parliament for the maintenance of that siege and had given his service as a surgeon to parliament's wounded soldiers. However, temporary lapses in judgment like his were to prove costly at the hands of commissioners, who treated excuses of all kinds with little sympathy. Question was therefore fined £135. The cases of three Gloucestershire men (Richard Banaster, John Chamberlayne and William Guise) further illustrate the way in which some individuals were unfairly charged and harshly treated (see Horrors of War 1, 3 & 6) (39)

Many of those charged with delinquency had lost so much through war-time plunder and sequestration of personal property that they were already deeply in debt. These, therefore, were not only unable to recover their estates through payment of a composition fine, but were also unable to support their families. By 1650, for instance, Richard Gay of Widcombe was languishing in prison for debt and was incapable of raising his £180 fine. His five children therefore petitioned the Committee for Compounding to release one-fifth of his former estate to secure their own survival. The chairman, John Ashe, intervened personally on their behalf. 'The petitioners', he wrote, 'are my near neighbours and are in very great want; and their father to my knowledge in very great misery by reason of his debts and imprisonment'. Lyncombe Farm was therefore released from sequestration for their support. Good neighbourliness like this often prevailed, even among those who had been on opposite sides during the war. A group of keen parliamentarians on Bath City Council, for instance, wrote a letter in 1649 supporting Robert Fisher (a former colleague) in his plea to be excused from appearing before the Committee of Compounding in London. He was, they said, 'aged three score and fourteen years and upwards; by reason of his said age, impotence and weakness of body, he is not any ways able to travel without danger of his life'. (40)

A similar story unfolded in Wiltshire, where 47 delinquents were referred to the Committee of Compounding, raising a total of £37,500 in fines - including £3,725 from Sir Francis Seymour. By comparison, quite small amounts were also raised from ordinary individuals. Although John Estcourt from Newton, for example, had fought with the royalist army, he only possessed a modest personal estate worth £50 10s 0d, including a small flock of sheep, a couple of horses and a pile of books. His fine was just £8 8s 4d. Henry Manning of Salisbury was even more impoverished. He too had joined the royalist forces, but with a total fortune of just two horses, a colt and £5 in cash, his fine was limited to £3 6s 8d. Robert Chander of Wilton had no money at all. He had greatly distressed his father, the town's puritan minister and a keen supporter of parliament, by quitting his studies at Christ Church College, Oxford and joining the royalist army there. Although he subsequently fought in the Battle of Lansdown, he eventually deserted and sought shelter under his father's roof. When he was charged with delinquency, his father came to his rescue by paying £50 in lieu of a fine for his son.

The attractions of life in Oxford had also appealed to Thomas Sackville. He claimed in his evidence that he had left his home in Edington in favour of the town where the king just happened to have his headquarters - partly to speed up his wife's recovery and partly so that he could make use of the university library for his own study. The committee were totally unconvinced, fixing his fine at £400. Several Wiltshire men claimed that their pro-royalist activities during the war had been undertaken as a means of helping the local community. Sir Thomas Hall of Bradford-on-Avon admitted that he had accepted a position in 1643 as commissioner to press local men into the king's army. He insisted, however, that he had not only been pressurised into doing this after receiving menacing letters from the king, but that he had also been persuaded by his own neighbours to accept. They felt that he would then be able to use his influential position to protect them from some of the harsher demands made by troops out in search of free quarter. Similarly, Edward Yerbury of Trowbridge said that he had accepted a commission to search out parliamentarian sympathisers in order to protect them from unreasonable treatment. Indeed, he was supported in his evidence by petitions from many inhabitants of the neighbouring hundreds, who stated that 'by his means and persuasion' they had been 'much eased' in the fines imposed on them. The Committee for Compounding, however, rejected these special pleas. Hall was fined £660 and Yerbury £190. (41)

The case of Edmund Bower of Allerton in Somerset clearly illustrates the procedure adopted when sequestration took place. Bower, a modest yeoman farmer, was convicted of delinquency for serving as a major in the king's army. Although the sequestration order was issued on 20th August 1645, his case was not heard by the Committee of Compounding until 11th March 1647, when he was fined £188 (half to be paid immediately and half within three months). Having paid in full, he was finally cleared and his estates returned on 30th November 1648, over three years after his original conviction. During this time, his estates were managed by the sequestration sub- committee for the hundred of Bempstone, led by sequestrators Robert Stone and Robert Neades.

One of their first tasks, on 3rd October 1645, was to draw up an inventory of Bower's personal possessions, a task entrusted to the assessors, Walter Stayle and John Whittinge. Bower's main residence consisted of a parlour (with table, sideboard, cupboard and 12 stools), a hall (with table, sideboard and stools), a kitchen (with pans, kettles, pots, pewter mugs, barrels and tubs) and six bedrooms (suitably furnished). In the farmyard, he had a store of wheat, barley, beans, hay, 6 oxen, 6 cows, 4 steers, 14 yearlings, 5 calves, 6 pigs, 1 colt and a plough harness. All this was valued at £128 8s 4d. The next task was to dispose of these goods and distribute the proceeds. There was an immediate crisis when a local farmer, George Day, claimed that three of the steers were his and immediately drove them away, losing the sequestrators £6 in value. Some of the remaining livestock and farm produce was sold to cover expenses (raising £48 15s 0d), some (wheat, barley, beans and 4 pigs, valued at £4 16s 0d) was delivered 'for use of the committee at Axbridge and some (valued at £6 15s 0d) was delivered to Mrs Bower 'by order of the committee'. Although Bower was still presumably with the royalist army, his wife continued to live in Allerton and needed support. The sequestrators therefore raised a further £50 for her maintenance from the sale of various household goods.

In the meantime, the officials had been giving their minds to one further task, namely the valuation of Bower's real estate. He owned a total of 190 acres of meadow and pasture and 92 acres of arable land, spread between Allerton, Wedmore and Tarnock, with an annual rental value of £160. His holding in Wedmore was rented out to six tenants, who handed over their back rent of £19 10s 0d to the sequestrators on 29th September. The other land, which had clearly been farmed by Bower himself, was now managed by the local sequestrators with the committee itself receiving future profits for support of the county's war effort. This aspect of their work was to prove extremely beneficial to the local community. The sequestrators' accounts show that they spent £30 10s 11d in the initial months on 'managing the estates' and that they employed 21 named individuals from the villages (plus other groups who were not identified) to undertake numerous tasks - mowing the meadow, making the hay, looking after the cattle, reaping the wheat, threshing the corn, raking after the plough, dyking, fencing, lopping the trees, using the plough to 'fetch home the hay', shodding the horses, mending the wain and helping 'to find Mr Bower's cattle' (which had strayed during the crisis of sequestration).

All-in-all, the sequestrators raised, during the first two months, £118 5s 0d from the sale of goods and rent received. They then distributed £120 10s 11d on expenses, including Mrs Bower's maintenance and a lump sum of £40 for the coffers of the committee. Over the next three years, much more would have been raised for their funds from both farm profits and rent. It is also worth noting that Bower owned a further smallholding in the Brent hundred, which was administered by another sequestration sub-committee, amounting to 18 acres of land farmed by himself and one tenement rented by a tenant. The local sequestrator found tenants for all the land, thus producing an annual rent of £10 6s 8d. (42)

The Wiltshire Sequestration Committee employed slightly different methods from those used in Somerset, when it came to dealing with the personal property of the accused. Instead of confiscating and disposing of all goods and chattels, the committee frequently accepted a fine (or 'quietus'), amounting to perhaps one -third of the value. The owner was then permitted to resume possession of the remainder, while he awaited the judgment of the Committee for Compounding on the matter of his real estate. This policy in Wiltshire is well illustrated by the case of Sir James Long of Draycott, although it also illustrates the ruthless behaviour of soldiers garrisoned in the area, who regarded property of local royalists as a fair target for plunder. In view of the fact that Long was not only the king's sheriff in Wiltshire, but also commander of a cavalry regiment, the Sequestration Committee, meeting at Malmesbury in October 1644, had no hesitation in ordering the sequestration of his rents, livestock and personal goods.

However, following Long's capture by Cromwell's forces in March 1645, the committee offered a deal to his wife (Mrs Dorothy Long) - namely that, in exchange for an immediate fine of £100 followed by similar payments on an annual basis, they would return her house and goods and guarantee protection. Mrs Long accepted, much to the fury of her husband in prison. However, a few months later in November, the agreement was violated by musketeers under Thomas Vaughan on behalf of the Malmesbury garrison. They seized not only a great variety of household goods from Draycott (including beds, curtains, bedlinen, chairs, tapestries, spits, tables, trunks, stools and cushions), but also their cattle from the Forest of Braydon. The personal property was immediately sold in Malmesbury to five individuals, including the governor, who bought 'a small cabinet and wooden standing' for £1. The sale raised £43 7s 10d in all, although Mrs Long claimed that the total losses amounted to £400. In spite of the fact that the Wiltshire Sequestration Committee denounced the soldiers' action as illegal, Long was unable to obtain any redress. When later he appealed to the Committee for Compounding, its Chairman (John Ashe, Member of Parliament for Westbury in Wiltshire) refused to intervene. Shortly afterwards, in November 1646, the Committee heard his case in full, fixing his composition fine at £714. (43)

Family Feuds

The Civil War sometimes provided a glorious opportunity for families and neighbours to pursue longstanding feuds, using the smokescreen of local military activity to further their ends - feuds which continued to rumble on long after the war had ended. In Iron Acton in Gloucestershire, for instance, two half brothers, Thomas and William Hobbs, had been in dispute since 1638 over the land bequeathed by their father, part of which had gone to William and part (eventually) to Thomas's younger son. By the summer of 1643, the disputed land (75 acres of arable and meadow occupied by William) had suddenly become a frontier zone, lying midway between a parliamentary garrison at Yate Court and a royalist garrison at Acton Court in Iron Acton. In an attempt to seize the whole inheritance, Thomas eagerly grasped the chance which the Civil War now provided to drive his half-brother out.

When eventually the whole dispute came to court (in November 1648), witnesses testified to the fact that Thomas had made an unscrupulous attempt during the war to expel William by using royalist troops. According to Thomas Bracie, a local weaver, Thomas Hobbs was 'intimate with the cavaliers' and 'did continually vex and persecute' William (who was 'well-affected to the parliament') 'with soldiers of the king's party'. William Slade, a husbandman, stated that he often saw William 'cruelly oppressed with soldiers'. The results of all this were devastating. First of all, the land could not be properly farmed during the whole period when royalists garrisoned Acton Court (1643-45), nor could animals be grazed for fear of loss, 'the cavaliers riding through the same to and from their garrison'. In consequence, the land 'did lie to ruin and waste'. Furthermore, although William himself fled for a while, because he 'durst not continue at his dwelling', the soldiers frequently visited his house 'looking to take him'. All this meant that, 'having no stock in his ground', he made little or no profit.

Secondly, through a deliberate programme of victimisation by royalist troops and officials, William (when at home) was greatly oppressed by excessive demands for contribution payments and free quarter - even though he was already 'in great poverty'. A 'multiplicity of soldiers' on their way to the port for transportation to Ireland were thrust in his direction for accommodation, a fact witnessed by his daughters, one of whom estimated that he was paying out at least £20 per annum in taxes and billeting costs. Such was his poverty that his wife and daughter often subsidised the payment demands out of money they had earned from spinning and carding. Nevertheless, William held out against this pressure until the royalist garrison was removed in 1645. His situation then eased. (44)

***

Family feuds, maimed soldiers, impoverished widows, broken bridges, neglected fields, disrupted churches, embittered losers, exhausted villages and homeless families - these were just some of the fruits of 'an unhappy civil war'. Whatever the long-term gains to the power and privileges of parliament or to the toleration of different beliefs in religion; whatever the short-term gains to businessmen, craftsmen and industrialists, who made money out of the war, many ordinary people in the three western counties had been scarred by their experiences.

Nor were defeated royalists the only ones to be affected in this way. Bulstrode Whitelocke aptly summed up the lot of the victors:

Thus we may see that, even after almost a conquest, yet they apprehended no safety; such are the issues and miseries of a civil war, that the victors are full of fears from those whom they have subdued: no quiet, no security. O let our prayers be to God, never to have such calamitous times again.

(Bulstrode Whitelocke, 'Memorials of the English Affairs', 1682)

*After the Civil War, Richard Wiseman (**see next page**), became Prince Charles's medical attendant in exile. After the Restoration, he was promoted to Sergeant-Surgeon. (Reproduced by kind permission of the President and Council of the Royal College of Surgeons of England).*

THE HORRORS OF WAR 9

BADLY WOUNDED

AT TAUNTON, MAY 1645

Richard Wiseman joined the royalist army in late 1643, working as an army surgeon on campaigns in Dorset, Devon, Somerset and Cornwall. In his memoirs, he later described the treatment he administered to one soldier, who was found with horrific gunshot injuries to the face at the siege of Taunton, where Wiseman was serving under Lord George Goring:

'At the siege of Taunton, one of Colonel Arundel's men, in storming the works, was shot in the face by case-shot. He fell down and, in the retreat, was carried off among the dead; and laid in an empty house by the way until the next day: when, in the morning early, the colonel marching by that house heard a knocking within against the door. Some of the officers, desiring to know what it was, looked in and saw this man standing by the door without eye, face, nose or mouth. The colonel sent to me (my quarters being nearest) to dress the man.

I went, but was somewhat troubled where to begin. The door consisted of two hatches: the uppermost was open and the man stood leaning upon the other part of the door, which was shut. His face, with his eyes, nose, mouth and foremost part of the jaws, with the chin, was shot away and the remaining parts of them driven in. One part of the jaw hung down by his throat and the other part pushed into it. I saw the brain working out underneath the lacerated scalp on both sides between his ears and brows. I could not see any advantage he could have by my dressing. To have cut away the lacerated parts here had been to expose the brain to the air. But I helped him to clear his throat, where was remaining the root of his tongue. He seemed to approve of my endeavours and implored my help by the signs he made with his hands.

I asked him if he would drink, making a sign by the holding up of a finger. He presently did the like and immediatelt after held up both his hands, expressing his thirst. A soldier fetched some milk and brought a little wooden dish to pour some of it down his throat; but part of it running on both sides, he reached out his hands to take the dish. They gave it him full of milk. He held the root of his tongue down with one hand and with the other poured it down his throat (carrying his head backwards) and so got down more than a quart.

After that, I bound his wounds up. The dead were removed from thence to their graves, and fresh straw was fetched for him to lie upon, with an old blanket to cover him. It was the summer. There we left that deplorable creature to lodge: and while we continued there, which was about six or seven days, he was dressed by some of the surgeons with a fomentation made of vulnerary plants (1), with a little brandy-wine in it, and with stupes of tow (2) dipped in our common digestive.'

(1) plants used in the healing of wounds (2) rough cloths made of flax for washing

Source: Sir T Longmore, *Richard Wiseman: Surgeon and Sergeant-Surgeon to Charles II* (1891), pp 44, 46-7

THE CIVIL WAR IN GLOUCESTERSHIRE, SOMERSET & WILTSHIRE, 1642-4:

CHRONOLOGY OF MAIN EVENTS

(Note: the dates given by contemporary sources are not always exact and are sometimes contradictory)

1642

February: *National background:*
(2nd) - the Commons drew up a Militia Bill, by which they sought to gain control of the county militia (the trained bands); (27th) - the king refused to accept it.
Gloucestershire:
The king appointed Lord Chandos to be Lord Lieutenant of Gloucestershire.
Somerset:
(25th) - Sir Thomas Wroth presented a Somerset petition to the Commons expressing concern at the king's breach of parliamentary privileges. The Earl of Bedford was appointed Lord Lieutenant of Somerset by parliament.
Wiltshire:
Earl of Pembroke of Wilton House appointed as parliament's Lord Lieutenant of Wiltshire. (24th) - the town of Salisbury sent a petition to parliament in support of its policy.

March: *National background:*
(5th) - the Commons passed the Militia Ordinance, sanctioning a list of Deputy Lieutenants in each county to organise and control the trained bands
Somerset:
The Deputy Lieutenants appointed in Somerset included Alexander Popham, Sir John Horner, John Ashe, John Pyne and William Strode.

June: *National background:*
(9th) - a parliamentary Ordinance was passed to raise plate, money and horses by voluntary contributions at 8 per cent interest ('the Propositions'). (11th) - the king condemned parliament's Militia Ordinance as illegal and granted individuals in each county a Commission of Array to muster the trained bands on his behalf.
Somerset:
(13th) - a petition from 200 Somerset royalists (including the Pouletts, Berkeleys, Phelipses and Dodingtons) was presented to parliament urging it to end its quarrel with the king.

July: *National background:*
(15th) - parliament appointed the Earl of Essex as commander of all its forces.
(20th) - County Committees were appointed by parliament to raise men and money on its behalf.
Gloucestershire:

(14th) - parliament granted powers for the volunteers of the city of Gloucester to train when and where they pleased.
Somerset:
(12th) - Marquess of Hertford left York with a Commission of Array to raise the forces of both Somerset and Wiltshire for the king. (20th) - parliament appointed a committee of twelve in Somerset (including Alexander Popham, John Harington, Sir John Horner, John Ashe, Sir John Wroth and John Pyne) to raise men and money according to the Militia Ordinance and the Propositions. (25th) - Hertford arrived in Bath (where the county assizes were in session) with the king's commission of array; the Grand Jury of Somerset lodged a petition with the assizes, protesting that the commission was illegal.
Wiltshire:
(11th) - parliament sent Sir Edward Hungerford and Sir John Evelyn to execute the Militia Ordinance for raising forces in Wiltshire. (18th) - in Marlborough, the powder magazine was secured for parliament and the Militia Ordinance executed. In Salisbury, Robert Hyde (the Recorder) tried to raise the town for the king by publishing the commission of array - but was imprisoned by the Commons; parliamentary supporters then seized control and raised a company of volunteers.

August:

National background:
(2nd) - Hertford was appointed King's Lieutenant-General of his forces in the West with instructions to raise an army there. (22nd) - the king raised his standard at Nottingham to signal the official start of the war.
Gloucestershire:
(5th) - a Committee of Defence was established in Gloucester; the city watch was doubled. (9th) - Lord Chandos attempted to execute the king's commission of array, but his carriage was attacked by the mob in Cirencester. He was succeeded in the task by Sir Ralph Dutton. (10th) - Lord Saye and Sele was appointed Lord Lieutenant by parliament. (12th) - Sir Robert Cooke and Nathaniel Stephens were sent by parliament with 'Instructions' to co-ordinate the defence of the county; Deputy Lieutenants were also named to execute the Militia Ordinance. (25th) - Cooke and Stephens called a meeting to advocate 16 propositions for the county's defence.
Somerset:
(1st) - Hertford, backed by a number of leading west country gentlemen, established his headquarters in Wells, where Sir Ralph Hopton, John Digby, Sir Francis Hawley and Henry Lunsford assembled a cavalry force. Parliament's county committee ordered a meeting of its leading supporters in Shepton Mallet, where a minor confrontation took place with Hopton. (4th) - the first blood of the war in Somerset was shed at Marshall's Elm, near Street, where seven members of John Pyne's force, on their way to the parliamentary rendezvous, were killed by Henry Lunsford's royalists. (5th) - 12,000 parliamentarian supporters assembled in arms at Chewton Mendip under Alexander Popham and Sir John Horner to confront the 900 royalist followers in Wells; Hertford quickly

withdrew to Sherborne via Somerton; Popham's men ransacked Wells Cathedral and the Bishop's Palace. (12th) - Sir John Foster, the Assize Judge, pronounce the commission of array illegal.

Wiltshire:

Devizes was garrisoned for parliament. (5th) - Salisbury Corporation began to fortify the city. (5th) - 300 members of the Wiltshire trained bands (with Sir Edward Hungerford, M.P. for Chippenham, and John Ashe, M.P. for Westbury) joined the rendezvous of parliament's forces at Chewton Mendip. (10th) - parliament sent the Earl of Pembroke as Lord Lieutenant to complete the organisation of the county militia, before handing over command to Denzil Holles.

September:

Gloucestershire:

(5th) - the county militia commenced training at Gloucester and Chipping Sodbury - but the defence scheme largely failed. (23rd) - preparations were made for the defence of Berkeley Castle.

Somerset:

(6th) - The Earl of Bedford and Col. Charles Essex, after briefly laying siege to Hertford in Sherborne, withdrew to Yeovil. (7th) - Hopton's royalist force from Sherborne skirmished with Bedford's troops at Babylon Hill, east of Yeovil. (19th) - Hertford's force left Sherborne, reaching Minehead (22nd) via Hinton St George; (23rd) - Hertford escaped to Wales by boat, while Hopton took the cavalry and dragoons into Cornwall.

Wiltshire:

Devizes was fortified by Sir Edward Baynton for parliament and its magazine enlarged. Sir Edward Hungerford began strengthening the defences of both Chippenham and Malmesbury.

October:

National background:

(23rd) - the first major battle of the war, which was fought at Edgehill, was indecisive. (29th) - the king established his headquarters at Oxford.

Gloucestershire:

The Earl of Stamford was appointed parliamentary commander for the defence of Gloucestershire, Herefordshire, Shropshire and Worcestershire.

Somerset:

(24th) - parliamentary gentry from Somerset, Gloucestershire and Wiltshire, who had established 'a mutual association' under the control of an organising committee, wrote to the Corporation of Bristol, urging them to join; the Corporation procrastinated, preferring to remain neutral. Leading royalists in Somerset were arrested, including Sir Edward Berkeley, Sir Charles Berkeley, Sir Francis Dodington and Sir Edward Rodney.

Wiltshire:

Parliament's Propositions were implemented by Sir John Evelyn in Salisbury, by Sir Neville Poole in Marlborough and by Sir Edward Baynton and Sir Edward Hungerford in the north-west of the county. Marlborough was fortified for parliament.

November: *Gloucestershire:*

(8th) - Bristol Corporation, anxious to retain its neutrality, sent a peace petition to both king and parliament; and (24th) decided to strengthen its defences by building a line of earthworks around the city in an attempt to keep out *all* intruders. Colonel Thomas Essex was appointed Governor of Gloucester with a garrison of two regiments.

(15th) - parliamentary supporters raised £15,000 in the county from loans based on the 'Propositions'.

Somerset:

(26th) - the parliamentary gentry of the three counties (strongly led by Popham, Ashe, Horner, Strode and Hungerford) put further pressure on Bristol to join their association both by sharp correspondence and by threatening troop movements near Pensford.

Wiltshire:

Marlborough was garrisoned for parliament and Salisbury's defences strengthened. (2nd) -the king published a pardon for the inhabitants of Wiltshire, excepting Sir Edward Hungerford, Sir Henry Ludlow, Sir John Evelyn and Walter Long.

December: *National background:*

(24th) - parliament passed an Ordinance to preserve the western parts of the kingdom by raising further money.

Gloucestershire:

(9th) - parliament sent 2,000 troops under Col.Thomas Essex to establish a garrison and become Governor in Bristol, thus ending their neutrality. Colonel Edward Massey became Deputy Governor to the Earl of Stamford in Gloucester. A parliamentary Ordinance established a County Committee for Gloucestershire to co-ordinate their war effort. Cirencester was fortified by parliament with Colonel Fettiplace as Governor. (31st) - the Marquess of Hertford quartered at Stow-on-the-Wold with Welsh royalist forces.

Wiltshire:

(5th) - Marlborough was seized for the king by Henry Wilmot with a detachment from Oxford (the first garrison in England to fall). (20th) - the Earl of Stamford (parliament's commander-in-chief in the West) reviewed the Wiltshire trained bands at Devizes.

1643

January: *National background:*

(17th) - the Cornish royalists invited Sir Ralph Hopton to become commander of their newly-raised army. (27th) - a parliamentary Ordinance empowered county committees to tax those who had not contributed loans to the Propositions.

Gloucestershire:

(1st) - a parliamentary garrison at Cirencester successfully raided Lord Byron's troops at Burford. Hertford unsuccessfully summoned the parliamentary garrison at Gloucester. (6th) - Prince Rupert failed in his attempt to capture Cirencester.

Gloucester Corporation began a policy of stockpiling food supplies. (27th) - Colonel Thomas Essex, Governor of Bristol, was arrested for irregular conduct. Massey (with garrison forces from Gloucester, Cirencester and Tewkesbury) captured Sudeley Castle (the seat of Chandos) after a short siege.

Somerset:

(27th) - a committee was set up to impose fines, amounting to one-twentieth of their estates, on those royalists who had not cooperated fully with the Propositions. (27th) - a parliamentary Ordinance permitted the Somerset Committee to retain (for the defence of the county) any money raised.

Wiltshire:

(10th) - parliament passed an Ordinance to raise two regiments of horse and one regiment of dragoons in Wiltshire under Sir Edward Baynton (as commander-in-chief) to secure the county against invasion from Oxford. Sir Edward Hungerford and Sir Edward Baynton were soon involved in a bitter personal dispute. (31st) - Hungerford was appointed commander-in-chief of parliament's forces in Wiltshire in place of Baynton.

February:

National background:

(11th) - parliament established the Western Association under Sir William Waller to organise the war in five western counties, including Gloucestershire, Somerset and Wiltshire - particularly in view of the threat to its grip on the West posed by the advance northwards of Sir Ralph Hopton's new Cornish army of royalists. (24th) - parliament issued an ordinance establishing the weekly assessment - a tax on individuals based on property value to fund additional forces; committees were established in each county to appoint local assessors and collectors.

Gloucestershire:

(2nd) - Prince Rupert took Cirencester by storm, leaving Colonel Kirk as governor. (3rd) - parliament withdrew their garrisons at Sudeley and Berkeley Castles. (6th)- Rupert called meetings of the leading gentry in the Cotswolds and agreed on contributions to raise £3,000 immediately, followed by £4,000 per month. (7th) - Tewkesbury was taken for the king by Sir William Russell and garrisoned by Sir Matthew Carew. (7th) - Lord Herbert's Welsh forces advanced through Coleford and the Forest of Dean to Highnam House before unsuccessfully summoning Gloucester. (11th) - parliament appointed Waller as Sergeant-Major-General of five western counties with powers to raise money to support ten new regiments. (11th) - Berkeley Castle was re-garrisoned for parliament by Lieutenant-Colonel Forbes. (12th) - the king prohibited all subjects from trading with Gloucester. Colonel Nathaniel Fiennes replaced Essex as Governor of Bristol. (23rd) - a parliamentary Ordinance empowered Fiennes to raise a regiment of horse in the county and to seize the horses of delinquents. (24th) - the county was instructed to pay £750 and the city of Gloucester £62 10s 0d per week towards the weekly assessment.

Somerset:

(24th) - the Somerset Committee was required to raise £1050 per week for the weekly assessment out of a national total of £33,518; the Somerset Committee appointed John Ashe as treasurer for the Eastern Division and Roger Hill for the Western Division.

Wiltshire:

(3rd) - Prince Rupert (from Oxford) captured Malmesbury for the king, leaving Col. Henry Lunsford as governor with a garrison of 400 foot and a troop of horse. (13th) - Sir Edward Hungerford and Col. Edmund Ludlow entered Salisbury with their force, taking contributions from the city. (23rd) - the parliamentary garrison in Devizes was withdrawn by Hungerford, who felt unable to make good the defences; the town was subsequently occupied for the king by Lunsford. (24th) - the Wiltshire Committee was instructed to raise £725 per week as its contribution to the weekly assessment to support the war effort. This committee was to consist of Sir Edward Hungerford, Sir Edward Baynton, Sir Nevill Poole, Sir John Evelyn, Edward Ashe and seven others.

March: *National background:*

(27th) - parliamentary Ordinance set up county committees to confiscate and manage the estates of royalists.

Gloucestershire:

(2nd) - the king ordered Prince Maurice to secure the county against the threat posed by Waller's march westwards. (7th) - a royalist plot to seize control of Bristol, organised by Robert Yeoman and George Bourcher, was thwarted by Fiennes. (15th) - Waller established his headquarters at Bristol. (22nd) - the king appointed William, Viscount Grandison, as commander-in-chief of both Gloucestershire and Wiltshire with six regiments of horse based on Cirencester. (25th) - Massey and Waller, in a joint attack on Highnam House, captured 150 officers and 1,444 men.

Wiltshire:

(9th) - Waller's army entered Salisbury on his march westwards, recruiting arms and horses in the city for parliament; relieved Sherston (20th), captured Chippenham and retook Malmesbury, leaving Hungerford in charge. (10th) - the king ordered the implementation of the commission of array for Wiltshire - 37 commissioners appointed to secure the county and maintain the garrisons. (23rd) - Malmesbury was surrendered by Hungerford's men to the royalists, who abandoned it shortly afterwards to free troops for the relief of Reading.

April: *National background:*

(1st) -a parliamentary Ordinance was passed for sequestering the estates of royalist delinquents, including those in Somerset, Gloucestershire and Wiltshire.

Gloucestershire:

(10th) - Maurice skirmished with Waller at Newnham-on-Severn. (12th) - Massey and Waller captured Tewkesbury, leaving a garrison of 1,000 men under Sir Robert Cooke. (13th) - Waller suffered a setback against Maurice in a skirmish at

Ripple Field, near Upton. (19th) - the royalist garrison at Cirencester was abandoned in view of the cost and the town was reoccupied by Waller. Massey was promoted to Governor of Gloucester. A Town Regiment was raised in Gloucester under the command of Henry Stephens.

Somerset:

(15th) - Alexander Popham's soldiers plundered the cathedral and Bishop's Palace in Wells. (16th) - Popham led a force of Somerset militia to Sherborne to deal with a suspected royalist attempt to seize control; he occupied both the town and the castle.

Wiltshire:

(5th) - Hungerford, now based in Bath, launched raids on Wiltshire, plundering royalists' estates at Woodhouse (28th) and Longleat (30th).

May:

Gloucestershire:

(30th) - Robert Yeomans and George Bourcher were executed in Bristol for their leadership of the abortive royalist rising.

Somerset:

(10th) - Popham's soldiers again plundered the Cathedral and Bishop's Palace in Wells. William Strode led a force of Somerset militia to assist Hungerford in the siege of Wardour Castle.

Wiltshire:

(2nd) - Hungerford began the siege of Wardour Castle. (3rd) - a parliamentary Ordinance appointed Sir Edward Hungerford and Edward Goddard to speed up the collection of the weekly assessment in Wiltshire. (8th) - Wardour Castle was captured for parliament by Hungerford, leaving Ludlow as governor. (17th) - Marlborough was reoccupied for the king by Hertford and Prince Maurice (en route to strengthen Sir Ralph Hopton's Cornish army on its western campaign), before moving on to garrison Salisbury (21st). (27th) - the royalist army was reviewed at Dogdean.

June:

Gloucestershire:

Waller, with the Tewkesbury garrison, left the county to halt the advance of Hopton's Cornish army.

Somerset:

(4th) - Hopton's royalist army entered Somerset at Chard, where it was joined by the reinforcements sent by the king from Oxford under the command of Hertford and Maurice. Facing this threat, the Somerset militia had mustered at Shepton Mallet (under Popham and Strode) and Taunton (under Pyne, Wroth and Edward Popham). (5th) - Edward Popham withdrew the Taunton garrison, enabling the royalists to occupy the town with Sir John Stawell as governor. (6th) - Bridgwater was abandoned by the parliamentarian garrison in panic, leaving Sir Edmund Wyndham to take over as governor; and Thomas Luttrell meekly surrendered Dunster Castle to Col. Francis Wyndham, who was made governor. (8th)- Waller arrived back in Bath from Gloucester and staged a rendezvous of his western forces on Bathampton and Claverton Downs. (9th) - Edward Popham and Strode assembled 3,000 militia at Glastonbury to halt the advancing royalists, who now numbered 6,500 men. (11th) - Hertford's army advanced to Somerton. (12th) - the outnumbered parliamentarian forces gradually withdrew through Wells and on to the Mendips, where a bloody cavalry skirmish took place; afterwards, the royalists withdrew to Wells and the parliamentarians to Bath. A truce was declared for the exchange of prisoners. (30th?) - the royalist army advanced to Frome.

July:

National background:
(15th) - Prince Rupert left Oxford to assist the royalist western army for their planned attack on Bristol.

Gloucestershire:
(23rd) - royalist forces under Rupert, Maurice and Hertford surrounded Bristol, which was subsequently captured (26th).

Somerset:
(2nd) - Hertford's army reached Bradford-on-Avon, where it camped the night before advancing next day (3rd) towards Bath; a skirmish was fought in the river valley below Claverton. (4th) - after camping the night at Batheaston, Hertford advanced onto the foothills of Lansdown only to be thwarted by Waller, who had shifted his ground during the night to block the royalists' path; they therefore withdrew to Marshfield, four miles north of Bath. (5th) - the Battle of Lansdown was fought on the northern slopes of the down; the royalist advance was halted and the plan to capture Bath was aborted. (10th) - the royalists appointed Edward Wyndham as sheriff with Lord Poulett, Edward Phelips, Sir John Stawell and seven others as king's county commissioners to liquidate the estates of parliamentarians in aid of the war effort.

Wiltshire:
(8th) - Hopton's army, after suffering the reverse at Lansdown, retreated to Chippenham; and then to Devizes (9th), where it was besieged by Waller. (12th) - a royalist cavalry force under Henry Wilmot from Oxford assembled at Marlborough with the aim of relieving Devizes. (13th) - the royalists routed Waller's army at Roundway Down, near Devizes (which subsequently remained in royalist hands until September, 1645); they then moved back across the county through Chippenham and on to Bath. (21st) - Royalist forces from Oxford under Rupert recaptured Malmesbury. (26th) - after the fall of Bristol to Rupert's army, the soldiers from its parliamentarian garrison were escorted out as far as Warminster. (31st) - the king stayed in Malmesbury with a none too friendly welcome.

August:

National background:
(3rd) - a parliamentary Ordinance authorised the raising of further money through a renewal of the weekly assessment. (10th) - a parliamentary Ordinance legalised conscription to the army. (20th) - parliament appointed Waller as commander of a new army in the south. (23rd) - a parliamentary Ordinance for the relief of Gloucester authorised the use of 9,500 troops from the London trained bands.

Gloucestershire:

(2nd) - the king entered Bristol; Rupert was appointed Governor with Hopton as his Deputy-Lieutenant. (8th) - the king's army advanced towards Gloucester, capturing Berkeley Castle and leaving Captain George Maxwell as Governor. (10th) - houses in the suburbs of Gloucester were destroyed by order of the Council; the king unsuccessfully summoned the city to surrender; the siege commenced. (26th) - the Earl of Essex left London with 8,000 men to relieve Gloucester.
Wiltshire:
Longford House and Wilton House were garrisoned for the king (until October 1645). (17th) - the king ordered a permanent weekly contribution from several counties (including £1,200 per week from Wiltshire) to maintain a field army of 14,000 men.

September: *Gloucester:*
Essex reached Brackley Heath (1st), where reinforcements enlarged his army to 15,000; and then Prestbury Hill (5th), ten miles from Gloucester. (6th) - the king lifted the siege, withdrawing to Sudeley Castle. (8th) - Essex's army entered Gloucester, bringing fresh supplies. (10th) - Essex left to give chase to the king's army, which was now heading for London. Essex first captured Tewkesbury, before entering Cirencester (15th), where he captured 400 men and horses with 40 cartloads of provisions.(16th) - the royalists recaptured Cirencester, leaving a garrison under Sir Jacob Astley as governor. Sir John Winter was appointed royalist governor of Lydney in the Forest of Dean, under Sir William Vavasour as colonel-general of the Welsh forces. Parliament established a committee under Thomas Pury to hear complaints against abuses by the Gloucester garrison.
Somerset:
(29th) - Hopton was appointed lieutenant-governor of Bristol with Sir Francis Hawley as his deputy.
Wiltshire:
(17th) - The Earl of Essex (commander-in-chief of parliament's forces), on his return to London after relieving the siege of Gloucester, spent the night at Swindon. (18th) - Rupert attacked Essex's parliamentary army on Aldbourne Chase to delay their return to London (a prelude to the 1st Battle of Newbury). Sir John Penruddock was appointed sheriff by the king. (29th) - the king appointed Hopton as commander of a field army in Wiltshire and the neighbouring counties.

October: *Gloucestershire:*
Tewkesbury was again occupied by 1,500 royalists commanded by Vavasour.
Somerset:
Somerset's weekly contribution was raised to £2000. Hopton commenced an extensive impressment policy to raise men for his new army (supported by Sir Edward Stawell and Sir John Poulett).

December: *Gloucestershire:*
(14th) - the trial commenced of Nathaniel Fiennes on charges of cowardice; found guilty and sentenced to death, but

eventually granted a pardon. (20th) - regiments of royalist infantry from Ireland under Colonel Mynne reached Thornbury, before going on to Tewkesbury and Painswick.
Wiltshire:
The royalists began the siege of Wardour Castle with assistance from Somerset troops under the command of Robert Phelips.

1644

January:

National background:
(22nd) - the king formally opened his Oxford Parliament.
Gloucestershire:
A Grand Committee was appointed by parliament to investigate abuses in war taxation. Prince Rupert was based in Tewkesbury, plundering the countryside. (9th) - royalist commissioners ordered the impressment of 1,800 men from the county.
Wiltshire:
(13th) - the king instructed Hopton and Penruddock to conscript as many men as necessary in Wiltshire for Hopton's new army.

February:

Gloucestershire:
(22nd) - parliament authorised money and supplies to be sent to Gloucester in an armed convoy (including powder, match, muskets, coats, shoes and shirts). Massey, the city's Governor, authorised the imposition of excise duties on meal, beer and malt to support the garrison.

March:

National background:
Prince Maurice succeeded the Marquis of Hertford as the king's Lieut-General of the West.
Gloucestershire:
(20th) - the king appointed a new body of commissioners for the county. (27th) - Sir John Winter was appointed royalist Governor of the Forest Division of the county.
Wiltshire:
(12th) - the king issued orders for the conscription of 667 men in Wiltshire for his own army. (18th) - Wardour Castle, the last parliamentarian garrison in the county, surrendered to royalist forces from Somerset under Sir Francis Dodington (assisted by miners from the Mendips, who undermined the fortifications); with the end of this three-month siege, Wiltshire was now entirely under the king's control.

April:

Gloucestershire:
Vavasour was appointed commander of all royalist forces in the county (with Winter as his subordinate in the Forest of Dean). (7th) - the royalists established permanent garrisons at Tewkesbury and Sudeley. Parliament's convoy of relief supplies managed to slip through the blockade into Gloucester - Vavasour was dismissed. Rupert was appointed as royalist commander in South Wales with Colonel Mynne as his deputy. (23rd) - Queen Henrietta Maria stayed in Bristol.
Wiltshire:
Waller's troops, after success in the Battle of Cheriton, marched into Salisbury.

The church at Highworth was fortified and garrisoned for the king. (10th) - the king reviewed his army of 6,000 men at Marlborough, before returning personally to his headquarters in Oxford - although the army remained in Marlborough for several weeks to keep an eye on the movements of Waller.

May: *National background:*

(1st) - the king established a Western Association (of Somerset, Devon, Dorset and Cornwall), under Maurice's control, with a central organising committee operating from Exeter. Somerset was to provide 9000 troops by impressment.

Gloucestershire:

Massey commenced a drive against royalist garrisons, taking their outposts at Westbury (7th), Little Dean (7th) and Newnham (8th); burning Winter's iron mills in the Forest of Dean (9th); and seizing both Beverstone Castle (23rd) and Malmesbury (24th). Lord Chandos defected to parliament. (10th) - parliament passed an Ordinance for the raising, maintaining and financing of forces for the Gloucester garrison.

Wiltshire:

Ludlow was appointed High Sheriff of Wiltshire by parliament. (24th) - Col. Edward Massey, in a thrust from his Gloucester garrison to support parliament's drive against Oxford, took Malmesbury (which then remained in parliament's hands until the end of the war) - Col. Nicholas Devereux was appointed governor there under Massey's control; Massey then went on to capture Chippenham, before arresting George Lowe, MP for Calne, in his own constituency and the king's county committee *en bloc* in Devizes. A foothold had now been re-established for parliament. (30th) - the king issued a further order to conscript 667 men in Wiltshire for his own army.

June: *Gloucestershire:*

(4th) - Massey captured Tewkesbury for parliament. (6th) - Waller met Essex at Chipping Norton; (7th) - together they chased the king through Cirencester and Stow-on-the-Wold to Evesham, before returning to take Sudeley Castle (9th).

Somerset:

(7th) - Essex began his western campaign to relieve Lyme and prevent the king's Western Association from taking root; he camped with his army at Chard for two weeks. Maurice strengthened the garrison of Bridgwater by weakening those elsewhere (including Taunton).

July: *National background:*

(1st) - parliament established a county committees in the West to raise money in Wiltshire, Somerset, Dorset, Devon and Cornwall for a new local army through the renewal of the weekly assessment for three months. (2nd) - parliament's allied armies won the Battle of Marston Moor, near York. (12th) - the king left Evesham and headed westwards with his army in pursuit of Essex.

Gloucestershire:

(1st) - the king left Evesham in pursuit of Essex to the south-west, passing through Coberley, Salperton, Badminton and

Bath with 7,000 men.

Somerset:

Essex sent Robert Blake and Sir Robert Pye to besiege and capture Taunton Castle, which was surrendered by the deputy governor, Sergeant-Major Reeve (8th), leaving Blake as parliamentary governor. The king, on the trail of Essex, stayed in Bath (15th), from where he despatched reinforcements to assist Dodington in the capture of Woodhouse garrison in Wiltshire; he moved on to Mells (14th); Bruton (19th); Ilchester (23rd), where he addressed the local people on King's Moor; and Chard, from where he moved into Devon (25th); demands for money were sent out to towns and villages *en route*. Essex, meanwhile, had left the county and had relieved Lyme (23rd).

Wiltshire:

(1st) - parliament appointed a new committee for Wiltshire to raise a Weekly Assessment for 3 months in support of a new army. (7th) - parliamentary cavalry under Ludlow and Popham were routed between Warminster and Salisbury by Hopton's forces; (17th) - the royalists, under Sir Francis Dodington, then captured the Woodhouse garrison, near Horningsham. (15th) - parliament's Wiltshire Committee was authorised to raise troops and money for the defence of the county and the maintenance of the Malmesbury garrison. The committee voted Massey as commander-in-chief of the Wiltshire forces. (30th) - Ludlow was appointed colonel of a regiment of Wiltshire horse.

August:

National background:

(19th) - a parliamentary Ordinance established an Association of Western Counties to counter the royalists' similar organisation. (31st) - Essex was defeated by the king at Lostwithiel in Cornwall.

Gloucestershire:

(2nd) - Colonel Mynne threatened Gloucester, but was killed when defeated by Massey at Ridmarley. Parliament increased its weekly assessment for the county from £750 to £1,000 per week.

Somerset:

The royalists established a supply depot for the king in Bridgwater. (14th) - a parliamentarian force of 2,000 cavalry and dragoons under Lieut.-Gen. John Middleton arrived from Hampshire to cut the king's line of supply; it attacked a supply convoy under Dodington at North Pemberton, but was repulsed.

Wiltshire:

Chalfield House was garrisoned for parliament by Col. Devereux.

September:

Gloucestershire:

(4th) - Massey appeared before Bath, but then withdrew to Marshfield with the intention of facing Bristol; he returned instead to Gloucester. (24th) - Massey captured Monmouth, having defeated Rupert's forces at Beachley, where they were establishing a base to command river links between Bristol and

Wales.
Somerset:
(4th) - Massey marched from Gloucester in an attempt to seize Bath for parliament, but withdrew. Colonel Edmund Ludlow's cavalry from Wiltshire captured both Stourton and the royalist garrison at Witham Friary. The survivors of Essex's cavalry, defeated by the king at Lostwithiel, rode through the county (23rd). The king's victorious army re-entered Somerset, camping at Chard before marching on into Dorset (30th); the king ordered the commencement of the siege of Taunton, directed by Edmund Wyndham with 4-5,000 men.
Wiltshire:
(5th) - Chalfield House was temporarily evacuated by the parliamentarian garrison on the approach of royalists from Bath, but it was restored by Massey (Governor of Gloucester), Chalfield thereafter remaining in parliament's hands until the end of the war. (7th) - Ludlow was at Salisbury with three troops of horse. (10th) - having staged a rendezvous of parliament's local forces at Salisbury, Waller's army passed through the county on his way to strengthen the garrisons at Weymouth, Lyme and Poole and to relieve Plymouth from siege. (24th) - Waller camped in Shaftesbury with his own cavalry in an attempt to check the king's return to Oxford (after the latter's victory over the Earl of Essex at Lostwithiel). Sir Walter Long replaced Sir John Penruddock as the king's sheriff, but was quickly succeeded by his son, Sir James.

October:
National background:
(10th) - Hopton was appointed field marshal of the king's western army with powers to impress and raise troops for the strengthening of local garrisons.
Gloucestershire:
(2nd) - parliament passed an Ordinance for a new weekly assessment on the city and county of Gloucester to support their forces there. (14th) - Massey defeated Winter, who was attempting to re-fortify Beachley.
Somerset:
(14th) - Royalist gentlemen from Somerset, who had presented a peace petition to the king at Sturminster Newton, staged a meeting at Wells to draft a petition to parliament. (28th) - the king reached Bath with an escort of 500 after the Second Battle of Newbury, leaving for Oxford with Rupert (30th).
Wiltshire:
(10th) - Waller was forced to fall back from Shaftesbury to Winterbourne Stoke in the face of the king's advance with superior forces; he then retreated to Andover, complaining that Ludlow's Wiltshire regiment had not joined him. (15th) - the king, returning from Cornwall, entered Salisbury, placing his guns in the garrisons of Longford House and Wilton House nearby; he made preparations to relieve his garrison in Donnington Castle, near Newbury.

November:
Wiltshire:
(10th) - the king marched with his army into the county,

quartering first at Wanborough and then at Marlborough (12th), from where he planned to relieve Basing House. He established garrisons at Longford Castle under Colonel Griffin and at Marlborough under Colonel Dabridgecourt. (17th) - the king ordered the immediate conscription of 200 men around Marlborough. Wilton House was evacuated by the royalist garrison.

December:

Gloucestershire:
(4th) - the king authorised a 'new establishment' to support his Bristol garrison. The construction of the Royal Fort was completed in that city.

Somerset:
(9th) - after much lobbying in parliament by William Strode of Barrington, Waller sent a force of 1200 cavalry under Maj.-Gen. James Holborne (including Ludlow's Wiltshire troops) to relieve Taunton, which was quickly achieved (14th).

Wiltshire:
The parliamentarians garrisoned Sir John Evelyn's house at West Dean, Mr Blake's house at Pinnel (near Calne), Lacock House and Rowden House (near Chippenham). The castle at Devizes was strengthened by the royalists and garrisoned under Sir Charles Lloyd. Major Wansey and Major Dowett, with a parliamentarian force, defeated Colonel Francis Cook at Salisbury, enabling Ludlow to establish a garrison in The Belfry there. (31st) - Ludlow was routed in an attack by Marmaduke Langdale's royalists, who proceeded to pillage the town and establish a garrison there. General George Goring's royalist cavalry entered Devizes (22nd) and attacked Pinnel House, near Calne (29th).

1645

January:

National background:
(15th) - parliament appointed Waller to lead a force of cavalry and dragoons into the West to hold the royalists in check until the New Model Army was ready to campaign.

Gloucestershire:
Sir Jacob Astley arrived in Cirencester with 1,500 royalist infantry. Sir Henry Bard established a royalist garrison at Campden House, Chipping Campden and commenced a reign of terror in the neighbourhood.

Somerset:
Holborne remained in south Somerset with his cavalry, forcing Wyndham to loosen his siege of Taunton and base most of his troops at Chard as a precaution. Hopton established a garrison at Langport, appointing Sir Francis Mackworth governor.

Wiltshire:
(3rd) - the parliamentarian garrison at Pinnel House surrendered. (10th) - the king appointed Maj. Hen as governor of Highworth and Col. Charles Lloyd as governor of Devizes. Lloyd began a process of transforming the old castle into a fortress (January-March). Goring's royalist forces moved across the county, basing themselves for a time (from 15th) in Salisbury and committing 'horrible outrages and barbarities' on the countryside.

February: *Gloucestershire:*
Massey defeated Winter at Lancourt-upon-Wye.
Wiltshire:
(5th) - Lacock Abbey was garrisoned by the royalists with Lieut.-Col. Jordan Boville as Governor. (15th) - Rowden House, a parliamentarian garrison near Chippenham, was captured by the royalists and dismantled.

March: *National background:*
(4th) - the king sent Charles, Prince of Wales, to Bristol as general of the Western Association; Goring was appointed overall commander of the king's forces in the West. Waller (now joined by Cromwell) was ordered to march immediately into the West as a counter to Goring.
Gloucestershire:
(2nd) - Sir Charles Lucas was appointed royalist Governor of Berkeley Castle. (4th) - Charles, Prince of Wales, (the newly-appointed General of the association of the four western counties) set up his headquarters in Bristol.
Somerset:
Lord Goring's royalist army of 4,500 men entered Somerset, basing themselves on Chard and Crewkerne. Royalist forces from Bristol and Bridgwater recommenced the siege of Taunton with help from Goring's infantry and artillery and Sir Richard Grenvile's forces from Devon and Cornwall.
Wiltshire:
(10th) - Waller and Cromwell marched to Amesbury on their way to relieve Taunton. The royalist garrison was evacuated from Salisbury. (12th) - from their new base in Salisbury, Waller and Cromwell defeated royalist forces near Trowbridge, capturing Sheriff James Long. (19th) - Waller detached Cromwell to rendezvous with parliament's western forces at Cerne Abbas in Dorset, while he proceeded to Bristol in the hope of bribing members of the garrison to open the gates.

April: *National background:*
(4th) - parliament established the first professional army, the New Model Army, under the command of Sir Thomas Fairfax.
Gloucestershire:
(2nd) - Rupert and Maurice entered the Forest of Dean to plunder and ravage the countryside.
Somerset:
Goring's cavalry based itself around Bruton, making attacks on Waller's forces billeted in villages on the Wiltshire border; Waller counter-attacked, forcing Goring to move back to Glastonbury and Wells. (10th) - the close siege of Taunton commenced with 8,000 troops successively under the command of Grenvile, Goring and Hopton. Grenvile's troops captured Wellington House. (23rd) - Prince Charles met the king's commissioners of Somerset, Devon, Cornwall and Dorset at Bridgwater to discuss a plan to raise 6000 troops. (28th) - Fairfax was ordered to march west with the New Model Army to relieve Taunton. (30th) - Goring left the siege of Taunton with his cavalry, having been ordered by the king to join his

field army in Oxford for a campaign in the North.
Wiltshire:
Chalfield House was briefly besieged by Goring' royalists. (9th) - Waller and Cromwell were based with their army in Salisbury from where they kept a watchful eye on Goring's activities in Somerset. On the following day they stayed in Wilton House. Waller's army was shortly afterwards amalgamated into the New Model Army. Sheriff James Long was released from prison in exchange for Col. Thomas Stevens (captured at Rowden in February).

May: *Gloucestershire:*
(8th) - the king, having left Oxford with an army of 8,000 to relieve Chester, quartered at Stow-on-the-Wold. Campden House was burnt to the ground by Bard as his royalist garrison retreated. Winter burnt his own house at Lydney to prevent occupation by the enemy.
Somerset:
(6th-10th) - the royalists launched a fierce assault on Taunton. (7th) - Fairfax, on his way to Taunton, was ordered by parliament instead to pursue the king's field army as it left Oxford; a small force of just 4,500 men under Col. Ralph Weldon was detached to relieve Taunton (later increased to 6,000 by local troops); (9th) - they quartered at Chard; (10th) - the royalists broke up the siege of Taunton, as Weldon's relief force approached. (17th) - Goring, having been sent back into the West by the king, assembled his army of 8,000 on King's Moor, near Ilchester. (19th) - heavy but indecisive skirmishing took place between Goring's troops and those of Weldon near Ilminster.
Wiltshire:
Rise of the Wiltshire Clubmen, including 700 in Salisbury. (9th) - Sheriff Long captured Chippenham and Lavington. (25th) - a mass meeting of Clubmen from Wiltshire and Dorset at Gussage Corner in Dorset, where articles of association were adopted and a declaration issued.

June: *National background:*
After its victory at Naseby over the king's army (11th), the New Model Army started out on its western campaign (30th). Massey was appointed commander of parliament's Western Association with powers to impress local levies.
Gloucestershire:
Massey, promoted to Maj.-Gen., joined Fairfax's New Model Army. He was replaced as Governor of Gloucester by Col. Walter Lloyd and then by Col. Thomas Morgan (18th). Fairfax and the New Model camped at Chipping Campden, Northleach and Lechlade (23rd-25th); a regiment of horse was sent to blockade Lucas at Berkeley Castle, while Fairfax moved westwards in pursuit of Goring's army.
Somerset:
Clubmen Associations were formed throughout the county with some 5,000 Clubmen assembling at Castle Cary (2nd) and presenting a petition to Prince Charles at Wells against the violent behaviour of Goring's troops; (3rd) - representatives of

the Clubmen met Prince Charles at Bridgwater. (18th) - Prince Rupert met the Clubmen of north-east Somerset at Wraxall, near Bristol, and later (28th) on Lansdown, near Bath, but his overtures were each time rejected. (30th) - a large gathering of Clubmen on Sedgemoor was addressed by Humphrey Willis. Goring resumed a blockade of Taunton.

Wiltshire:

A gathering of Clubmen took place at Upavon. (13th) - leaders of the local Clubmen met at Salisbury the commanders of two rival garrisons and arranged a temporary treaty for the peace of the county until their peace petitions to king and parliament had been heard. (27th) - Sir Thomas Fairfax and the New Model Army, in pursuit of Goring's forces in the south-west, captured the royalist garrison at Highworth. (28th) - Fairfax moved on to Marlborough.

July:

Somerset:

(4th) - Goring abandoned his half-hearted siege of Taunton, withdrawing to Yeovil. (5th) - Fairfax marched into Somerset, linking up with Massey's forces to create a combined force of 14,000 men based on Crewkerne; (7th) - advanced to Yeovil; (10th) - defeated Goring's 7,000 men at Langport (Goring himself escaping to Dunster); (11th) - met a deputation of Clubmen on Sedgemoor; (21st) - commenced the assault on Bridgwater, which surrendered (23rd) after a heavy bombardment; (26th) -marched south to Martock in pursuit of Goring, but turned back, at the same time detaching Col. Pickering's brigade to commence the siege of Sherborne; (28th) - set up his headquarters in Wells as a prelude to an attack on Bath, whose garrison had already been strengthened by Rupert (21st) . (29th) - Cols. Rich and Okey were sent by Fairfax with a reconnaissance party of cavalry and dragoons to investigate the strength of Bath, which was quickly surrendered in panic (to everyone's surprise) by its governor, Sir Thomas Bridges (30th).

Wiltshire:

A petition of the Wiltshire Clubmen expressed a desire for peace, the maintenance of the protestant religion, the king's prerogatives, the privileges of parliament and the liberties of the people. (12th) - royalist forces under Long again captured Chippenham.

August:

National background:

(26th) - a parliamentary Ordinance renewed the weekly assessment in the western counties for a further six months.

Gloucestershire:

(20th) - Fairfax's army reached Hanham , establishing its headquarters first at Stapleton and then at Ashley Down, before commencing the siege of Bristol (garrisoned by Rupert).

Somerset:

(2nd) - Fairfax marched from Wells via Queen Camel to complete the siege of Sherborne (which finally surrendered on 15th). (18th) - Fairfax returned to Somerset, marching through Castle Cary and Shepton Mallet with the object of laying siege to Bristol. (20th) - Nunney Castle surrendered to Col.

	Thomas Rainsborough with a detachment of the New Model Army after a bombardment. (26th) - Somerset was assessed for £1,250 per week in the new weekly assessment. (28th) - the New Model Army captured Portishead Fort with the assistance of the local Clubmen. *Wiltshire:* (12th) - royalist forces under Sir James Long captured Chippenham. (26th) - Wiltshire was assessed for £750 per week in the new weekly assessment..
September:	*Gloucestershire:* (4th) - Rupert rejected Fairfax's summons to surrender Bristol; (10th) - Fairfax began to storm the city; (11th) - Rupert surrendered Bristol; (15th) - Maj.-Gen. Philip Skippon was appointed as acting Governor of Bristol for parliament. (23rd) - Col. Rainsborough besieged Berkeley Castle, taking it by storm. *Somerset:* A large gathering of Clubmen from north-east Somerset gathered at Chewton Mendip to be addressed by Oliver Cromwell, before agreeing to give active support to the New Model Army; a second meeting took place at Dundry Hill. (11th) - local Clubmen assisted in the capture of Bristol after a short siege. (13th) - after the fall of Bristol, Fairfax decided that, before continuing his campaign into the West, he would first clear out royalist garrisons in Wiltshire and Somerset which blocked his line of communications to London. (15th) - Farleigh Castle was recaptured by its owner, Sir Edward Hungerford, with support of troops from the New Model Army. *Wiltshire:* (17th) - Cromwell with 500 troops camped at Trowbridge, before capturing Devizes (23rd) by assault. (24th) - the royalist garrison at Lacock Abbey surrendered to Col. Pickering.
October:	*Somerset:* Blake and Col. Sydenham were ordered to march with 600 men to commence the siege of Dunster Castle under its governor, Francis Wyndham. *Wiltshire:* (18th) - Longford House (the last royalist garrison in Wilts) surrendered to Cromwell.
November:	*Somerset;* (6th) - the close siege of Dunster Castle commenced.
December:	*Gloucestershire:* (3rd) - parliament confirmed Maj.-Gen. Philip Skippon's appointment as Governor of Bristol. *Wiltshire:* (24th) - royalist forces from Oxford raided Calne.
1646	
January:	*National background:* (15th) - Hopton was appointed by the Prince of Wales to command the royalist forces of the Western Association, numbering 3,000 cavalry and 2,000 infantry. *Wiltshire:* (20th) - royalist forces from Oxford under Col. James Long

raided Marlborough, Salisbury, Warminster, Devizes and Leigh.

February:
National background:
(16th) -Fairfax defeated Hopton's army at Torrington.
Somerset:
(2nd) - parliament withdrew its garrison from Bath. (5th) - a relief force of 1800 royalists under Col. Finch, sent by Hopton from Devon, took Blake's besieging army by surprise at Dunster, destroying his siege works and bringing in fresh supplies to the garrison.

March:
National background:
(2nd) - the Prince of Wales fled to the Scilly Isles. (12th) - Hopton surrendered the remnants of the army of the Western Association on generous terms.
Gloucestershire:
The king ordered Astley to leave Cirencester and collect the remaining royalist forces in Wales, before joining him in Oxford. Morgan, Governor of Gloucester, quickly re-occupied Cirencester for parliament. (21st) - Astley's force from Wales, in attempting to reach Oxford, was intercepted and routed by Cols. Birch and Morgan near Stow-on-the-Wold.
Somerset:
(2nd) - parliament ordered the dismantling of the fortifications at Bridgwater.

April:
Somerset:
(16th) - Blake, met Fairfax at Chard on his return from Torrington; (17th) - Blake was joined by Philip Skippon's infantry regiment from the New Model Army to resume the siege of Dunster by putting on a show of force; (19th) - Wyndham surrendered Dunster Castle.
Wiltshire:
Fairfax and the New Model Army marched through the county on their way to reduce Oxford (the last field army to cross the county).

May:
Somerset:
(29th) - the fortifications at Bath were dismantled.

September:
Wiltshire:
The garrison at Chalfield House was dismantled.

October:
Wiltshire:
Garrisons at Malmesbury and Highworth House were dismantled.

November:
Wiltshire:
Parliament's Wiltshire troops were disbanded at Marlborough and those of Massey's western army (based on Gloucester) at Devizes.

References

ABBREVIATIONS

BodL	Bodleian Library
BL	British Library
BRO	Bath Record Office
BrRO	Bristol Record Office
CJ	Journals of the House of Commons
CCAM	Calendar of the Committee for the Advance of Money
CCC	Calendar of the Committee for Compounding
CUL	Cambridge University Library
CSPD	Calendar of the State Papers Domestic
CSPV	Calendar of the State Papers Venetian
E.	British Library, Thomason Tracts
EHR	English Historical Review
GRO	Gloucestershire Record Office
HMC	Historical Manuscripts Commission
LJ	Journals of the House of Lords
n.d.	no date of publication given
PRO	Public Record Office
SANHS	Somerset Archaeological and Natural History Society Proceedings
SP	State Papers
SRO	Somerset Record Office
TBGAS	Transactions of the Bristol and Gloucestershire Archaeological Society
TRHS	Transactions of the Royal Historical Society
VCH	Victoria County History
WA	Wells Archives
WANHS	Wiltshire Archaeological and Natural History Society Proceedings
WRO	Wiltshire Record Office

1 FORCED TO DECIDE: FOR KING OR PARLIAMENT?

(1) A.R. Warmington, *Civil War, Interregnum and Restoration in Gloucestershire, 1640-1672* (1997), pp 7, 9, 13-19; John M. Paddock, *The Storming of Cirencester in 1643: an Episode in the Civil War* (Cirencester, 1993), p 1

(2) David Underdown, *Somerset in the Civil War and Interregnum* (Newton Abbot, 1973), pp 12-15; John Wroughton, *A Community at War: the Civil War in Bath and North Somerset, 1642-1650* (Bath,1992), pp 24-38; CSPD, 1644-5, p 83; David Underdown, *Revel, Riot and Rebellion, 1603-1660* (Oxford, 1985), pp 293-4

(3) Underdown, *Revel, Riot and Rebellion*, pp 5-8, 294

(4) Wroughton, *Community at War*, pp 25-28; CSPD, 1619-23, p 391; SRO, Session Roll, 43 ii, f 166 (The petition of the Vicar of Frome, 1622); E.H. Bates-Harbin, *Quarter Sessions Records for the County of Somerset*, vol. 1, p 323

(5) Wroughton, *Community at War*, p 28; T.G. Barnes, *Somerset, 1625-1640* (Oxford, 1961), pp 156-7; Buchanan Sharp, *In Contempt of all Authority*

(California, 1980), pp 6-7; R.B. Pugh & Elizabeth Crittall (eds.), *The Victoria County History of Wiltshire*, vol. 5 (1957) p 132

(6) Warmington, *Civil War in Gloucestershire*, pp 28516, 18, 22

(7) PRO, SP16.185.40; SRO, Sessions Roll, 64, ii, F 200, 204

(8) *VCH Wiltshire*, vol. 5, p 132

(9) SRO, D/D/Ca 194, Comperta, 1615; *Wroughton, Community at War*, pp 56-65; Underdown, *Revel, Riot and Rebellion*, pp 77-9; Bates-Harbin, *Quarter Sessions Records*, vol.1, p 250; vol. 2 pp 109, 138-9, 144, 269; BRO, Chamberlain's Accounts, 1617, 1618, 1624, 1628; BRO, Council Book, no. 1, April 1634; *VCH, Wiltshire*, vol. 3, pp 34-42

(10) *VCH Wiltshire*, vol. 5, p 131

(11) Wroughton, *Community at War*, pp 57-62

(12) For a more detailed account of what follows at Shepton Mallet and Chewton Mendip, see Wroughton, *Community at War*, pp 19-20, 69-74; C.E.H. Healey (ed.), *Bellum Civile* (Somerset Record Society, vol. 18, Taunton, 1902) - Hopton's account; BL, E.109 (24), *A Letter from the Committee in Somersetshire*, 1st August 1642; BL, E.111 (7), *A Relation of all the Proceedings in Somersetshire and Bristol*, 11th August 1642; BL, E.111 (5), *A Perfect Relation of the Proceedings of the Cavaliers that were in Wells*, 7th August 1642; BL, E.111 (4), *Joyful News from Wells*, 12th August 1642

(13) For a more detailed analysis of the theories of localism and neutralism see Wroughton, *Community at War*, pp 78-80, 83-5

(14) Wroughton, *Community at War*, pp 87-90; John Vicars, *Jehovah-Jireh, God in the Mount* (1644), p 134: BL, E109(34), *A True Relation of Divers Passages in Somerset, 5th August, 1642*

(15) James Waylen, *Chronicles of the Devizes* (1839), p 265; VCH, *Wiltshire*, vol. 5, pp 138-40

(16) F. Hancock, *Minehead in the County of Somerset* (1903), p 265; *Strange and Bloody News from Minehead* (1642)

(17) WA, Acts of the Corporation, book 7, 1635-1644, ff 214-5

(18) John Corbet, *An Historical Relation of the Military Government in Gloucester* in John Washbourn, *Bibliotheca Gloucestrensis* (1825), pp 16-17; Warmington, *Civil War in Gloucestershire*, pp 15-18, 41-2

(19) Corbet, *Military Government of Gloucester*, pp 6-7

(20) Warmington, *Civil War in Gloucestershire*, p 37

(21) Warmington, *Civil War in Gloucestershire*, pp 34-7; T.D. Fosbrooke, *An Original History of the City of Gloucester* (1819; reprinted Dursley, 1976), p 28

(22) *A Particular Relation of the Action before Cirencester...written by an Eyewitness* (1643)

(23) John Lynch, *For King and Parliament: Bristol and the Civil War* (Stroud, 1999), pp 9-10, 20; Wroughton, *Community at War*, pp 75-77; John Latimer, *The Annals of Bristol* (Bristol, 1900), pp 160-4; Patrick McGrath, *Bristol and the Civil War* (Bristol, 1981), pp 3, 10-12; BrRO, Common Council Book, no. 4, 1642-49, ff 1-2, 5, 11-16, 18-19, 21; HMC, 13th Report, App.1, pt. 1, Duke of Portland, vol. 1(1891), p 65

(24) *LJ*, vol. 4, p484; John Morrill, *The Revolt of the Provinces* (1976), pp 98-106; Ronald Hutton, *The Royalist War Effort, 1642-1646* (1982), pp 159-172

(25) Underdown, *Somerset in the Civil War*, pp 98-100, 106-8; *Underdown, Revel, Riot and Rebellion*, pp 156-9, 167-8, 276-7; Joshua Sprigge, *Anglia Rediviva: England's Recovery* (1647), p 63; *LJ*, vol. 7, p 484; W.C. Abbott, *The Writings and Speeches of Oliver Cromwell*, vol. 1 (New York, 1937), p 369; BodL, MS Dugdale, 19, f 182

(26) Underdown, *Somerset in the Civil War*, pp 98-100, 106-8

(27) For a more detailed description see Wroughton, *Community at War*, pp 128-32; PRO, SP28.175; SP28.154

(28) C.H. Firth (ed.), *Ludlow's Memoirs*, vol. 1, p 75; BL, Add. MSS, 22084, ff 12, 20 (at rear)
(29) D.M. Ross, *Langport and its Church* (Langport, 1911), pp 282-3; Mary Siraut (ed.), *The Trevelyan Letters to 1840* (Taunton, 1990), pp viii, 126
(30) Underdown, *Somerset in the Civil War*, p 44; Emmanuel Green, 'Colonel William Strode' in *SANHS*, 30, pt 2, (1881), p 54
(31) Wroughton, *Community at War*, p 98
(32) Wroughton, *Community at War*, pp 50-4; *VCH Wiltshire*, pp 136, 140; George Harrison, *Royalist Organisation in Gloucestershire and Bristol*, (unpublished MA thesis, Manchester University, 1961), pp 58-9; George Harrison, *Royalist Organisation in Wiltshire*, (unpublished PhD thesis, London University, 1963), p 135; BodL, Harleian MSS, 6804, f 118; Lynch, *For King and Parliament*, p 45
(33) Corbet, 'Military Government in Gloucester' (in Washbourne, *Bibliotheca Gloucestrensis*, pp 116-7)

2 FORCED TO FIGHT: WARTIME CONSCRIPTION

(1) T.G. Barnes, *Somerset, 1625-1640* (Oxford, 1961), pp 107-116; C.H. Firth, *Cromwell's Army* (1962 edn.). pp 8-9; Robert Ward, *Animadversions of War* (1639), p 30; John Washbourne (ed.), *Bibliotheca Gloucestrensis* (1825), p 10; J.E. Jackson, *The Hungerford Family: Collections for their Personal History*, vol. 2 (unpublished MSS in Devizes Museum, 1885), p 276
(2) BL, Add. MSS., 28,273, ff 105-118, subsidy assessments and other memoranda by J. Locke, 1623-1655; BRO, Bath Chamberlain's Accounts, 1636-42
(3) WA, Acts of the Corporation, book 7, 1635-44, f 231; PRO, SP28.175, Portbury compensation claim; HMC, 5th Report (1876), The MSS of Edmund Cholmondeley, p 346
(4) C.H. Firth & R.S. Rait (eds.), *Acts and Ordinances of the Interregnum*, vol.1 (1911), pp 100-101; *LJ*, vol. 5, p 637
(5) Patrick McGrath, *Bristol and the Civil War* (Bristol, 1981), p 7; BrRO, Common Council Proceedings, 04264 (4), f 4
(6) BRO, Bath Chamberlain's Accounts, 1642-3
(7) John Wroughton, *A Community at War: the Civil War in Bath and North Somerset, 1642-50* (Bath, 1992), pp 73-4; David Underdown, *Somerset in the Civil War and Interregnum* (Newton Abbot, 1973), pp 41-2
(8) *A Copy of a Letter read in the House of Commons*, 20th August 1647
(9) *LJ*, vol. 5, pp 544-5; W. St. Clair Baddeley, *A Cotteswold Manor being the History of Painswick* (Gloucester, 1929), p 188; D.M. Ross, *Langport and its Church* (Langport, 1911), p 284; Peter Young & Norman Tucker (eds.), *Richard Atkyns & John Gwyn* (1967), p 7; BodL, MS Dugdale, 19, ff 8, 37; George Harrison, *Royalist Organisation in Gloucestershire and Bristol* (unpublished MA thesis, Manchester University, 1961), pp 55-6; Robert Steele (ed.), *A Bibliography of Tudor and Stuart Proclamations*, vol. 1 (Oxford, 1910), p 279; I.G. Philip (ed.), *The Journal of Sir Samuel Luke* (Oxford Record Society, vol. 29, 1947), p 37
(10) CUL, Western MSS, add.89, f110
(11) Firth & Rait, *Acts & Ordinances*, vol. 1, pp 6-8, 60-61, 74-6, 84-5; PRO, SP28.175, assessments
(12) Mary Siraut (ed.), *The Trevelyan Letters to 1840* (Taunton, 1990), pp 128-9
(13) GRO, D115, Declarations and Orders, no. 12; George Harrison, *Royalist Organisation in Wiltshire* (unpublished PhD thesis, London University, 1963), pp 192, 277
(14) Peter Young & Norman Tucker (eds.), *Richard Atkyns and John Gwynne* (1967), p 12; Ronald Hutton, *The Royalist War Effort, 1642-46*

(1982), p 28; Firth & Rait, *Acts & Ordinances*, vol.1, pp 79-80; Firth, *Cromwell's Army*, p 18
(15) Hutton, *Royalist War Effort*, pp 92-3; BodL, Dugdale MS, 19, ff 43, 50; PRO, SP23.114,
f 989; Harrison, *Royalist Organisation in WIltshire*, pp 251-60; Harrison, *Royalist Organisation in Gloucestershire*, p 101
(16) James Waylen, *A History Military and Municipal of the Ancient Borough of the Devizes* (1859), p 195; Harrison, *Royalist Organisation in Gloucestershire*, p 101; BL, Add MSS, 15,750, f 18; G.D. Stawell, *A Quantock Family* (1910), p 394; BL, Add. MSS, 22084, f 20 (at rear)
(17) Firth & Rait, *Acts & Ordinances*, vol. 1, pp 241-2, 489-96; W.C. Trevelyan & C.E. Trevelyan (eds.), *The Trevelyan Papers*, part 3 (Camden Society, 1872), p 237; CSPV, 1643-47, p 146; Firth, *Cromwell's Army*, p 3
(18) Waylen, *History of Devizes*, p 210; John Lynch, *For King and Parliament: Bristol and the Civil War* (Stroud, 1999), p 2
(19) Howard Cunnington, *Records of the County of Wiltshire* (1932), p 157
(20) Cunnington, *Records of Wiltshire*, p 189
(21) PRO, SP28.175, assessments.
(22) H.E. Nott (ed.), *The Deposition Books of Bristol*, vol. 1, 1643-7 (Bristol, 1935), p 151; H.G. Tibbutt (ed.), *The Letter Books 1644-45 of Sir Samuel Luke* (1963), p 665
(23) Clive Holmes, *The Eastern Association in the English Civil War* (Cambridge, 1974), p 168; Firth & Rait, *Acts & Ordinances*, vol. 1, pp 675-7
(24) Waylen, *History of Devizes*, p 198; Harrison, *Royalist Organisation in Wiltshire*, p 320
(25) Waylen, *History of Devizes*, p 195; Holmes, *The Eastern Association*, pp 152, 167
(26) Holmes, *The Eastern Association*, p 167; WRO, G22/1/205/2, Marlborough General Account Book, 1643; A.W. Mabbs (ed.), *Guild Stewards' Book of the Borough of Calne, 1561-88* (Devizes, 1953), p 61; PRO, SP28.175, assessments
(27) Mabbs, *Guild Stewards' Book, Calne*, p 61; PRO, SP28.175, assessments; Cunningham, *Records of Wiltshire*, p 14
(28) *Trevelyan Papers*, part 3, p 247
(29) BL, Add. MSS., 15,750, f 27, Griffin's letter to Digby, 12th November, 1644
(30) CSPD, 1644, p 474-5; 1644-5, p 131; BodL, MS Dugdale, 19, ff 127-8; Tibbutt, *Sir Samuel Luke*, p 261; PRO, SP28.129(5), Accounts of Thomas Blayney
(31) Henry Foster, *A True and Exact Relation of the Marchings of the Trained Bands* (1645) in Washbourne, *Bibliotheca Gloucestrensis*, pp 254-60
(32) Young & Tucker, *Richard Atkyns & John Gwyn*, pp 22, 28
(33) Foster in Washbourne, *Bibliothetica Gloucestrensis*, 265-7; Charles Carlton, *Going to the Wars* (1992), pp 95-6; Firth, *Cromwells' Army*, pp 215-20
(34) Bulstrode Whitlocke, *Memorials of the English Affairs* (1682), p 132, F.T.R. Edgar, *Sir Ralph Hopton: the King's Man in the West, 1642-1652* (Oxford, 1968), p 127
(35) W.D. Macray (ed.), Earl of Clarendon, *The History of the Rebellion and the Civil War in England*, vol. 3 (OXford, 1969 edtn.), p 111; *A True Relation of the Storming of Bristol* (1645); Douglas Stevens, *War and Peace in West Somerset*, 1620-1670 (Minehead, n.d.), pp 59-60; Washbourne, *Bibliotheca Gloucestrensis*, introduction pp 37, 372
(36) PRO, SP 28. 228, pt 3 (4), f 738; SP 28.154, f 22; SP28.147, ff 242-4
(37) GRO, G3/SO2, Draft Minutes, 1635-70, ff 32-3; Carlton, *Going to the Wars*, p 246
(38) C.H. Firth (ed.), *Outline of the Civil War in Wiltshire* (Oxford, 1894), pp 23-6; Cunnington, *Records of Wiltshire*, p 217; E.H. Bates-Harbin (ed.), *Quarter Sessions Records for the County of Somerset* (Taunton, 1907-

8), pp 208, 315
(39) Young & Tucker, *Richard Atkyns & John Gwyn*, pp 27-8
(40) J. Thompson, *The Other Army: Camp Followers of the Civil War* (Leigh-on-Sea, n.d.), pp 19-27
(41) George Parker, 'Early Medieval Institutions, the Medieval Hospitals and Barber Surgeons' in *TBGAS*, vol. 44 (1922), pp 160-6.
(42) PRO, SP28.129 (5); SP28.154 (2) - accounts of the Gloucester garrison
(43) Rory McCreadie, *The Barber-Surgeon's Mate of the 17th Century* (Upton, 1997), pp 48-55
(44) I.G. Philip (ed.), *The Journal of Sir Samuel Luke*, vol. 1 (Oxford Record Society, vol.31. 1951), pp 29-30, 115, 146, 149-50; BodL, MSS Eng Hist, C53 f17, Sir Samuel Luke's Diary, 1643-4; John Dorney, 'A Brief and Exact Relation of the Siege of Gloucester' in Washbourne, *Bibliotheca Gloucestrensis*, p 225; Whitelocke, *Memorials*, p 141; HMC, 13th Report, App. pt. 1, Duke of Portland, vol. 1 (191), p 309; BrRO, 04264 (4), Common Council Proceedings, 1642-49, f 108; Firth, *Memoirs of Edmund Ludlow*, p 86
(45) Nott, *Deposition Books of Bristol*, vol. 1,157-8; PRO, SP28. 228, pt. 4, f 681; SP28.228, pt. 3 (4), f 679
(46) Young & Tucker, *Richard Atkyns and John Gwynn*, p 20; Howard Cunningham, *Some Annals of the Borough of Devizes* (Devizes, 1925), p 109; WRO, G22/1/205/2, Marlborough General Account Book, 1643
(47) J.H.P. Pafford (ed.), *Accounts of the Parliamentary Garrisons of Great Chalfield and Malmesbury, 1645-1646* (Devizes, 1966), *passim*
(48) HMC, 13th Report, pt. 1, Portland, vol. 1, pp 346-7; Steele, *Proclamations*, vol. 1, pp 281, 191, 303
(49) Young & Tucker, *Richard Atkyns and John Gwynn*, p 15; PRO, SP28.129 (5); SP28.154, ff 22, 25; SP28.228, pt. 3 (4) f 686; SP28.228, pt 4, f 764 - Gloucester garrison accounts; GRO, G3/SO2, Draft Minutes, 1635-70

3 FORCED TO PAY: WAR TAXATION

(1) For a more detailed analysis of the parliamentary tax-raising system, see John Morrill, *The Revolt of the Provinces, 1630-1650* (1976), pp 52-80.
(2) For a more detailed analysis of the royalist tax-raising system, see Ronald Hutton, *The Royalist War Effort, 1642-1646* (1982), pp 86-109, on which this summary is largely based; BodL, MS Dugdale, 19, ff 6-8
(3) PRO, SP28.175, Assessments, Somerset.
(4) BodL, MSS Dugdale, 19, ff 29, 43; HMC, 5th Report, The MSS of Reginald Cholmondley (1876), p 346
(5) PRO, SP23.114, f 987; George Harrison, *Royalist Organisation in Gloucestershire and Bristol, 1642-1645* (unpublished MA thesis, Manchester University, 1961), p 64
(6) Hutton, *Royalist War Effort,* p 92; James Waylen, *A History Military and Municipal of the Ancient Borough of the Devizes* (1859), p 196; Harrison, *Royalist Organisation in Gloucestershire*, pp 247-8; John Latimer, *The Annals of Bristol in the Seventeenth Century* (Bristol, 1900), p 189; Mary Siraut (ed.), *The Trevelyan Letters to 1840* (Taunton, 1990), p 129; Joshua Tomlin, *The History of the Town of Taunton* (Taunton, 1791), pp 113-4
(7) BodL, MS Dugdale, 19, ff 23, 46; George Harrison, *Royalist Organisation in Wiltshire* (unpublished PhD thesis, London University, 1963), pp 268-71; BL, Add. MSS, 22084, ff 2, 4, 9, 12, 16, 32, 53; Howard Cunnington, *Records of Wiltshire* (1932), p 213
(8) F.T.R. Edgar, *Sir Ralph Hopton: the King's Man in the West, 1642-1659* (Oxford, 1968), p 124; Harrison, *Royalist Organisation in Wiltshire*, pp 284-8
(9) C.H. Firth & R.S. Rait (eds.), *Acts and Ordinances of the Interregnum*, vol. 1 (1911), pp 6-8; Harrison, *Royalist Organisation in Wiltshire*, pp

116-7; J.E. Jackson (ed.), *Hungerford Family*, vol. 2 (unpublished MSS, 1885), p 280; Latimer, *Annals of Bristol*, p 160

(10) PRO, SP28.175; David Underdown, *Somerset in the CIvil War and Interregnum* (Newton Abbott, 1973), p 46; John Wroughton, *A Community at War: the Civil War in Bath and North Somerset* (Bath, 1992), pp 134-5

(11) Firth & Rait, *Acts and Ordinances*, vol.1, pp 67-8.

(12) PRO, SP28.175; Firth & Rait, *Acts and Ordinances*, vol.1, pp 38-9,60-61, 69-70; Harrison, *Royalist Organisation in Wiltshire*, pp 161-3.

(13) Firth & Rait, *Acts and Ordinances*, vol. 1, pp 79-80, 428-31, 475-8; Morrill, *Revolt of the Provinces*, pp 84-5; J.H.P. Pafford (ed.), *Accounts of the Parliamentary Garrisons of Great Chalfield and Malmesbury, 1645-1646* (*WANHS Records*, vol.2, Devizes, 1940), pp 48-9, 98-9; BL, Add. MSS, 22085, ff 47-68; PRO, SP28.154

(14) CCAM, pp 476, 550, 746, 753, 757-8, 760, 815, 855, 870, 1245

(15) Firth & Rait, *Acts and Ordinances*, vol.1, pp 85-100, 139-41, 223-41

(16) Eliot Warburton, *Memoirs of Prince Rupert and the Cavaliers*, vol. 2 (1849), pp 334-5; Harrison, *Royalist Organisation in Wiltshire*, pp 222-3

(17) Firth & Rait, *Acts and Ordinances*, vol. 1, pp 262-3; H.E. Nott (ed.), *The Deposition Books of Bristol*, vol. 1, 1643-7 (Bristol, 1935), p 13

(18) PRO, SP28.175

(19) PRO, SP28.175; SP28.228, pt.3(4), ff 760, 770; A.R. Warmington, *Civil War, Interregnum and Restoration in Gloucestershire, 1640-1672* (1997), p 59; Harrison, *Royalist Organisation in Gloucestershire*, p 109; BodL, MSS Eng, Hist., C53, Sir Samuel Luke's Diary, 1643-4, f 28

(20) Bod.L, Clarendon MSS, 28.85 (Ashe to Fiennes, 1st June 1643).

(21) Bod.L, Clarendon MSS, 22.71 (Ashe to Fiennes, 5th June 1643); PRO, 28.175, Account of Colonel William Strode, 1642-1643; SP28.147, ff 242-251, Account of Colonel John Fiennes

(22) Frederick H. Goldney (ed.), *Records of Chippenham* (1889), pp 209-211.

(23) Waylen, *History of Devizes*, p 199; PRO, SP28.175

(24) WA, Acts of the Corporation, book 7, 1635-1644, ff 258, 262, 263-4, 269; G.D. Stawell, *A Quantock Family* (1910), p 384

(25) BrRO, 04264(4), Common Council Proceedings, 1642-49, ff 76-7; PRO, SP28.228, pt. 3(4), f 726

(26) PRO, SP28.175; SP28.242; E179.172.142, subsidy,1641; Morrill, *Revolt of the Provinces*, p 84; Alan Everitt, *The County of Kent and the Great Rebellion, 1640-1660* (Leicester, 1966), pp 157-60

(27) Morrill, *Revolt of the Provinces*, pp 56, 65, 85; Hutton, *Royalist War Effort*, p 93; Firth & Rait, *Acts and Ordinances*, vol. 1, pp 162-3, 274-83; Underdown, *Somerset in the Civil War*, pp 81, 135; Falconer Madan, *Oxford Books*, vol. 2 (Oxford, 1912) no. 1639

(28) Hutton, *Royalist War Effort*, pp 97-104; Donald Pennington, 'The War and the People' in John Morrill (ed.), *Reactions to the English Civil War* (1982), pp 115-124; John Morrill, 'Mutiny and Discontent in English Provincial Armies, 1645-1647' in *Past and Present*, No 56, 1972), pp 52, 63

(29) WRO, G22/1/205/2, Marlborough General Account Book.

(30) Goldney, *Records of Chippenham*, pp 212-13; Harrison, *Royalist Organisation in Wiltshire*, p 224; BL, Harleian MSS, 6952, f 46

(31) Harrison, *Royalist Organisation in Gloucestershire*, p 108; PRO, SP28.129(5); SP28.228, pt. 3(4), f 760

(32) Waylen, *History of Devizes*, pp 201, 211-12.

(33) *Archaeologia* (1803), vol.14, pp 121-28; BL, E.61, *Mercurius Civicus*, 11th-17th July 1644; Bulstrode Whitelocke, *Memorials of the English*

Affairs, vol. 1 (Oxford, 1853), p 540; PRO. SP23.114, f 989
(34) CSPD, 1644-5, p 511 (Marsh to Nicholas, 22nd May 1645).
(35) Firth & Rait, *Acts and Ordinances*, vol.1, pp 811-2; PRO, SP28.175
(36) Waylen, *History of Devizes*, p 231; HMC, 13th Report, App. pt. 1, Duke of Portland, vol. 1 (1891), pp 283-5
(37) Warmington, *Civil War in Gloucestershire*, p 53-6; H.G. Tibbutt, *The Letter Books, 1644-5, of Sir Samuel Luke* (1963), p 382
(38) Warmington, *Civil War in Gloucestershire*, p 54; PRO, SP28.228, pt. 3(4), ff 787-983 *passim*
(39) PRO, SP28.228, pt. 3(4), f 770; SP28.175

4 FORCED TO SUPPORT: A CASE STUDY IN TAX COLLECTION

(1) PRO, SP28.138, Chalfield and Malmesbury Acount Books; J.H.P. Pafford (ed.), *Accounts of the Parliamentary Garrisons of Great Chalfield and Malmesbury, 1645-1646* (*WANHS Records*, vol. 2, Devizes, 1940)
(2) See the discussion on the question of dates in Pafford's introduction to his transcript, p 12
(3) See Pafford's helpful analysis on pp 40-1 of his introduction
(4) Pafford, *Accounts of Great Chalfield and Malmesbury*, pp 66-79

5 FORCED TO PROVIDE: FREE QUARTER

(1) Ronald Hutton, *The Royalist War Effort, 1642-1646* (1982), pp 96, 98; John Morrill, *The Revolt of the Provinces, 1630-1650* (1976), p 86; Clive Holmes, *The Eastern Association in the English Civil War* (Cambridge, 1974), pp 153-4; PRO, SP28.175, Assessments, Somerset; E.179.256/16 (book 23), Somerset Hearth Tax, 1664-5; David Underdown, *Somerset in the Civil War and Interregnum* (Newton Abbot, 1973), p 106
(2) PRO, SP28.242 (pt.1), pp 115-131, 161-186, 190-204, 320-347
(3) WA, Acts of the Corporation, book 7, 1634-44, ff 147-9; PRO, SP28.175, Assessments, Somerset; BL, E260 (39), *Perfect Proceedings*, 30 (14-21 May 1645)
(4) Eliot Warburton, *Memoirs of Prince Rupert and the Cavaliers*, vol.2 (1849), p 334; Robert Steele (ed.), *A Bibliography of Tudor And Stuart Proclamations* (Oxford, 1910), p 303
(5) C.H. Firth & R.S. Firth (eds.), *Acts and Ordinances of the Interregnum*, vol.1(1911), pp 489-96; PRO, SP28.175, Assessments, Somerset
(6) PRO, SP28.175
(7) BL, E.293(3), *A More Full Relation of the Great Battle* (1645), p 8
(8) W.A. Day (ed.), *The Pythouse Papers* (1879), pp 30-3
(9) PRO, SP28.175, Assessments, Somerset; John Morrill, 'Mutiny and Discontent in English Provincial Armies, 1645-47' (in *Past and Present*, no. 56, 1972) pp 51-2
(10) PRO, SP28.175, Assessments, Somerset
(11) Edward Green, 'On the History of Chard' in *SANHS*, vol. 28, pt.2 (Taunton, 1882), p 57
(12) BL, Harleian MSS, 6084, f 120
(13) PRO, SP28.175; SP28.242 (pt. 1), ff 109-10
(14) HMC, 13th Report, App.1, Duke of Portland, vol.1 (1891), pp 309-10, 346-7
(15) Philip Ralph, *Sir Humphrey Mildmay: Royalist Gentleman* (New Brunswick, New Jersey, 1947), pp 174-80
(16) W.C. Trevelyan & C.E. Trevelyan (eds.), *The Trevelyan Papers*, pt. 3 (1872), p 257; Howard Cunnington, *Records of Wiltshire* (1932), p 216; Ernest Baker, 'Bristol and the Civil War' in *The Bristol Times and Mirror*, 1 January 1925; Douglas Stevens, *War and Peace in West Somerset, 1620-70* (Minehead, n.d.), pp 63-4
(17) Green, 'History of Chard' in *SANHS*, vol. 28, pt. 2; Charles Carlton, *Going to the Wars* (1992), p

281
(18) G.R. Quaife, *Wanton Wenches and Wayward Wives: Peasants and Illegal Sex in early Seventeenth-Century England* (1979), pp 49-50, 123
(19) Howard Cunnington, *Some Annals of the Borough of Devizes* (Devizes, 1925) pp 114-15; Frederick H. Goldney (ed.), *Records of Chippenham* (1889), p 211; John K.G. Taylor, 'The Civil Government of Gloucester, 1640-1646' (in *TBGAS*, vol. LXVII, 1949), pp 85-6; Howard Cunningham, *Records of the County of Wiltshire* (1932), p 164; PRO, SP28.228, pt. 4
(20) PRO, SP28.154, claims by Bristol Innkeepers; SP28.147. f250, The Accounts of Colonel John Fiennes
(21) Goldney, *Records of Chippenham*, pp 213-4
(22) BRO, Bath Council Book, no. 1 (9th February, 1646); Rev. H. Harington, *Nugae Antiquae*, vol.2 (1779), pp 179-87
(23) John Lynch, *For King and Parliament: Bristol and the Civil War* (Stroud, 1999), pp 92-3

6. FORCED TO YIELD: REQUISITIONS, PLUNDER AND WANTON DAMAGE

(1) PRO, SP28.131 (pt. 3), London; Ronald Hutton, *The Royalist War Effort, 1642-1646* (1982), pp 97-8
(2) H.E. Nott (ed.), *The Deposition Books of Bristol*, vol. 1, 1643-47 (Bristol, 1935), pp 139-40, 169-70; PRO, SP23.156, f 361; J.E. Jackson, *A Guide to Farleigh Hungerford* (Chippenham, 1879), pp 12-13
(3) PRO, SP28.175; SP28.421 (pt. 1), f 110; *LJ*, vol. 5, pp 544-5
(4) C.H. Firth & R.S. Rait (eds.), *Acts and Ordinances of the Interregnum*, vol. 1 (1911), pp 85-100
(5) John White, 'A Relation of the Taking of Cirencester' in John Washbourne, *Bibliotheca Gloucestrensis* (Gloucester, 1825), pp 175-185; Nott, *Deposition Books of Bristol*, vol. 1, p 58
(6) PRO, SP28.175; J.J. Daniel, *The History of Chippenham* (1984), p 140
(7) PRO, SP28.175; SP28.242 (pt. 1), f 12
(8) James Waylen, *A History Military and Municipal of the Ancient Borough of the Devizes* (1859), pp 201, 208-9; James Bennett, *The History of Tewkesbury* (Tewkesbury, 1830), p 69; George Harrison, *Royalist Organisation in Wiltshire* (unpublished PhD thesis, London University, 1963), pp 335-8
(9) GRO, D115, Declarations & Orders, no. 9
(10) PRO, SP23.114, f 989; Firth & Rait, *Acts & Ordinances*, vol. 1, pp 489-96; W.C. Trevelyan & C.E. Trevelyan (eds.),*The Trevelyan Papers*, vol. 3, (Camden Society, 1872), pp 250-1
(11) PRO, SP28.175; SP28.242 (pt. 1), f 136; Waylen, *History of Devizes*, pp 208-9; Harrison, *Royalist Organisation in Wiltshire*, pp 96-7, 339-40
(12) BL, Harleian MSS, 6802, ff 286, 288-91, 293-5; Harrison, *Royalist Organisation in Wiltshire*, pp 310-14
(13) A.R. Warmington, Civil War, *Interregnum and Restoration in Gloucestershire, 1640-1672* (1997), p 77; T.D. Fosbrooke, *An Original History of the City of Gloucester* (1819; reprinted Dursley, 1976), p 28; Bennett, *History of Tewkesbury*, p 62; Eliot Warburton, *Memoirs of Prince Rupert and the Cavaliers*, vol. 2 (1849), pp 105-6; White, 'The Taking of Cirencester' in Washbourne, *Bibliotheca Gloucestrensis*, pp 175-85
(14) BodL, MS Dugdale, 19, f 128; MS Tanner, 60, f 75; GRO, D128, Guise of Elmore Papers, no. 4
(15) WRO, G23/1/40, Notes of goods and chattels taken by force from Salisbury, 31st December, 1644
(16) Peter Young & Norman Tucker (eds.), *Richard Atkyns and John Gwynn* (1967) pp 13, 16:
(17) BL, Harleian MSS, 6804, f 120
(18) Robert Steele (ed.), *A Bibliography of Tudor and Stuart Proclamations*, vol. 1 (Oxford, 1910),

pp 278, 287, 303
(19) Douglas Stevens, *War and Peace in West Somerset, 1620-1670* (Minehead, n.d.), p 27; C.E. Long (ed.), *Diary of the Marches of the Royal Army...kept by Richard Symonds* (Camden Society Series, 74, 1859), pp 30-1, 153; *A Narration of the Expedition to Taunton* (1645), pp 3-4
(20) GRO, D115, Declarations & Orders, no. 10; *Warburton, Memoirs of Prince Rupert*, vol. 2, p 334
(21) Alfred T. Lee, *A History of the Town and Parish of Tetbury* (1877), p 19; I.G. Phillips (ed.), *The Journal of Sir Samuel Luke*, (Oxford Record Society, vol. 29, 1947), pp 150-1
(22) GRO, D745/X4; Warburton, *Memoirs of Prince Rupert*, vol. 2, pp 276-7; W.St. Clair Baddeley, *A Cotteswold Manor being the History of Painswick* (Gloucester, 1929), pp 189-90
(23) BL, Harleian MSS, 6804, ff 114, 118
(24) GRO, GBR, B9/2; PRO, SP23.156, ff 361-3
(25) HMC, 9th Report, Marquess of Salisbury, part XXII, 1612-1688 (1971), pp 375-9
(26) Fosbrooke, *History of Gloucestershire*, p 29; Ian Roy, 'The English Civil War and English Society' in Brian Bond & Ian Roy (eds.), *War and Society*, vol. 2, (1975), pp 39-41; Ian Roy (ed.), *Royalist Ordinance Papers*, vol. 2 (Oxford Record Society, 1975), 365
(27) F. Hancock, *Minehead in the County of Somerset* (1903), pp 270-6; BL, Lansdown MSS, 676, f 21
(28) CSPD, 1644, p 214; W.D. Macray (ed.), Earl of Clarendon, *The History of the Rebellion and Civil War In England*, vol. 3 (Oxford, 1969 edtn.), pp 165-6
(29) Bennett, *History of Tewkesbury*, pp 61-3; PRO, SP28. 228 (pt. 4), f 704; BL, Egerton MSS, 2533, f 384
(30) Baddeley, *History of Painswick*, p 192; GRO, D128, Guise of Elmore Papers, no. 4
(31) C.H. Firth, *Outline of the Civil War in Wiltshire, 1642-1646*, (Oxford, 1894), pp 11, 13-14; John J. Daniell, *The History of Warminster* (1879), p 64
(32) Waylen, *History of Devizes*, pp 230-1
(33) BodL, MSS English History, C53, Sir Samuel Luke's Diary, f 17; Patrick McGrath (ed.), *Merchants and Merchandise in Seventeenth-Century Bristol* (Bristol, 1955), p 152
(34) PRO, SP28.175
(35) Trevelyan & Trevelyan, *Trevelyan Papers*, pt. 3, pp 316-7
(36) Hutton, *Royalist War Effort*, pp 97-104; Donald Pennington, 'The War and the People' in John Morrill (ed.), *Reactions to the English Civil War, 1642-1649* (1982), pp 115-124; John Morrill, 'Mutiny and Discontent in the English Provincial Armies, 1645-1647' in *Past and Present*, No 56 (1972), pp 52, 63; John Corbet, 'The Military Government of Gloucester' in Washbourne, *Bibliotheca Gloucestrensis*, pp 67-8, 72-4, 90, 107-9; Bulstrode Whitelocke, *Memorials of the English Affairs* (1682), p 223
(37) David Underdown, *Somerset in the Civil War and Interregnum* (Newton Abbot, 1973), pp 86-90; Sir Richard Bulstrode, *Memoirs and Reflections upon the Reign and Government of King Charles I and King Charles II* (1721), pp 134
(38) John Oldmixon, *History of England during the Reign of the Royal House of Stuart*, vol. 1 (1730-35), p 278
(39) *A Narration of the Expedition to Taunton* (1645), p 7
(40) Clarendon, *History of the Rebellion*, vol. 4, pp 13, 54-5, 63; HMC, 13th Report, App. pt. 1, Duke of Portland, vol. 1 (1891), pp 227-8

7 FORCED TO IMPROVISE: THE DISRUPTION OF TRADE

(1) WRO, G23/1/40, Notes of goods and chattels taken by force from Salisbury...
(2) BL, E.69, *Mercurius Civicus*, 21st-28th September, 1643; John Latimer,

The Annals of Bristol in the Seventeenth Century (Bristol, 1900), p 193

(3) PRO, SP28.147, f 250, The Full Accompt of Colonel John Fiennes; BRO, Council Book No 2 (22nd September 1642); PRO, SP23.180, f 604, Committee for Compounding

(4) Ian Roy, 'England turned Germany?' The aftermath of the Civil War in its European context' (in *TRHS*, 5th series, vol. 28, 1978), pp 137-8; Robert Steele (ed.), *A Bibliography of Tudor and Stuart Proclamations*, vol. 1 (Oxford, 1910), p 279

(5) *Mercurius Aulicus*, 16th March 1643; *LJ*, vol. V, 1642-3, p 670; *CJ*, vol. III, 1642-3, p17

(6) PRO, C107/20, The Cloth Books of James Ashe

(7) Steele, *Tudor & Stuart Proclamations*, vol. 1, pp 283, 296, 301

(8) Falconer Madan, *Oxford Books*, vol. 2 (Oxford, 1912), no. 1438; J.F. Nicholls & John Taylor, *Bristol Past and Present*, vol. 1 (Bristol, 1881), p 311; PRO, PC2/53, Privy Council Registers; John Corbet, 'The Military Government of Gloucester' in John Washbourne, *Bibliotheca Gloucestrensis* (Gloucester, 1825), pp 97-8

(9) Roy, 'England turned Germany?', pp 139-40; James Waylen, *The History Military and Municipal of the Town of Marlborough* (1854), pp 220-2; W.D. Macray (ed.), Earl of Clarendon, *The History of the Rebellion and the Civil Wars in England*, vol. 3 (Oxford, 1969 edn.), p 292; H.G. Tibbutt, *The Letter Books 1644-45 of Sir Samuel Luke* (1963), p 205; Washbourne, *Bibliotheca Gloucestrensis* , p 335; BL, 284(15), *Mercurius Veridicus*, no. 5, 10-16 May, 1645

(10) G.D. Ramsay, *The Wiltshire Woollen Industry in the 16th and 17th Centuries* (1965), pp 111-14; Howard Cunnington, *Records of the County of Wiltshire* (1931), p 189

(11) Washbourne, *Bibliotheca Gloucestrensis*, p 335; BL, E.26(9), *Perfect Proceedings*, 22-28 January, 1645; BodL, MSS English History, C53, Sir Samuel Luke's Diary, 1643-4, p 40; BL, Egerton MSS, 2533, ff 386, 390

(12) David Harris Sacks, 'Bristol's Wars of Religion' in R.C. Richardson (ed.), *Town and Countryside in the English Revolution* (Manchester, 1992), pp 106-7, 110

(13) H.E. Nott (ed.), *The Deposition Books of Bristol*, vol. 1, 1643-7, (Bristol, 1935), pp 23, 30-1

(14) Patrick McGrath (ed.), *Merchants and Merchandise in Seventeenth-Century Bristol* (Bristol, 1955), pp 150-5

(15) Nott, *Deposition Books of Bristol*, vol. 1, pp 11, 163-4

(16) BrRO, 04264(4), Common Council Proceedings, 1642-49, f 56; BodL, Clarendon MSS, 22, f 1708; PRO, SP28.129(5), Gloucester garrison accounts

(17) Latimer, *Annals of Bristol*, p 193; WA, Acts of the Corporation, Book 7, 1635-44, ff 262, 269; *CSPD*, 1644-5, p 511, Richard Marsh to Sir Edward Nicholas; Ian Roy (ed.), *The Royalist Ordnance Papers, 1642-46*, vol. 2 (Oxford Record Society, 1975), pp 388-9, 420

(18) PRO, SP28.154, The Accounts of Richard Aldworth

(19) GRO, D115, Declarations and Orders, no. 2; Roy, *Royalist Ordnance Papers*, vol. 1 (1963), pp 8, 36; John Lynch, *For King and Parliament* (Stroud, 1999) pp 122-137

(20) J.H.P Pafford (ed.), *Accounts of the Parliamentary Garrisons of Great Chalfield and Malmesbury, 1645-6* (*WANHS Records*, vol. 2, Devizes, 1940), pp 66-79

(21) PRO, SP28.222, pt. 3, f 441

(22) John Oldmixon, *History of England during the Reigns of the Royal House of Stuart* (1730), pp 208-12

(23) *CSPD*, 1644, p 12

(24) BL, E.61, *Mercurius Civicus*, 11th-17th July, 1644; *CSPD*, 1644-5, p 493, Culpepper to Digby; Peter Clark

& Paul Slack, *English Towns in Transition, 1500-1700* (Oxford, 1976), pp 89-90
(25) Bod.L., Rawlingson MSS, D.945, pp 32-7, Paman to Sancroft; BRO, Council Book, no 1, 1642-6; BL, Harleian Mss, 2135, f 35, Legge to Holme
(26) Howard Cunnington, *Some Annals of the Borough of Devizes* (Devizes, 1925), vol. 2, p 112; Latimer, *Annals of Bristol*, p 193; George Harrison, *Royalist Organisation in Wiltshire* (unpublished PhD thesis, London University, 1963), pp 362-3; A.R. Warmington, *Civil War, Interregnum and Restoration in Gloucestershire, 1640-1672* (1997), p 77; PRO, SP28.175, Yatton
(27) Cunningham, *Records of Wiltshire*, p 160
(28) HMC, 13th Report, App. pt. 1, Duke of Portland, vol. 1 (1891), pp 133-4; Corbet in Washbourne, *Bibliotheca Gloucestrensis*, pp 56-8, 87
(29) Madan, *Oxford Books*, vol. 2, no. 1228; PRO, SP28.114, f 991
(30) GRO, D115, Declarations and Orders, no. 7

8 FORCED TO DEFEND: THE SIEGE OF GLOUCESTER, 1643

(1) John Corbet, *A Historical Relation of the Military Government of Gloucester* (1645) in John Washbourn, *Bibliotheca Gloucestrensis* (Gloucester, 1825), p 150; Malcolm Atkin, *Gloucester under Siege: A City Council at War* (Gloucester, 1993), pp 1-2; J.R.S. Whiting, *Gloucester Besieged* (Gloucester, 1984), p 7; GRO, GBR B3/2, Council Minutes, 1632-1656, ff 241, 249; PRO, SP28.129(5), Accounts of Thomas Blayney, 1643
(2) Corbet in Washbourn, *Bibliotheca Gloucestrensis*, pp 11, 16, 25-6, 37, 48-9; Washbourn's introduction to *Bibliotheca Gloucestrensis*, pp 22-3, 163; Atkin, *Council at War*, pp 3-5; Malcolm Atkin & Wayne Laughlin, *Gloucester and the Civil War: A City under Siege* (Gloucester, 1992), pp 26, 35-6; Whiting, *Gloucester Besieged* , pp 5-6; GRO, GBR B3/2, ff 221-2, 231
(3) John Dorney, *A Brief and Exact Relation of the ...Siege laid before the City of Gloucester* (1643) in Washbourn, *Bibliotheca Gloucestrensis*, pp 208, 211, 214-5, 218-9, 224, 226-7; Corbet in Washbourn, pp 11, 46; Washbourn's introduction to *Bibliotheca Gloucestrensis*, p 139; Atkin, *Council at War*, p 13; Atkin & Laughlin, *Gloucester and the Civil War*, pp 72-4; GRO, F4/5, Gloucester Chamberlain's Accounts, 1642-3, ff 178, 220-2, 230; GRO, GBR, B3/2, ff 220-1, 228, 253, 255; John K.G. Taylor, *The Civil Government of Gloucester, 1640-1646* (*TBGAS*, vol. 67, Gloucester, 1949), pp 72-3, 81-3
(4) Atkin & Laughlin, *Gloucester and the Civil War*, pp 65-71; Washbourn, *Bibliotheca Gloucestrensis*, 379-85 and introduction, pp 52-3, 158; Dorney in Washbourn, p 211; Sergeant Foster, *A True and Exact Relation of the Marching of the Two Regiments* in Washbourn, pp 261, 272; GRO, GBR B3/2, f 266; GRO, G3/SO2, Draft Minutes, 1635-70, f 35; Whiting, *Gloucester Besieged*, pp 12, 14, 16-17;
(5) Dorney in Washbourn, *Bibliotheca Gloucestrensis*, pp 212, 214-5, 217, 220-2, 225, 227; Corbet in Washbourn, pp 47-8, 50-1, 56; Atkin, *Council at War*, p 6; Atkin & Laughlin, *Gloucester and the Civil War*, pp 108, 136-41; GRO, GBR B3/2, ff 237, 249, 252
(6) Dorney in Washbourn, *Bibliotheca Gloucestrensis*, pp 212, 221-2, 227; Washbourn's introduction to *Bibliotheca Gloucestrensis*, pp 55, 62-3; Atkin, *Council at War*, pp 12, 15; Atkin & Laughlin, *Gloucester and the Civil War*, pp 36-7, 47, 74, 106.
(7) Dorney in Washbourn, *Bibliotheca Gloucestrensis*, pp 209,213, 218, 223-5, 227; Corbet in Washbourn, pp 12, 14-16, 22, 25-6, 28-30, 40-43, 50; GRO, GBR B3/2, f 245; Taylor, *Civil Government of Gloucester*, pp 69, 96-109; Whiting, *Gloucester Besieged*, pp 11-14.

9 FORCED TO SHARE: LIVING UNDER THE SHADOW OF A GARRISON

(1) Charles Carlton, *Going to the Wars* (1992), pp 150-1; D.M. Ross, *Langport and its Church* (Langport, 1911), p 286
(2) See the Chronology for information on the involvement of these garrisons in the war.
(3) Carlton, *Going to the Wars*, pp 154-5
(4) Ronald Hutton, *The Royalist War Effort, 1642-1646* (1982), p 104; David Underdown, *Somerset in the Civil War and Interregnum* (Newton Abbot, 1973), pp 67-8, 72
(5) Emanuel Green, 'The Siege and Defence of Taunton, 1644-5' (*SANHS*, vol. 35, pt 2, Taunton, 1879), pp 34-5, 42; Emanuel Green, 'The Siege of Bridgwater, July 1645' (*SANHS*, vol. 23, pt. 2, Taunton, 1877), pp 12-13, 18; S.G. Jarman, *A History of Bridgwater* (1889), p 45; Bulstrode Whitelocke, *Memorials of the English Affairs* (1853 edn.), p 434
(6) C.H. Firth (ed.), *The Story of the Siege of Wardour Castle extracted from the Memoirs of Edmund Ludlow* (Newbury, 1887), pp 5-6
(7) PRO, SP28.144.9; SP28.175
(8) Ross, *Langport and its Church*, p 288; Carlton, *Going to the Wars*, p 153; Stephen Porter, *Destruction in the English Civil War* (Stroud, 1994), pp 31-2; Ronald Hutton, *The Royalist War Effort, 1642-1646* (1982), pp 189-90, quoting BL, E.266.24
(9) T.D. Fosbrooke, *An Original History of the City of Gloucester* (1819; reprinted Dursley, 1976), p 54; HMC, 9, *Marquess of Salisbury MSS*, pt. 12, 1612-68 (1971), pp 375-9
(10) Robert Steele (ed.), *A Bibliography of Tudor and Stuart Proclamations*, vol. 1 (Oxford, 1910), p 302
(11) J.H.P. Pafford (ed.), *Accounts of the Parliamentary Garrisons of Great Chalfield and Malmesbury, 1645-1646* (Devizes, 1966), pp 28-30
(12) Sir Thomas Fairfax, *A True Relation of the Storming of Bristol* (1645), p 16; Porter, *Destruction in the Civil War*, pp 2-6, 42; Malcolm Atkin & Wayne Laughlin, *Gloucester and the Civil War: a City under Siege* (Stroud, 1992), pp 68-9; John Wroughton, *A Community at War: the Civil War in Bath and North Somerset, 1642-1650* (Bath, 1992), pp 122-126; James Russell, *The Civil War Defences of Bristol* (Bristol, 1995), pp 31, 33-4.
(13) Green, *Siege of Bridgwater*, p 18; John Collinson, *The History and Antiquities of the County of Somerset*, vol. 3 (Bath, 1791), pp 76-7
(14) Peter Harrington, *Archaeology of the English Civil War* (Princes Risborough, 1992), pp 30, 33; Porter, *Destruction in the Civil War*, pp 18-19;A.R. Warmington, *Civil War, Interregnum and Restoration in Gloucestershire, 1640-1672* (1997), p 78
(15) Green, *Siege of Taunton*, p 40; Green, *Siege of Bridgwater*, p 16; Ross, *Langport and its Church*, p 307
(16) John M. Paddock, *The Storming of Cirencester in 1643: an Episode in the Civil War* (Cirencester, 1993), pp 8-18
(17) BL, E.248.8, *Marleborowes Miseries: or, England Turned Ireland, Written by Those who Suffered* (1643)
(18) C.H. Firth (ed.), *Outline of the Civil War in Wiltshire, 1642-1646* (Oxford, 1894), pp 8-9, 21-2; Howard Cunnington, *Records of the County of Wiltshire* (1931), p 200
(19) Green, *Siege of Taunton*, pp 42-5; Porter, *Destruction in the Civil War*, p 36; *A Narrative of the Expedition to Taunton* (1645), p 4
(20) Peter Gaunt, *The Cromwellian Gazetteer* (Gloucester, 1987), pp 59-60; John Washbourn (ed.), *Bibliotheca Gloucestrensis* (Gloucester, 1825), pp 328-9 (*Ebenezer. A Full and Exact Relation of the Proceedings of Colonel Massey, 7th-25th May 1644*) and pp 93-4 (John Corbet, *An Historical Relation of the Historical Government of Gloucester*)
(21) Joshua Sprigge, *Anglia Redivia:*

England's Recovery (1854 edn.), p 60; Gaunt, *Cromwellian Gazetteer*, pp 56, 59, 145, 170, 172; Washbourn, *Bibliotheca Gloucestrensis*, pp 88-9, 372; Eliot Warburton, *Memoirs of Prince Rupert and the Cavaliers*, vol. 2 (1849), pp 238-42; W. St Clair Baddeley, *A Cotteswold Manor being the History of Painswick* (Gloucester, 1929), pp 193-4, 197
(22) Firth, *Civil War in Wiltshire*, pp 38-9
(23) Porter, *Destruction in the Civil War*, pp 39, 46-8; Edward Hyde, Earl of Clarendon, The *Life of Edward, Earl of Clarendon*, vol. 7 (1759), p 122; Warburton, *Memoirs of Prince Rupert*, vol. 2, pp 251-2; Sprigge, *Anglia Rediviva*, pp 116-7
(24) A.H. Powell, *The Ancient Borough of Bridgwater* (Bridgwater, 1907), pp 251-5; Green, *Siege of Bridgwater*, pp 17-20
(25) Green, *Siege of Bridgwater*, pp 15, 20; Sprigge, *Anglia Rediviva*, p 18
(26) Green, *Siege of Taunton*, p 45
(27) Firth, *Siege of Wardour Castle*, pp 5, 7-8, 10
(28) Alan Wicks (ed.), *Bellum Civile: Sir Ralph Hopton's Memoirs of the Campaign in the West* (Leigh-on-Sea, 1988), p 47; G.A. Harrison, *Royalist Organisation in Gloucestershire and Bristol, 1642-45* (unpublished MA thesis, Manchester University, 1961), pp 168-71; H.G. Tibbutt (ed.), *The Letter Books 1644-45 of Sir Samuel Luke* (1963), *passim*
(29) GRO, D115, Declarations and Orders, no. 1; Steele, *Tudor and Stuart Proclamations*, vol.1, p 279; BodL, MS Dugdale, 19, f 182; GRO, G3/SO2, Draft Minutes, 1635-70, f 36; SP28.129(5), Thomas Blayney's accounts
(30) Wroughton, *Community at War*, pp 118-9
(31) John Latimer, *The Annals of Bristol in the Seventeenth Century* (Bristol, 1900), 170-6; for a fuller account, based on the latest research, see John Lynch, *For King and Parliament: Bristol and the Civil War* (Stroud, 1999), pp 45-59
(32) Latimer, *Annals of Bristol*, pp 197, 203; Warburton, *Memoirs of Prince Rupert*, vol. 3, pp 167-8
(33) Firth, *Siege of Wardour Castle*, p 7
(34) Gaunt, *Cromwellian Gazetteer*, p 148; Firth, *Siege of Wardour Castle*, p 7; Joshua Toulmin, *The History of the Town of Taunton* (Taunton, 1791), p 117
(35) James Coleman, 'A royalist account of the withdrawal of the King's forces from Taunton, 13th December 1644' (*EHR*, 13, 1898); Sprigge, *Anglia Rediviva*, p 19
(36) Wroughton, *Community at War*, pp 123-4; Green, *Siege of Bridgwater*, p 22
(37) Latimer, *Annals of Bristol*, p 179
(38) Clarendon, *Life*, vol. 7, p 122; Green, *Siege of Bridgwater*, p 20
(39) Latimer, *Annals of Bristol*, p 191; C.E.M. Chadwyck Healey (ed.), *Bellum Civile: Hopton's Narrative of his Campaign in the West* (Somerset Record Society, vol. 18, 1902), p 85
(40) Firth, *Siege of Wardour Castle*, pp 4, 7-8, 10
(41) Clarendon, *Life*, vol. 7, p 129; Healey, *Bellum Civile*, p 47
(42) Lynch, *For King and Parliament*, p 91; Clarendon, *Life*, vol. 7, p 130: Latimer, *Annals of Bristol*, pp 180-1
(43) Patrick Morrah, *Prince Rupert of the Rhine* (1976), pp 1213-4; Warburton, *Memoirs of Prince Rupert*, vol.2, pp 261-2
(44) BL, E.90 (7), *A Relation of the Taking of Cirencester* (1643)
(45) S.C. Minnitt, 'Civil war coin hoard from Taunton' in *SANHS*, vol. 125 (1981); John Miles Paddock, *The Story of Cirencester in 1643* (Cirencester, 1993), p 22. The hoards from Ashbrook and Weston-sub-Edge are displayed in the Cirencester Museum.
(46) Latimer, *Annals of Bristol*, pp 180-1; S.G. Jarman, *A History of Bridgwater* (1889), pp 51-2; Green, *Siege of Bridgwater*, pp 22, 24
(47) Thomas Fairfax, *A True Relation*

of the Storming of Bristol (1645), p 22; John Corbet, 'Historical Relation of the Military Government of Gloucester' in John Washbourne, *Bibliotheca Gloucestrensis* (1825), p 98
(48) Green, *Siege of Taunton*, pp 47-8; BL, E.344 (6); George Newton, *Man's Wrath and God's Praise; or, a Thanksgiving Sermon Preached at Taunton* (1646), pp 13-14

10 FORCED TO ENDURE: THE LINGERING EFFECTS OF WAR

(1) Charles Carlton, *Going to the Wars: the Experience of the British Civil Wars, 1638-1651* (1992), pp 90, 211, 221; BL, E.69, *Mercurius Civicus*, 21st-28th September 1643; Peter Clark & Paul Slack, *English Towns in Transition, 1500-1700* (Oxford, 1976), pp 89-90
(2) BrRO, 04264 (4), Common Council Proceedings, 1642-49, f 79; H.E. Nott (ed.),*The Deposition Books of Bristol*, vol. 1,1643-7 (Bristol, 1935), p 4; H.G. Tibbutt (ed.), *The Letter Books, 1644-5, of Sir Samuel Luke* (1963), p 551; H.C. Maxwell Lyte, *A History of Dunster*, pt. 1 (1909), p 186; John Latimer, *The Annals of Bristol in the Seventeenth Century* (Bristol, 1900), p 196; Joshua Sprigge, *Anglia Rediviva: England's Recovery* (1647), p 112; Thomas Fairfax, *A True Relation of the Storming of Bristol* (1645), p 14
(3) C.H. Firth & R.S. Rait (eds.), *Acts and Ordinances of the Interregnum*, vol.1 (1911), pp 36-7; E.H. Bates Harbin (ed.), *Quarter Sessions Records for the County of Somerset*, vol. 3, 1646-1660 (Somerset Record Society, vol. 28, 1912), p 6; Carlton, *Going to the Wars*, pp 228-9
(4) SRO, DD/X/MKN 17, Quarter Sessions Petitions, ff 42, 89, 156; Howard Cunnington, *Records of the County of Wiltshire* (1932), pp 173, 216
(5) PRO, SP28.228, pt 3 (4)
(6) Carlton, *Going to the Wars*, pp 209, 223-9; SRO, DD/X/MKN17, Quarter Sessions petitions, f 118
(7) O.L. Dick (ed.), *John Aubrey - Brief Lives* (1950), p 19; Carlton, *Going to the Wars*, p 207; Peter Young & Norman Tucker (eds.), *Richard Atkyns and John Gwyn*, p 20; BL, E249, *A Perfect Diurnall*, 10th-17th July 1643
(8) SRO, DD/X/MKN 17, Quarter Sessions Petitions, f 119
(9) Carlton, *Going to the Wars*, pp 221-9; 'A Particular Relation of the Action before Cirencester in Gloucestershire' (1642) in John Washbourne, *Bibliothetica Gloucestrensis* (Gloucester, 1825), p 172
(10) C.H. Firth, *Outline of the Civil War in Wiltshire, 1642-46* (Oxford, 1894), 33; C.H. Firth (ed.), *The Story of the Siege of Wardour Castle* (1887), p 9; W.D. Macray (ed.), Clarendon's *History of the Rebellion and Civil War in England*, Vol. 3 (Oxford,1969 ed.), pp 101-7
(11) SRO, DD/x/MKN 17, Quarter Sessions Petitions, ff 115, 116, 121, 147
(12) Cunnington, *Records of Wiltshire*, p 216
(13) Carlton, *Going to the Wars*, pp 228-9, 347; SRO, DD/X/MKN 17. Quarter Sessions Petitions, f 106
(14) SRO, CQ 3/1/23, Quarter Sessions Rolls, 1666-81, passim
(15) Cunnington, *Records of Wiltshire*, p 172; CSPD, 1644-5, p 43; Washbourne, *Bibliotheca Gloucestrensis*, introduction, p 101; J.D. Fosbrooke (ed.), *An Original History of the City of Gloucester* (1819; reprinted Dursley, 1976), p 55; Stephen Porter, *Destruction in the English Civil War* (Stroud, 1994), pp 65-6, 96-7
(16) Bates Harbin, *Quarter Sessions Records*, vol. III, p 126
(17) CSPD, 1656-7, p 207; HMC, 3rd Report, Corporation of Bridgwater, p 319
(18) SRO/X/MKN 17, Quarter Sessions Petitions, f 129; Bates Harbin, *Quarter Sessions Records*, vol. III, pp 85, 126, 20
(19) Latimer, *Annals of Bristol*, p 210;

G.D. Stawell, *A Quantock Family* (1910), p 403
(20) Cunnington, *Records for Wiltshire*, pp 171-2, 174
(21) Bates Harbin, *Quarter Sessions Records*, vol. III, p xxxi; A.L. Humphreys, *The Materials of the History of the Town of Wellington* (1889), pp 87-8
(22) Bates Harbin, *Quarter Sessions Records*, vol. III, pp 7, 153;
(23) Cunnington, *Records for Wiltshire*, pp 164; Carlton, *Going to the Wars*, pp 344-5; Bates-Harbin, *Quarter Sessions Records*, vol.3, p 201
(24) Bates Harbin, *Quarter Sessions Records*, vol. 3, pp 2, 6, 11; J.S. Cockburn (ed.), *Somerset Assize Orders, 1640-1659* (Frome, 1971), p 15; Tibbutt, *Letter Books of Sir Samuel Luke*, pp 68-9, 381
(25) Douglas Stevens, *War and Peace in West Somerset, 1620-70* (Minehead, n.d.), p 63; J.S. Cockburn (ed.), *Western Circuit Assize Orders, 1629-48* (1976), pp 250, 260
(26) BrRO, 04264 (4), Common Council Proceedings, 1642-49, ff 135-6; Joshua Sprigge, *Anglia Rediviva: England's Recovery* (1647), p 129
(27) PRO, C7/178/125; PRO, SP28.214; CCC, 1643-60, pt 1, p 85
(28) Menna Prestwich, *Cranfield: Politics and Profits under the Early Stuarts* (Oxford, 1960), pp 567-70
(29) Humphreys, *History of Wellington*, p 88
(30) Eliot Warburton, *Memoirs of Prince Rupert and the Cavaliers* (1849), vol. 2, p 284; C.E. Long (ed.), *Diary of the Marches of the Royalist Army...kept by Richard Symonds* (Camden Society Series, 74, 1859), p 101; D.M. Ross, *Langport and its Church* (Langport, 1911), p 294; John Wroughton, *From Civil War to Age of Reason: Bath Abbey, 1600-1800* (Bath, 1997), pp 8-11; Latimer, *Annals of Bristol*, p 211; George Harrison, *Royalist Organisation in Wiltshire* (unpublished PhD thesis, London University, 1963), p 298
(31) *A Full and True Account of the Sacking of the Church at Taynton* (1643); John Wroughton, *A Community at War: the Civil War in Bath and North Somerset, 1642-50* (Bath, 1992), p 88; HMC, Wells, vol. 2, pp 426-7
(32) Wroughton, *Bath Abbey*, pp 10-11
(33) Sir William Dugdale, *A Short View of the Late Troubles* (Oxford, 1681), p 559
(34) Maurice Exwood & L.H. Lehmann (eds.), *The Journal of William Schellinks' Travels in England, 1661-1663* (Camden 5th Series, vol. 1, 1993), pp 99, 107, 131; Wroughton, *Community at War*, p 177
(35) Wroughton, *Community at War*, pp 178, 180-1; Mary Siraut (ed.), *The Trevelyan Letters to 1840* (Taunton, 1990), p 128
(36) John Walker, *An Attempt towards recovering an Account of the Numbers and Suffering of the Clergy* (1714), pp 73, 200, 227, 242, 254, 273, 282, 289
(37) Wroughton, *Community at War*, pp 177-184; David Underdown, *Revel, Riot & Rebellion* (Oxford, 1985), p 255
(38) David Underdown, *Somerset in the Civil War and Interregnum* (Newton Abbot, 1973), pp 126-8; Wroughton, *Community at War*, pp 171-2
(39) Underdown, *Somerset*, pp 127-8; Emanuel Green, 'On the History of Chard' in *SANHS*, vol. 28, pt 2 (Taunton, 1882), pp 60-65; F. Hancock, *Minehead in the County of Somerset* (1903), p 277
(40) Wroughton, *Community at War*, pp 173-4
(41) James Waylen, 'The Wiltshire Compounders' in *WANHS Magazine*, vol. 23 (1887), p 334; vol. 24 (1889), pp 61, 79, 312, 318, 341; VCH, Wiltshire, vol. 5, pp 143-4
(42) PRO, SP28.214; SP23.4 (38); SP23.191 (461); CCC, vol. 3, p 1686
(43) PRO, SP28.217A, pt 2, ff 236-7; SP28.216; Waylen, 'Wiltshire Compounders', *WANHS Magazine*, vol. 24, pp 308-9
(44) PRO, C22.640 (pt. 2), no. 39; C7/178/125 - Hobbs v Hobbs

BIBLIOGRAPHY

1 Unpublished Manuscripts

Bath Record Office
Bath Council Book, No. 1, 1631-49
Bath Chamberlain's Accounts, 1569-1662

Bodleian Library, Oxford
Aubrey 2
Clarendon MSS
Dugdale MS
MSS English History
Rawlinson MSS
Tanner MS

Bristol Record Office
Common Council Book, No. 4, 1642-49

British Library
Additional MSS
Egerton MSS
Harleian MSS
Lansdowne MS
The Thomason Tracts (contemporary newsbooks and pamphlets)

Cambridge University Library
Western MSS

Gloucestershire Record Office
Council Minutes, 1632-1656
Declarations and Orders
Draft Minutes, 1635-1670
Chamberlain's Accounts, 1642-43

Public Record Office
SP 16: State Papers Domestic, Charles I
SP 18: State Papers Domestic, Interregnum
SP 20: Papers of the Committee for the Sequestration of Delinquents' Estates
SP 22: Papers of the Committee for Plundered Ministers
SP 23: Papers of the Committee for Compounding
SP 28: Commonwealth Exchequer Papers (County Committees)
C 7 & 107: Chancery Papers
E 179: Assessments
PC 2: Privy Council Registers

Somerset Record Office
Quarter Sessions Petitions
Comperta, 1615
Sessions Roll, 64, ii

Wells Archives
Acts of the Corporation, 1635-1644

Wiltshire Record Office
Marlborough General Account Book, 1643
Notes of goods and chattels taken by force, December 1644

2 Printed Contemporary Sources, Calendars etc.

A Narrative of the Expedition to Taunton (1645)
Archaeologia, vol. XIV (1803)
Bates Harbin, E.H. (ed.): *Quarter Sessions Records for the County of Somerset*, vol. 3, 1646-60
Bond, Shelagh (ed.): *The Chamber Order Book of Worcester, 1602-1650* (Worcester, 1974)
Bulstrode, Richard: *Memoirs and Reflections upon the Reign and Government of*

King Charles I and King Charles II (1721)
Calendar of the Committee for Compounding , 1643-1660, 5 vols
Calendar of the Committee for the Advance of Money
Calendar of State Papers Domestic, 1642-47
Calendar of State Papers Venetian, vols. 26 & 27
Calendar of the Manuscripts of the Dean and Chapter of Wells, vol.2 (HMC, 1914)
Cockburn, J.S. (ed.): *Somerset Assize Orders, 1640-1659* (Frome, 1971)
Cockburn, J.S. (ed.): *Western Circuit Assize Orders, 1629-48* (1976)
Corbet, John: *An Historical Relation of the Military Government of Gloucester* (in Washbourne, 1825)
Cunnington, Howard, *Records of the County of Wiltshire* (1931)
Davies, G. (ed.): *Memoirs of the Family of Guise of Elmore, Gloucestershire* (Camden Series, vol. 28, 1917)
Day, W.A. (ed.): *The Pythouse Papers* (1879)
Dorney, John: *A Brief and Exact Relation of the Siege of Gloucester* (in Washbourne, 1825)
Dick, O.L. (ed.): *John Aubrey - Brief Lives* (1950)
Dugdale, Sir William: *A Short View of the Late Troubles* (Oxford, 1681)
Exwood, Maurice & Lehmann, L.H. (eds.): *The Journal of William Schellinks' Travels in England, 1661-1663* (Camden 5th series, vol. 1, 1993)
Fairfax, Sir Thomas: *A True Relation of the Storming of Bristol* (1645)
Foster, Henry: *A True and Exact Relation of the Marching of the Trained Bands* (in Washbourne, 1825)
Firth, C.H. (ed.): *Memoirs of Sir Edmund Ludlow*, 2 vols. (Oxford, 1894 edn.)
Firth, C.H. (ed.): *The Story of the Siege of Wardour Castle extracted from the Memoirs of Edmund Ludlow* (Newbury, 1887)
Firth, C.H. & Rait, R.S. (eds.): *Acts and Ordinances of the Interregnum, 1640-1660*, vol.1, (1911)
Goldney, Frederick H. (ed.): *Records of Chippenham* (1889)
Healey, C.E.H. (ed.): *Bellum Civile* (Somerset Record Society, vol. 18, Taunton, 1902)
Historical Manuscripts Commission Reports:
3rd Report Corporation of Bridgwater
5th Report: The MSS of Edmund Cholmondeley
9th Report: The MSS of the Marquess of Salisbury
13th Report: The MSS of the Duke of Portland
Wells Dean and Chapter, vol. 2
Journals of the House of Commons, vols. 2-7
Journals of the House of Lords, vols. 4-10
Jackson, J.E. (ed.): *The Hungerford Family: Collections for their Personal History*, vol. 2 (unpublished MSS in Devizes Museum, 1885)
Long, C.E. (ed.): *Diary of the Marches of the Royal Army...kept by Richard Symonds* (Camden Series, 74, 1859)
Mabbs, A.W. (ed.): *Guild Stewards' Book of the Borough of Calne, 1561-1688* (Devizes, 1953)
Macray, W.D. (ed.): Earl of Clarendon, *The History of the Rebellion and the Civil War in England*, 6 vols. (Oxford, 1969 edn.)
Madan, Falconer: *Oxford Books*, 2 vols. (Oxford, 1912)
Marleborowes Miseries: or, England Turned Ireland, Written by those who Suffered (1643)
Newton, George: *Man's Wrath and God's Praise: or, a Thanksgiving Sermon Preached at Taunton* (1646)

Nott, H.E. (ed.): *The Deposition Books of Bristol*, vol. 1, 1643-7 (Bristol, 1935)
Nottestein, Wallace (ed.): *The Journal of Sir Simonds D'Ewes* (Yale, 1923)
Pafford, J.H.P. (ed.): *Accounts of the Parliamentary Garrisons of Great Chalfield and Malmesbury, 1645-46* (Devizes, 1966)
Philip, I.G. (ed.): *The Journal of Sir Samuel Luke* , vol. 2 (Oxford Record Society, 1947)
Prynne, William: A *Legal Vindication of the Liberties of England against Illegal Taxes* (1649)
Roy, Ian (ed.): *Royalist Ordinance Papers*, vol. 2 (Oxford Record Society, 1975)
Rushworth, John: *Historical Recollections of Private Passages of State* (1701)
Siraut, Mary (ed.): *The Trevelyan Letters to 1840* (Taunton, 1990)
Sprigge, Joshua: *Anglia Rediviva: England's Recovery* (1647)
Steele, Robert (ed.): *A Bibliography of Tudor and Stuart Proclamations*, vol. 1 (Oxford, 1910)
Stocks, H. (ed.): *Records of the Borough of Leicester, 1603-1688* (Cambridge, 1923)
Tibbutt, H.G. (ed.): *The Letter Books 1644-45 of Sir Samuel Luke* (1963)
Trevelyan, W.C. & Trevelyan, C.E. (eds.): *Trevelyan Papers*, part 3 (Camden Society, 1872)
Vicars, John: *Burning Bush or Parliamentarie Chronicle* (1646)
Vicars, John: *Jehovah-Jirah, God in the Mount: or England's Parliamentarie Chronicle* (1644)
Walker, Edward: *Historical Discourses upon Several Occasions* (1705)
Walker, John: *An Attempt towards recovering an Account of the Numbers and Suffering of the Clergy* (1714)
Washbourn, John: *Bibliotheca Gloucestrensis* (Gloucester, 1825)
White, John: *A Relation of the Taking of Cirencester* (in Washbourne, 1825)
Whitelock, Bulstrode: *Memorials of the English Affairs from the Beginning of the Reign of Charles the First*, vol.1 (Oxford, 1853)
Wicks, Alan (ed.): *Bellum Civile: Sir Ralph Hopton's Memoirs of the Campaign in the West* (Leigh-on-Sea, 1988)
Young, Peter & Tucker, Norman (eds.): *Military Memoirs of the Civil War: Richard Atkyns and John Gwyn* (1967)

3 Secondary Works (Place of publication is London unless stated)

Adair, John: *Roundhead General: the Campaigns of Sir William Waller* (Stroud, 1997 edn.)
Atkin, Malcolm & Laughlin, Wayne: *Gloucester and the Civil War: A City under Siege* (Stroud, 1992)
Atkin, Malcolm: *Gloucester under Siege: a City Council at War* (Gloucester, 1993)
Baddeley, W. St. Clair: *A Cotteswold Manor being the History of Painswick* (Gloucester, 1929)
Baker, Ernest: 'Bristol and the Civil War' (in *The Bristol Times and Mirror*, 1 January 1925)
Barnes, T. G: *Somerset, 1625-40* (Oxford, 1961)
Bennett, James: *The History of Tewkesbury* (Tewkesbury, 1830)
Carlton, Charles: *Going to the Wars: The Experience of the British Civil Wars, 1638-1651* (1992)
Clark, Peter & Slack, Paul: *English Towns in Transition, 1500-1700* (Oxford, 1976)
Coleman, James: 'A Royalist Account of the withdrawal; of the King's Forces

from Taunton, 13th December 1644' (in *EHR*, 13, 1898)
Collinson, John: *The History of Somersetshire*, vols. 1 & 2 (1791)
Cunnington, Howard: *Some Annals of the Borough of Devizes* (Devizes, 1925)
Daniel, John J: *The History of Chippenham* (1884)
Daniel, John J: *The History of Warminster* (1879)
Edgar, F.T.R: *Sir Ralph Hopton: The King's Man in the West, 1642-1652* (Oxford, 1968)
Emberton, Wilfred: *The English Civil War Day by Day* (Stroud, 1995)
Everitt, Alan: *The County of Kent and the Great Rebellion, 1640-1660* (Leicester, 1966)
Finberg, H.P.R. (ed.): *Gloucestershire Studies* (Leicester, 1957)
Firth, C.H: *Cromwell's Army* (1962 edn.)
Firth, C.H: *Outline of the Civil War in Wiltshire, 1642-1646* (Oxford, 1894)
Fosbrooke, T.D: *An Original History of the City of Gloucester* (1819; reprinted Dursley, 1976)
Gaunt, Peter: *The Cromwell Gazeteer* (Gloucester, 1987)
Green, Emanuel: 'On the History of Chard' (in *SANHS*, vol. 28, pt. 2 (Taunton, 1882)
Green, Emanuel: 'The Siege of Bridgwater, July 1645' (in *SANHS*, vol. 23, pt. 2, Taunton, 1887)
Green, Emanuel: 'The Siege and Defence of Taunton, 1644-45' (in *SANHS*, vol. 35, pt. 2, Taunton, 1879)
Gardiner, S.R: *History of the Great Civil War, 1642-49*, 4 vols. (1894)
Hancock, F: *Minehead in the County of Somerset* (1903)
Harington, H: *Nugae Antiquae* (1779)
Harrington, Peter: *Archaeology of the English Civil War* (Princes Risborough, 1992)
Harrison, George: *Royalist Organisation in Gloucestershire and Bristol* (unpublished MA thesis, Manchester University, 1961)
Harrison, George: *Royalist Organisation in Wiltshire* (unpublished PhD thesis, London University,1963)
Holmes, Clive: *The Eastern Association in the English Civil War* (Cambridge, 1974)
Hughes, Anne: *Politics, Society and Civil War in Warwickshire* (Cambridge, 1987)
Humphreys, A.L: *The Materials of the History of the Town of Wellington* (1889)
Hutton, Ronald: *The Royalist War Effort, 1642-1646* (1982)
Jackson, J.E: *A Guide to Farleigh Hungerford* (Chippenham, 1879)
Jarman, S.G: *A History of Bridgwater* (1889)
Jennings, R.W: *The Cotswolds in the Civil War* (Cirencester, 1976)
Latimer, John: *The Annals of Bristol in the Seventeenth Century* (Bristol, 1900)
Lynch, John: *For King and Parliament: Bristol and the Civil War* (Stroud, 1999)
Lyte, H.C. Maxwell: *A History of Dunster*, pt. 1 (1909)
Lee, Alfred T: *A History of the Town and Parish of Tetbury* (1877)
Longmore, Sir T: *Richard Wiseman: Surgeon and Surgeon-General to Charles II* (1891)
Mann, J. de L: *The Cloth Industry in ther West of England from 1640 to 1880* (Oxford, 1971)
McCreadie, Rory: *The Barber-Surgeon's Mate in the 17th Century* (Upton, 1997)
McGrath, Patrick: *Bristol and the Civil War* (Bristol, 1981)
McGrath, Patrick (ed.): *Merchants and Merchandise in Seventeenth-Century Bristol* (Bristol, 1955)

Minnitt, S.C: 'Civil War Coin Hoard from Taunton' (in *SANHS*, vol. 125, 1981)
Morrah, Patrick: *Prince Rupert of the Rhine* (1976)
Morrill, John: 'Mutiny and Discontent in English Provincial Armies, 1645-1647' (in *Past and Present*, no. 56, 1972)
Morrill, John (ed.): *Reactions to the English Civil War, 1642-1649* (1982)
Morrill, John (ed.): *The Impact of the English Civil War* (1991)
Morrill, John: *The Revolt of the Provinces* (1976)
Nicholls, J.F. & Taylor, John: *Bristol Past and Present*, vol. 1 (Bristol, 1881)
Oldmixon, John: *The History of England during the Reigns of the Royal House of Stuart* (1730)
Paddock, John Miles: *The Storming of Cirencester in 1643: an Episode in the Civil War* (Cirencester, 1995)
Page, W. (ed.): *The Victoria County History of Somerset* (1911)
Parker, George: 'Early Medieval Institutions, the Medieval Hospitals and Barber Surgeons' in *TBGAS*, vol. 44 (1922)
Pennington, Donald: 'The War and the People' (in Morrill, ed., *Reactions to the English Civil War*)
Porter, Stephen: *Destruction in the English Civil Wars* (Stroud, 1994)
Powell, A.H: *The Ancient Borough of Bridgwater* (Bridgwater, 1907)
Prestwich, Menna: *Cranfield: Politics and Profits under the Early Tudors* (Oxford, 1960)
Pugh, R.B & Elizabeth Crittall (eds.): *The Victoria County History of Wiltshire*
Quaife, G.R: *Wanton Wenches and Wayward Wives: Peasants and Illegal Sex in early Seventeenth-Century England* (1979)
Ralph, P.L: *Sir Humphrey Mildmay: Royalist Gentleman* (New Brunswick, 1947)
Ramsay,: *The Wiltshire Woollen Industry in the Sixteenth and Seventeenth Centuries* (1965)
Ross, D.M: *Langport and its Church* (Langport, 1911)
Roy, Ian: 'England turned Germany? The aftermath of the civil war in its European context' (in *TRHS*, 5th series, vol. 28, 1978)
Roy, Ian: 'The English Civil War and English Society' (*War and Society*, vol. 2 (1975)
Russell, James: *The Civil War Defences of Bristol* (Bristol, 1995)
Sacks, David Harris: 'Bristol's Wars of Religion' (in R.C. Richardson, ed., *Town and Countryside in the English Revolution*, Manchester, 1992)
Sharp, Buchanan: *In Contempt of all Authority* (California, 1980)
Stawell, G.D: *A Quantock Family* (1910)
Stevens, Douglas: *War and Peace in West Somerset, 1620-1670* (Minehead, n.d.)
Styles, Philip: *Studies in Seventeenth Century West Midlands History* (Kineton, 1978)
Symonds, Henry (ed.): 'A By-path of the Civil War' (in *SANHS*, vol. 65, pt. 2, Taunton, 1919)
Taylor, John K.G: 'The Civil Government of Gloucester, 1640-46' (in *TBGAS*, vol. 67, 1949)
Thompson, J: *The Other Army: Camp Followers of the Civil War* (Leigh-on-Sea, n.d.)
Toulmin, Joshua: *The History of the Town of Taunton* (Taunton, 1791)
Underdown, David: *Revel, Riot and Rebellion, 1603-1660* (Oxford, 1985)
Underdown, David: *Somerset in the Civil War and Interregnum* (Newton Abbot, 1973)
Warburton, Eliot: *Memoirs of Prince Rupert and the Cavaliers*, 2 vols. (1849)
Warmington, A.R: *Civil War, Interregnum and Restoration in Gloucestershire,*

1640-72 (1997)
Waylen, James: *A History Military and Municipal of the Ancient Borough of the Devizes* (1859)
Waylen, James: *A History Military and Municipal of the Town of Marlborough* (1854)
Waylen, James: 'The Wiltshire Compounders' (in *WANHS*, vols. 23 -4, 1887-8)
Whiting, J.R.S: *Gloucester Besieged* (Gloucester, 1984)
Wroughton, John: *A Community at War: the Civil War in Bath and North Somerset, 1642-1650* (Bath, 1992)
Wroughton, John: *From Civil War to Age of Reason: Bath Abbey, 1600-1800* (Bath, 1997)
Wroughton, John: *The Stuart Age, 1603-1714* (1997)

Index